Fatal Tide

DAVID LEACH

WHEN THE RACE OF A
LIFETIME GOES WRONG

VIKING
CANADA

VIKING CANADA

Published by the Penguin Group

Penguin Group (Canada), 90 Eglinton Avenue East, Suite 700,
Toronto, Ontario, Canada M4P 2Y3 (a division of Pearson Canada Inc.)

Penguin Group (USA) Inc., 375 Hudson Street, New York,
New York 10014, U.S.A.

Penguin Books Ltd, 80 Strand, London WC2R 0RL, England

Penguin Ireland, 25 St Stephen's Green, Dublin 2, Ireland
(a division of Penguin Books Ltd)

Penguin Group (Australia), 250 Camberwell Road, Camberwell, Victoria 3124, Australia
(a division of Pearson Australia Group Pty Ltd)

Penguin Books India Pvt Ltd, 11 Community Centre, Panchsheel Park,
New Delhi – 110 017, India

Penguin Group (NZ), 67 Apollo Drive, Rosedale, North Shore 0632, Auckland,
New Zealand (a division of Pearson New Zealand Ltd)

Penguin Books (South Africa) (Pty) Ltd, 24 Sturdee Avenue, Rosebank,
Johannesburg 2196, South Africa

Penguin Books Ltd, Registered Offices: 80 Strand, London WC2R 0RL, England

First published 2008

1 2 3 4 5 6 7 8 9 10 (RRD)

Copyright © David Leach, 2008

Illustration of map on page xix by Deborah Crowle, 2008

Portions of this book appeared previously in a different form in
explore: Canada's Outdoor Magazine.

Manufactured in the U.S.A.

LIBRARY AND ARCHIVES CANADA CATALOGUING IN PUBLICATION

Leach, David, 1968–
Fatal tide : when the race of a lifetome goes wrong / David Leach.

Includes biographical references.
ISBN 978-0-670-06629-2 (bound)

1. Arseneault, René, 1980–2002. 2. Adventure racing—Accidents—New Brunswick—
Saint John Region. 3. Fundy Multi-Sport Race. 4. Athletes—New Brunswick—
Rothesay—Biography. I. Title.

GV1038.2.F85L42 2008   796.5   C2008-900345-4

ISBN-13: 978-0-670-06629-2
ISBN-10: 0-670-06629-X

Visit the Penguin Group (Canada) website at **www.penguin.ca**
Special and corporate bulk purchase rates available; please see
www.penguin.ca/corporatesales or call 1-800-810-3104, ext. 477 or 47

For my parents,
who were always there
to send me away on my own adventures
and welcome me home again

Contents

Part Three: The Storm

Part Four: The Reckoning

Introduction

In 1997, I happened to catch a TV documentary on the Discovery Channel about the ups and downs of an unusual wilderness competition called the Eco-Challenge. Like millions of other viewers, I was captivated by the dramatic footage of this so-called "expedition with a stopwatch." I even pictured myself among the hardy co-ed teams of five that chased each other over storm-swept mountains, down glacial-cold rivers, and through the dense coastal forests of British Columbia for pride and prizes. Like most armchair adventurers, I did little more than daydream and wait for the next broadcast of the annual race. Some viewers, however, were inspired enough by the televised spectacle to get off their sofas and compete in, even to organize, similar events.

Five years later, I was working as an editor at *explore*, an outdoor travel magazine based in Toronto. At the magazine, we had tracked the rapid growth of this new sport, called "expedition racing" or "adventure racing," as it evolved from multi-day, multi-sport team events such as the Eco-Challenge (often a week or longer, with dropout rates of seventy percent) to include softer, single-day sprint races, off-road triathlons, and urban treasure hunts. In an issue that spring, our magazine publicized one such introductory event near Saint John, New Brunswick. At the time, I knew little about the Fundy Multi-Sport Race beyond a brief description on the website of the outdoor retail store that was sponsoring the event. Several months later, I learned that a fatal paddling accident had overshadowed the very race we had helped to promote. According to police reports and news articles, participants had completed the trail-running and mountain-biking stages when a sudden storm had struck the Bay of Fundy and turned the final kayaking section treacherous.

By 2002, the pop-cultural fascination with all things extreme had reached its zenith. Oddball activities ranged from the insane (parachuting off electrical towers) to the inane (ironing clothes atop mountain peaks), and reality TV hits such as *Survivor* and *Fear Factor* pitted ordinary people against each other in physical and psychological ordeals. Adventure racing often fell under this extreme-branded umbrella. Marketing of races played up the dangers—one event was called the Canadian Death Race—and the sport had been featured in ESPN's X Games, the annual Olympics of extreme sports. In reality, adventure racing shared more in common with sober, adult endurance activities such as marathon running and sea kayaking than such reckless Generation Ritalin hobbies as street luge and skydiving. In fact, I had never before heard about a fatal accident at a competition. Was Canada the site of the sport's first death?

Our magazine had encouraged readers to attend, so we felt a responsibility to determine what had happened at the race, how the fatal misadventure could have been prevented, and who—if anyone—was to blame. That proved to be difficult. When we contacted the organizers, the young couple was too upset to go on the record. Family members of the deceased weren't talking, nor were the RCMP, nor the Canadian Coast Guard, nor the New Brunswick coroner's office. We were left with more questions than answers.

Something about the incident bothered me, so I decided to keep digging. As I made inquiries and trawled adventure-racing websites for witnesses, not everyone seemed pleased that a journalist was asking questions about their sport. "I was at the race & I was in the kayak portion when the shit went down," one participant wrote on an internet discussion group. "My concern is if you talk to this gentleman & put a negative spin on the race you could be hurting the organizers' future, not to mention the future of adventure racing." Other respondents were less skeptical about the glare of outside interest. "Circling the wagons in some sort of defence against negative media attention is a recipe for negative media attention," replied another racer on the same online forum. "The more people that are aware of the consequences of being in the wilderness, the better."

Soon I began to field messages from participants who had been at the event. For some, it had been just another race that they had endured, even enjoyed, until news of the accident trickled back to the finish line and colored forever their memories of that day. For others, the signs of potential calamity seemed obvious in hindsight. All agreed that they had made their own choices, to turn back or push on through the storm, and that they bore the consequences of their actions. Many had returned home, having approached the lip of disaster on the turbulent bay, with a more complex understanding of what risks they take in their outdoor adventures.

Residents along the Fundy coast were more blunt in their assessments. "I'm a fisherman," said one lobster-boat captain who had helped to rescue kayakers. "We're taught to respect the sea and know what it can do and not to challenge it. These people were doing the exact opposite. It makes me angry to see that." Other locals echoed his outrage. The Bay of Fundy, they insisted, is not a playground for adrenaline-seeking yahoos and yuppies. And yet eco-tourism, guided adventures, and action sports of every variety were gaining prominence on the East Coast, across the continent, and around the world.

The whole concept of adventure tourism suggests a paradox. Can you really organize an adventure? How do you simulate the thrills of the outdoors without the risks that are an essential part of any wild place? And in competitive events, might not the ego-driven desire to be first across the finish line trump the caution that is a necessity of safe wilderness travel?

Five years and more than a hundred interviews later, I understand better the broad reach and deep impact of this one small tragedy, as well as the larger issues it raises. The sequence of decisions and inde-cisions, actions and inactions, mistakes and pure bad luck that led to the death by adventure on the Bay of Fundy drew hundreds of people into its orbit: sixty-eight racers and their families, dozens of race offi-cials and volunteers, two fishing villages, the Canadian Coast Guard, the Canadian Forces, the RCMP, the local fire rescue detachment, ambulance attendants, emergency room doctors, coroners, Crown prosecutors, lawyers, and insurance adjusters, the vast bureaucracy of a province and a nation. Few of the people intimate with the events of that day would ever be the same again.

The story of the race only loomed larger and more mysterious as I chased it from one coast to another and back again. It continues to gather momentum. Organizers, outfitters, wilderness teachers, back-country guides, amateur adventurers, and eco-tourists of all sorts—everyone, in fact, who cares about the responsibilities we share when we step into the outdoors—may be affected by the final answer to the question: What really happened at the Fundy Multi-Sport Race?

Cast of Characters

Main Organizers and Safety Staff

Jayme Frank, marine biologist and kayak guide, co-organizer, from Kenora, Ontario

Sara Vlug, teacher and kayak guide, co-organizer, from Dipper Harbour, New Brunswick

Bob Vlug, Sara's father, co-owner of Eastern Outdoors, from Dipper Harbour, New Brunswick

Deanna Vlug, Sara's mother, co-owner of Eastern Outdoors, from Dipper Harbour, New Brunswick

Owen Vlug, Sara's brother, Zodiac operator, from Dipper Harbour, New Brunswick

Jason Stanley, employee of Eastern Outdoors, Zodiac operator, from Quispamsis, New Brunswick

Key Racers

Mark Campbell, solo, Canadian Forces network manager, from Halifax, Nova Scotia

Shawn Amirault, solo, telecom manager, defending champion, from Halifax, Nova Scotia

Peter Hancock, solo, technical manager, from Bathurst, New Brunswick

René Arseneault, solo, grocery store employee, from Rothesay, New Brunswick

Jim Currie, solo, pharmaceutical manager, from Halifax, Nova Scotia

Robin Lang, tandem (with partner), piping designer, former white-water paddling champion, from Rothesay, New Brunswick

Dana Henry, solo (unofficial), kayak sales rep, U.S. whitewater paddling champion, from Vermont

The Tallywhackers, tandem: *Bob Carreau*, environmental manager, and *Bob Leclair*, technical superintendent, from Bathurst, New Brunswick

Boon Kek, solo, university student, from Singapore

Joe Kennedy, tandem (with partner), wildlife biologist, from Hampton, New Brunswick

Malcolm Brett, tandem (with Bob Vlug), college department head, from Rothesay, New Brunswick

Baymen and Women

Keith Mawhinney, captain of the *Benevolence*, from Chance Harbour, New Brunswick

Mark Mawhinney, cousin of Keith, captain of the *Quaco Duck*, from Chance Harbour, New Brunswick

Bob Mawhinney, brother of Keith, captain of the *D.P. Clipper*, from Dipper Harbour, New Brunswick

Andrew and *Peter Mawhinney*, sons of Bob, crew members on the *D.P. Clipper*

Keith Nicholls, sternsman on the *D.P. Clipper*

Edward Jacques, sternsman on the *High Sierra*, from Chance Harbour, New Brunswick

Cindy Jacques, wife of Edward

Search-and-Rescuers

Gilles Arseneault, deputy chief, Musquash Volunteer Fire Rescue Department

Constable Wayne Burke, RCMP, Lepreau Detachment, from Dipper Harbour

Wendell Sperry, maritime search coordinator, Canadian Coast Guard, Joint Rescue Coordination Centre, Halifax, Nova Scotia

Elaine Small, sister-in-law of Bob Mawhinney, registered nurse, from Maces Bay, New Brunswick

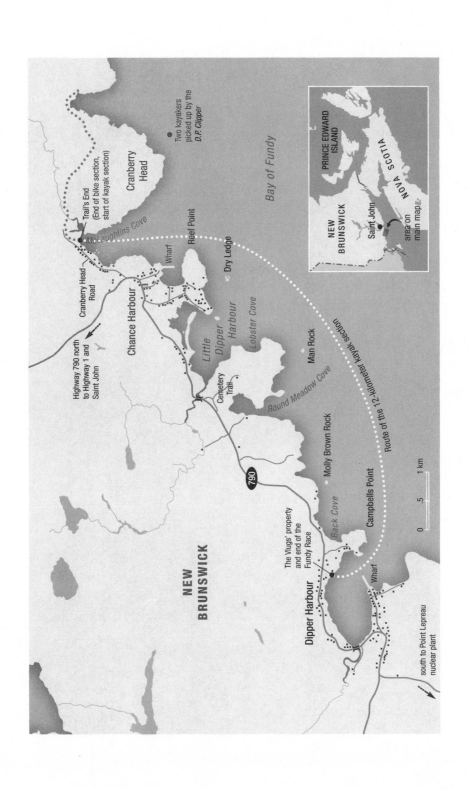

NEW BRUNSWICK

Highway 790 north to Highway 1 and Saint John

Cranberry Head Road

Chance Harbour

Wharf

McLaughlins Cove

Trail's End (End of bike section, start of kayak section)

Cranberry Head

Reef Point

Dry Ledge

Little Dipper Harbour

Lobster Cove

Cemetery Trail

Man Rock

Round Meadow Cove

Molly Brown Rock

Campbells Point

Route of the 12-kilometer kayak section

Two kayakers picked up by the D.P. Clipper

Bay of Fundy

790

Back Cove

The Vlugs' property and end of the Fundy Race

Dipper Harbour

Wharf

south to Point Lepreau nuclear plant

0   .5   1 km

PRINCE EDWARD ISLAND

NEW BRUNSWICK

Saint John

NOVA SCOTIA

area on main map

Rising Tide

In the trough of the wave, the adventurer tells his story; his words give a permanence to the illuminating moments of action he has lived.

—Paul Zweig, *The Adventurer: The Fate of
 Adventure in the Western World*

At first it didn't seem strange to the captain that a kayaker, alone in the rebounding swells off Cranberry Head, was waving at his lobster boat. Experienced paddlers along these shores knew to alert larger vessels if they didn't want to be swamped or run down by a distracted fisherman. And a kayaker would have to be plenty experienced—either that or a damned fool—to be paddling solo on an afternoon as squally as this one.

A southwest wind had steepened the seas, and the captain had pulled the last of his traps a few hours early so that his crew could get home before it worsened. He steered close to shore where he knew an eddy of ebb water would run for an hour or two against the incoming tide. He didn't beat the storm, though. A squall line had darkened the hills and blotted out the sky, while spume sheered off the tops of two-meter-high waves. Crackling with electricity, the storm had spit cold rain across his boat's deck. And then it had blown out to sea.

As the captain closed on the kayaker, he could tell, even through the rain-smeared windshield of the wheelhouse, that something wasn't right—the sideward angle at which the man tilted, the urgency of his gestures. And then he saw it. The kayaker's other hand was gripping the red life jacket of a second person, a hunched shape that was half-submerged in the tumult of the waves.

It suddenly made sense. The strange gray projection he had seen bob past the boat a few minutes ago, like the fluke of a whale or mysterious flotsam pulled by the legendary tides of the Bay of Fundy—that must have been the second man's kayak. At the time, the captain had assumed it was another floating log. He had considered snagging the stump with a gaff and flagging it with orange tape as a warning to other boats. But the heaving seas had made the maneuver too chancy, even for a fifty-ton vessel like his own, so he kept the boat on course for safe harbor.

Now the captain understood that the danger implied by that murky shape had already struck. An hour or two before, he had heard chatter on the VHF radio about some sort of race on the bay. These two paddlers must have been part of that competition. He wondered how long the capsized kayaker had been immersed in the cold Atlantic waters. The two men had drifted to fewer than thirty meters from the shoreline. Along this stretch of Fundy coast, the land rose abruptly in a toothy battlement of broken rock, twenty meters high in spots. In an emergency, the exposed foreshore offered no crescent of sand or level turf on which an unlucky mariner could beach a foundering boat. You either made it around Cranberry Head to Chance Harbour or you sank. If the wind and tidal current drew the kayakers any closer to the jagged fringe, the adjacent waters would prove too shallow and the waves, which ricocheted erratically off the cliffs, too powerful for the captain to risk a rescue. His crew would be left to watch helplessly as the thrust of the surf crushed the two frightened men against the rocks.

The captain swung the boat sidelong to the paddlers, both in their early twenties, to shelter them from the wind-blown waves. His first mate tossed a rope. The captain could tell this effort wouldn't work. The young man still in the kayak would have to release his companion to snag the rescue rope. It was clear he wouldn't risk losing his friend to the pounding waves, not even for a moment. Instead, the first mate grabbed a three-meter gaff pole used to haul buoys, hooked one of the cords that ran along the kayak's plastic hull, and dragged it to the stern of the lobster boat.

"We're going to grab your buddy," the captain shouted, "but don't let go 'til we tell you to!"

The crew stood shoulder to shoulder. "Wait for the swell," the captain told them. The undulating bay lifted and dropped the fishing boat and the smaller kayak, and the men timed their actions with the next crescendo. When the boats grew level, they grabbed the soaking limbs of the loose kayaker and heaved him onto the deck. He wore only a thin cycling T-shirt and shorts under his life vest, and his skin had gone bone-china white. His eyes stared at the gray sky, but he didn't speak, didn't even twitch.

The lobster crew steadied their boots on the pitching deck and waited for the right moment to reach for the remaining kayaker. Again, they grabbed fistfuls of life jacket and hauled the other boy over the boat's tailgate. He flopped onto the deck and rubbed sea spray from his eyes. His skin was darker toned and he wasn't wearing much more than his friend. A light polyester jacket and bike gloves were all the extra insulation he had on. The captain turned back to the wheelhouse.

"We can't leave the kayak!" the still-conscious paddler insisted.

"Don't worry about it," said the captain. "Someone will pick it up."

"No, no!" The young man's voice was low, and he struggled to pass words through the chatter of his teeth. Convulsions washed over his body. "It's not mine."

They didn't have time to argue, so the captain hooked the kayak with the gaff and dragged it aboard, too. His first mate had carried the unconscious kayaker under the awning behind the wheelhouse and wrapped him with rain jackets and life vests, anything dry he could pull from the boat's utility closet. The first mate then bear-hugged the rescued lad and tried to share body heat.

"Is he okay?" the friend asked. "I was just talking to him."

The boat was maybe a kilometer or two from the breakwater of Chance Harbour, the closest safe berth. Back at the wheel, the captain tried to raise help on his VHF radio, but the bluffs of Cranberry Head blocked the line-of-sight signal, and the operator at Fundy Traffic in Saint John couldn't make out his pleas. He flicked on his cell phone and speed-dialed his home number. His wife picked up on the second ring.

"Debbie," he told her, "get an ambulance down to Chance Harbour now!"

And then he dropped the throttle and aimed for the wharf.

PART ONE
The Call to Adventure

Go, as adventure will thee lead.

—Henry Lovelich, *The History of the Holy Grail*

Now in myth and ritual the great instinctive forces of civilized life have their origin: law and order, commerce and profit, craft and art, poetry, wisdom and science. All are rooted in the primeval soil of play.

—Johan Huizinga, *Homo Ludens: A Study of the Play Element in Culture*

ONE

The Island

First-time visitors to New Brunswick unfamiliar with the province's corporate geography must often wonder: Who is this "Irving" and what *doesn't* he own?

No matter from which compass point you approach the port city of Saint John, you can't help but notice the Irving signature etched across the landscape, the sea coast, and the skyline. Many of the outlying second- and third-growth jack pine and spruce forests have been signposted as territory for the huge lumber operations of J.D. Irving Ltd., twenty-five thousand square kilometers of stumpage throughout the Canadian Maritimes and Maine. Along the highway, driving south from the provincial capital of Fredericton or east from the American border, your car will zip past the diamond-shaped signs advertising yet another gas station operated by Irving Oil Ltd. As you cross Saint John on either of its two bridges, your senses will be overtaken by the tangy effluent aroma of the Irving pulp and paper mill, nestled into an otherwise scenic crook of the Saint John River. If you drive west from the airport, you will see, tucked into the valley between Loch Lomond Road and the slate gray sea, the lighted spires and domes of a petrochemical Taj Mahal, the largest oil refinery in Canada. Six enormous white cylinders hunker along the service road, a black letter painted on each drum, spelling out a huge graffito: I R V I N G. Should you cross the Bay of Fundy by sailboat or on the three-hour ferry ride from Digby, Nova Scotia, an equally gargantuan six-cylinder billboard welcomes you to the working harbor that the Irvings dominate. However you arrive in the city, it's clear in whose pocket Saint John sits.

In 1881, James Dergavel Irving, a third-generation Maritimer of Scottish descent, bought a sawmill in Bouctouche, New Brunswick, and grew his business from this one operation. His hyper-ambitious son K.C. took over and became the corporate patriarch who leveraged the family's small holdings into an industrial juggernaut worth more than four billion dollars, a private conglomerate that (since K.C.'s death in 1992) is still run by his three sons and their children and grandchildren. In an era of instant internet wealth, the Irvings are a throwback to the gilded age of New World industrial barons and family fortunes, like the Carnegies or the Rockefellers. They are either resourceful or rapacious, depending on your point of view, but undeniably powerful. Their forests produce the paper, pulped in their mills, that feeds their printing presses, which ink the dozen or so newspapers the Irvings own. Their tankers sit in their shipyards (or once did, for Saint John recently concluded a long history of shipbuilding that had earned it a reputation as "the Liverpool of North America") and in the deep-water harbor dredged by Irving money. They own sawmills and diaper plants, building supply stores and a french fry manufacturer, trucking firms and a rail line, an executive airplane service, a communications firm, countless real estate holdings, and a hockey team. The Irvings are everywhere in New Brunswick. Like the Fundy tides, the family's reach is long and their power—often quiet, sometimes not—nearly unfathomable.

As in any company town, especially one locked in the rusting doldrums of a long economic slide, the seventy-four thousand citizens of Saint John retain a crusty ambivalence to the come-from-nothing clan of billionaires who lords over their lives. The Irving conglomerate keeps on its payrolls five thousand people in the city alone; its bosses have likely laid off that many over the years, too. "The Irvings are bastards," locals will tell you, "but they're *our* bastards." Better to serve a master you know than a faceless corporate board in Toronto or New York.

If there is one Irving product that the residents of Saint John rally around, it's the two and a half square kilometers of peninsular parkland on the western edge of the city. Set aside by the company in 1992, the area once known as Taylors Island is still called that by citizens uncharmed by its rechristening as Irving Nature Park. (Not everything, they figure, needs the family trademark.) This puzzle piece of forest, beachfront, and cliff-edge juts into low-tide mudflats, thick with avian life, and splits the brackish tidal estuary of Saints Rest Marsh and Manawagonish Cove from the deeper waters of the Bay of Fundy. The Irvings fund the upkeep, hire naturalists, and let the public wander around eight animal-themed trails. The red spruce and balsam fir of the Acadian forest shade these walking routes, while breakers perform a steady drum roll on the polished rocks of Saints Rest Beach. Here, you can escape the industrial thrum of the city and absorb the more natural rhythms of this confluence of rare, even endangered ecosystems.

On a Saturday morning in early June, you could expect to encounter a handful of visitors already heading into the park: a jogger or two, a few dog walkers, maybe a retired couple whose passions have turned to bird watching, even the flash of a cyclist poaching an illicit ride on the pedestrian-only trails. Had you been there on June 1, 2002, driving southwest along Sand Cove Road a little before nine thirty in the morning, you would have spotted an unseasonably large gathering beside the Sheldon Point car lot and the service barn at the entrance to the park. That day, nearly a hundred people moved with more purpose than is typical for such an hour on a weekend. They seemed underdressed for a wedding party, and the gear they unloaded from truck beds and car trunks suggested the group had gathered for more action than an ordinary picnic. Mountain bikes were removed from roof racks, assembled, and tested. Several kayaks lay across the dewy turf. Listeners formed a semicircle around one boat and attended to a brief safety demonstration. Men and a few women stood alone or in pairs, wearing polyester shorts or wind pants and light jackets. They pretzeled limbs and torsos in rituals of physical and mental preparation. Some participants seemed young and lean and hungry to display their gym-fought fitness. Others appeared less certain of success. They were older or heavier, more anxious and less revved up. They wore cheap shoes and T-shirts that no serious runner would show off at a start line. They seemed casual athletes at best, not hard to keep pace with in whatever competition was to come.

"Five minutes 'til the start!" somebody called. A murmuring swept across the crowd.

Beyond the bluff edge of Sheldon Point, an early fog still hung like gauze across the horizon. Already, a stiff breeze off the hills and the heat of the sun had begun to dissipate the haze and expose the dark expanse of the bay. The spring wind's breath felt cool against the cheek. Sunshine sparkled across car windshields. The scene held the promise that summer was near, if not quite here, and that the cold, gray days of winter were finally done. It was a perfect morning for a walk in the park, you had to agree. And a damn fine day for a race.

TWO

The Guides

August 30, 2001, St. Moritz, Switzerland. Wish you were here. The Alps are spectacular. But nobody warned us about the cows. If Sara Vlug and Jayme Frank had time to pen postcards during their European adventure, that was how one of their hasty missives might have read. The fit young couple had traveled across the Atlantic, from their home along the Fundy shore, all the way to the Swiss Alps. They hadn't planned an idle vacation of hopping among cafés, cathedrals, and museums. Vlug and Frank had signed up to compete in what had been billed as the "world championship of adventure racing," and they expected more vigorous navigational challenges than catching the right train. Days and nights of trekking, rock climbing, off-road biking, and whitewater paddling. The camaraderie of international athletes racing against the clock. Roving camera crews broadcasting their efforts around the globe. And more than four hundred and twenty kilometers of snow-capped backcountry terrain to cover.

The Discovery Channel World Championship had attracted the most accomplished multi-sport athletes to Europe's most famous mountain range for seven days of competitive adventure. The first team of four to cross the finish line under its own steam would win bragging rights and a star turn in the global broadcast of the big race. The winners could also better leverage the sponsorship dollars that made attending such far-flung events affordable. For now, the young couple from New Brunswick relied largely on the support of Eastern Outdoors, the Vlug family's retail store and outfitting company, and had spent thousands of their own dollars on airfares and entry fees to get to St. Moritz. They were long shots to win but hoped to give the more experienced teams a scare. If everything went well, the Swiss trip would be their coming-out party as serious competitors.

The race began with a sprint down a three-thousand-meter mountain slope. Then competitors scrambled back up the heights of the Alps. Midway through the first night's trek, Team EasternOutdoors.com was trudging across an alpine pasture when distant lowing turned to more aggressive grunts. A herd of curious cattle encircled and began nudging the fatigued racers. In the pitch black, sharp horns poked and prodded their backpacks and spandex. Trekking—perhaps even running—with the bulls was an unexpected obstacle that hadn't appeared on any map.

Two of the Fundy region's top kayak guides, Sara Vlug and Jayme Frank could have been a poster couple for the sport of adventure racing or the active outdoor lifestyle in general. Standing together, they looked like brother and sister, in the way well-matched twosomes often do. At twenty-six, Jayme Frank had a prematurely receding carpet of orangey hair and was lean yet solid, with a perpetual touch of red in his fair-skinned cheeks, like fresh windburn or a healthy flush from a long run or bike ride—which was often the case. Sara Vlug, a year older, was more compact, a coil of barely suppressed energy, impatient to pounce upon her next adventure. In race photographs, she was often at the vanguard of her team, muddy, sweaty, still grinning, her reddish-blond hair spilling out from her bike helmet.

Frank was from Kenora, Ontario, a logging and mining town nestled against Lake of the Woods, the labyrinth of fifteen thousand islands that borders Manitoba and Minnesota. Knowing how to navigate through forest and water is a point of pride in his hometown. Frank had moved east to study marine biology in New Brunswick. As captain of his university basketball team in Saint John, he had been a shooting guard who had won the Most Valuable Player of the Year. After meeting Vlug, he had also become an adept sea kayaker, thanks to her family's interest in the sport, and now led paddling trips for Eastern Outdoors while he trained as an adventure racer and looked for full-time work as a marine biologist.

Sara Vlug was a Bay of Fundy girl through and through. She had graduated with her teaching degree and still lived, with Frank, at her parents' seaside property in Dipper Harbour. Deanna, her mother, was a direct descendant of the community's first settler, a Loyalist who had arrived in 1786 after fighting in the American War of Independence. Bob Vlug, Sara's father, had a Dutchman's love of the sea. He was a longtime sailor and kayaker, and a proud promoter of both sports. She shared her dad's passion for paddling, his quick laugh, and his notoriously fast-boiling temper. Her parents had started Eastern Outdoors as an equipment retailer and outfitter out of their garage in 1979. In Saint John's Brunswick Square shopping mall, the Vlugs later opened a store that sold paddling and camping gear. They also ran kayak tours from the beach in front of the family home and out of an outlet in St. Andrews.

Sara Vlug and Jayme Frank were what demographers describe as early adopters. The couple had been introduced to adventure racing back in 1998, when the obscure sport was gaining buzz from the televised success of the Eco-Challenge. They had entered a four-day race in southwestern Quebec called the Canadian Quest—three hundred kilometers of paddling, bushwhacking, and off-road bike riding. Just finishing was an accomplishment that few competitors got to savor. Most sane couples would consider such sleepless suffering a violation of the Geneva Conventions rather than a romantic holiday. Frank and Vlug couldn't wait to do it all again.

The couple had always been keen on competitive sports and outdoor exploration, so the chance to merge two passions seemed ideal. They could train and travel together. The emphasis on endurance and team strategy, rather than brute strength and speed, put female athletes on an even footing with male teammates and rivals. Adventure racing especially suited Vlug's wild-at-heart spirit. "Before, I was a freak," she confessed to a local reporter. "I always liked running around in the woods, but I tried to hide that side of me. Now I have a purpose. I no longer have to be embarrassed about it." The payoff for the sacrifice and suffering, she explained, was a better understanding of her own physical and psychological limits, as well as a deeper relationship with her teammates, including her boyfriend. "Some people don't understand why we fork out thousands of bucks to get brutalized," Frank said, "but it's fun."

Four years after their first race, the couple continued to sacrifice time and money to feed their appetite for adventure. They trained three hours every work day and often squeezed in sixteen hours of running, cycling, and paddling on weekends. "It's tough scrounging the time and money to do it," Frank told a sports writer. "But it's very addicting." The couple aspired to compete at a top international race. Like most competitors, they had their ambitions fixed on the Eco-Challenge, considered the Super Bowl of adventure racing for its technical difficulty, its global prominence, and its all-American hype. "It's been a dream for a long time," said Vlug to another reporter. "We want to be one of the top teams in Canada. Because of our age, we've got another fifteen or twenty years to compete on an international level."

In 2001, sponsored by the Vlug family's business, Team EasternOutdoors.com got its first chance to compete in the big leagues of their little sport. By completing a pair of qualifying races, they became eligible for a spot in the first ever Discovery Challenge World Championship. Stakes were high for everyone. The organizers and Discovery Channel (which no longer owned the broadcast rights to the popular Eco-Challenge) wanted to prove they could host a new race as challenging and as safe as other major events. Young racers hoped to establish reputations by beating veteran teams. "I'm a very competitive person and would like the opportunity to race against the best in the world," Vlug confided on her internet profile. "After adventure racing for four years, we feel ready to take the next step," added Frank. With two teammates, the pair of Fundy kayak guides trained with renewed vigor. "We'll have to contend with glaciers and rope work," Frank anticipated. "There are no marked trails.... It's dangerous but they make things very safe. It's a controlled danger."

In the end, not all the dangers could be controlled.

After some bovine probing, Team EasternOutdoors.com made a midnight getaway from the curious cows and later laughed about the incident. What they couldn't laugh at—and hadn't prepared for in their largely sea-level training—was the debilitating effects of the altitude. The European Alps don't reach Himalayan heights, but the thin air still sapped the athletes' energy. Their legs felt as stiff and unwilling as raw logs. Symptoms of mountain sickness squeezed the breath from their lungs and muddled their brains. Reluctantly, after less than forty-eight hours, the young Canadians pulled out of the race.

It might have been for the best. The early exit meant that Vlug and Frank never reached the aptly named Via Mala Gorge. There, competitors had to rappel into a narrow canyon and swim two kilometers in glacier-fed waters. Racers who hadn't dropped out by then (only nine of forty-one teams would finish) were exhausted and cold after twenty-four hours of alpine trekking. They huddled until daybreak and then shimmied into the gorge. One determined racer was throwing up even as he pulled on a wetsuit and life vest.

Scottish triathlete Carolyn Jones seemed similarly out of sorts as she floated on her back down the last hundred meters of the canyon stream. She missed the final pullout, so she flipped over and tried to swim. The force of the rushing water took control and pinned Jones head first and face down between two rocks. A nearby TV cameraman attempted to free her with his tripod to no avail. Her teammates were too hypothermic to help. By the time she was pulled to safety, Jones's face had been submerged for twenty minutes. She was airlifted to a hospital and remained in a coma for several weeks. She later regained consciousness, although she sustained brain damage and would need constant medical care.

Despite its inherent risks, the sport of adventure racing had remained free of tragedy and controversy for a dozen years. Injuries were an accepted part of wilderness events but tended to be minor: sprained ankles on treks, busted bones and torn muscles on mountain-biking routes, mild hypothermia during longer races, a touch of altitude sickness in alpine events, dehydration, heat exhaustion, the odd virus, and simply getting pooped beyond the ability to take another step. Still, many racers considered it a matter of luck that nobody had yet died in their still-young sport. The world champi-onship in St. Moritz only emphasized that fact. Several top-level participants at the Swiss race complained to a journalist from *Sports Illustrated* that events were becoming increasingly dangerous. Racers were pushing harder over more precarious terrain, while organizers were looking to outdo the drama and challenge of rival races. "Someone's going to die in one of these," one racer predicted. "Everyone knows it." Other people wondered if the near-fatal accident would increase public scrutiny of their sport. "Maybe we'll see some sort of governing body develop," mused a veteran competitor. "That means some really boring races for a while, until we get a set of standards. But maybe it's time for that. Maybe it's time for people to realize adventure racing is risky."

The tragedy-clouded Swiss event proved a disappointment for the sponsors (the Discovery Channel never produced another race) and many of the competitors, among them the early dropouts from Team EasternOutdoors.com. Vlug and Frank returned from Europe determined to improve their reputation internationally. They also continued to promote the sport around the Maritimes. In 2000, the couple had organized a pair of races using the Vlug family's kayaks and contacts: a thirty-six-hour overnight event (called the Atlantic Canada Adventure Challenge) and an eight-hour beginners' race (the Fundy Multi-Sport Race). Twenty-five people participated in the introduc-tory event. Two months before the Swiss trip, Frank and Vlug had hosted the short race again and attracted even more participants. For

2002, they promoted the Fundy challenge broadly. They posted notices in recreation centers and in internet groups. They left brochures at the Eastern Outdoors store and physiotherapists' offices. They visited high schools and talked up the sport among students.

There wasn't much money to be made, if any, as a race organizer, not when they were charging a hundred dollars for two-person teams and seventy-five for solo competitors. That wasn't why they put on events. "It's to build a community of racers who want something different from a triathlon," Vlug explained to a reporter. "To introduce people to a thirty-six-hour adventure race, you maybe need to start out with an eight-hour race.... Our goal is to have people go to bigger races, like the Eco-Challenge." After Vlug and Frank's letdown in Switzerland, the end of winter and the arrival of next year's racing season must have seemed like forever to the ambitious young adventurers.

THREE

The Runner

Three times a week, René Arseneault ran a thirteen-kilometer loop, from the bungalow his father had built near the end of Dobbin Street—his parents had separated four years ago, in 1998—and out to Old Rothesay Road. There, he turned west, with the broad Kennebecasis River to his right, and continued along the former highway, past the shore-side park and the tree-shaded manors that overlooked the water. The Kennebecasis Valley had long been the summer getaway and retirement retreat for the wealthier residents of Saint John, and the town of Rothesay formed a leafy and less foggy suburb of the larger, more industrial city. At the midway point of his run, Arseneault liked to stop at Colwell's, a corner store and butcher, and quaff a bottle of spring water before he turned for home.

Along the route, he nodded to fellow joggers or to neighbors who knew him from the supermarket in nearby Quispamsis where he stocked produce. If anyone asked, he told them he was training for a marathon—*the* marathon. In 2001, he had completed the half-course at the Marathon by the Sea, a popular race that skirted the nineteenth-century facades of uptown Saint John and offered spectacular vistas—whenever runners weren't gasping for breath or cloaked in summer fog—of the Bay of Fundy. Arseneault, then twenty-one, had placed fifth in his age division. This summer, he planned to tackle the full twenty-six miles.

Nobody could remember when Arseneault had begun to run seriously, perhaps because he had always seemed in motion, a merry prankster with limitless energy and an often abbreviated attention span. His father, Jean-Guy, with whom he lived, couldn't stop him from performing distracting finger-tip drum solos on the dashboard of his truck. His many friends knew that, come Saturday night, René would be the one to make sure that everyone went out dancing—and stayed out late—at one of the nightclubs in Saint John. Or if it was New Year's Eve and midnight struck, he would be the first to streak naked from the house party, flop backwards into a snow bank, and carve drunken angels on the winter canvas. He was loquacious, and when he talked, his hands danced for emphasis, in a very French manner, as he chomped on an ever-present sliver of gum.

His mother, Jacqueline, marveled at how René seemed to have an itinerary for every moment of his life. He might argue about many things—anything, in fact—but he never complained about being bored. Even on the rare day when he didn't have a set plan, he would hop astride his apple-red Kawasaki Ninja and ride his motorbike to Fundy National Park, descend the switchbacking road to the bay, and return home. "Ah, mom, what a beautiful ride I had!" he would say. Life was too short for sitting still.

He got that *joie de vivre*, Jacqueline reckoned, from his Acadian grandfather, who had died eight years earlier. Jean-Guy's dad, a favorite of René's, had been an industrial therapist who dabbled in poetry and sketched satirical cartoons. Years ago, whenever his grandson got rambunctious, Grandpa Raphael, perhaps wearing his T-shirt that read "Take Me Drunk I'm Home," would hang René by his shirt collar or denim overalls from the hook of a bedroom door until he calmed. In the winters, he took his grandson ice fishing. René may not have learned patience from their trips, but the mini-expeditions instilled in the boy a passion for hiking, camping, and other outdoor pursuits.

René had also inherited his grandfather's wicked tongue, a censor-less wit that got him into and out of trouble. Raphael had once looked at his grandson, three years old at the time, and teased, "René, why do you have such a big nose?"

René hadn't missed a beat. "But *papère*," he had replied, "everyone tells me I look just like you!"

In one of his earliest photos, taken when he was eight months old, Arseneault smiles and squats in a tiny sweater embossed with "Super Sport." It was a sign of things to come. He developed into a gifted young athlete with a keen competitive spirit, honed in a family of four sports-mad boys. When he was four years old, he had abandoned his tiny training bike and learned to pedal a far bigger ten-speed. "René," his dad had warned, "you're going to rupture yourself!" He didn't care. In the summer, Arseneault would build pitching mounds beside his parents' house to practice his fastball. In the winter, he played pickup hockey on the backyard rinks his father flooded for the boys, and then rooted with his dad for the Montreal Canadiens whenever their team appeared on *Hockey Night in Canada*. The drywall in the unfinished basement of the family house was still black-marked and scratched from years of errant pucks, basketballs, and skateboards. When he had graduated from Kennebecasis River Valley High, a public school of fifteen hundred students, Arseneault had accepted an award as the best all-around athlete.

Even today, he rarely traveled anywhere without a ball or a Hacky Sack, something to throw or kick around, to turn idle moments into spirited competition. Twenty-one years after posing as a Super Sport and now a man—fit and handsome and perhaps overly conscious of both—the label still applied. "René, I swear, was born with a ball in his mouth," his mother often said. He could pick up a new sport and master it in months. A few years ago, to everyone's surprise, it had been badminton. Nobody wanted to tell him, but chasing a birdie didn't seem all that macho. Still, Arseneault had practiced until he was beating many of the top players at the local club. "You almost want to invent something he won't be good at," André, the oldest of René's three brothers, would joke. That would be tough. Arseneault loved to come out on top—in a game, a race, or an argument.

"René, is it always about winning?" his mother would ask.

"Mom," he replied, "you don't train this hard to lose."

In the early spring of 2002, whenever Arseneault dropped by his mom's house after a shift at the grocery store, he would study a wrinkled sheet of paper downloaded off the internet. It listed details and included a map for something he called the "Fundy race."

"What's that?" his mother asked.

"It's like a triathlon," he explained, "but different."

He pored over the fine print, traced a finger along the route, and composed lists of the equipment he still needed to buy or borrow. His mother recognized the attention he brought to his preparations. After her son came home with a paycheck, he liked to sit at her kitchen table and draw out a careful budget—how much for motorcycle payments, driver's insurance, his other expenses—at first always working the numbers so he had enough money left over for one case of beer. Jacqueline Arseneault could tell that her son was taking this new race seriously because he gradually curtailed and then stopped drinking altogether. He wouldn't even enjoy an after-work bottle of Alpine lager, his favorite local brew. He had shown the same teetotaling discipline in the weeks leading up to the previous year's half-marathon. Only after he had finished that race would he let his mom buy him a pint.

René told Jacqueline about the organizers, Jayme and Sara. The young couple traveled across the country, around the world even, to compete in races. In the weeks before the Fundy event, Arseneault frequently dropped into the Eastern Outdoors store, where Sara Vlug worked, to learn more about the race. In high school, Arseneault had struggled with classroom routines and homework exercises. Now three years since graduating, he felt like he was spinning his wheels. While he never lacked for things to do, with plenty of hobbies and outings and other weekend distractions, he was still searching for what to do in a larger sense. The two young race organizers seemed to have found a vehicle for their own athletic passions. Arseneault just needed to discover his own. He knew he didn't want to rinse lettuce at the grocery store for the rest of his life. He had enrolled at the community college to upgrade his math and English credits. He thought he might like to complete a technical program afterwards, maybe work for the cable company like his older brother André.

His mother didn't worry too much. René was fit and determined and took good care of himself. Tightly muscled from working out, he stood five foot eight and a little over one hundred and seventy pounds. He watched what he ate—no junk food binges, especially when training—and often chided Jacqueline about her smoking. His mom had faint yellow stains on her fingers and the etched facial lines of a longtime smoker. Even if she couldn't emulate it, she admired her son's commitment to healthy living. With a group of friends, Arseneault had flown down to Cuba for the March break and he still had a remnant of the deep tan he had brought through customs along with a bottle of rum for his mom. That accent of bronze, his fashionably slim sideburns, and the blond highlights he'd applied to the tips of his brown hair gave him the dark-eyed Mediterranean looks of a Formula One driver. A few years ago, Jacqueline had managed to convince all four boys to dress up and pose for a photographer. André had complained that he looked fat. Denis had thought his smile was askew. Guy, the youngest, had shrugged with indifference. Only René had beamed at the results. "I don't know about the rest of you," he said, "but I look great." René was the most outgoing of the four. Every year he had performed in his high school's musical and, always the flirt, attended four proms with four different girls. Jacqueline knew that his confidence would see him through the race—and whatever might come next in his life.

Most of his friends didn't pay too much attention either to his talk about the race. It was just another of René's big ideas. They had long ago given up trying to keep pace with his plans. Erin Dobson, though, found the image of René competing by kayak on the Bay of Fundy a little odd. Dobson and Arseneault had dated for two years but had broken up after a squabble on New Year's Eve. They remained close and hung out with the same pack of high school pals from

Rothesay. In their summers together, they had visited almost every park in New Brunswick. Arseneault loved to be in the outdoors, doing anything—or almost anything. Dobson knew Arseneault wasn't a big fan of the water. While they had all grown up along the Kennebecasis River, he had never learned to swim well, aside from a few lessons in an uncle's backyard pool. Dobson's parents kept a sailboat, a power boat, and jet skis docked on the Kennebecasis, but Arseneault had always been reluctant to venture out on the boats. When he did, he often wore not one but two or even three life vests. Dobson and Arseneault had gone canoeing a few times for short jaunts along the river's shore, and he took the same precautions. In her favorite photo of him, Arseneault stands on a rock that turtles out of the shallows near her parents' house. He grins that wild and carefree, slightly cocky smile she had fallen for—Arseneault was her first true love. But even here, he still wears a life jacket. Besides, the Kennebecasis—a placid river protected between the long walls of the valley, a popular moorage for American sailors traveling up the Eastern Seaboard—was a far different and far safer stretch of water than the Bay of Fundy. Out on the bay, the ten-meter tides can pull vessels off course and the summer fogs can obscure dangers of all sorts. Even steep-hulled lobster boats can vanish in a gale.

Not much frightened René. But water came close.

"So why are you doing this race?" Dobson had asked, a week before the event.

"I've taken some kayak lessons," he said. "I'll be fine."

That Arseneault would want to conquer his fear of water didn't surprise her. She trusted that he knew that he was getting into. In fact, she was sure he would do well. He might even win.

A week and a half before the race, Jacqueline Arseneault had gotten a call from her oncologist. She had been treated for breast cancer for the last year and a half. The prognosis had seemed grim at first, and she had tried to prepare her family for the worst. Now, after rounds of chemotherapy and biopsies and months of anxious waiting, the final tests had come in. Her doctor gave her a clean bill of health. A weight lifted from her mind. For months, she had been forced to contemplate leaving behind her four boys. Now she could imagine a future with them again.

Still, the experience only heightened her sense of tenuous mortality. She worried about her boys. Not so much the older two. Denis was a business student in Halifax. André, always the serious one, lived at home but worked as a videographer and field reporter for the local cable TV company. René was more headstrong and speed-loving than either of them, a born risk taker. Jacqueline could barely hide her concern whenever he peeled out of her driveway on his Kawasaki, even though she knew how much he loved that bike and how he promised to drive it wisely. Guy, her youngest, took most after René—he idolized and teased his older sibling in equal measure, as brothers do. Both were fueled by a heedlessness and a competitive fire.

When René visited the next evening, Jacqueline was brooding about the number of young people from town who had died in late-night car accidents on Loch Lomond Road. In the past few years, that dark stretch of pavement, winding from the airport into Saint John, had claimed several lives, all of them near René's age. Speed and alcohol and the invincibility of youth had contributed to these tragedies in different measures. The names of the dead were well known in Rothesay. Jacqueline tried her best not to imagine the awful scenario that had been repeated too many times: the ambulance lights flaring down Loch Lomond, the metal wreckage along the road, the midnight visit from the police, and the long hopeless drive to the morgue.

"What's going on out there?" she asked René.

"I don't know," he said.

"What are their parents going through?" she wondered. "What are their mothers going through?"

He didn't have an answer.

She asked him about the upcoming race. Was it safe? What about kayaking on the bay?

"Mom, it's going to be okay," he assured her. "It's along the shore."

A few days later, René visited his mother's house again. He sat at her kitchen table, talking yet again about the race. Tonight, he seemed distracted by a late-night premonition of his own.

"Mom," he told her. "I had a terrible dream."

"What was it?" she asked

"Just one of those crazy dreams." That was all he would say.

On Friday, May 31, 2002, René dropped by his mother's house in the early evening. He removed a couple of pull-tab lottery tickets from one of the pockets on his new red and black motorcycle jacket. He often surprised his mom with gifts. "Let's see if you're lucky," he said. He seemed more restless than usual. He sat down and then bounced back to his feet. His talk circled back to the next day's race. Nothing else could hold his attention.

"Check these out," he said. He showed off a new pair of deep-treaded hiking shoes, which had cost a good chunk of his last paycheck. He had picked them up for the race at the Eastern Outdoors store. He let his mom admire the canary-yellow cycling socks he had bought, too, which matched the jersey he had borrowed from his brother André.

"You paid ten dollars for a pair of socks?" his mother marveled. Theirs had never been a family to toss money at passing fancies.

"Mom," he said, "I have to look good!"

Finally, he realized he should get enough sleep before the big day, so he gave his mother a goodnight kiss on the cheek. Jacqueline watched her son disappear into the dark and listened for the throttle of his bike.

Past midnight, in the early hours of June 1, Jean-Guy Arseneault returned from his shift on a construction job at the airport. René was still awake.

"Why're you up?" Jean-Guy asked.

"Can't sleep," René said.

He told his dad—for the twentieth time, it seemed—what the race would involve: the running, the cycling, the paddling, all day and all out. His voice hummed as if caffeinated. He seemed to be playing out the coming race in his imagination, over and over again. Finally, he decided he needed to sleep. His father wished him well and promised to pick him up at the end of the race.

The next morning, René grabbed his duffel bag and drove his father's Chevy pick-up to his mother's house. While less athletic than his younger brother, André was the most avid cyclist in the family, so he had agreed to lend René his mountain bike and helped load it onto the truck. Finally, René folded and tied a red bandana around his forehead to mop sweat. It gave him an outlaw look, which he didn't mind either. He stood in the doorway to the basement, bouncing on the balls of his hiking shoes, eager to go. "C'mon, André, let's move!" he urged. His mother awakened on the couch where she had fallen asleep in front of the TV. "Give it your best shot!" she called as her two sons headed off.

André and René drove to Saint John and reached the Sheldon Point barn around 8:30 a.m. The morning air was cool and damp, but the white disc of the sun had started to pierce the fog.

"You ready?"

André had to drive back to Rothesay and leave the truck with their dad. Then he would check in at work, pick up a video camera and van, and return to the race. He hoped to shoot footage at every stage. Later that afternoon, he had to film the national fencing championships at the university. Both events promised more action than the typical community happenings he covered. Both should make for good TV.

"You bet," René assured him.

"Well, good luck," said André.

René hoisted the duffel bag over his shoulder and rolled the mountain bike toward the registration table. At last he would meet the other racers, the people he would soon be chasing and who—by the final section on the bay, he hoped—would be chasing him.

FOUR

The Sport

In 1982, viewers of ABC's *Wide World of Sports*, the popular weekend TV roundup of athletic highlights, were transfixed by the extraordinary ordeal of young Julie Moss. The event was the Hawaii Ironman, then a little-known race that had debuted four years earlier to settle a bet about who were the fittest athletes: swimmers, runners, or cyclists. The first Ironman triathlon had combined three already exhausting competitions: the Waikiki Rough Water Swim (3.8 kilometers), the Around-Oahu Bike Race (one hundred and eighty kilometers) and the Honolulu Marathon (forty-two kilometers). Fifteen athletes started and twelve completed the original course, with the winner crossing the last of the three finish lines in eleven hours, forty-six minutes, and forty seconds. (The top men now do the route in just over eight hours.) However, it would be the efforts of an Iron Woman that would revolutionize interest in the sport and set the benchmark against which all future performances in endurance races would be measured.

Julie Moss, a twenty-three-year-old American college student, had gone to Hawaii to compete as part of her research into exercise physiology. To everyone's surprise, as she entered the final marathon stage, she held a twenty-minute lead over the next female racer. A few hundred meters from the finish, Moss began to falter. After eleven hours, the sweat-drenched triathlete was succumbing to a loss of fluids. Cheering onlookers urged her on and tried to drape a Hawaiian lei around her thin neck, oblivious to the twilight zone of suffering into which she had passed. Her eyes appeared haunted. Her thin legs wobbled and began to feel like spaghetti. Suddenly, she collapsed in a heap of splayed limbs. She wearily pulled herself to her feet and continued at a walking pace. She tried to run again (foolishly, she would later admit), then staggered, tumbled to the ground, and was helped up once more. After another fall, utterly spent but unwilling to quit, Moss began to crawl the final twenty meters, only to be passed by her nearest rival. By the end, Moss had lost control of almost every bodily function, except her indomitable will to finish the race.

Twenty-five years later, the footage of Moss's struggle to the line remains powerful. Her crawling finish inspired thousands to take up the sport of triathlon. They were drawn to discover whether they, too, could spur their bodies onward when every synapse and muscle fiber screamed at them to stop. The televised conclusion also cemented the reputation of the Ironman as the toughest race in the world. Any new event that wanted to make the same boast would have to offer competitors their own Moss-like moments of suffering and redemption, and then advertise their ordeals to the world.

We might like to think we invented the Age of Extreme. The urge to push the human body to its outer limits, however, has been around far longer than the current fad for Ironman triathlons, action sports, and reality TV. Public tests of human endurance are as old as the Greeks. Long before the Ironman, the most legendary measure of physical stamina was the marathon. The inspiration for the famous footrace was the tale of brave Pheidippides, the professional runner who dashed to Athens, in 490 B.C., to alert his countrymen and women of the Greek victory at the Battle of Marathon. "Rejoice, we conquer!" he shouted—then keeled over from exhaustion and into the realm of legend, the first recorded death of an extreme athlete. That noble effort inspired the organizing committee for the resurrected Olympics in 1894 to recreate Pheidippides' legendary (although likely apocryphal) run from Marathon to Athens. Over the next century, the marathon became the universal yardstick of endurance, as well as shorthand for any long-distance event. People would compete in swimming marathons, ski marathons, canoe and kayak marathons, and the Depression-era spectacle of dance marathons. Runners can now line up for arctic marathons, desert marathons, and mountain marathons. Marathons can be divided into half-marathons or expanded (twice the distance, often more) into ultramarathons. *Marathon*, as an adjective, now emphasizes any activity that has been pursued with relentless and impassioned endurance.

Even before the *fin de siècle* resurrection of the Olympic marathon, newspapers published accounts of long-distance running and walking races. These events became known by the unfortunate title of "pedestrianism." In 1762, a British ambler won the first recorded 160-kilometer footrace in just under twenty-four hours. Seven years later, another Englishman walked his way into celebrity (and settled a bet) by strolling six hundred and thirty-seven kilometers from London to York and back. Six-day races were especially popular, as fit Christians could complete the routes without running on the Sabbath. "The runners back a hundred, two hundred years ago were phenomenal," marveled Ian Adamson, one of the world's top adventure racers and an amateur historian of obscure endurance sports. "They had none of the technology we have—the moisture-wicking clothing and shock-absorbing shoes. People ran in flat leather shoes and drank whiskey. They did everything wrong." And a few competitors likely crawled across the finish line, too.

The same year as Julie Moss's miracle finish, Mark Burnett, a young paratroooper from a working-class family in England, quit the British Army, after tours of duty in the Falklands War and

Northern Ireland, and bought a one-way ticket for the New World. He planned to seek work in Central America as a "military adviser" (read: soldier of fortune). His mother, however, had vague misgivings about his new job and told him as much. Burnett promised to look into a different line of work. He skipped out on Central America and stayed in Los Angeles, where an expat friend helped the young Brit land a position as the nanny for a wealthy Beverly Hills couple. For two years, he worked as California's most combat-ready *au pair* and earned extra money by selling manufacturer-rejected T-shirts along Venice Beach. He sank those profits into a real estate deal and started his own marketing company.

By 1991, the thirty-two-year-old Burnett was living the American dream, warts and all—a well-off workaholic in the City of Angels, with a fast car in the driveway and an even faster-approaching existential crisis. On a February morning, he picked up the Sunday edition of the *L.A. Times* and read the opening lines of a feature article, the first in a four-part series, called "The Ultimate Race": "A gentle rain began to fall soon after midnight, streaking the mud on my glasses and softening the sound of my horse's hoofs on the jungle floor...." The story described an exotic and arduous ten-day wilderness competition, in which co-ed teams of amateur athletes sleeplessly navigated through the rivers and rainforests of Costa Rica by foot, bike, boat, and horse. Burnett was transported by the descriptions of the participants' epic suffering and by Gérard Fusil, the event's swashbuckling creator.

A French journalist with globe-spanning ambitions, Fusil had been reporting on the Whitbread Round the World sailing race in 1987 when he had an epiphany. "I got the idea to organize an adventure competition for people who would only use physical and mental strength and no mechanics," he recalled. "A race where you have to live in your environment as a family, instead of just passing through it." In 1989, he had arranged five million dollars in sponsorship, laid out a course in New Zealand, and attracted thirty-five teams of five, with at least one woman in each, for his inaugural Raid Gauloises. While other multi-day, multi-sport outdoor competitions (such as the Alpine Ironman, also in New Zealand, and the Alaskan Mountain

Wilderness Classic) had preceded his own race, Fusil's ambitions were grander. The following year, the Raid decamped to the volcanoes and cloud forests of Costa Rica, and Fusil arranged for a team of international reporters, including one from the *L.A. Times*, to compete and field on-the-ground stories.

Mark Burnett knew from his market-tracking research that the future looked bright for a trinity of trends: environmental awareness, extreme sports, and personal development through physical challenge. The Raid Gauloises provided the perfect storyline through which to experience all three themes. (Fitness freaks did raise their eyebrows that the famous French cigarette maker was the title sponsor of the race.) Burnett took the newspaper article as a favorable omen. "Somewhere deep within my paratrooper soul still beat the heart of an adventurer," he realized. "I needed to bring it forth before it was too late." He had always envied the showy creative power of Hollywood's TV and film producers. He decided to launch his own event. To make the theme of self-discovery through wilderness adventure even more explicit, he would call his race the Eco-Challenge.

First, Burnett needed to experience a race for himself. He signed up for the next Raid Gauloises, in the Arab state of Oman, cobbled together four teammates, and christened them with a name guaranteed to gall the French organizers, competitors, and fans: Team American Pride. Midway through a stormy sea-kayaking stage, however, one disgruntled member quit and disqualified the team. When race organizers found the solo racer alone on a beach, they launched a hunt to locate the missing Americans. "No one had ever died during a Raid," Burnett recalled, "and it seemed a cruel act of fate for the novice American team to be the first." It was a false alarm. The remaining members of Team American (Wounded) Pride eventually staggered across the finish line—in last place. For the following year in Madagascar, Burnett drafted a U.S. dream team that included three Navy SEALs. This crew, although not without its own squabbles, fared better. They finished ninth, the first U.S. team to complete the race as a group. More importantly, media coverage on ESPN and NBC introduced North America to a strange new French export, expedition racing.

Burnett now understood the logistical challenges of putting on a wilderness event. To ensure he did it right, he bought the franchise rights for an American version of the Raid. Secretly, he wanted to create an Eco-Challenge that was bolder and better than the Raid Gauloises. He would double the number of TV crews shadowing the teams and make the big race fit the small screen. "I wanted to produce a dynamic television show about racers questing after this Holy Grail," he recalled in his memoir, *Jump In! Even If You Don't Know How to Swim.* "I wanted *Eco* to be more epic, more dramatic, more bombastic: a David Lean film come to life."

When it made its American debut in 1995, however, the Eco-Challenge was not universally embraced by locals. In Utah, Burnett thought he had found the ideal site. The spooky desert wilds and mesas promised a picturesque backdrop, and the stateside location would ease the logistics of TV production and event management. By choosing Utah, however, the producer waltzed into a political hornet's nest in an already polarized corner of the country. Burnett had the support of the state's Republican governor, but that fact only made liberal-minded environmentalists suspicious. The race promoted self-propelled travel and crossed federal lands already used by all-terrain vehicles. Still, green groups found fault because competitors would infringe on the habitat of bighorn sheep and peregrine falcons. Utah ranchers, on the other hand, assumed that Burnett was just another of the environmental activists with whom they had been feuding, an opinion based largely on the "Eco" in the race's name and its broadcast deal with MTV, the video-age apotheosis of urban decadence. Paying for impact assessments and lobbying efforts drained Burnett's finances, and he stared down a million-dollar budget shortfall and a bureaucratic logjam of land-use applications. Only a last-minute sponsorship deal and federal permits issued four days before the start saved the race from imploding.

Despite the early hurdles, the first race in Utah proved a popular success. When only seventeen of fifty-three teams finished a course that Burnett had boasted "ate the Ironman triathlon for breakfast," the Eco-Challenge cemented its reputation as a rival to the title of world's toughest race. Shortly afterwards, cable sports network ESPN invited

Burnett to produce another race in Maine for the network's inaugural X Games. He whipped up a second race in six months. With the ESPN contract, he paid off the debt from the Utah event. At MTV, the cable network was gravitating away from music videos to reality TV melodramas such as *The Real World*. For the next Eco (as the race became known to fans), executives demanded that Burnett feature only participants who fit MTV's demographic of good-looking twenty-somethings (presumably, female, drunk and dressed in bikinis). That restriction didn't fit with Burnett's broader vision of adventure racing. Burnett found a more willing collaborator with Discovery, the international cable channel, which could broadcast the Eco-Challenge to a global audience of one hundred and forty million households in a hundred and thirty different countries. Adventure racing was ready to make a truly international debut. Now Burnett had to design a wilderness course and produce a documentary of the race that would live up to his hype.

"A vision quest, a journey into nature. Push yourself until the pain comes, until you think you cannot survive, and then go on. Here the ego will let go. Here you will be purified. Here is the moment of true prayer, where you will feel the power of the universal law. It is here where your quest begins ... and ends."

In February of 1997, a barrel-voiced narrator intoned the philosophy of a new tribe of modern adventurers. Around the world, the Discovery Channel broadcast, in five episodes, an event that led seventy teams of five through the Coast Mountains near Whistler, British Columbia. TV viewers were introduced to the nine-day competition (filmed the previous summer) as *Eco-Challenge: The Adventure Race* and learned that teams had paid ten thousand dollars "to complete the most grueling course designed in the fifteen-year history of adventure racing."

What captured audiences' interest in the race wasn't simply the natural landscapes of coastal British Columbia or the mystery of who might win. Rather, the show accented the human drama of amateur athletes working together or falling apart under the stress of completing an expedition against the clock. The British Columbia–based

Eco-Challenge provided the narrative template that Burnett would use in his later reality TV hits. His secret? He found compelling and quirky personalities, removed them from their ordinary lives, faced them off against each other under intense conditions, and then hired enough camera crews to capture every emotional meltdown. "Life is competition," he later observed in his memoir. "And the *Eco-Challenge*—as the perfect blend of sport, human dynamics, and adventure—is the epitome of competition.... Whether competing in the Eco-Challenge, vying for a CEO's position, or racing for the last spot in a crowded mall parking lot, everyone on earth is in the game."

The British Columbia race witnessed a close battle between three top teams, including the eventual winners Team Eco-Internet, led by Ian Adamson, the inexhaustible Australian who was establishing his reputation as the Michael Jordan meets Tiger Woods of adventure racing. The broadcast also wove together storylines that followed people to whom couch-bound viewers could better relate. Team Houston, a rookie squad of four bankers and one lawyer, promised comic relief, especially in the form of Michelle Blaine, a coiffed and perky Texan who packed a cosmetic kit for mid-race touch-ups and seemed destined for disaster. "I have to wear my lipstick," the doe-eyed attorney explained. "It's a team joke—this race is the antithesis of being a princess." And yet Blaine outlasted two male teammates, who dropped out due to exhaustion and injury.

Other competitors weren't so lucky. Throughout the broadcast, Burnett made cameos to warn about the obstacles set for his racers. "This is not Club Med," he promised. "This is not a vacation. There is no guaranteed finish." A medley of scenes drove home that fact: Racers gone catatonic from dehydration. Gimpy competitors helicoptered off mountainsides. Grown men weeping into calloused palms from sleepless exhaustion. Friendships fraying like cheap T-shirts as exasperated teams abandoned slower members.

Later in the race, the Eco-Challengers were further splintered by an alpine storm—rain, lightning, hail, winds of eighty kilometers per hour—that caught teams exposed on glaciers and mountain peaks. "Mother Nature at her most frightening," as the show's narrator observed. Burnett made the tough decision to cancel the second mountain stage, as well as the whitewater rafting section down the Elaho River, now engorged with storm runoff. He faced discontent from teams who wanted to finish the entire course, not a truncated version. One British Arctic explorer complained about training so hard, only to have "the fun bits" cancelled. Burnett held firm.

Even as the TV broadcast emphasized the wilderness dangers, Burnett played up a safety-first message. "In a race of this magnitude," he explained, "weather and safety are the overwhelming concerns." Before the event, he and his production team had landed in Whistler, Canada's pre-eminent alpine playground, and cherry-picked the best climbing and paddling experts to help rig cameras, occupy checkpoints, and ensure that competitors passed unharmed through the exposed high-country and whitewater sections. "People want these great Indiana Jones–like adventures," explained Kevin Hodder, a local mountain guide who would become the course designer for future Eco-Challenges. "Our product was a safer way to have one of those adventures."

The televised documentary of the nine-day race proved a hit for the Discovery Channel and earned Burnett his first Emmy nomination. Hundreds of weekend athletes discovered a new outlet for their energies. Subsequent Eco-Challenges were flooded with entries. While other expedition-style events existed, the television exposure of the Eco-Challenge elevated Burnett's race above those of his competitors. "It branded the sport around the world," recalled one veteran racer. "It was the race everyone aspired to do. Even Joe Q. Public knew about it." Soon, similar (and shorter) events such as the Fundy Multi-Sport Race began to sprout up across North America and beyond.

As Mark Burnett built on the foundation of his early Eco-Challenges, his restless imagination circled a new project that could explore similar themes of team dynamics and wilderness endurance in an even more dramatic environment. In 1995, a Fox TV executive had told Mark Burnett about an idea for a show being shopped around by a British production company, co-owned by rock star–philanthropist Sir Bob Geldof. Sixteen people would be split into two teams and dropped on a desert island with minimal provisions, and then followed by camera crews while they competed in various challenges and voted each other off the show one by one. A million-dollar pot would stoke their psychological brinkmanship. A version of the concept, called *Expedition Robinson*, aired in Sweden in 1997 and became a huge, if controversial, success. A French take on it was filmed in the Turks and Caicos Islands using an underwater pearl-diving cage. Burnett was intrigued. On business trips or while scouting Eco-Challenge locations—Australia, Morocco, Patagonia— he would glance out the plane window and imagine crash-landing on a scrubby island or getting shipwrecked on a barren atoll. Where would he fit into that new society? he wondered. Who would lead and who would follow? And who, above all, would survive?

The fascination with survival stories is as old as Jonah and the whale. Tales of shipwrecks and castaways cut off from civilization have an especially firm grip on our imaginations. Shakespeare used it as a plot device in *The Tempest* (based on a Virginia-bound ship that foundered off the Bermudas in 1609), while Daniel Defoe's 1719 novel *Robinson Crusoe* (inspired by the four-year odyssey of marooned Scottish sailor Alexander Selkirk) provided the template for three centuries of desert-island fantasies, from Tom Hanks in *Castaway* to innumerable *New Yorker* cartoons. In the twentieth century, the travails of polar explorers drew readers to serialized depictions of their suffering, and Ernest Shackleton's plucky determination against all odds in Antarctica made him the survivor *par excellence*, subject to frequent revivals of hero worship.

As an ex-commando and adventure guru, Mark Burnett was inspired by the theme of modern castaways stripped to their essential selves in a survival scenario. He used his Eco-Challenge experience to pitch an even more ambitious reality TV series. "My *Survivor* would be bigger, more dramatic and more epic than any nonfiction television ever seen," he promised anyone who would listen. He even coined a new word to describe the televised marriage of real people in dramatic situations: *dramality*. (It never caught on.) When the debut season was serialized on CBS in the summer of 2000, the show became a monster ratings success, the most-watched summer TV show ever. More than fifty million viewers tuned into the finale to watch Richard Hatch, the clothing-optional schemer, outwit, outlast, and outplay his way to the million-dollar first prize.

By then, office workers across the continent were wagering on *Survivor* pools, and newspapers scrambled to offer local angles on the cultural phenomenon that everyone was talking about. In Saint John, before the final episode, a reporter from the *Telegraph-Journal* tracked down Sara Vlug to get the young adventurer's take on the show. Vlug said she wouldn't want to be trapped on an island with any of the devious finalists, but confessed that, as an adventure racer, she wouldn't mind attempting a *Survivor*-style challenge. "I think it's a real test of your mental capabilities," she said. "You can see the stress."

FIVE

The Student

He could blame it on the whales.

It was the whales that had sold Boon Kek on the notion of moving around the world to Saint John, New Brunswick, a city he had never visited and knew little about. After two and half years of military service in his native Singapore, he had been demobbed and still felt hungry for adventure. Canada seemed like a good country to find it while earning a university degree—he wanted to see the world, yes, but he was a pragmatist at heart.

Most international visitors tend to bring along a few stereotypes when they arrive in the Great White North: igloos and polar bears, Anne of Green Gables and toothless hockey players, the mountains of Banff, the Falls of Niagara, and red-uniformed Mounties watching over them all. Kek's image of Canada derived mostly from a brochure with a classic Bay of Fundy photo: a backdrop of wilderness shoreline and a whale—likely a humpback, the clown of the sea—breaching out of the sparkling waters. That had been enough. He could have chosen to study in one of Canada's multicultural metropolises. But to the twenty-one-year-old from Singapore, a city was a city. He wanted to experience something different, something wild.

He had grown up in a congested port metropolis of four and a half million citizens—Vancouver on steroids—and lived with his parents and younger brother in one of the Legoland apartment towers that rim the harbor. His father was a spice trader; his mother, a school administrator. They had always emphasized the importance of education and spoke English with their two sons at home. Even before reaching Canada, Kek was fluent, although he still spoke with a softly accented voice. The schools in his rule-heavy birth country had adopted the uniforms and rigid decorum of the British system, with its focus on team sports and outdoor games to forge in students a sterling physical and moral character. The curriculum included coursework from Outward Bound, the adventure school founded in Wales by exiled German educator Kurt Hahn. Conceived to train British seamen in survival during World War Two, Outward Bound had spread the four pillars of its philosophy around the globe: physical fitness, self-reliance, compassion, and personal development through outdoor expeditions. Kek learned the basics of wilderness travel and joined the school's outdoor club for hikes in the forest reserves and hills yet to be engulfed by the sprawling city or on camping trips to Indonesia and Malaysia. He kayaked in the protected coves and harbors and nearly two hundred kilometers of coastline beyond the industrial heart of his island nation. He loved to cycle, too, although the casual trail riding he did back home bore little resemblance to the rocky, rooty, muddy, and steep trails that real mountain bikers sought for thrills in North America.

After high school, Kek completed a three-year business diploma. For his national service, he enlisted as a paratrooper and rose to the rank of third sergeant. His tour of duty helped to solidify his character, to draw out the still-shaky confidence of his teenage years, and to make Kek see what he could do when he set his mind to it.

He remained reserved, intensely rational, more inclined to listen first than to speak. At five-foot-seven and one hundred and fifty-five pounds, with a squarish head, wire-rimmed glasses, and a smattering of acne scars across his caramel cheeks, he would never cut an imposing figure. He looked more like an accounting intern than a battle-ready skydiver. Still, nearly three years of military service had left him with the calm, unflappable demeanor of a potential leader and an appetite for the unknown.

Given the opportunity to study overseas, Kek picked New Brunswick. His parents weren't thrilled that their son would be twelve time zones away, but they were happy that he would be furthering his education. In early January of 2001, he arrived in Saint John for his first semester of studies in psychology. As winter thawed into spring, the wilderness beyond Saint John revealed itself much as he had imagined. Parkland and forest trails were minutes from anyone's door. The wide expanse of the bay exerted a subtle presence on daily life in the city—salting the air, misting the skies, turning the river on its head—although Kek had yet to spot a whale leaping out of its dark waters.

Culture shock was inevitable. The population of Saint John was still largely Caucasian, as white as the early British-sympathizing settlers, mostly Scots and Scotch Irish, who fled the post-Revolution United States and gave their new home its nickname: the Loyalist City. (Benedict Arnold, the traitor to the American cause, lived in the city for six years after being exposed as a British spy.) Even one hundred and twenty-five years later, Saint John had yet to be as transformed by new immigrants as Canada's larger polyglot cities. The annual influx of overseas students, many Chinese speaking, tend to stick together in cliques. Kek tried to be an exception. He was keen to visit the province's wild places and meet new people. He made sure to drop by the Eastern Outdoors shop often, where he scanned the bulletin board for upcoming events. He hoped to try a triathlon come summertime and was intrigued to read about the Fundy Multi-Sport Race. Kayaking, biking, running—he already did all three. And the race would be run along the Bay of Fundy, the slice of the Atlantic that had drawn him to Canada in the first place.

He competed solo in the 2001 event. The three-part course was challenging, and the other competitors seemed friendly. Still, Kek felt one nagging disappointment. He had paddled, biked, and then run for hours. He had pushed his body as hard as he ever had. By the end, he had been jogging the final stretch through Irving Nature Park with a handful of stragglers. They looked at their watches, kept running, looked at their watches again. They weren't going to make it. Not under the official eight-hour mark at least. As they shuffled up the final hill at Sheldon Point, they knew that the race was already done. The organizers were packing up. Yes, Kek had finished—fifteen minutes shy of the cut-off time. He wasn't sure if it felt like a victory or a defeat.

The following year, when the store announced another Fundy race, Kek wanted a rematch. The morning of June 1, Kek got a lift from two friends who were also competing. The three men fueled up with breakfast at the Diplomat, a diner that overlooked the Saint John River and Reversing Falls. Kek pecked at his food. His thoughts were already on the trails, out on the bay. He wanted to compete against his friends. He wanted to compete against his previous time. This year, whatever it took, he would cross the finish line without a shadow of doubt about what he had accomplished.

SIX

The Start

"Okay, let me explain the rules!"

Sara Vlug had a firecracker of a voice that quieted the murmur of gathered racers. It was 9:15 a.m. The race was set to start in fifteen minutes. Standing in a black windbreaker and fleece, with a sun visor containing her red hair in the breeze, Vlug delivered a final set of instructions to the idling athletes. At the sound of her "Go!" they would run down Sand Cove Road, do a loop of Taylors Island, follow the beach back, and ascend the cliffside trail to the Sheldon Point barn. Twosomes and solo runners would retrieve their mountain bikes there and continue along the next stage. Follow the map, Vlug told them, and watch for volunteers and course marshals. These helpers would be stationed throughout the park, at intersections along the busy highway, and at South Musquash Road, where a logging road led—as previous competitors already knew—into a boggy and nearly impassable miasma.

"Remember, this isn't a triathlon," Vlug added. "We're not out there to wipe your noses."

The racers nodded. That's why they were there, for an adventure. The sixty-eight competitors, save for a handful of lean and cocky high-school boys, didn't look like the stereotype of the extreme-sports enthusiast: the tattooed and spiky-haired eternal teenager from Mountain Dew ads. Their ages ranged from seventeen to seventy, and averaged out in the mid thirties. The two-person teams and solo racers included university undergraduates, medical school students, army cadets, college instructors, fitness teachers and physiotherapists, pulp mill and refinery workers, several computer and high-tech consultants, a dozen business managers of various permutations, an insurance broker, a packaging designer, a forestry worker, a funeral director, a government biologist, and an air traffic controller.

In this crowd, Vlug could spot friends and repeat customers. Mark and Shawn, up from Halifax. Rob, a local paddling legend. Bob, her dad, and Mac, his running partner. Dana, a kayak sales rep from the States. And standing out amid the winter-white faces, Boon Kek, the student from Singapore. Others, like René Arseneault, she recognized from the store. Many had signed up for the first time. Most lived in the Saint John or Rothesay area. A few had driven from Bathurst, Moncton, Fredericton, and other towns north or east of the city, or around the horseshoe of the Bay of Fundy from Nova Scotia.

The year before, the kayaking section had been the race's first stage, with paddlers setting off from the beach in Irving Park for twenty-five kilometers along the Fundy coast. Afterwards several runners and triathletes had complained about leg cramps and tight muscles from being squeezed into a cockpit right off the start. For the 2002 event, the organizers had shortened the sea kayaking to twelve kilometers and made it the last leg instead, one that would conclude on the lawn of the Vlugs' house.

That Friday, Sara Vlug and Jayme Frank had hosted an introductory kayaking course. Only one team had shown up. Earlier that morning, after completing registration, the race participants had listened to Frank deliver a five-minute briefing about kayaking safety. He had demonstrated how to cinch the nylon spray skirt around their waists and over the kayak's cockpit. He had pointed out the rescue tools that would accompany each boat: a hand pump, a throw line, a life jacket, and a safety whistle. "These are very loud and people can hear them," he had said. The single kayaks, more narrow and prone to tipping, would also include a paddle float. Frank had shown how to use this inflatable device in case of a capsize. "Are there any questions?" he had asked. There had been none.

Vlug reinforced his message that the bay was a serious body of water. "The water is extremely cold, so be careful," she warned. "If you need help, blow your whistle or go to shore. If you hear someone blowing a whistle, or if someone capsizes, stop and help them. If you don't, you'll be disqualified and banned from any races we organize in the future."

The racers nodded and shifted in their running shoes to keep their muscles warm.

"Most of all, have fun," said Vlug, "and we'll see you in Dipper Harbour for the barbecue and awards!"

The main attraction of any outdoor race is the challenge of traveling up, over, and around wilderness obstacles. It's a rare chance to feel immersed, even lost, in nature. The reality tends to be more prosaic. In almost any wilderness race, aside from a few exotic multi-day international events, the terrain might lead competitors beyond the concrete and steel of the urban grid, but it can rarely be described as pristine. (A smaller subclass of events, which inspired the TV success of CBS's *The Amazing Race*, occupies city streets or suburban sites, with competitors leaping from canoes into subway cars or even rappelling down office towers.) Over the last quarter-century, cheap airfares and eco-tourism have complicated the search for authentic backcountry experiences. Even the most remote regions of the globe, from Mount Everest to Antarctica, have become fair game for package trips and wannabe adventurers. To stand out, an organized expedition race must concoct a mixture of the natural and unnatural that feels both novel and challenging to connoisseurs of ready-to-wear wilderness thrills.

The Fundy Multi-Sport Race was no exception. At the 2002 race, the first stage led runners through a tree-shaded arcade of rooty trails, where a misstep could sprain an ankle. Still, it wasn't that tough. The running route looped through a publicly accessible park, owned and operated by a mega-corporation that had made its fortune hewing lumber and refining oil. The trails were padded with cedar shavings and blazed with carved posts, logos, and cute animal names for each loop. (How macho can you really feel dashing down something called the Squirrel Trail?) Once out of the trees, the runners would strike the beach and pass an exposed quarry and a quartet of radio towers. The bicycling stage took racers away from the city's limits but not beyond its reach. The route passed a cemetery, curved around a waste-water facility, crossed a busy highway, followed an abandoned railway line, and connected with dusty country lanes. Even the difficult final few kilometers, through swampy logging roads and overgrown ATV trails, had once been part of a horse-and-cart thoroughfare that had joined early fishing settlements with Saint John. The cyclists would dismount bikes on a beachfront at the end of a cottage-lined road. Many would find wives or husbands, dads and moms, waiting there. Small children would be playing in the pebbles between the kayaks. Not the most extreme of scenes.

If any stage of the race posed a true wilderness challenge, it was the twelve kilometers of sea kayaking on the Bay of Fundy. Even here, between the scrubby headlands and coves, it would be hard to ignore the evidence of human impact. To the east, the twin stacks of the Coleson Cove oil-burning plant released white plumes that could be seen for miles. Just beyond the finish line, at Point Lepreau, the only nuclear reactor in the Maritimes jutted into the bay and fed power into the same grid. Between these energy-generating behemoths, a broad byway had been carved through the interior forest to make room for the electrical towers and lines. On the bay itself, salmon farmers had been colonizing the coast and lobbying to expand their fish pens into the remaining coves. Debates flared across the op-ed and letters pages of the *Telegraph-Journal* about the industrial exploitation of the once-wilderness shoreline. The paddlers would also notice smaller signs of how human hands had tamed the bay over the last century. The wooden stakes of herring weirs. The red-and-white bell buoys at the entrances to Chance Harbour and Dipper Harbour. The automated beacon on Reef Point, where a staffed lighthouse had once stood. The houses and small cottages cut into acreages along this broken shoreline. And the lobster boats raising traps or returning with fresh hauls. One good Fundy gale, however, could make all these mechanical intrusions—and certainly a convoy of plastic kayaks—seem like corks bobbing on a wild and forbidding sea.

In our age of Air Miles and overpopulation, cultivating a sense of true wilderness can require a squinting effect, a sort of mental photo-cropping. You narrow your field of vision until your otherwise alert senses filter out the taints of civilization from the natural panorama you prefer to see. Once you return home, your memory can excise the hydro lines and groomed trails, the granola-bar wrappers and food-scrounging wildlife. You can almost fool yourself—and certainly others—that you're a true explorer, even if you've only arrived at the end of well-trodden trade route in an overcrowded national park or kayaked a stretch of coastline with "for sale" signs hidden behind the evergreen scrim. That's part of the appeal of an outdoor competition. A race demands a focus, a mental triage, a break from the digital multitasking of our workday lives. You learn to attend to the immediate obstacles ahead and tune out all distractions. Competitors see only what lies just beyond their handlebars or over their partners' shoulders and remain blind to the street signs and buzz of traffic behind the forest's edge. In this way, the mundane reality of a glorified treasure hunt transforms into an urgent expedition through a wild labyrinth. A mere game becomes both more serious and more fun to play.

To an outsider, the earnest pursuit of such activities can seem a little odd. In the first adventure race I tried, we were dropped off by school bus on a dirt road in the cottage country of southwestern Ontario. Then we set off for the next six hours across pockets of conservation land, through farmers' fields (complete with wary bovines), and down the grassy slopes of a ski resort in summer hibernation. At one point, a horde of racers burst through a gap in the woods on a quest for the next checkpoint. Our legs were lacerated from raspberry thorns. Our numbered yellow bibs flapped in the breeze. Charging down a grassy slope toward our arbitrary goal, we must have appeared like a grade school dodge-ball team storming the beaches of Normandy. We felt that determined. We looked that silly. Nothing would stop us from reaching the finish line—at least until one of my teammates hit a rock on her bike, hurtled over her handlebars, and fractured her thumb. Even then, she wanted to keep going.

The same squinting effect applied as the Fundy race began. Sixty-eight runners kicked up the gravel of Sand Cove Road, spread apart, found their paces, chatted with partners, fell quiet, and focused on the route ahead. They imagined the miles of land and sea they would traverse. They tuned out the distractions of city life, which they had come here to escape in the first place. They tried not to see the forest—or where it had been replaced by the parking lot, the power lines, the highway overpass—for the trees. They became absorbed in the game.

Everyone had to agree. That last hill was a son of a bitch.

Muscles burning with lactic acid, the runners managed to jog, walk, or stagger the final few hundred meters up to the promontory and finish the fifteen-kilometer loop of Irving Nature Park. Sara Vlug was there to welcome them. All morning she had been on the go to make sure the race started smoothly. Then she had driven around Taylors Island, snapped photos of the racers, and hustled back to the start line. She watched her father chug up the hill and urge his partner to the top. "Jeez, what a country!" the store owner and race sponsor exclaimed with a smile. The last stragglers crested the rise, passed through the checkpoint, mounted their bikes, and rode off. Sara Vlug finally had a chance to catch her breath, but only for a moment. A news reporter from the local cable channel had a few questions.

"Can I get you to talk just to me?" asked André Arseneault. "Not to the camera, because it looks too odd."

Vlug glanced away. Long pause. The sound of the breeze rattled and popped in the microphone. She smiled and shivered dramatically for the camera.

"Okay, I'm rolling," Arseneault said. "Just spell your name and give me what role you play in this event."

It was nearly eleven. Vlug seemed more relaxed now that the race was under way. In another hour and a half the race leaders should reach the beach in Chance Harbour, where Jayme Frank would be waiting for them with the kayaks. Already the competition had split between the seriously fit and the seriously fatigued. Vlug gave the reporter a rundown of their race. "It's a great way for triathletes to make the transition into adventure racing and get a little taste of following a map," she explained. "It's a fast-paced race. It's not quite a triathlon because the trails aren't marked. It's not a traditional road, bike, swim." With a finger, she traced the running route on a wooden map of the park.

In the weeks leading up to the Fundy race, a big concern for the two organizers had been the prospect of fog. Dense banks could make kayaking tricky and the rest of the race damp and unpleasant. In a chowder-thick mist, paddlers might lose sight of the shore. The well-churned Atlantic waters of the Bay of Fundy create some of the foggiest weather in the world. Much of it arrives in the summer months, when prevailing southwesterly winds push warm, wet air up the Eastern Seaboard until it collides with the cool bay and releases a haze of water droplets. In July, the foggiest month, Saint John can make the famous marine climates of London or San Francisco look like the sun-parched Gobi Desert. Locals claim the fog gets so dense you can lean against it. Only St. John's, Newfoundland, with which the similarly baptized Fundy city is often confused, gets socked in with more fog. It's no surprise, then, that the world's first steam-driven foghorn was invented in Saint John. Or that in the 1930s, bay residents made baby formula from condensed fog, assuming the air-distilled water must be as pure as possible. (Today, the Fundy fog has become so tainted by nitric and sulfuric acid from vehicle exhaust and the coal-fired electrical plants west of the bay that its lemon-juice acidity can strip foliage from coastal birch forests.) In the 1960s, entrepreneurial locals even marketed a string of misty motels as cooled by "nature's air conditioning." In July of 1967, fog enshrouded the city in a wet white blanket for a record twenty-seven straight days. When the nearly forgotten sun finally peeked through again, pedestrians in uptown Saint John broke into applause.

The two organizers of the Fundy race had emailed participants a warning to bring a compass in case of foggy conditions. Poor visibility might make navigating the coastline less than obvious. The night before the race, Jayme Frank had checked the marine forecast. It called for thirty-kilometer-per-hour winds out of the southwest and a smallcraft weather warning by the afternoon, not ideal conditions for kayaking. He had discussed the forecast with Vlug. The couple had agreed to gauge the weather again in the morning. Not long after daybreak, Frank had driven the coast highway from Dipper Harbour to the park. He could see dawn spreading across the bay. The seas had looked fine. Not exactly flat, but with few whitecaps and no serious swell. He had paddled the bay in far, far worse conditions many times before. They should be good to go.

Now, as the day pushed past eleven, Sara Vlug stood in the sun as it streamed through the dissipating mist and illuminated the bay. Good fortune seemed to have shone on the race. Misty weather shouldn't pose an obstacle to the paddlers.

"Luckily, the fog cleared up this year," Vlug said into the camera with a laugh. "Hopefully, the wind won't blow them over in the kayaks."

PART TWO
The Quest

Kayaking was an existential highpoint for the northernmost peoples of this planet, and the sleek kayak is one of the most beautiful watercraft designs ever to exist; simply to see its streamlined shape is a pleasure. Speed is written in every line, and for all that the kayak was primarily an instrument for hunting, it was speed, whether in a sprint or a long course, calm or rough, that the kayaker reveled in.

—E.Y. Arima, *Inuit Kayaks in Canada*

'A man who is not afraid of the sea will soon be drownded,' he said, 'for he will be going out on a day he shouldn't. But we do be afraid of the sea and we do only be drownded now and again.'

—John Millington Synge, *The Aran Islands*

SEVEN

The Leaders

T hey had come to win.

That much was clear as the two men hurtled down the last stretch of logging road and skidded their mountain bikes into the transition zone. They were the first racers to arrive, a minute past 12:30 p.m., and over the past three hours they had left the rest of the field far behind. Still, they moved with purpose, handing off bikes to a volunteer and toweling off the mud. Every second mattered, even in an endurance race that might last five hours or more. The two men had raced together before, that much was obvious, and they weren't here for the simple joy of participating. Many event organizers like to console runners-up with the feel-good mantra: "Just finishing is a victory." That loser's sentiment didn't wash with the two leaders. Mark Campbell and Shawn Amirault had come to win it all. They would be satisfied with nothing less.

McLaughlins Cove had been carved into the larger curve of Chance Harbour and was doubly protected from full exposure to the Bay of Fundy. Twenty or so people mingled near the beach where the merging of Cranberry Head Road and a graveled logging lane, known to locals as Trail's End, marked the end of the bike stage. Amid this crowd, the two race leaders spotted Jayme Frank, standing by the empty kayaks. They could use his expertise right now.

"What's the fastest?" asked Campbell, eyeing up the rainbow array of boats along the pebbly high-water line.

Amirault and Campbell both knew a slimmer boat would cut through the water with less drag but have a greater risk of capsizing; as the width of its hull narrows, a kayak sacrifices stability for increased speed and nimbleness. Reaching the finish line first remained their focus.

"Try these," said Frank. He gestured to several sleek and light boats labeled "Pursuit."

Many of the spectators assumed Campbell and Amirault were racing as a team and would launch a two-seat tandem kayak. The two friends had partnered at other events. Months ago, however, they had decided to compete solo for the Fundy race. As they pulled a pair of single-cockpit boats toward the water, their real showdown was about to begin.

An hour earlier, the bay had reached low tide, a difference of six meters or more from the high-water mark here at McLaughlins Cove. Drawn back into the deep Atlantic, the slack ocean waters were now returning to the bay and would peak again at 5:30 p.m. The two leaders hauled the plastic kayaks fifty meters down the muddy, sloping beach and into cold, ankle-high surf. A weak stream wriggled through a brackish marsh and out of the second-growth forest from which they had cycled. To their right, a line of cottages and a few curious owners stood along the rocky shoreline between the waters of Chance Harbour and the paved access road. A steady breeze blew from the southwest, although the full force of this wind couldn't be felt in the lee of the cove. Waves less than a meter tall rolled toward the beach and collapsed into a burble of foam. Nothing menacing, just a steady march of postcard-pretty whitecaps stirring the surface of the water.

Campbell and Amirault settled into their kayaks and hitched the nylon spray skirts around the cockpits. They glanced at the race map. Aim straight out to the bay, bend a hard right, follow the coastline to the finish line—the route seemed simple enough. They pushed loose and paddled hard through the oncoming surf. If they looked back, they might have seen a tandem safety kayak launching from the beach and then several other volunteers wrangling a ten-foot inflatable Zodiac and its small outboard engine toward these same shallows. No other racers had arrived. They had a good lead yet.

If you wanted to typecast for the sport of adventure racing, you could do worse than Mark Campbell and Shawn Amirault. The two friends from Halifax, Nova Scotia, fit the key categories in the demographics of the average racer: thirty-something guys who support their passion for after-hours adventure with day jobs in the high-tech industry. Adventure racing has always drawn participants from a wide spread of ages and backgrounds, men and women both. However, the sport boasts a preponderance of high-tech workers. The techno jocks of the information age have tried to shuck the stereotype of the IT worker as a pocket-protector-wearing nebbish. These neo-nerds tend to be bored by the golf gatherings of their fathers' era and the lowbrow laughs of a company softball team. Adventure racing better suits their temperament: they're well educated, independent minded, intensely competitive, hungry for exotic experiences. They are a risk-seeking variant of the classic Type-A go-getter, what Frank Farley, the former president of the American Psychological Association, dubbed Type-T personalities—goal-driven thrill seekers.

Thirty-four-year-old Mark Campbell was a civilian network manager for the Canadian Forces. Shawn Amirault, three years his junior, worked for the region's major telecom company. While their day jobs weren't uncommon among adventure racers, their accomplishments as athletes pushed the far limit on the athletic bell curve of the typical techno jock. Thickset and tightly muscled, just under six feet, Campbell tipped the scales around two hundred pounds. He was rarely mistaken for a computer geek. A neatly trimmed goatee and a well-receded hairline that framed the curve of his forehead gave him a Lenin-esque profile, if one imagined the Russian revolutionary leader had spent less time composing communist tracts and more in the weight room. Campbell was an accomplished road cyclist and a master's level cross-country skier. A decade ago, he had begun to compete in the longer Ironman triathlons. After he saw the Raid Gauloises on TV, Campbell figured that adventure racing would be a natural extension of his multi-sport training. In 1998, he had paired with Amirault for a wilderness event in Nova Scotia and they had finished in seventeen hours. For all his athletic ambitions, Campbell still maintained a sense of humor. The previous June, he had done the Fundy race with his wife under a whimsical team name: The Bald and the Beautiful.

Amirault was more compact than his friend, quiet spoken, with short-cropped, gelled hair and a hyper-fit, slightly bronzed generic handsomeness. He looked as if he had stepped from the fitness pages of a men's magazine, the high-school jock who hadn't let his body go soft. He had been a downhill ski racer, and still competed in mountain bike events and cross-country ski marathons—two sports that require the legs of a thoroughbred and the lungs of a pearl diver. Adventure racing was a natural fit for him, too. The previous two years, he had driven to Saint John with another buddy to compete in the Fundy Multi-Sport Race as a team. Both times they had taken home first prize—last year, winning by nearly forty minutes. He was the reigning champ, back to defend his title.

This year, Amirault and Campbell had decided to compete in the solo category. First, they could fuel a friendly rivalry. Second, they wanted to see if a solo racer could outpace the best of the two-person teams. Single competitors had a slight advantage in the running and biking legs because they didn't have to race at the pace of a slower partner. But once on the water, that advantage would melt away. The two-person teams could make up time in tandem boats, out-muscling solo kayakers with two paddle strokes to their every one. It would be tough to hold a lead against such odds.

Once the two leaders punched through the surf zone, the kayaking proved easier, and they bent to the task of paddling the twelve kilometers to the finish line at Dipper Harbour. Their boats rode up and over a regular train of waves, as they progressed away from the beach. Campbell and Amirault stayed close, paddling side by side, not talking much, just trying to maintain a regular cadence to their strokes. Such rhythm is key to stability in any kayak, but especially these solo racing boats. Keep your paddle turning in the water, as steady as a sternwheeler. Pause for too long, daydream for even an instant, and you could get knocked over by a rogue or sneaker wave.

As they exited the mouth of McLaughlins Cove, they could see to their right the breakwater that guarded the public wharf. This was Chance Harbour proper, home to a small contingent of the area's lobster fleet. Chance was so named because any captain took a gamble dropping anchor in a spot that couldn't block the full brunt of a southwest gale; two winters earlier, a storm had demolished nearly fifty meters of dock. That was why the bulk of the area's thirty or so full-time lobstermen usually moored their boats in Dipper Harbour, the race's finish line, which had earned its title (depending on who you asked) from its cup-like scoop, for a species of native duck, or because it was deeper (and safer) than other berthages.

As the two racers pushed toward the western headland, the waves increased in amplitude. There, a small navigational beacon at Reef Point marked the exit and the entrance to Chance Harbour. Rounding the point, the two leaders got a taste of the true sea conditions along the exposed Fundy coast. The waves increased in size—three meters and higher. Every time their boats climbed a crest, Campbell and Amirault would steal quick glances behind them, but they couldn't see any other kayaks. When one of their boats dipped into the deep troughs, it disappeared from the sight of the trailing paddler.

"Hey, Shawn, let's stick together through this," Campbell shouted, "and save the sprint for the finish!" Amirault agreed to buddy up.

The problem for Campbell and Amirault was not the size of the waves but their erratic behavior. The two leaders had rounded Reef Point and reached Dry Ledge, the first bare patch in a minefield of shallow water, exposed rock, and hidden shoals that can prove perilous under the wrong conditions, even to thick-hulled lobster boats. On calmer days, visitors often mistook the bare backs of the ledges for breaching whales. That afternoon, however, the strong southwest wind rubbed against these rocky shallows and created confused seas.

Beyond the shelter of Chance Harbour, kayakers could expect turbulent waters between Reef Point and the next protrusion of land, known as Man Rock, about halfway to Dipper Harbour. Since the 1800s, baymen have told the tale of a shipwreck off this point. Every sailor managed to swim to shore, except for one unlucky soul. To this day, when the tide shifts, you can see emerging from the bay the profile of a forehead, nose, and chin—the drowned man of Man Rock. Once paddlers passed Dry Ledge and committed their boats on a westward course for Dipper Harbour, there would be almost nowhere to beach safely until they had put this ill omen in their wake. As the waves rebounded off the shoreline and ledges, they began to haystack—charging from different directions, colliding in a froth of powerful whitewater.

Campbell and Amirault couldn't read the bay anymore. It had become nearly impossible to know when to stroke hard and when to jam one of the paddle's blades into the water in a stabilizing brace. Their focus shifted from the race. The struggle, for now, was to stay afloat.

The two leaders didn't panic. They reckoned the state of the seas wasn't likely to improve soon, and they both kept an eye on the gnarled projection of barely exposed rocks they were approaching. They would likely find calmer waters if they detoured offshore, maybe a kilometer or more. Experienced kayakers know to head out to the open sea to skirt such dangers. However, Amirault and Campbell realized it might be safer—and perhaps faster—to cut back toward shore, beach their boats, and carry them instead across the boot-shaped peninsula between Chance Harbour and Little Dipper, the next cove. Would this improvisation be allowed? Or might they be disqualified? Campbell and Amirault had competed in enough adventure races to know that the sport assumed a flexibility and creativity on the part of both the rule-enforcing organizers and the navigating racers. As long as they didn't skip a section of the course, the portage should be legal.

They aimed for shore. But now they faced a new problem. When the leaders had been paddling forward, they could zigzag along the coast by turning the bows of their kayaks to meet the oncoming waves and then adjusting their bearings into a more or less straight course. However, to head toward land, they had to put their backs to the waves, a position that even expert kayakers don't like to be in for too long. A swell coming from the stern might speed your progress, but it can feel like being rear-ended by a wall of water. In these "following seas," the back of the boat lifts as though gripped in a giant's hand, the paddler pitches forward, and the kayak begins to slide with increasing velocity, up to three times its normal speed, down the face of the wave. In controlled bursts, it can be an addictive adrenaline rush. Some kayakers buy specially designed surf boats—shorter, lighter, more agile—and ride the same tall waves and watery funnels that surfers hang ten on. But you must be able to react quickly, before the wave swings your kayak by the stern and twists you sideways into its breaking crest. This unstable position, known as a broach, is the most common cause of capsizes.

Both the race leaders were reconsidering their decision to choose the faster boats. The narrow kayaks drifted off-line and slipped sideways into the force of each wave. To keep from tipping, the racers kept glancing back at the approaching waves and correcting their bearings with a quick brace stroke. Amirault was surfing his boat toward a patch of beachhead that might make a safe landing spot, when he heard a shout from behind.

"Shawn!" Mark Campbell's voice cut through the cacophony of wind and waves. "I'm in the water!"

EIGHT

The Bay

The Bay of Fundy, one of the most legendary bodies of water on our blue planet, has earned its notoriety, in part, from the simple fact that it's shaped like a tub. Oceanographers, sailors, camera-toting tourists, and trivia aficionados all know the bay as the well-advertised home to the world's highest tides. (Ungava Bay, on the northern Labrador-Quebec border, actually shares this honor.) In Nova Scotia's Minas Basin, where the Bay of Fundy sharpens to an arrowhead at its easternmost cul de sac, differences of seventeen meters are regularly recorded between the high and low watermarks; globally, the oceans' tides average less than a meter. In 1869, a tropical cyclone known as the Saxby Gale, aided by low atmospheric pressure and a near-perfect alignment of earth, sun, and moon, pushed water levels in the basin upward of twenty-two meters, a surge that would have swamped a six-story building. The rapid tidal transit within this oceanic nook likely convinced sixteenth-century Portuguese navigators to label the bay on their maps as *Rio Fondo* or "deep river." At low tide, when the bay water rushes back into the Gulf of Maine and the North Atlantic, its retreat exposes a thousand square kilometers of bare but not lifeless ocean floor. That's enough intertidal real estate to turn the metropolis of Hong Kong into the lost city of Atlantis, twice a day.

The world's tides, of course, are caused by the gravitational pull of the moon. The oceans bulge where they are both nearest and farthest from the moon, and press downward elsewhere, while the earth's rotation ensures that these high and low points alternate in a regular two-a-day rhythm. (The sun has a similar effect but only half as strong because of its greater distance from earth.) The moon's own circling around the earth delays this high-low schedule by about fifty-one minutes every day. That's why tide tables are needed to anticipate the oceans' behavior. What draws the waters of the Bay of Fundy up more dramatically than anywhere else are the physical dimensions of the geological vessel into and out of which the tides flow. The bathtub-shaped scoop of the bay runs from the Gulf of Maine, where it opens onto the Atlantic Ocean near the United States–Canada border. It then narrows as it arches between the mudflats and red cliffs of New Brunswick's south shore and the northern edge of Nova Scotia. In its central depths, near Grand Manan Island, the bay plumbs bottom at two hundred and twenty meters. Finally, it funnels eastward and grows shallower as it enters the tightening corrals of Chignecto Bay and Cumberland Basin to the north, and Minas Basin and Cobequid Bay to the south. Once set in motion, liquid in any basin, even one as big as a bay, has a characteristic period of oscillation—the time it takes to run from end to end. It will slosh back and forth, regular as a metronome, with the surface rising at one end and then the other, while the middle depth remains the same. In the Bay of Fundy, the oscillation equals the time it takes a single wave to undulate from the bay's mouth all the way to Cobequid Bay, where a neck of land joins the rest of North America to the peninsula of Nova Scotia, and then for the same wave to rebound back to Maine.

By sheer coincidence, this stopwatched time is almost exactly the 12.4 hours between any day's two high tides. That synchronicity has powerful consequences. In Fundy's two-hundred-and-eighty-kilometer-long tub, the tick-tock of watery tonnage coincides with the moon-driven swaying of the tides. This matching rhythm, or resonance, creates what scientists call a seiche effect, from the Swiss-French verb for "to sway." The resonance amplifies both the bay's high and low watermarks. The next time you're sprawled naked in your own tub, with soapy water sloshing back and forth, you can create your own private seiche effect by giving the water an extra push in synch with its natural rhythm and watching as it sloshes—likely across your bathroom tiles—to greater heights.

The native Mi'kmaq people, who settled the shores of the Bay of Fundy nearly ten thousand years before the first Europeans arrived, have long relied on a bathtub-based theory of their own to fathom the source of the bay's great power. They tell the story about the god Glooscap, who, between his many adventures, decided he needed a bath. He ordered Beaver to construct a wooden dam across a river that rushed into the bay, so he could savor a freshwater dip. This water stoppage didn't sit well with Whale, with whom Glooscap already had a testy relationship. "Why have you stopped the river from coming into my domain?" demanded Whale. Glooscap didn't want trouble, so he leapt from his improvised tub and ordered Beaver to tear down the dam. His toothy companion didn't act fast enough for the impatient sea creature. Whale swung her tail and obliterated the dam. The unleashed saltwaters of the Bay of Fundy rushed upriver, led by a frothing tidal bore—a flood-tide wave that runs against a river's natural flow. Before departing, Whale beat the surface of the bay with her tail and set in motion the metronomic sloshing of the Fundy waters.

One hundred billion tons of seawater commute through the bay on an average tide, more than two thousand times the discharge of the St. Lawrence River and equal, according to some estimates, to the daily outflow of all the rivers and streams on earth. Fourteen billion tons collect in the far eastern reaches of the bay and cause the adjoining land to tilt like a diving board. The energy potential of all that moving water has been estimated at thirty thousand megawatts per day, the output of two and a half dozen electrical plants, although only a small fraction of that tidal power has ever been harnessed, via nineteenth-century mills and modern turbines. The relentless flushing effect stirs a planktonic bouillabaisse that feeds fifteen species of whale and maintains the steady seasonal temperatures of the Bay of Fundy, cold by any standard. Sun-warmed shallows are soon drawn back into its frigid heart and returned nearly twelve hours later as ice water. Summertime bay water rarely rises above 12°C. Few swimmers dare the chill of a Fundy dip for more than a minute or two.

The unique character of the Bay of Fundy, as layered with myth and mystery as the Mediterranean, can't be reduced to mere statistics. To be understood, the tides must be experienced up close. The biggest draw for Fundy visitors is the spectacle of Hopewell Rocks. At low tide, you can descend from the heights of the red-cliffed cape and walk across the naked ocean floor. Here, the receding bay exposes a geological sculpture garden of top-heavy flowerpot formations, towering spires, and natural bridges, like the hoodoos of the Badlands or the arches of Utah. In 1604, French cartographer Samuel de Champlain dubbed the Rocks *Les demoiselles*—the Young Girls. "He was either at sea too long," one tour guide told me, "or he had a great imagination." Return to the park six hours after low tide, and the promenade around the Rocks will be submerged. You can then join a sea-kayaking tour—the sport is increasingly popular—and paddle through the erosion-formed red-umber arches. Before and after shots of the Hopewell Rocks have become the signature image of the Fundy tourism industry. It takes such time-lapse trickery to appreciate the true dimensions of the tidal shifts, which can't be reckoned in a brief visit. "People say that the great tides of the Bay of Fundy are a great sight," observed author Calvin Trillin, a frequent visitor to the Maritimes, "except it takes six and a half hours to see it."

Not all of the bay's tricks require such patience. In the five-kilometer gap between Deer Island, New Brunswick, and Eastport, Maine, an ocean trench and underwater hill set in motion a tidal whirlpool called the Old Sow. That swirl of turbulence expands to seventy-five meters in radius on an average day, the largest in the western hemisphere and one of only five major whirlpools anywhere in the world. The pool can usually be spotted three hours before high tide, the waters twisting clockwise, at speeds of up to twenty-eight kilometers per hour, as though Glooscap had pulled the plug on his Fundy-sized bathtub. With stronger tides and higher winds at work, a deeper vortex will appear in the whirlpool's center, while smaller gyres—known to locals as piglets—dance around it, along with boils, spouts, holes, and standing waves. The Old Sow poses little threat to most motorized boats, although it can give a careless kayaker or sailor a furious spin.

One of the most striking demonstrations of Fundy's power remains the great bay's ability to stall the outflow of the rivers that feed it and chase freshwater back from where it came. In downtown Moncton, fifty kilometers inland of the bay, you can watch from the public promenade as a low rumbling announces the arrival of the tidal bore. A meter-high crest of froth rolls up the Petitcodiac River at fifteen kilometers per hour. Over the years, the concrete causeway built along the banks has caused the river to silt up and mute this tidal bore—time and tide may stand for no one, but the modern city can dent its force. More famous still, the port city of Saint John is home to the odd phenomenon known as the Reversing Falls. Here, in a rocky elbow, the rising tide not only halts the Saint John River's seaward flow but actually pushes the river back up a waterfall that measures, at low tide, a drop of four and a quarter meters. In the shadow of Reversing Falls Bridge, tourists snap portraits of the boiling, spinning collision of river rush and tidal push. More adventurous visitors can book a jet-boat joy ride through the turned-back falls, while experienced kayakers travel to Saint John from around the world to test their whitewater skills in the ever-changing mix of stationary waves and whirlpools. One enterprising outfitter has recently begun to take curious (and well-insured) thrill seekers up and down the falls in a giant inflatable hamster wheel called the Bubble.

Sea kayaking offers another way of getting intimate with the Bay of Fundy. While the sport has grown more slowly on the East Coast of Canada than on the West, eco-tourism operators have sprung up to rent boats and lead tours. The mercurial nature of the bay, however, still intimidates newcomers to the sport. The *Sea Kayaking Safety*

Guide, published by the Canadian government, warns against paddling alone and recommends that Fundy kayakers first acquire a tide table so they can anticipate currents that run at up to eight knots. "Wind may also rise abruptly within minutes," caution the authors, "and when counter-current, may create standing waves that make it difficult to maneuver. Moreover, the often inhospitable coast has the highest cliffs of the Maritime coastline." Fog can grow so dense that kayakers can't see the bow of their own boats. "The ocean is often deceptive," the guidebook states. "Feeling assured upon leaving shore at high tide when everything is calm, you may come to feel as if in a giant whirlpool only three hours later." Matched with poor skills or worse luck, that combination of fog, wind, tidal current, and rocky coast can turn a pleasant day of paddling on the Bay of Fundy into a fight for survival—just as the race leaders were about to discover.

NINE

The Capsize

For novice kayakers, the capsize is the moment they most fear. On a first trip, the prospect of tipping while inside a whitewater or sea kayak often transforms brave hearts into nervous claustrophobes, especially paddlers accustomed to the open spaces of a canoe or a raft or the plastic sit-a-board kayaks used on cottage lakes or at Caribbean resorts. If you flip these other craft, you might be tossed from the boat into the surrounding water or, at worst, be forced to swim from under an overturned raft. Ocean and river kayaks, by contrast, are designed to hold occupants more securely in place, even when a boat goes bottom-up.

To enter a sea kayak, you must squirm your legs into the cockpit of a narrow plastic or fiberglass hull. Then you wedge your feet against pegs that control the rudder (if the boat is fitted with one) and jam your knees against the hull or a pair of plastic braces that let you control the boat through subtle shifts of the body. To a first-timer taller than a jockey, this confined and splay-legged posture feels about as comfortable as being stirruped into a gynecologist's chair. If this weren't unnerving enough, you are then held even more tightly in place by the spray skirt that keeps water from flooding into the cockpit. Used with most sea and whitewater kayaks, the skirt (also called a deck) is just that—a knee-length oval of nylon or neoprene, designed in varying degrees of waterproofness, that girdles the waist. In these flouncy outfits, a band of kayakers idling on shore looks like the cast from an avant-garde production of *Swan Lake*. When you take a cold wave over the bow of your kayak and watch the seawater slosh off the stretched fabric of the skirt, you quickly forget about fashion statements and appreciate the skirt's duck-like ability to shed water.

Once you slide into the boat, the edge of the skirt must be lifted over and sealed around the raised coaming of the cockpit, like the lid of a Tupperware container. An elasticized band or a belt of shock cord secured with a plastic cord-lock holds the skirt in place. The skirt should fit tightly enough that it doesn't come free in rough conditions, yet remain loose enough that you can open it partially mid-trip when you need to retrieve gear, pump out water, or answer nature's call. If you capsize, the skirt should stay in place, so that you can twist back upright by performing a so-called Eskimo roll. If you have to escape the kayak instead, the skirt must pop free with ease before your last breath runs out. That's the part that new paddlers don't like to think about. Once flipped, the buoyancy of a boat reverses its intended effect. It forces you *under* the water, and the drum-taut spray skirt suddenly feels like a dangerous snare. Inexperienced kayakers have died in this way. Unable to free themselves from a too-tight skirt after capsizing, they panic in the dark water, take a mouthful into their lungs, and drown, caught upside down in their overturned boats like bats in a cave. But such accidents are rare.

Neoprene spray skirts are more waterproof (and more expensive) but tend to fit more snugly and are more difficult to peel off. To avoid having clients trapped in an overturned boat, guides and instructors often outfit neophytes with nylon skirts, which pull free more easily. All the racers at the Fundy Multi-Sport Race had been outfitted with such nylon skirts, except for a few experienced paddlers who had brought their own neoprene decks. While some participants complained about the waterproofness of these nylon skirts, nobody could argue that they fit too tightly. At the safety briefing before the race, Jayme Frank had described to the racers how to perform what kayakers call a "wet exit"—a rather bloodless term for a situation often fraught with panic. After capsizing, you must remain calm, lean forward while submerged, and reach for the loop of fabric at the end of the spray skirt. (When you first cinched the skirt, you should have been careful not to tuck the loop inside the cockpit; otherwise removing the skirt suddenly becomes a desperate clawing for any loose edge.) You then jerk the loop—sometimes attached to a wooden or plastic dowel—away and upward, like the pull tab on a pop can. The skirt should peel toward your body and off the cockpit's coaming, the raised edge that keeps out the water. You can then simply roll forward while underwater, draw your legs free of the boat's embrace, and rise buoyantly to the surface.

That's the theory. Few kayakers who capsize for the first time remain placid enough to pull the ripcord on their skirts. They're usually out of the boat before they know what hit them. The first time I paddled a kayak was also the first time I capsized—fortunately, in the Pacific shallows around British Columbia's Gulf Islands, one of the most popular sea-kayaking locations in the world. Among a group of experienced friends, I was a self-conscious rookie, anxious about the snugness of my spray skirt, uncertain whether I could ever untangle my long legs from the boat's tiny cockpit in an emergency. And then it happened. An awkward stroke threw my kayak off balance. I panicked. I began to go over.

All I recall about the episode is the sensation that someone had injected a vein in my neck with a pint of pure adrenaline. My body flushed with an unfamiliar strength. Suddenly, I knew I could chew a hole through the plastic hull if that's what it took to reach the surface again. In the end, I didn't have to. As soon as my body rolled sideways into the water, it convulsed and kicked free of the kayak, yanking the spray skirt from the boat's hold on it. There was no thinking about it, no calmly reaching for the skirt's pull tab, just raw survival instinct.

Get. Me. Out. Of. Here. The next thing I knew, I was floating in the embrace of my life jacket, sputtering but relieved to be out of the boat. A few meters away, the puppy-dog eyes of a harbor seal stared at me with a smile between its whiskers. If this was a wet exit, I had mastered the move.

And that's exactly what Mark Campbell did, too.

At the Fundy race that afternoon, there were only a handful of competitors who held in their quiver of paddling skills what kayakers call a "bombproof roll," the ability to perform an Eskimo or Greenland roll instinctively and repeatedly even in the worst sea conditions. They get knocked over—they flip back up, spinning like sea otters, time and again. There are a dozen variations of this tricky-to-learn submarine maneuver, but the fundamental sequence involves what one kayak writer has characterized as a "comma-shaped sweep of the paddle and a simultaneous flick of the hips." Even the Inuit, who invented the kayak four thousand years ago, weren't universally adept at rolling. (Their descendants also prefer that kayakers not use the culturally offensive term *Eskimo* to label the technique.) In Greenland, where the subsistence economy traditionally depended almost entirely on hunting by kayak, paddlers still deploy long, narrow, fast-moving boats that are prone to tipping, and so they have developed more than thirty ways to roll, both solo and with help from hunting companions. By contrast, because the sea ice disappeared only briefly every summer in the Canadian Arctic, the Inuit there relied less on kayaks and by the mid twentieth century had abandoned their use almost entirely. On Baffin Island, they built wide, flat-bottomed boats that were slower but nearly untippable, and there is little evidence that they knew how to roll. The Koryak people in Siberia likewise paddled short, fat boats, stabilized with rocks as ballast, and avoided rough seas whenever possible.

The previous summer, Mark Campbell had enrolled in a kayaking skills course before competing in a five-day adventure race along Newfoundland's north shore. As a longtime Ironman triathlete, Campbell was already a tireless swimmer. He was a good paddler, too, but not a Greenland-worthy pro. And a bombproof roll? That was a skill he hadn't mastered.

Campbell was following Amirault's kayak, aiming for shore, and timing his strokes with the rollercoaster of waves. One second, he was riding a two-and-a-half-meter crest, fully in control. The next, the wave collapsed, like the floor of a burning building. As it dropped, the breaking wave spun his kayak sideways and, before he could react, he was window-shaded—paddler lingo that suggests the cartoon velocity with which a kayak can spin over, like Wile E. Coyote caught in a set of roll-up blinds. In an instant, Campbell was underwater. He went over so unexpectedly that he didn't have time to consider a roll. Instead he kicked free of the cockpit and burst up through the surface of the water. The cold bear-hugged the breath from his body. He gasped for new air, made sure he didn't lose his boat, and looked for land. "Shawn!" he called toward his friend's kayak. With relief, he watched the boat make a tricky U-turn. In less than a minute, they were reunited. The two friends had been competitors when they had first entered the race. Now, they would act again as a team.

Trying to climb back into the flooded cockpit of a capsized kayak is about as easy as balancing atop a greased log in high heels. The stability of the vessel has been almost entirely compromised. "Can you hold on to my boat?" Campbell asked his friend. Then he pulled the paddle float—all the single kayaks were supplied with one—from under the shock cord of the back deck. This inflatable float and the paddle it attached to were all he should need to get back into his flooded boat. Campbell put the float's valve to his lips and began blowing into it.

Paddle floats come in a variety of shapes and designs, usually a rectangular sheath of foam or an inflatable bag built to slide over a paddle's blade. Refined and promoted in the early 1980s by Cam and Matt Broze, a fraternal pair of kayak designers in Washington State, the paddle float has become the most common tool for capsized solo kayakers to rescue themselves. The idea is to improvise an outrigger, like the ones attached to dugout canoes by Polynesians, the world's most proficient big-water paddlers. Once inflated, the rescue float is hitched to one blade of the paddle and the other blade is then secured under the web of fixed cord behind the cockpit. Voilà, instant outrigger. A capsized kayaker can use the paddle and its now-buoyant blade as an extended arm to keep the kayak from flipping again, climb aboard the rear deck, and slide back into the cockpit.

As Mark Campbell discovered, safety skills learned in the calm, heated waters of an indoor swimming pool don't always translate to a survival situation. Amirault kept his kayak from drifting, while Campbell blew into the valve of the paddle float. One breath. Two. Three. Nothing seemed to be happening. The rectangle seemed no less floppy than before. What was wrong with the damn thing? Campbell couldn't help but think now of his neoprene wetsuit—the one that was rolled up and stuffed into his gear bag, sitting on the beach back at McLaughlins Cove. He could use it now. He could already feel the cold water of the bay leaching the warmth from his body. After less than ten minutes of immersion, his hands and feet tingled. With every second, tasks as simple as holding and blowing into the paddle float became clumsy to execute.

Anyone familiar with the perils of cold-water rescues knows the Rule of Twenty-Five. Water acts as a far superior conductor than air and will sap heat from an unprotected human body at a rate twenty-five times faster. On the water, most people worry most about drowning. But as experienced kayakers understand all too well, hypothermia is the real threat, its effects swift and debilitating. While a capsized paddler wearing a life jacket might bob for days without fear of drowning in tropical waters, someone immersed in 10°C seas will be unlikely to remain conscious and survive for more than a few hours. Only insulation, either natural or artificial, can prolong exposure times in the waters of the world's northern seas. Here, hypothermia extinguishes any athletic advantage. Survival of the fittest becomes survival of the fattest. Lean, nutrition-obsessed athletes who count calories with an auditor's eye are most vulnerable to the effects of the cold. Anyone who lugs an extra layer of body fat, by contrast, can stave off hypothermia for longer. Famous open-water swimmers, usually women such as Canada's Marilyn Bell and Lynne Cox of the United States, tend to have barrel-bodied, seal-like physiques. A simple equation has evolved in the bodies of mammals best suited to survive in this environment: the more blubber the better.

Campbell fell somewhere in the middle of the spectrum of body types. He couldn't be described as portly, but he was still bulkier in muscle mass than most of the reed-thin triathletes he competed against. That extra flesh would provide a measure of insulation when he needed it most. His five-millimeter wetsuit would have been better. There had been no requirement to wear a wetsuit for the kayak section of the Fundy Multi-Sport Race. It wasn't even suggested on the gear list. Campbell had stuffed his suit into his equipment bag anyway, in case. But when he had arrived at the kayak zone, the high sun of the early afternoon was beating down on his body, already slick with sweat from the run and the ride. The thought of squeezing into a tight rubber bodysuit hadn't appealed to him. The trailing racers had yet to appear, but they might at any second. There had been no time to waste and so he had left the wetsuit in the sack. Now he wished he hadn't been so hasty.

"Take this, Shawn. You try it!"

Campbell passed the paddle float to his friend. His hands were going numb and he had to get out of the water now. There was no time to keep fussing with equipment that didn't work. (He later realized that he hadn't unplugged the float's blowhole.) He wasn't panicking, but his situation had started to seem serious. Campbell had done New Year's Day polar bear swims—organized cold-water dips for groups of nearly nude masochists—so he knew how quickly a human body sheds its heat into frigid waters. Without the paddle float, it would be difficult to get back into his kayak without capsizing again. And the shore was still too far away, and likely too rugged, to swim for.

The day had begun so well. It had been a fine morning, nearly clear and warming, and Campbell had felt strong—strong enough to win. Together, he and Amirault had flashed through the first two stages and seemed on the way toward their goal of beating all the teams to Dipper Harbour. They had finished the running and biking legs so fast, in fact, that they had launched onto the bay ahead of the safety boats. And who knew how far behind the other competitors were lagging? That gap had seemed fine at the time. But thrown by an errant wave into the wild and open bay, Mark Campbell would have been happy to see someone else out on these dangerous waters. Anyone.

TEN

The Trail's End

André Arseneault had missed his brother. By the time he arrived back at Irving Nature Park with the red Rogers TV van, the fittest racers were already on their bikes and gone. René, he figured, must be among that lead group. André had always been the quiet brother, and the job of a videographer suited his personality—the entire world shrunk to the tiny box of his viewfinder, whole lives packaged into a few minutes of edited tape. He shot footage of older and slower runners staggering up the last hill. Then he wrapped up an interview with Sara Vlug, the race's co-organizer. He still needed action shots. Vlug was heading to McLaughlins Cove and told Arseneault to follow her vehicle. On the highway, he realized his own van hadn't been fueled up, so he stopped for gas and lost track of her. Soon he was lost entirely. Finally, near Musquash Swamp, he spotted a line of mountain bikers. Two race volunteers waited beside a parked truck and directed the cyclists down a turn.

"Do you know the way to the beach?" he asked.

"Sorry," the volunteers said. He could follow the cyclists, but they would soon be pedaling onto an old logging road that would mire his van in muddy ruts. There had to be a shortcut.

"Is there someone we can call to find out?"

"We don't have a phone."

"You can use mine," said André. "What's the number to call?"

"Sorry," the race volunteers repeated. "We don't know."

That was odd, thought Arseneault. He continued along the highway toward Chance Harbour, turned down a side lane of cottages and, where the pavement petered out, found the beach at McLaughlins Cove. Two slivers were rising and falling over the swells toward the horizon, so he filmed the race leaders and then set up a few takes of the incoming tide and low-angled footage of the rainbow array of kayaks. Soon these boats would all be out on the bay. For now, Trail's End had the lazy atmosphere of a company picnic.

Twenty minutes later, another racer arrived and handed off his mountain bike for safekeeping. Arseneault filmed the man, thin and angular and in his late thirties, as he stripped off a sweat-soaked red and black jersey and revealed a pair of cycling bib shorts, like old-time wrestler's tights. He pulled on a baby-blue fleece sweater and added a matching ball cap. He was hustling, but without the urgency of the first two racers. "It's a beautiful day," he mused aloud. He didn't seem as interested as Mark Campbell or Shawn Amirault in choosing the lightest, fastest kayak available.

"Are they all the same?" he asked a volunteer. "What's the easiest for a lousy kayaker?"

"You want something wide," suggested the race official, "and a little bit shorter."

"That's for me," said the racer.

"You're in third place," Arseneault told him

"Get out of here!" the man said with a laugh. "You've got to be kidding!"

Suddenly, André Arseneault noticed another arrival and recognized the peacock-bright jersey, now sprayed with mud, and the bike, both of which he had loaned to René. Filming his brother would be an unexpected bonus for the story. André hustled across the beach to welcome him.

Peter Hancock was as surprised as anyone when he arrived at the kayak zone just before 1:00 p.m. and discovered that—except for a few race volunteers, spectators, and a news cameraman—he had the beach to himself. He knew he wasn't going to catch the leaders today. But for someone who wasn't a runner, who had lost his map, and who was competing in his first adventure race, Hancock felt pretty good about his performance so far. Then he heard he was in third place. Who would have guessed? All that remained were twelve kilometers of sea kayaking between him and a finish worth bragging about.

At a fraction under six feet and a hundred and sixty pounds, Hancock looked spidery, all arms and legs. His glasses and Clark Kentish haircut, and the self-deprecating way he described many of his outings, as though always a step from disaster, suggested he was a bit of a klutz. He was anything but. Underneath that casual demeanor beat the heart of a serious competitor—just not a serious adventure racer. Hancock had been a varsity swimmer throughout his youth and had taught sailing, too, when he lived in Nova Scotia ("Canada's ocean playground," according to license plates), so he felt confident on rough water. What he had always loved most was cycling. He had road-biked at a high amateur level since his early twenties. Every year, he would average twelve thousand kilometers of riding—the length of the Trans-Canada Highway and halfway home again. His fitness had tailed off a shade in the past two years; ascending the corporate ladder and fatherhood will do that to a guy. Still, his remaining skill, strength, and savvy on a bike had propelled him into third place in a race he had never intended to enter and for which he hadn't trained.

A volunteer helped Hancock carry the heavy plastic boat down to water deep enough to launch. The surf washed over their ankles in a low wall of froth. "Can I get through this stuff?" he asked.

"Yeah, yeah, just keep your nose into it and paddle hard," came the reply. "And make sure you pump out your boat when you get to flatter water."

Hancock charged through a spray of seawater and was on his way.

The thirty-eight-year-old cyclist had been a last-minute entry to the Fundy Multi-Sport Race. Weeks earlier, a quartet of his friends from Bathurst, New Brunswick, had signed up as two teams and suggested he join them. He wasn't into adventure racing, Hancock said, and he didn't have a partner. "Oh, come on—it'll be a laugh," the others insisted. "You can go solo." Five days before the race, Hancock had agreed.

Friday after work, the five friends had driven south through the forested interior of the province, past Miramichi and its legendary fly-fishing river, into Moncton and then along Highway 1 to Saint John. They planned to stop at a restaurant, where they would surprise one of the gang with a gag birthday gift—pink Barbie streamers to attach to the handlebars of his mountain bike. On the four-hour drive, split between two cars, they had joked and laughed as they always did. Hancock had to raise his voice, because the bikes on the roof rack were rattling in the stiff southwest breeze. On the fuel-efficiency gauge, he could see more evidence that his new car was fighting a headwind. "Jesus," he said, "it's going to be a hell of a thing tomorrow, if the wind is like this."

The next morning, the first stage of the race had gone smoothly. The well-laid chip trails, with forest-fringed views of the bay, were easy on the eyes and forgiving on Hancock's nearing-forty knees. In fact, he had felt faster than he had in a long time. He had finished the fifteen-kilometer route not far off the pace of the leaders. That strong start, especially for an out-of-practice runner, alerted Hancock that the field of competitors at this race, while enthusiastic, consisted largely of weekend warriors like himself. Many were far less committed than Hancock to training. Few seemed to be truly outstanding athletes. It was, as had been promised, a beginner's race.

On his mountain bike, Hancock had quickly overtaken most of the racers ahead of him. He wasn't a mountain biker by inclination. He preferred the speed and strategy of biking on asphalt. The first thirty kilometers of the bike stage, though, had suited his style of cycling. It was flat, mostly on the graveled trail of a converted rail bed. Even buffered by a corridor of trees, Hancock could sense the headwind. He would have made even better time if he hadn't dropped his map along the way. However, it seemed that gaffe didn't matter much. In traditional adventure races, wilderness orienteering is a key part of the experience. If you lose your map, you can expect a long day (or more) of wandering hopelessly through undifferentiated brush in search of elusive checkpoints. The Fundy Multi-Sport Race was more of an off-road triathlon. The course was clearly marked (for the most part), with volunteers directing cyclists at key points, especially the two highway crossings.

Once Hancock had reached the mucky labyrinth of logging roads near Musquash Swamp, he had to wait at each intersection until a trailing rider caught up with him, so they could confer using the other racer's map. It was usually the same young guy, a good-looking kid with a red bandana under his helmet. They would ride together for a while or push their bikes through the mud. For parts of the swampy section, they could have used a machete or an all-terrain vehicle—or better still a jet pack—to overcome the fallen trees, clawing brush, and knee-deep, shoe-slurping, quicksand-like goop. Eventually, Hancock pulled ahead. The kid had younger legs, but Hancock's experience outweighed that age advantage. He could tell that the kid, while fit, wasn't a regular cyclist by glancing at his shoes (low-cut hiking boots rather than cleat-soled cycling shoes) and how he mashed down on his pedals rather than spinning in even, efficient circles. When Hancock reached the kayaks, the kid was nowhere in sight.

Now out on the water, Peter Hancock wished he wasn't quite so alone.

In the cove, the water had seemed less turbulent. But as he paddled toward the mouth of Chance Harbour, the swells continued to rise. With every wave that burst over his kayak's bow, Hancock could feel cold water seep through the thin nylon of the spray skirt and start to pool in the bottom of his boat. He remembered the race official's advice, stopped every so often to pop his spray skirt, and used the hand pump to bilge water from his cockpit. He made slow, herky-jerky progress toward the mouth of the harbor. The race was beginning to seem less fun than it had an hour ago. The problem, he realized, was the gnarled-looking headland of Reef Point and the ledges beyond it. He had been told to paddle beyond this landmark and then follow the shoreline westward to the finish line. But the half-submerged rocks, now a roiling spectacle of whitewater, projected straight into the bay. To avoid getting near to them, he would have to paddle offshore a kilometer or more.

"This is crazy," he thought. "I'm going to kill myself."

His body hummed with adrenaline, and even in his light cycling apparel, he felt warm in the wind. But the water that seeped through the spray skirt told him how cold an unexpected dip into the Bay of Fundy would be. Hancock had been close to hypothermic before. On a solo bike ride up Mount Diablo, near San Francisco, the weather had turned nasty and, blue lipped and shaking, he had barely made it back down to warmer altitudes. He knew how quickly a failing body temperature turned your mind to mush and your hands to useless slabs of meat.

Two kilometers into the kayak leg, Hancock decided to pull the plug. He turned his boat around. His race was done.

He hadn't retreated far before he met another solo kayaker coming out of McLaughlins Cove. "Where you going?" the puzzled newcomer asked.

That afternoon, one of the strongest sea kayakers at McLaughlins Cove wasn't even in the race. Six foot three, two hundred and ten pounds, with yoke-broad shoulders straining the blue fabric of an untucked work shirt, John Brett was likely one of the strongest men there, period. For ten years, he had raced mountain bikes and gone on kayaking trips with his father and friends. Now twenty-five, in his final term of a forest engineering degree, Brett knew the wilderness of New Brunswick, land and sea, better than most guys twice his age. But he had never been to an adventure race before. A day earlier, Brett had eloped with his fiancée and gotten married in Fredericton. By all rights, he should have been on his honeymoon. He had only come down to Saint John to announce the nuptials to his parents. Then he had driven with his mother, his new wife, and their springer spaniel to Trail's End so they could all act as cheerleaders for his father.

Malcolm Brett—Mac to his friends—was the fifty-four-year-old head of the engineering department at the local community college and an avid kayaker. He had agreed to compete in the race with Bob Vlug, the owner of Eastern Outdoors and a friend with whom he often paddled. Two summers ago, Mac had joined Bob, Sara Vlug, and Jayme Frank to complete, in a pair of tandem kayaks, a risky seventy-kilometer, eleven-hour crossing of the entire Bay of Fundy. Four months later, on New Year's Eve of the year 2000, Mac Brett and Bob Vlug organized a chilly midnight paddle near Reversing Falls to welcome the new millennium. Brett and Vlug were fit for their age, and had used the Fundy challenge as an excuse to keep in shape. Brett had joked that the two graying friends ought to call their partnership Team Nearly Dead. For all their training, they expected to lag behind the younger legs on the running and cycling stages. On the water, though, the savvy paddlers should catch many of the racers ahead of them.

John Brett figured his dad was unlikely to hit the water with the first set of competitors. Among the leaders, Brett did spot a face that he knew, even spattered with mud. René Arseneault had wheeled to a stop on his mountain bike and was buzzing with excitement. Brett's mother had taught Arseneault in grade school. Brett had also worked for a local dairy that supplied the grocery store where Arseneault stocked produce. They would often chat during his milk runs. In all that time, Arseneault had never mentioned he was a paddler. The kayaking community around Saint John was small enough that Brett and his dad could name almost all of the regulars. Most kayakers eventually came through the Eastern Outdoors store in town or the Vlugs' seaside home in Dipper Harbour. Throughout the race, Brett would be surprised by how few faces he recognized from the local kayaking scene. How many of these racers, he later wondered, had any real experience on the bay?

"Man, that is muh-UH-*dee!*" Arseneault exclaimed. Dancing on the spot, he unstrapped his helmet and handed his dirt-encrusted sunglasses to his brother André. "Oh, that was crazy!"

Brett helped René lug a light gray solo kayak down to the water's edge. André trailed them with a video camera.

"How was it?" Brett asked.

"I think a lot of people are going to stop in the middle of that—especially the women," he said. "I think the women are getting really discouraged." René's cheeks were speckled with wet dirt, and the bandana around his forehead dripped with sweat. "How am I doing?" he asked.

"You're in fourth place, buddy," Brett told him.

That fired him up more. Arseneault stepped into a spray skirt, climbed inside the kayak, and fumbled to hitch the skirt around the cockpit. "Do it around the back first," Brett suggested. Arseneault didn't seem to understand, so Brett helped seal the water-resistant skirt.

"Have you paddled much before?" he asked.

"Not a lot," Arseneault admitted.

"Do you think you can handle this?"

"Yeah, I've been out a bit."

"If you get into problems, look for the Zodiac."

Brett had watched race volunteers muscle the ten-foot inflatable boat into the shallows of the cove. The operators were now tugging on the outboard's cord. Brett lifted the kayak's stern and launched Arseneault through the surf. "Good luck!" André called, still recording the scene. René's arms flailed and his paddle slapped at the water until he found a more comfortable rhythm. His technique wasn't pretty, but he managed to push through the breaking water and to hold a straight line toward the mouth of the harbor. He never looked back.

ELEVEN

The Rescuers

John Brett wasn't the only kayaker to size up the racers at the Fundy race and question their paddling experience. Earlier that morning, Robin Lang had glanced around the start line at his fellow competitors. He didn't need to see them lift a paddle to know that few had logged many hours in a kayak. Many looked in fine shape—runners and cyclists and triathletes probably. Like Brett, however, Lang hadn't recognized many faces from the region's small paddling community. And when he reached the kayaking stage, that fact began to worry him.

The forty-six-year-old from Rothesay knew his way around rough water as well as anyone. Over the last two decades as a competitor and coach, Lang had likely squeezed into more kayak cockpits than (with an exception or two) all the other racers combined. As a young man, he had paddled in his native Scotland as a top-level downriver canoeist and then competed for ten years on the Canadian whitewater team, winning nine national championships and attending five world championships. Over the past decade, even with a full-time job as a piping designer at the refinery, he had put in long hours in his boat as a flatwater coach and a marathon paddler. For the Fundy challenge, he had convinced a twenty-six-year-old friend—another Popeye-armed marathon paddler and quadrathlete from Dartmouth, Nova Scotia—to join him in a tandem.

The two men arrived at the kayaking stage with only five or six other racers ahead of them. Lang knew how cold the bay water could be. He told his out-of-town partner, more accustomed to inland lakes, to pull on a long-sleeved shirt and any extra clothes. Few of the paddlers that followed them would take the same precaution. They launched into the cove but hadn't paddled far when they saw, to their left, one guy tip over in a solo boat. The inflatable rescue Zodiac zipped toward the capsized racer. Farther ahead, they recognized another solo racer, whom they had been chasing on the bike stage but who had proven too fast to catch—Peter Hancock. They weren't about to follow him. Instead of angling parallel to the shoreline toward the finish, he seemed to be aiming straight into the bay. If he kept that bearing, Lang figured, he would paddle all the way to Nova Scotia. It didn't inspire confidence. These two guys—one capsized, the other off course—were apparently the best racers here.

And then Lang spotted two people he hadn't expected to meet again until finish line: the race leaders. Mark Campbell had pulled himself onto the back deck of his flooded kayak and was straddling it like a burro. Shawn Amirault hovered nearby and was readying the paddle float to stabilize his friend's boat. Lang and his partner helped to haul Campbell into the cockpit. His body was still twitching from the fifteen-minute dunk in the bay. Otherwise, he seemed calm and clear-headed.

"What are you going to do now?" Lang asked, in his mid-Atlantic brogue.

"I'm heading to shore," said Campbell.

"What about you?"

"I'm going with him," said Amirault.

In the distance, the buzz of the Zodiac closed on their position. Lang was reluctant to leave the men but figured they should be safe now. He was more worried about the competitors still to come. Most were far less accomplished than either Campbell or Amirault. There was little more to do, though, than push on. Lang and his partner had a race to finish. And with the leaders out of the running, it was a race they planned to win.

Earlier that year, Jason Stanley, a nineteen-year-old from Quispamsis, had been hunting for a job. He kept dropping off résumés at the Eastern Outdoors shop in Saint John until he finally got called in for an interview and hired. He had little kayaking experience, so Jayme Frank and Sara Vlug took the new employee paddling a half-dozen times to get him comfortable on the Bay of Fundy. With summer around the corner, Stanley mostly helped on shoulder-season kayak tours that set out from the outlet down the coast in St. Andrews. He ferried food and gear in his boat while the older, more experienced guides attended to the clients. For four months, he worked at Eastern Outdoors, saving money to pay his first year of university tuition.

A few weeks before the Fundy race, Frank had asked if Stanley would volunteer at the event. Maybe "asked" and "volunteer" weren't the right words. All the store employees, it was clear, were expected to pitch in. It wouldn't look good if he refused. Stanley was told he only had to do tick names from a checklist. He could do the job in his sleep. He might have to. The night before the race, Stanley had cleaned kayaks and set up a large geodesic tent near the beach. The prep work had gone late and the organizers suggested that he stay overnight in Dipper Harbour. A number of out-of-town racers had already pitched tents on the Vlugs' seaside acreage. Stanley declined, but by the time he got home, an hour's drive away, he realized he still had the keys to one of the store's trucks. Jayme Frank called. Stanley needed to get back to Dipper even earlier, around 4:00 a.m., so the organizers could use the truck to haul kayaks.

It never happened. Stanley slept through his alarm and didn't wake until 7:00 a.m. He left his parents' house in a panic and by the time he reached Dipper Harbour, the race had begun. "Don't worry," Deanna Vlug assured him. Jayme Frank was less thrilled by the late arrival of his helper. The organizer might act relaxed among his adventure-racing friends, but Stanley found his boss could be arrogant and abrupt. Together, they toted a trailer of kayaks to McLaughlins Cove, where Stanley separated pumps, paddles, and life jackets and arranged boats on the beach. Around 12:30 p.m., a pair of competitors cycled down the dirt road, grabbed solo kayaks, and charged into the water. Not long afterward, two other race volunteers—one was an Eastern Outdoors employee, the other a friend of the organizers—launched a double kayak to patrol within the cove.

"Jason," Jayme Frank announced, "I need you in the Zodiac."

The change in plans caught Stanley off-guard. He had no experience in a Zodiac; no on-the-water certification of any kind. He was slight of build—five foot eight and a hundred and forty pounds—but at least he had packed warm clothes: a synthetic shirt, a fleece pullover, a windproof jacket, and hiking pants. The soft-spoken son of a pastor didn't want to make a fuss, not after his own screwup this morning. Stanley agreed to head out in the Zodiac, the only motorized boat in the race.

The Zodiac's other operator was Owen Vlug, son of Bob, brother to Sara. He was a hulking, taciturn young man, a bit older than Stanley, with a brush cut and thick glasses, who worked at Ocean Steel, an Irving-owned plant along the Saint John River. Together with another race volunteer, the men hauled the small red Zodiac down the beach and muscled it into water deep enough to engage the twenty-horsepower outboard motor. The boat was ten feet at its longest, with the cramped square footage of a double bed. In jeans and a bomber jacket, Vlug steered from the stern while Stanley weighed down the bow as the boat punched through the surf and the waves.

Even in the cove, the Zodiac took on water. Stanley noticed that the boat's drain hole lacked a plug. In its place, someone had stuffed a folded length of plastic hose, which had popped loose. Water burbled up the hole. In a self-bailing boat, the drain hole must be plugged before it is launched. Once the vessel gathers speed, the plug can then be removed and a momentum-generated vacuum will suck excess water out through the hole. But as the Zodiac fought through the swells, its small engine never generated enough speed for the drain to work properly. Cool water pooled around the two men's ankles. Stanley grabbed a hand pump and began bilging furiously. At best, he realized, he was fighting the incoming seawater to a stalemate, but that was better than the alternative.

The Zodiac suddenly stopped. Only a kilometer or two off the beach, a kayaker had tumbled into the water, and Vlug had gone to his aid. Stanley kept his head down and focused on pumping seawater out of the idling boat. When he looked up, the racer was back in his kayak and Vlug was readjusting the spray skirt around his cockpit. Stanley recognized the young guy in the red bandana: René Arseneault. They had gone to high school together, although René was a few years older, a well-liked athlete who ran with the popular crowd. More recently, Stanley had chatted to Arseneault when he had dropped by the store.

"Do you want to keep going?" Vlug asked.

"I'm fine! I'm fine!" Arseneault insisted. He seemed keen to make up lost time.

The Zodiac's operators let him head off. Other kayakers were emerging from McLaughlins Cove and paddling almost directly out to the bay to avoid the two-meter-tall breaking waves near Reef Point. "Stay close to the shore," Stanley shouted, "but not too close!" The original plan had been for the motorized Zodiac to patrol the second half of the kayak stage, while the tandem rescue kayak kept a lookout in Chance Harbour. The Zodiac hadn't traveled far, however, before Vlug spotted two more solo kayakers in trouble. The racers were closer to shore than the rest of the competitors, maybe a couple hundred meters away from a vertical wall of shale. Vlug angled the craft in their direction. Stanley recognized the race leaders.

"My friend capsized," Shawn Amirault said, "and he's very cold."

"Are you all right?" Owen Vlug asked.

"I'm okay," said Mark Campbell. "I can make it."

To everyone else, he seemed nearly epileptic with shivering. "No, you should get in here," insisted Vlug.

Campbell didn't argue. The Zodiac operators cleared space for him on the floor. It wasn't the most comfortable perch—the Zodiac had collected nearly ten centimeters of water on its metal deck. Stanley opened the dry bag that held the boat's emergency supplies. The watertight seal hadn't been secured properly, and the contents (a fleece blanket, a first-aid kit, some granola bars) were soaked. He gave the damp blanket to the hypothermic paddler. It was better than nothing.

Vlug tied Campbell's kayak behind them with a tow rope. The Zodiac made little progress over swells that were now the height of a man, even more—the tallest waves Stanley had ever seen. The empty kayak flopped like a cheap float toy, filled with water, and nearly disappeared beneath the surface. The submerged kayak now acted like a drogue—an emergency device, like a drag racer's brake chute, used in stormy weather to slow and steady kayaks until conditions improved. The Zodiac's occupants, however, wanted to be back on dry land as fast as possible, and the kayak wasn't helping. Stanley madly hand-pumped the water that kept sloshing into their vessel. Vlug fought with the outboard's handle to maintain the boat's course. Finally, he hauled the kayak in by its tow rope, emptied the cockpit of water, and pulled the boat into the Zodiac. He steered the outboard with one hand and cradled the kayak in his other arm, while Campbell held the other end in his lap.

They picked up speed. Each time they punched through a wave, water cascaded over the three men, Campbell shouted from the shock of the cold, and Stanley bruised his elbows and knees against the aluminum floor. The empty kayak bounced and smashed across their shoulders and heads and threatened to knock them all out of the Zodiac.

"This is not working!" Stanley pleaded. Vlug wanted to keep trying. He didn't want to abandon one of his dad's rental kayaks. "Screw the boat!" Stanley yelled. "Throw the friggin' thing over and let's find some place to land!"

Soon they had bigger worries. A large wave swamped the outboard and stalled the engine. The motorless Zodiac wobbled amid the haystacking waves, as Vlug yanked on the outboard's starter cord. Once. Twice. All they could hear was the hiss of sea spray and the rumble of breaking waves. Finally, the outboard coughed, sputtered, and engaged. They didn't get far before another breaker drowned the engine. Vlug tried to restart it again. Stanley, now seriously frightened, wondered if the safety boat would need to be rescued. But by whom? They had no VHF radio or cell phone or walkie-talkie or flares to alert the onshore organizers or the patrol kayak or anyone else.

"This is a nightmare!" muttered Campbell. Stanley had to agree.

Vlug kept hauling on the cord of the outboard.

Nothing. Vlug yanked again. Nothing.

Finally, the gurgle of the small outboard echoed off the water. Kayakers were still paddling toward the bay and at least one racer was following the wake of the rescue boat back to the beach. Even with the outboard revved, the Zodiac couldn't outpace these paddle-pushed craft. Slowly, the Zodiac chugged far enough into the lee of McLaughlins Cove that the threat of swamping diminished. When they hit the shallows, Jayme Frank dashed down and wordlessly helped to drag the Zodiac onto the beach. It had taken them an hour to travel two, maybe three kilometers. Stanley dashed to a pickup truck and cranked up the heater. Campbell borrowed Stanley's fleece jacket and climbed into the cab of the truck. Both organizers approached the Zodiac's operators.

"Why aren't you out on the water?" Sara Vlug asked.

"I'm too cold," Owen told his sister. "I'm not dressed for this."

"I'm too scared," Stanley agreed. "I don't want to go back out."

Sara Vlug seemed frustrated, angry even, by their reluctance to return to the bay. She flipped a hand in Jason Stanley's face, turned, and walked away.

Jim Currie had hit the Big Four-O, lost some hair, even put on a bit of a paunch. That didn't slow him down much. And it didn't stop his mother from worrying either. For more than two decades, she had fretted about her son's athletic escapades. Why would she stop now? A married father of three and a pharmaceutical manager from Halifax, Nova Scotia, Currie still caught grief for almost every race. He had grown up in New Brunswick, and his parents had retired to a cottage an hour outside of Saint John. After the Fundy race, they planned to rendezvous with Jim at the finish line. His mom wouldn't breathe right until she saw him back on solid ground.

At McLaughlins Cove, Currie pulled on a Gore-Tex jacket, a toque, and neoprene gloves, and then paddled out of Chance Harbour in a solo kayak until he met another racer going the wrong way. He could tell that the guy, in his late thirties and more lightly dressed, wasn't comfortable in his own solo boat. "What's the matter?" Currie asked.

"I'm getting soaked," admitted Peter Hancock, "and I can't work this steering thing."

"You need to drop your rudder," said Currie.

He pointed to the rectangle of metal, still in the locked position on the stern of the kayak—clear evidence that Hancock didn't know his way around a sea kayak. Currie reached over, unlatched the rudder, and flipped it into the water. Then he helped to pump dry the cockpit, adjust the rudder pedals, and fit the spray skirt back over the cockpit.

"You want to come with me and we'll stay together?" asked Currie.

"Okay," said Hancock, "but it's pretty rough out there."

"Let's make a pact," Currie suggested. "Let's just put the race aside and finish this thing. If one of us turns around, we both turn around."

Hancock had already been having second thoughts about his second thoughts. His competitive fire sparked again in the company of another racer. Maybe Currie was right. Maybe it wouldn't be so bad if they paddled together.

Like Hancock, Currie was a middle-aged, after-work athlete, although one more familiar with sea kayaking and wilderness-style events than the cyclist from Bathurst. His thinning hair, sharp chin, and sly wit suggested a stockier version of Hollywood actor James Woods. Since university, he had competed in marathons, triathlons, and, more recently, adventure races. He had intended to do the Fundy Multi-Sport Race with a friend, but the team arrangement hadn't panned out, so he had signed up as a soloist. Maybe racing alone wasn't the smartest idea—just ask his mother—but this was a short course with little navigation. It shouldn't be hard. Like Hancock,

Currie also had the gift of the gab and entertained friends and family members with comic tales of his competitive ups and downs. Occasionally he exaggerated the dangers to send his mom into conniptions. He loved a good story, and wilderness races offered plenty of material. Not every event had a happy ending, though. His mother, he had to admit, wasn't paranoid for no reason.

Twenty years before, at a triathlon in northern New Brunswick, Currie had exited the lake, wriggled out of his swimming gear, and was circling the route on his bike when his wife waved to him from the sidelines. "Someone died!" she yelled. During the fifteen-hundred-meter swim, a competitor from Quebec had floundered and then disappeared into cold Lac Baker—a victim of a heart attack or muscle cramp. No lifeguards or patrol boats had been on the water, standard safety measures at triathlons today. The race had been sponsored by the local McDonald's franchise, and the store had hired a barge for its costumed employees. When the restaurant characters saw the triathlete start thrashing and then disappear under the water, one mascot leapt into the lake to help, but he couldn't swim in his bulky, sodden suit and had to be yanked back onto the barge.

"Can you imagine being the guy drowning?" Currie often wondered. "'God, the Hamburglar's coming to get me—I *must* be dead!'"

Currie and Hancock paddled together for another half hour. As they rounded Reef Point and skirted the boisterous waves near Dry Ledge, the sea conditions only worsened. In the troughs of two-and-a-half-meter waves, the racers would lose sight of each other. They spotted the Zodiac closer to land, a kayak hanging off its stern and its outboard spinning in the air atop each big crest—a scene that didn't inspire confidence. They had reached the make-or-break point of the race, Hancock realized, and it marked a line he wasn't willing to cross, not without a safety boat nearby. He waved his paddle at his new partner.

"I'm turning back!" he shouted.

"Yeah, sure," Currie agreed. "Let's do it."

In dozens of races, Currie had never *not* finished an event, and he wasn't keen to blemish that record. Rather than give up, he would have preferred to beach his kayak on shore and drag it through the woods until he crossed the finish line. But he had made a commitment—and he could tell that Hancock was too nerved up to continue. If Currie had been alone, he might have pushed on. Not now. A pact was a pact.

They paddled out of the wind and into the lee of the cove, not far behind the Zodiac. They could see a convoy of racers, in single and double kayaks, surging toward the bay. "It's worse the farther you get!" Hancock told the passing paddlers. Few did more than nod at his warnings. Even his pals from Bathurst resisted his pleas. Currie passed along similar warnings to racers, including a young guy in a red bandana. "Are you going to be okay?" he asked. "It's really rough out there."

"I'll be fine," René Arseneault replied.

A few minutes later, Currie encountered a young Asian man in a trailing boat. Again, a warning. This time Boon Kek assured him he was okay and kept paddling.

Two hundred meters from dry land, the dumping surf ejected both Hancock and Currie. They swam and dragged the water-loaded boats up the sloping beach. Only then did they understand how truly cold the bay was. The safety Zodiac was out of the water, empty, its engine disengaged. Currie knew Jayme Frank from other events. He had once taken the experienced athlete out for breakfast so that Frank could share training tips and racing secrets. Currie felt he could be forthright with him. "Jayme," he said, "it's too dangerous out there for this kayaking section."

It was 2:00 p.m., an hour and a half since the first kayaks had launched from McLaughlins Cove, and Frank's casual demeanor had vanished. His face was etched with urgency. "We cancelled it," he said. "We're trying to get people off the water."

Both Currie and Hancock were shivering from their wet exit, so they climbed into the cab of an idling truck and waited for a lift to Dipper Harbour. Mark Campbell was already inside, wrapped in blankets. His body had recovered much of its warmth, although he had left a little pride back on the bay. His sense of humor at least remained intact.

"Welcome to the Shame Wagon!" he joked to the new arrivals.

"There's no shame in self-preservation," replied Hancock.

That sentiment would stick with Currie. Later, when the gravity of the day's events became clear, Jim Currie would look for Peter Hancock in the crowded house at the end of the race, find him again, and shake his hand. In an afternoon filled with lapses in judgment—some minor, some major—only Hancock had shown the good sense to slip the leash of his own ego and make the right call, one that likely saved him. The decision to turn back.

TWELVE

The *Benevolence*

Since before Canada could call itself a nation, Mawhinneys have been fishing the Bay of Fundy. If you stroll down the wharves at Chance or Dipper Harbour and blindly cast with a rod and reel, you will likely hook a Mawhinney by the collar of his rain slicker—and then the bayman will offer advice on how to improve your angling technique. Bumping into Mawhinneys can't be helped in these parts. The surname peppers the phone book for the seaside villages, a column almost as long as for Arseneaults in the Acadian parishes of New Brunswick. The Mawhinney name also graces a local street sign, a cove, and dozens of headstones, and appears on the shipping registry for many of the commercial vessels that berth along the Bay of Fundy.

The original Mawhinneys came to Canada in the early 1800s from the highlands of Scotland, via Northern Ireland, a family of the famed clan MacKenzie. Their surname translates most literally as "abundant in gorse"—the hardy, abundant (some say invasive) yellow-budded shrub with spines and pea-like pods. Upon arriving in Maces Bay, the Mawhinneys spread like their namesake shrub between the rocky headlands and beside the natural harbors west of Saint John. Families of eight or nine children were the rule rather than the exception. "They were such prolific breeders," observed one relation who tried to graph their genealogy, "that there are one heck of a lot of Mawhinney kin." As did other Scots, Irish, and Scotch-Irish immigrants, the Mawhinneys found on the coastlines of the Canadian Maritimes a fog-bound, wind-sculpted, wave-battered home not unlike the one they had left. It was a land less crowded, one where a man could be his own master, if he and his family were willing to risk the Atlantic crossing and then carve a living from a hard land and harder sea. "It has been said of the Mawhinney men," wrote another local historian, "that all one needed to make a start on his own was a stove, a bed, and a bag of potatoes."

Like most of his ancestors and relations, Keith Mawhinney had fished for lobster for as long as he could balance on two legs. He had grown up with his six siblings near the Chance Harbour wharf and now lived in a small bungalow a five-minute stroll up the road from the water. His eighty-year-old father still set and retrieved traps, and Keith and his four brothers had all apprenticed with their dad. Now forty-five, Keith Mawhinney had lobstered full-time since graduating from high school, and did so from his own forty-two-foot boat, whitewashed with maroon stripes, a real beauty called the *Benevolence*, which he anchored down the highway in Dipper Harbour.

It's hard to say which are more wily and elusive sea creatures: lobsters or the men who hunt them down. The *Homarus americanus* (American lobster) can be found in the Atlantic waters of the Bay of Fundy and down to North Carolina, and has long been both a staple on the dinner plates of coastal residents and a way to harvest a living from the saltwater depths. Lobsters were once so pervasive that six packs could be plucked from rockweed that washed ashore and were dismissed as cheap charity food for widows, orphans, and the poor. Unruly servants demanded they be served the fat-clawed inverte-brates no more than three times a week. In the nineteenth century, European aristocrats acquired a taste for lobster as a gastronomic delicacy. By the 1840s, the first commercial fishery had opened in Maine, and thanks to the advent of canning, the export industry took off soon afterward.

Like farmers, lobstermen can seem a superstitious tribe. Even in bountiful seasons, they look ahead to next year with foreboding. They're simply realists, baymen insist, not pessimists. And they've got history to back them up. When the first curious Europeans arrived on the New World's shores, wide-eyed Scandinavian and Portuguese seamen could have walked from Newfoundland to Nantucket on a highway of cod and taken a side trip to Saint John on a garden path of salmon backs. That's a bad joke now to the unemployed fishermen up and down the East Coast. While lobsters haven't suffered the same precipitous declines as cod and salmon, they do show a boom-and-bust cycle that nobody has puzzled out. By 2002, even though captains were pulling in historically high catches, almost everyone predicted that the good times wouldn't last forever.

The jobs of the baymen, at least, are neither as back breaking nor as unrelenting as they once were. Motorized winches, wire traps, and computerized depth sounders have removed much of the muscle ache, constant repair, and guesswork from the business. The new wire traps are lighter to haul and longer lasting, although the design hasn't changed much from the arch-topped, wood-slatted classics that decorate the porches of many Maritime homes. Baited with everything from herring to animal hide, the traps tease lobsters out of their homes on the ocean floor and through a hooped hole into a two-chambered house, divided into a parlor and a kitchen. Most young lobsters can skitter out of a trap, while larger adults may become too confined to retreat through the funnel of netting. If a captain pulls in a pound or two worth of salable lobsters in every trap, that's a good day on the water.

Even without their methodical East Coast drawl, Fundy lobstermen can sound as though they speak an alien language, a sort of maritime Klingon, with idioms varying between towns and coves. On the docks or over the VHF radios, you might overhear boat owners or buyers talk about chicks (one-pound lobsters), deuces (two pounders), selects or markets (lobsters between a pound and a quarter and three and a half pounds), keepers and counters (above the legal catch size of three and a quarter inches), shorties, snappers, and tinkers (those that fall below and should be thrown back), cripples—which include culls (single-clawed lobsters) and ministers, pistols or bullets (unfortunate brawlers that have lost both their big crushers and smaller pincers)—horses or jumbos (extra-large males, up to twenty-five pounds or more), and eggers or berried females (which carry spawn under their tails and should also be tossed back). If the Inuit really have forged a dozen words for snow, that essential element of their Arctic home, it's little surprise that baymen have at least as many ways to say lobster.

Finding lobsters was only one of the challenges of Keith Mawhinney's job, and often the least aggravating. He also had to stickhandle through the bureaucracy and regulations of the Department of Fisheries and Oceans. And the ringed nets of salmon farms were being constructed up and down the coast, spoiling prime lobster grounds and getting in the way of fishing boats. More recently, Mawhinney had noticed a proliferation of recreational kayakers. Their numbers were linked to the trips launched from the house of the Vlug family in Dipper Harbour. He found it a bit of a bother to keep an eye out for the narrow, low-lying vessels that were rarely picked up on radar. He couldn't understand why paddlers often chose kayaks in sea-camouflaged shades of blue, green, or gray rather than more eye-catching fluorescent hues. Then again, he knew next to nothing about kayaks. A bit of a loner, Mawhinney had as many opinions as lobster traps and he was never shy about dropping a few into his conversation to see what he brought up. His crusty charm could both welcome strangers and keep them at a gaff's length from his own business.

On the morning of June 1, Mawhinney had been fishing alone due more to economics than a taste for solitude. That spring, the water was still a touch too cold yet for the lobsters to migrate inshore and start trapping, and it wasn't worth hiring a sternsman to draw up mostly empty cages. He had left at dawn—there's a reason that newsrooms along the East Coast still call the late-night detail the lobster shift—and checked his traps all morning near Musquash Harbour, halfway to the city. By 1:30 p.m., the wind had picked up, and Mawhinney was guiding his boat past Chance Harbour and back to Dipper Harbour. Between the bell buoy that marks the entrance to Chance Harbour and the Alice Roger Ledges, the site of an old shipwreck, he glimpsed a flash of something. He didn't think "kayak" at first—he rarely encountered paddlers in seas this rough. A little farther, another conglomeration of color stood out amid the steely water and white-foaming waves. This time, he angled inshore for a better look.

Sure enough, a group of paddlers had gathered in a tight formation. Mawhinney wanted to be sure they were all right. From the wheelhouse, he could discern four kayaks: three singles and a double. One of the sodden paddlers looked as sour as a wharf rat caught in a barrel of brine.

"What the hell are you all trying to prove?" he called over the side of his boat. "Do any of you need a hand?"

By now, Shawn Amirault was meant to be safely on shore, sipping hot chocolate at the finish line, basking in the glory of his third straight victory—this one solo—at the Fundy Multi-Sport Race. On the kayak section, though, he had already relied twice on good Samaritans. First, Robin Lang, the paddling champion, had swept in to help Mark Campbell after he had capsized. Then the safety Zodiac had ferried his friend back to shore. Amirault had planned to beach his boat nearby and abandon the course, too. Once the Zodiac had motored away, Amirault could see Lang and his partner in the distance. He could follow their tandem kayak and still finish the race. For a fierce competitor, second place would feel far better than a DNF, the dreaded "did not finish." Amirault hadn't reckoned how his solo boat could be so much slower than a double kayak, let alone a tandem propelled by two of the country's fittest paddlers. He soon lost sight of Lang's boat beyond the barebacked crests of the restless bay. Now he was truly alone.

And that's when a rogue wave blindsided him, too.

Amirault's kayak broached before he could react. He had less experience sea kayaking than Campbell, and so a roll was not an option. Instinctively, as the boat tipped over, his submerged body kicked free. A former ski racer, Amirault thought he knew what true cold felt like. But the Bay of Fundy was a different order of frigid, an immediate shock to his body's furnace, as though he had stepped onto the surface of the moon. He knew he had to get out of this water as fast as possible. Each time he tried to climb aboard the kayak, he slipped off the back deck and into the bay. It had been tricky enough to return Campbell into his cockpit with three helpers. Alone in the water, Amirault's fingers were already numbed to near uselessness, and he wondered how the hell he would rescue himself. It was all he could do not to panic.

Amirault wasn't as alone as he felt. Other racers had begun to catch up. He didn't see them yet, but three separate boats were converging on his foundering solo kayak. He couldn't have dreamed up a better rescue posse. The leading co-ed team in the race reached him first. They were a pair of university friends from Halifax; one was a summer-time kayak instructor. In a solo boat, a thirty-two-year-old whitewater paddler from Moncton, New Brunswick, also came to Amirault's aid. The third kayak to arrive, another solo vessel, contained the most dexterous boat handler on the water that day. Dana Henry, twenty-seven, was the son of Jim and Kay Henry, the Vermont founders of Mad River Canoes. Like his father, Dana was a competitive paddling champion. In 2001, he had swept seventeen events at the flatwater, whitewater, and downriver U.S. championships. Henry wasn't even an official entrant in the Fundy race. He had only been in Saint John as part of his day job as a rep for Necky Kayaks, and the Vlugs had invited him to take part. Once he had reached McLaughlins Cove, other kayakers were shocked at the speed with which this mysterious solo paddler from the States shot through the waves, like a high-powered Sea-Doo compared to their own lumbering progress.

Together, the four kayakers rafted up, helped Amirault back into his boat, and pumped the cockpit dry. He was in no condition to continue. The cold water had knocked his senses for a loop. That was when they saw the lobster boat bearing down. One problem: how did you get a hypothermic, nearly delirious paddler out of his sea-level kayak and then over the meter-and-a-half sidewall of the lobster boat, while the forty-two-foot fishing vessel and the plastic kayaks bounced in the swells like kindergartners on a trampoline?

Keith Mawhinney sidled the *Benevolence* as close as he dared to the racers. Then he extended his gaff, the three-meter pole with a sharp, rounded hook on the end. "Grab hold of this!" he called. Amirault did exactly that. Adrenaline gave his cold-numbed fingers the snap-lock grip of a lobster clawing its prey. Mawhinney pulled him close to his boat, but he couldn't convince the shivering kayaker to let go of the gaff and reach for his hand. The hooked stick had become an umbilical cord that the hypothermic racer refused to release.

"You have to let go!" yelled Mawhinney.

The tug-of-war continued for several minutes. The other racers could only watch. If Amirault didn't let go of the gaff, they realized, it might spear him through the arm. Meanwhile, the four kayaks rolled up and down with the waves and crashed like driftwood against the lobster boat's hull. On the back of a crest, the *Benevolence* rose, until the boat's bottom loomed over the paddlers, its propeller exposed, and then the huge boat belly flopped down again. A meter or two closer, and it would crush the kayaks like a raft of Popsicle sticks.

Finally, Amirault relinquished his grip and Mawhinney yanked him into the boat. The lobsterman snagged the empty kayak and lifted it aboard, too, and then wrapped the wet, shivering racer in dry rags and a jacket. Amirault curled up, convulsed, and spilled the meager contents of his stomach across the deck. Mawhinney knew he needed to get his passenger to shore soon. First, he asked the remaining kayakers if they wanted a lift to safety, too. They all declined. Mawhinney then backtracked toward Chance Harbour in case any others needed help. Five minutes later, he encountered another tandem kayak.

"Is everybody okay?" he asked.

"We're fine!" the two paddlers insisted. "Everything's fine!"

Their tone of glib self-assurance annoyed the fisherman. If these guys all thought they knew what they were doing, then Mawhinney would leave them to the bay and worry instead about getting the hypothermic racer to Dipper Harbour. He pulled a U-turn, aimed for home, and muttered under his breath about the stupidity of kayakers heading out in these conditions.

Those fifteen minutes felt like an eternity to Amirault, an all-weather athlete who had never witnessed his body react so violently to the cold. While it would be hours before he felt normal again, his thinking started to clear as the boat approached the wharf. He appreciated the predicament from which he had been plucked. There was no way he could have lasted another half hour in that water. Simply getting him aboard the *Benevolence* had been trouble enough. Amirault made a mental note to thank his rescuer—maybe when his teeth quit chattering—and buy the fisherman a case of beer. He spotted two familiar faces arriving at the wharf. Robin Lang and his partner had entered Dipper Harbour but overshot the beach at Campbells Cove where the race was supposed to end. They were even more surprised to see Amirault. He had beaten his two rivals to Dipper Harbour and would again be the first to the end of the Fundy Multi-Sport Race. It was just not the way he had ever imagined finishing.

A race volunteer offered to drive Amirault around the harbor to the Vlugs' house. The volunteer seemed calm about the situation and assured Mawhinney that somebody was overseeing the event and that a safety boat was out on the bay. Everything was fine. Satisfied, Mawhinney dropped anchor and called an end to his eventful day. Later, he would second-guess his decision not to return the bay and look for other paddlers.

"I guess now I should have done more," he would reflect. "But I was under the assumption that they knew what they were doing."

THIRTEEN

The Dread

In adventure races, running relays, dragon boat meets, and amateur competitions of every sort, there is a long and proud tradition of the silly, ironic, even salacious team name. Top-flight athletes must christen their teams after the corporate sponsors that have ponied up money for good publicity. Other amateurs dub their groups after the noble causes and charities for which they are raising money and awareness. Everyone else has two options. Give your team a mythically memorable title for inspiration. Or take the low road and use a bad pun, a double entendre, or a self-deprecating in-joke so that everyone knows that finishing with your sense of humor is more important than finishing first.

At the Fundy race, several of the two-person teams had gone with the first philosophy: Team Storm (which helped rescue Shawn Amirault), Team Odyssey, the Outlaws. Others had decided to tweak the funny bone: the Sea Monkeys, the Tortoise and the Turtle, the

Guys That Won't Finish, Team Grumpy Old Men (two brothers-in-law who were neither old nor especially grumpy). Perhaps the oddest team name on the registration list—and certainly the most risqué, although few people realized it—belonged to the Tallywhackers.

In Bathurst, New Brunswick, 365 kilometers north of Saint John on the Baie de Chaleur, a gang of thirty- and forty-something employees from the zinc mine, lead smelter, and nearby power plant had discovered a shared interest in the outdoors. Unlike many co-workers, their wilderness jaunts didn't involve hooks or bullets and a case of cheap beer—although they might crack open a few cold ones after a half-marathon or a backpacking trip. Bob Leclair, a thirty-four-year-old technical superintendent at the smelter, had read about the Fundy Multi-Sport Race on the internet and thought it sounded like the kind of weekend event his friends would enjoy—more of an off-road triathlon or introduction to adventure racing. Competitors wouldn't need any special skills. Leclair asked Bob Carreau, a forty-six-year-old environmental manager at the mine, to be his partner. A busy father of four, Carreau had run triathlons for nearly twenty years and, at five foot nine and one hundred and sixty-five pounds, he still had the gym-fit physique of a guy half his age. Outdoor challenges helped to burn off his hyperactive sense of adventure—what friends described as "attention deficit disorder done good." The Two Bobs, as they were known, agreed to race as a tandem. They were joined by two more friends, a pair of thirty-something engineers who would team up as the Bob Hunters. Finally, the quartet cajoled Peter Hancock, a technology manager at the smelter, to compete in the solo category. When asked for a name, Leclair and Carreau called their partnership the Tallywhackers.

A few years earlier, on their first backpacking trip together, the Two Bobs had hunched around a campfire and swigged from a bottle of Talisker, a single-malt scotch, until they began slurring to each other: "Hey, Bob, pass the Tallywhacker!" It became a running joke—literally. To memorialize the next day's hangover, the Two Bobs borrowed the name for a Tuesday-night running club they formed not long afterward. Members of that group would pencil in "Tallywhackers" for any competition they entered: 10Ks, relays, triathlons, half-marathons, ski loppets. In Bathurst, the extended clan of athletically inclined friends even hosted an end-of-season barbecue and Oscar-style awards night called the Tallywhackies. A typical trophy was the Premature Evacuation Award, given to a member who had accidentally skipped an entire running loop at a triathlon. Only later did someone Google "tallywhacker" and discover, with some embarrassment, what the word actually meant: obscure slang for an especially long penis. By then the name had stuck.

Team Tallywhacker arrived at Trail's End a half an hour behind Peter Hancock. André Arseneault was still filming new arrivals. "We went through the biggest swamp I've ever seen," Bob Leclair told the camera. "But if it doesn't hurt, it's not fun." Leclair had only sea kayaked four times before and was debating what to wear. Digging through his duffel bag, he saw his toque but instead pulled on a floppy Gilligan's Island sunhat.

Bob Carreau glanced at McLaughlins Cove and saw kayaks pushing through the breakers. Standing in bike shorts and a light shirt, he tried to imagine how cold it might get. "Is this going to be enough," he asked a race volunteer, "or should we wear a coat?"

"It's up to you," the volunteer replied.

"Well, what would *you* wear?" Carreau pressed.

"Yeah," admitted the volunteer, "I'd wear a coat."

The Bobs pulled on thin nylon jackets, and Carreau hopped into the front cockpit. The elder Tallywhacker had sea kayaked a dozen times and figured his upper-body strength would help to motor them both to the finish line. That confidence took an immediate dousing, as the friends launched through the surf and water swamped their twin cockpits. Rather than stop to pump out, the Two Bobs pressed on. They hadn't paddled far when they spotted a familiar face heading in the wrong direction.

"Guys, turn back!" Peter Hancock shouted. "It's absolutely nuts!"

The Two Bobs waved but kept paddling.

"Well, what do you think?" Carreau asked.

"If I was out here alone, there's no friggin' way I would do this," Leclair admitted. "Does it seem all right to you?"

The double kayak felt stable. They assumed that working together, they could finish. "Let's head a little farther," Carreau suggested, "and see how it goes." There were other boats on the water now, paddling for Dipper Harbour. They couldn't all be wrong, could they? A few minutes later, another tandem boat passed them.

"Are you guys kayakers?" the Bobs asked.

"Yeah," one of the paddlers replied. "We've been out quite a bit."

"Should we be out here?" Carreau asked.

"I think it's all right," came the reassuring answer.

And so they continued.

They rounded Reef Point and met the tumult near Dry Ledge that had convinced their friend to turn back. Every time a wave broke over the boat, bay water leaked through the spray skirts and numbed their ankles and feet. They watched the remaining kayaks pull farther ahead. The saltwater caught in the kayak was slowing them down. Carreau estimated that a hundred liters had collected in the plastic shell—225 pounds of extra weight. That shifting ballast compromised the boat's stability. As the water sloshed back and forth in their cockpits, the Two Bobs fought to keep the bow pointed into the waves and prevent the boat from tilting onto its side and capsizing. They considered pumping out the boat, but if they opened their spray skirts in the messy seas, they would get more water dumped into the kayak. They had no idea how far the finish was. And the shoreline, maybe a kilometer off, was raggedy-edged and lacking in a sandy sanctuary on which to land a boat. Paddling onward seemed the best of several bad options. The Two Bobs' banter had vanished. As they focused on staying afloat, both men barely spoke.

"Hey, Bob?" Leclair called from the rear cockpit.

"Yeah …?" replied a voice dulled of its familiar edge.

"Are you okay up there?" Leclair asked.

"Uh, yeah …"

Leclair didn't believe it. He knew his fellow Tallywhacker better than that. They had raced together over some rough spots. When Carreau got frustrated—and these conditions would vex anyone but an expert kayaker—he didn't go quiet. Instead, the high-energy business manager was more likely to get angry and vocal: at himself, at his partner, at the obstacles they faced, whatever it took. He would clench his molars, curse like a true miner, and then urge his aching body across the finish line by force of will. The dead tone in Carreau's voice was new. It signaled to Leclair that something wasn't right with his now-silent partner, that their race was skidding sideways.

"I don't feel good out here," Leclair admitted. "Actually, I'm scared out of my mind."

Among the Inuit, the near-constant perils of Arctic kayaking—the sea ice, the frigid ocean, the fierce weather, or the unpredictable mammals that they hunted—preyed upon the imaginations of even the most talented paddlers. As far back as 1765, cases were documented of a strange kayaking-related malady, much like post-traumatic stress disorder. It usually struck when paddling alone, often after a recent fright or the loss of a relative or hunting partner. A kayaker would begin to worry unnecessarily about capsizing, shake uncontrollably, feel his arms go numb and his palms sweat, and see spots pinwheeling before his eyes. The kayak might appear distorted, as though it were growing taller and skinnier, the bow extending Pinocchio-like toward the horizon. The paddle itself suddenly felt as uselessly light as a goose feather. The strange disorientation often gave the sense that the kayak was leaning precariously to one side. In a sudden urge to correct this lopsided stance, a hunter sometimes tipped the boat. Inuit kayakers may have died on perfectly calm seas from such panic attacks.

The sight of shore or another kayaker usually brought an end to the episode, and yet the psychological effects could linger for a decade or longer. Some kayakers returned to solo paddling but with diminished confidence. Others could only travel with a companion. A few gave up kayaking entirely. Several diagnoses were floated for the cause of the syndrome: too much coffee, tobacco, or sex, or perhaps the corrupting influence of European contact upon the Inuit's traditional skills. There was no known cure. Danish medical observers dubbed the mysterious mental illness *kajakangst* or "kayak dread." The Greenland masters of ocean paddling knew it simply as *nangiarneq*: "to be afraid in dangerous places."

René Arseneault was getting frustrated, too.

He had performed so well in the running and biking stages. When he launched onto the bay, he had been in fourth place. Sixty-four other racers were still behind him. Everything since then seemed to conspire to slow his sprint to the finish. He hadn't gone far, maybe a hundred meters, when one of the rolling waves knocked his boat enough to unbalance his paddle stroke. His center of gravity wobbled, the kayak tipped, and he spilled out of the cockpit into the water. The shock of the bay was immediate—an instant ice-cream headache. He wasn't on the Kennebecasis River anymore, that much was certain. A safety Zodiac quickly appeared. The boat's operator got Arseneault seated again and his kayak pumped out and asked if he wanted to continue. He was cold and wet but he wasn't about to give up so close to the end. Damn right, he wanted to keep going.

Arseneault hadn't gone far when a new problem arose. His kayak kept angling off course against the stiff headwind, an especially precarious situation as the waves steepened. Something was wrong with his rudder or the pedals that shifted it. He stopped, popped his spray skirt, and peered into the shadows of the cockpit. Half an hour had passed since he had launched from McLaughlins Beach. Other boats were overtaking him.

A tandem kayak sidled up. The two race volunteers in the safety kayak had noticed his herky-jerky progress. "How are you doing?" they asked.

"I'm having trouble with this rudder," Arseneault said. "I can't get my feet on the pedals."

One of safety officials leaned over, craned his head between Arseneault's legs, and reached inside the cockpit to adjust the foot pegs.

"Are you okay?" the other race volunteer asked.

"Yeah."

"Are you sure you want to continue? The waves are getting rough out there."

"I've come this far," Arseneault insisted. "I want to finish the race."

He paddled away and saw the Zodiac struggling back into the cove, and then the two solo kayakers returning. They were warning everyone of the rough conditions beyond the point. Around 1:50 p.m., as another tandem kayak caught up, Arseneault was still fighting the waves with his paddle.

Joe Kennedy, a thirty-seven-year-old wildlife biologist and experienced canoeist, had competed in a dozen adventure races, including the last two Fundy challenges. He had won the solo category the previous year—the only soloist out of six to finish under the eight-hour time limit. This year, he was racing as Team Forty with a friend from Fredericton. They had launched a double kayak a half-hour behind Arseneault and had made up that gap in just twenty minutes. Their boat had taken on water punching through the surf and more was leaking through the spray skirts. Kennedy recognized the problem. Whenever a wave spilled over the kayak's deck or ocean spray pooled on the stretched nylon of the skirt, water seeped through the stitching holes that rimmed the fabric. He had rented kayaks from Eastern Outdoors once before and had experienced the same leakage. Afterward, he had told a store employee that the nylon skirts needed sealant applied around the threading to keep out water. The message, it seemed, hadn't gone anywhere.

Maybe Arseneault had gotten cold for the same reason. It was hard to tell. Kennedy chatted with him about the wind and waves and asked how he was doing. "Yeah, it's not very nice out," the young racer agreed, but he didn't say much more. His taste for chit-chat had soured. What struck Kennedy as odd was the young racer's weak paddling technique. Kennedy assumed that anyone who had chosen to go solo would be a strong paddler. Arseneault, however, was leaning backward in his cockpit and turning the paddle shaft with twists of his arms and wrists. Good technique requires a kayaker to sit spine-straight and pivot the upper torso with each stroke. The abdominal muscles drive the momentum of the vessel up through the chest, shoulders, and then arms. Relying instead on the wrists and biceps will quickly tire a paddler.

It wasn't the time for a lesson. The three kayakers wished each other well, and Team Forty plowed through the waves, leaving Arseneault behind. Not long afterward, they met a lobster boat steaming in the opposite direction.

"Do you need any help?" the captain asked.

"No, we're fine," Kennedy insisted.

After the race, the name of the boat would strike Kennedy as funny. Captains tend to christen their boats after their mothers, their wives, or maritime puns—sometimes a combination, like the *Betty Sea*. This boat had a more poetic moniker painted across its bow. *Serendipity* or something like that.

He was close. The boat was Keith Mawhinney's vessel, the *Benevolence*. After Kennedy assured him all was well, Mawhinney quit his search for competitors in trouble and returned to Dipper Harbour. The kayakers who were left behind to face the rising tide and the approaching storm would soon wish he hadn't. Many would have welcomed a touch of serendipity, benevolence, or both.

Boon Kek was farther back in the pack, hustling to catch up. The running and biking sections had taken longer than he had anticipated. The logging roads had been a mud bath. Alone, he had strained to heave his bike over fallen logs and push it through thigh-deep craters. There were still teams and solo racers behind him, but they seemed unlikely to complete the whole course. Kek had trained too hard to give up. When he reached the kayak section at 1:37 p.m., more than an hour after the race leaders had arrived, he felt anxious to gear up and get away. Jayme Frank helped Kek to settle into a kayak. His would be one of the last boats allowed to leave.

As he paddled away, Kek could see other kayaks, mostly doubles, heading out of the cove. He knew from a marine science class that the waves would be rougher inside the cove as they rose and broke against the shallow incline of the beach—that was the theory, at least. He figured it should be calmer on the bay. Now, he hoped to make up lost time. He spotted the Zodiac and the two solo kayakers abandoning the race.

"Why are you heading back?" he asked Jim Currie and Peter Hancock.

"It's too rough out there," they told him. "We're not going to do it."

Boon Kek wasn't concerned—not yet. He bent his head into the wind and tried to keep his paddle strokes deep and steady. When he rounded Reef Point, waves began to break over the deck of his boat, the ocean spray strafed his cheeks, and water leaked through his spray skirt. The seas, if anything, were rougher beyond the cove. He realized, then, how cold the bay was and paused several times to pump water from his cockpit. During one of these five-minute pit stops, a tandem kayak came up alongside his boat. The two race volunteers asked how he was doing.

"I'm okay," he told them. "How far is the finish?"

"You're a quarter of the way there at least," one said. "Maybe a third. You want to continue?"

"Yeah, no problem," he said. "I can go on."

The safety kayak headed toward Dipper Harbour, and Kek followed until it disappeared beyond the swells. The sun was still out, but the wind and the waves off Reef Point and Dry Ledge had picked up. Kek heard what sounded like a whistle—something more than just the shrilling of the powerful breeze. He looked around and couldn't see anything. It must be coming from the shore, he thought, and so he kept paddling. More whistling. Louder now. He looked around again. This time another kayaker was paddling toward him from farther offshore, riding over the swells, blowing his safety whistle and waving to catch his attention. Kek stopped. The solo racer drew up to the seaward side of his kayak, and they grabbed each other's boat for stability.

"Do you have anything to eat?" the racer asked.

Something had happened to René Arseneault in the half hour between talking with Joe Kennedy and flagging down Boon Kek. His natural bravado was gone. His enthusiasm for the race—so obvious to those who had spoken to him in the weeks leading up to it, to anyone who had seen him on the beach, even to the Zodiac operators who had restored him to his kayak—had vanished, too. He felt cold, hungry, tired. And he was willing to admit that the race had bettered him.

Kek offered an energy bar. Arseneault gobbled it down and handed back the wrapper. Labored breathing slowed his speech. "How far do you think we are?" he asked.

"We're a third, maybe halfway there," Kek said.

"Man, I'm ready to turn back," Arseneault admitted.

"That doesn't make sense," Kek said. "It will be just as far going back as finishing."

They discussed the options. Arseneault agreed to continue. They could tough out the last stretch together. Ready to set off again, Kek loosened his hold on the other kayak and let go.

PART THREE
The Storm

In exchange for exposing oneself to the loss of life, the player intends to hunt on Death's territory and bring back a trophy that will not be an object, but a moment; a moment impregnated with the intensity of self because it bears within it the insistent memory that, through courage or initiative, he or she succeeded for a moment in extracting from Death or physical exhaustion the guarantee of a life lived fully.... These sacred experiences, detached from all explicitly religious references, are abundant in the domain of dangerous physical activities.

—David Le Breton, "Playing Symbolically with Death in Extreme Sports"

I'll never lose sight of my Chance Harbour home
And the young man that I'd grown to be
And the friends and the neighbours that I left behind
And my folks in our home by the sea.

—Wayne Burke, "A Maritimer's Lament"

FOURTEEN

The Extreme Gene

Jim Currie's parents had wanted to celebrate all day. That morning, news had arrived from Jim's younger brother in Vancouver that the Curries were grandparents, yet again. They had to wait before popping a cork, though. They had driven down to the wharf in Dipper Harbour to attend the triumphant arrival of their own boy— forty years old, a father of three, but a boy to them all the same. Around 3:30 p.m., a storm blew off the hills. It seemed to come out of nowhere, propelled by furious winds, a curtain of black that erased the blue sky within seconds. Even protected by the rock-walled breakwater and wooden wharves, the lobster boats pitched from side to side, tethered by their lines and anchors. Waves surged over the exposed top of the pens where the day's catch was housed before the lobsters were sold. Beyond the breakwater, the bay churned like a cauldron at full boil. Earlier, the Curries had seen a few double kayaks round Campbells Point, enter the harbor, and touch land on the far beach. Nobody else was arriving. The squall only got angrier. But where was Jim?

Currie's father felt his stomach tighten as he scanned the black sea for a sign of his son. He turned to his wife, who looked equally concerned. "Oh my god," he said, "we've had one born today, but now we've lost our Jim!"

The Curries drove their SUV around the harbor to the Vlugs' house. To their amazement and relief, they found Jim showered and awaiting his lift. His mother was pleased, and puzzled, that her son had finally shown enough good sense on one of his outdoor escapades to quit rather than risk an accident. Still, she was appalled by the disarray at the finish line. The Vlugs' house looked like the aftermath of a prolonged battle. Dozens of exhausted and shivering racers, some barely coherent, spilled out of the rooms in various states of undress.

"You're nuts, you know that?" she told her son. "I can't believe you keep doing these things!"

The tirade continued as they retraced the coast road to retrieve Jim's bike. They didn't get far. On the shoulder, a clutch of people flagged down their Ford Explorer. Currie recognized Sara Vlug, one of the organizers, standing beside two middle-aged racers. The men looked like stray dogs swept away by a flash flood and miraculously pulled from its raging current. Vlug asked if they would chauffeur the sodden dropouts back to Dipper Harbour. The Curries agreed. One man climbed into the backseat, but his friend needed to be helped into the rear cabin of the SUV, where he crouched on all fours, dripping seawater and shaking so hard that his skull beat a tattoo against the ceiling. The Curries turned up the heater and passed back dry blankets.

Once he closed the hatch, Currie's father asked, "Is it that bad out there?"

Vlug's voice dropped. "No," she said, "it's not that bad."

As the Explorer ferried the two racers to the finish line, their mutterings told a different tale. "We were in way over our heads," they admitted. "What the hell were we doing out there? We don't know how to deal with that shit!"

"See? *See?*" said Currie's mother. "You're gonna get yourself killed!"

After they dropped off the rescued racers, Currie managed to calm her again on the ten-minute drive back to McLaughlins Cove. "They wouldn't call it an adventure race," he always told her, "if it wasn't an adventure." Yes, the weather was turning belligerent. But he had gotten off the water long before the storm. The two racers they had helped were cold and wet but fine, too. Everyone was fine.

As Currie loaded his bike into the Explorer, a man rushed up to the driver's side window. "Is this a four-wheel drive?" he demanded.

"Yeah," replied Currie's father. "Why?"

The man gestured down the dirt road. "A guy just flipped over on his bike," he said, "and we think he's broken his back!"

Currie cringed.

His mother shot him a glare that could cut diamonds. "See! You're gonna kill yourself!"

As Jim Currie knew, the call to adventure, as strong as any drug, can be difficult to explain. If you don't feel its pull, you wouldn't understand—at least that's the attitude both professional adventurers and weekend warriors assume about their thrill-seeking hobbies. Still, why do some people answer the siren song—to jump out of airplanes, to ski down avalanche-prone mountainsides, to dash breathlessly through forest labyrinths—while others remain content with their quiet lives of domestication?

Over the last decade, I've asked dozens of outdoor athletes and adventurers that question. Often I've tracked down peripatetic adrenaline junkies by cell phone or satellite link in the middle of a wilderness foray. In the comfort of my pajamas, I've interviewed these travelers standing atop mountain peaks, traversing polar tundra, or (in the case of one round-the-world explorer) rowing across the Atlantic while dodging hurricanes, container ships, and amorous giant turtles. Almost as often, I've caught them while they were recuperating from the injuries (frostbite, sprained joints, worse) that are the dues of their unconventional occupations and risky hobbies. They are articulate and amusing when they describe the ups and downs of previous expeditions, the close calls and peak experiences, the moments of ecstasy and the moments of doubt. They can detail with precision and passion the training and preparation they devote to trips and competitions, past, present, and future. Ask them, however, for a definition of true adventure, or inquire (as their spouses and parents must do) why they chase its tail, and their answers become more vague, less certain.

Why shouldn't they be? It is hard to rationalize such socially unproductive pastimes as backcountry skiing, whitewater kayaking, or adventure racing. Outdoor sports have always existed outside the definitions of ordinary morality. That's why French mountaineer Lionel Terray dubbed his clan of climbing colleagues the "conquistadors of the useless." For years, the stock reply to the whys and wherefores of any adventurous undertaking has been George Mallory's flip justification for trying to ascend (and ultimately perishing upon) Mount Everest: "Because it's there." The currency of that cliché, alas, has faded from overuse. Back in the 1930s, placing the first mountaineer atop the world's highest peak had been an expedition of national urgency for glory-hungry governments in the United Kingdom and elsewhere. Thirty years before that, the sprint for the poles had gripped the attention of pre-television audiences around the globe. The polar expeditions were the ultimate in extreme races, complete with bold winners (Roald Amundsen), tragic losers (Robert Scott), and trash-talking rivals who disputed each other's achievements (Robert Peary and Frederick Cook).

By the twenty-first century, most of the major accomplishments in wilderness exploration had been ticked off, at least the ones that don't require a rocket ship or a deep-sea submersible. Our tallest peaks have been conquered, our most distant lands discovered. We have paved paradise, practically to the base of Everest. Every attempt at adventure adds a footnote at best to the great expeditions of the past. To catch the attention of a fickle public, attention-getting outdoor "firsts" have become sliced absurdly thin. How much glory is there, really, in becoming the youngest diabetic to skateboard across the Sahara?

Our present age has been kind neither to adventure nor to adventurers. As a culture, most North Americans have retreated from seeking outward journeys in what little wilderness remains beyond our bloated suburbs. Instead, we look for inner worlds to explore, new depths of self-awareness to plumb. Our postmodern vision quests tend to be of a virtual sort—through movies, self-help books, psychedelic drugs, meditation retreats, inspirational seminars, websites, internet chat rooms. Without ever leaving the safety of their bedrooms or basements, video game players and online second-lifers pay to live vicariously through digital avatars, comic book symbols of their better selves, and to navigate imaginary worlds straight out of the ancient myths. "Our modern disregard for adventure reveals how thoroughly domesticated is this view we have come to take of our human and cultural limits," warned Paul Zweig, the literary critic and inveterate globe trotter, thirty years ago. "Man, we decided, is the laboring animal whose ability to create values depends upon his infinite capacity to buy and to sell: his time, his work, his very life. From this point of view, adventure is, at best, a recreation." These days, adventure is almost always packaged that way—as a recreation, an off-the-shelf consumer accessory, an experience bought and sold like any widget.

And yet people still long to push beyond the boundaries of the world they know. For full-time explorers and part-time weekend warriors, that call to adventure is no longer something out there—it's mostly something *in* here, either hardwired into our DNA or culturally habituated into our consciousness. For some people, it can feel like a relentless tug from a deep recess of the mind. In the mid 1960s, J.R.L. Anderson, a British journalist for *The Guardian*, succumbed to the call and embarked on several long-distance sailing journeys, including an attempt at age fifty-five to recreate the Vikings' six-thousand-five-hundred-kilometer crossing of the North Atlantic to the enigmatic coast they had dubbed Vinland. In 1970, after several risky boating expeditions, he gave this will-to-adventure a name: he called it the Ulysses factor, after the mythical Greek hero and Mediterranean wanderer. Anderson admitted that the exploring instinct didn't manifest in all or even a majority of the human population, and that it likely waxed and waned throughout history and among nations, cultures, and civilizations. "There is some factor in man," he mused in his book, *The Ulysses Factor*, "some special adaptation, which prompts a few individuals to exploits which, however purposeless they may seem, are of value to the survival of the race." He catalogued examples and types of this adventurous mutation in humankind, such as the ocean-crossing scholar Thor Heyerdahl, the English nomad Eric Shipton, and the French mountaineer Maurice Herzog. Each of these explorers shared a curiosity about the world, similar to the general scientific frame of mind that Anderson called the Archimedes factor, but they also had a drive to step beyond the comforts of civilized life and test their own limits.

"I think people by nature are inquisitive," agreed Ian Adamson, the world's premier adventure racer, who has described his twenty-four years in the sport as a "postdoctoral degree in living." "Consequently, humans moved from Africa half a million years ago and explored—pushed further and further to the outer reaches of the world. In the modern era, when you look at all the explorers, why do people try and push to the North Pole? It's a desire for adventure. And now there's not a whole lot left in terms of conquering peaks, poles, oceans—and yet we're still inquisitive beasts, we're still searching in science and nature. So now that we have so much more leisure time and money and resources, we're naturally drawn to doing things like adventure races because it's a challenge—exploring our souls and exploring a new environment or wilderness or country or culture or society or interpersonal relationships. It's all a discovery."

The Ulysses factor that supposedly flows through the blood of great explorers, as described by Anderson, can sound like an odd mystico-genetic urge, a bit like the Force from the later *Star Wars* sequels. The author-adventurer suggested neo-Darwinian justifications for such dangerous preoccupations as trans-Atlantic sailing and Himalayan climbing. "The grape that has too sheltered an existence does not produce good wine," mused Anderson. "The great vintages are from vines on exposed hillsides that have to struggle to survive. What is true of viticulture is true of human society: the over-sheltered individual does not thrive." His metaphorical leap of logic, from cultivating wine to courting death, isn't entirely convincing. In the end, the best grapes still get crushed.

From the perspective of evolutionary survival, the risks taken by explorers and adventurers appear counterintuitive. How do you pass on your genes if you have been buried by an avalanche or lost at sea? For those adventurers who push themselves too far and never return from their journeys into the unknown—the Mallorys and the Scotts and the Earharts, the thousands of other ill-fated and anonymous strivers—he might have reserved another category. Call it the Icarus complex, the sometimes fatal drive to touch the sun.

Still, Anderson may have been on to something. By the end of the 1970s, psychologists had begun to chart humankind's moth-to-the-flame urge to seek risks. Researchers variously described the impulse as sensation seeking, novelty seeking, or the Type-T (for thrill) personality. The Zuckerman-Kuhlman questionnaire became a widespread method to profile such tendencies in experimental subjects and psychiatric patients. With a litmus test for risk tolerance, scientists could explore what might cause variations in behavior. Studies of identical twins, the gold standard of nature-versus-nurture debates, revealed that the sensation-seeking trait in humans is highly genetic. While environment helps shape our appetite for danger, the line between whether we will want to ski the bunny hill or the double-black diamond run is more than fifty percent programmed into our genes—a greater genetic link than most other psychological characteristics.

In the late 1980s, biologists began a quest to link such behavior to a specific gene or mutation. They soon focused on the dopamine D4 receptor, a genetic marker that controls the intake of dopamine by the brain's reward center, the patch of gray matter associated with motivation and pleasure. A pair of Israeli scientists dubbed the DRD4 the "adventure gene." Health-conscious outdoor athletes will be dismayed to learn, however, that when studying this bit of risk-friendly DNA, scientists and psychologists tend to lump extreme sports with drug-taking, unprotected sex, gambling, reckless driving, and other unhealthy habits. "All the studies, they look at skydivers or something—and then they look at cocaine users," explained Cynthia Thomson, a former Rocky Mountain ski bum and now a risk-genetics researcher at the University of British Columbia in Vancouver. "The idea is that some people find an athletic outlet instead of using drugs." By the late 1990s, biologists were debating how strong, if any, an association could be made between variations in the DRD4 gene and the risky business of study subjects. Do tiny changes in the DNA mean that some people need a bigger thrill—a stronger drug, a steeper mountain—to get the same rush of pleasure as everyone else? For her research, Thomson collected DNA swabs and interviewed avid skiers, both those who were experienced yet cautious and others who were of a more extreme inclination. Next she planned to match genetic clues with their varying tastes for outdoor risk. Ultimately, she hoped some social good would come out of her pure science. Adventure-based wilderness programs such as Outward Bound, she suggested, could be aimed at kids who would otherwise chase illicit thrills. "That child may not respond to playing basketball or volleyball," Thomson said, "because they're not getting the adrenaline rush they need." Her findings may add one more mark on the trail of the mysterious extreme gene.

Most participants in expedition-style races, ultramarathons, and organized eco-adventures claim they are interested in more than the transient pleasures of an adrenaline rush. Seeking sensation or novelty is only part of the equation. Pushing the body to its physical limits opens doors of perception otherwise closed in daily life. Asked what they're chasing in endurance activities, outdoor athletes and amateur adventurers of a Zen frame of mind describe a phenomenon called the Flow. It can be experienced by a skier carving perfect S-turns across the canvas of a mountain slope. It might be the union of body and machine as a mountain biker weaves down a slalom course of tree trunks, gnarled roots, and exposed rocks. It could simply be the trance-like rhythm between landscape and gait that hill walkers and hikers fall into as they lope for hours along a forest trail. Pro athletes talk in a similarly fuzzy way about being "in the zone," when every shot feels certain of scoring, when they feel invincible. Marathoners describe pushing through "the wall," an invisible psychosomatic barrier, beyond which they encounter a sense of floating outside of time—of Flow.

The concept comes from the research and writings of American psychologist Mihály Csíkszentmihályi, who described Flow as an elusive mental state, a kind of preconscious harmony of mind and body that comes with intense psychic focus, physical mastery, and the rescuers learned that Stanley was part of the race, they peppered the employee from Eastern Outdoors with questions. "Who else is still in the bush?" they asked. "How many racers are on the water?"

Stanley apologized. He didn't know.

"Why don't you have a checklist?" demanded one firefighter. "We need to find out who's missing."

Meanwhile, as the biker was being removed from the woods, Gilles Arseneault had fielded a new emergency call. Another person was being brought to the wharf in Chance Harbour with hypothermia. Probably part of the same race. The unexpected development was exactly why the Musquash team needed the Accountability Board. Half his crew was occupied with the injured cyclist, but Arseneault still had rescuers as backup. Now they could run down to the wharf, a minute or two away, and act as first responders. His second crew would get there long before a new ambulance—likely dispatched from Saint John—could arrive. He gave his team the go-ahead, chalked down the assignment beside their tags, and waited for his first crew to emerge from Cranberry Head Road.

Once the cyclist had been loaded into the ambulance, the attendants headed for the wharf, too, and Arseneault departed with his crew and the Rescue One truck. Jason Stanley was left behind again.

It was nearly 5:00 p.m.—the official end of the race, although nobody cared by now who won or lost. Stanley stood alone among the scattered kayaks, watched the tide crawl up the beach, and wondered what to do next. He walked to a nearby cottage, asked to use the phone, and called the house in Dipper Harbour. Bob Vlug picked up.

"Where are my boats?" Vlug demanded. "Where are my boats?"

Jason Stanley hung up without answering.

SEVENTEEN

The Flood Tide

It happened in an instant.

Boon Kek released his grip from René Arseneault's kayak, and like that, Arseneault was gone. Before either racer could react, his boat spun on its axis and pitched sideways. The kayak wasn't broadsided by a rogue wave or a gust of wind, nothing so dramatic. A kayak is designed to be most stable in motion, balanced by the rhythm of alternating paddle strokes. Arseneault's kayak was stationary and bobbing amid the rolling waves. When Kek let go, it wobbled laterally, and Arseneault overcompensated in the cockpit until his shifting weight capsized the vessel. He disappeared under the water. Then he squirted free of the cockpit and was buoyed to the surface by his life jacket. His eyes were wide and frantic from the shock of the 9°C water.

"God, it's cold!" Arseneault exclaimed.

He tried to crawl back into his kayak, but the cockpit was filled to its coaming with water. He kept sliding off the slick plastic deck.

"Do you know how to use a paddle float?" Kek asked.

Kek had taken lessons in performing a rudimentary outrigger self-rescue—in the heated, still waters of a swimming pool, using a more stable tandem kayak. Arseneault didn't reply. Even if they had been experienced in the technique, Kek figured, the battering from the waves would have made the maneuver next to impossible. Arseneault unhitched the hand pump and tried to bilge the water from the cockpit. He had to pull his torso out of the water to jam the pump into the cockpit. Kek offered to try from the higher vantage of his own boat.

Aleut kayakers who plied the shores of Alaska and the Bering Strait had invented an early version of the kayak pump by hollowing out a cylinder of wood, which they used like an oversized straw to siphon excess water into the tube and throw it over the side. The designs of modern hand pumps have improved from their suck-and-toss origins, although the portable devices are hardly flawless. A typical plastic hand pump is about half a meter long and often wrapped in foam so it will float. The pump action of a small handle draws water up and jets it out a nozzle. Bilge rates range between twenty and forty liters per minute. With the largest pumps, a paddler can empty an average cockpit of one hundred and forty liters in under five minutes—in ideal conditions. The Canadian Coast Guard and the United States Coast Guard both require that kayaks be outfitted with some form of pump or bailing device. All of the boats at the Fundy Multi-Sport Race included hand pumps lashed to the front decks by bungee cords.

A hand pump, however, is a bit of a misnomer. It is better described as a *hands* pump. Using one often requires both hands to be free. When hands are off the paddle, a motionless kayaker runs an extra risk of capsizing. Kek took this chance and rammed his hand pump into the flooded kayak. After several minutes, he realized his efforts were futile. As much water as he could pump out of the boat, that much filled it again with every breaking wave. They were trying to hold back the tide with a small plastic tube.

"Man, I'm cold!" Arseneault repeated.

Kek didn't know what to say. Heading to shore didn't seem an option. They were perhaps a kilometer away from Dry Ledge, and other rocky patches stood between the two racers and the mainland. Waves launched rooster tails of spray up these jagged, hidden barriers. Beyond the rocks, the nearest shore offered little more than a shale cliff face on which to beach a kayak. They needed help. Both racers grabbed the whistles that dangled from their life vests and blew hard. Kek couldn't see other boats nearby. He couldn't see much in the pitching seas. He hoped that someone—the Zodiac perhaps or another racer—would hear the whistling and come to their aid. Arseneault, clinging to his overturned kayak, had been immersed in the bay for fifteen minutes now. Neither man had spoken much in the last few minutes. Kek wanted to say something, to assure Arseneault that they would both be okay, but his own facial muscles had stiffened in the cold. Between that lock-jawed tension, the shrilling winds, and his low-toned Asian accent, Kek felt his words wouldn't be understood.

They needed to do more than talk. Kek could now see that their kayaks were drifting backward past the rocky projection of Reef Point. The opening of Chance Harbour and the beachhead of McLaughlins Cove slowly scrolled past. They were helpless in the wind and the current to paddle for these safe harbors. If they drifted beyond Chance Harbour, they would leave the race route entirely, and the incoming tide and southwest wind would carry them toward Saint John. Nobody would be able to find them, no matter how loudly they whistled.

"We're off course," Kek told Arseneault. "I'm going to try to bring us to shore."

Kek asked Arseneault to tie the two kayaks together with a tow line. Despite nearly senseless fingers, the half-submerged racer managed to join the boats. He then grabbed onto the front of Kek's kayak, his body cradled under the bow, as the student from Singapore dug hard with his paddle and tried to propel them in the direction of the start line. They continued to drift east instead. The second kayak, heavy with water, stalled their attempts to change course. The flood

René Arseneault along the Kennebecasis River in Rothesay, New Brunswick, 2000. (Photo by Erin Dobson.)

Bob Carreau of The Tallywhackers talks with Jacqueline Arseneault, mother of René, during a recess at the inquest in Saint John, New Brunswick, June 2003. (Courtesy of the *New Brunswick Telegraph-Journal*.)

André Arseneault, René's eldest brother, prepares to give testimony at the first day of the inquest, June 2003. (Courtesy of the *New Brunswick-Telegraph Journal*.)

Jean-Guy Arseneault, René's father, in Rothesay, New Brunswick, January 2003. (Photo by David Leach.)

Sara Vlug and Jayme Frank, the organizers of the Fundy Multi-Sport Race, arrive at the courthouse for the inquest in Saint John, New Brunswick, June 2003. (Courtesy of the *New Brunswick Telegraph-Journal*.)

Adventure race organizer and reality TV pioneer Mark Burnett (left) with Fundy Multi-Sport Race participant and Canadian Forces network manager Mark Campbell at the final Eco-Challenge, Fiji, 2002. (Courtesy of Mark Campbell.)

Boon Kek in Saint John harbour, January 2003. (Photo by David Leach.)

Peter Hancock (left), and Bob Leclair and Bob Carreau of The Tallywhackers on the morning after the race, June 2, 2002. (Courtesy of Marc Lejeune.)

Shawn Amirault competing at an adventure race in Nova Scotia, 2005. (Courtesy of Shawn Amirault.)

Sea kayaks on the beach at McLaughlins Cove, where the paddling section of the race began, 2006. (Photo by David Leach.)

Jim Currie (right) and his father at the Currie family's cottage in New Brunswick. (Photo by David Leach.)

Bob Mawhinney, captain of the *D.P. Clipper*, stands at the wharf in Chance Harbour where he brought the two rescued kayakers. (Photo by David Leach.)

The *D.P. Clipper*, Bob Mawhinney's 50-ton lobster boat. (Photo by David Leach.)

RCMP constable (retired) Wayne Burke practises guitar at his home in PEI, 2005. (Courtesy of Wayne Burke.)

Gilles Arseneault at the station house of the Musquash Fire-Rescue Department, August 2006. (Photo by David Leach.)

A video still of René Arseneault at McLaughlins Cove, just before setting off in a sea kayak, June 1, 2002. (Courtesy of André Arseneault.)

tide grabbed its weight and drew them deeper into the bay's interior. Kek reluctantly unloosed the overturned kayak and set adrift a thousand dollars worth of borrowed boat.

As they scanned the bay, a darkness stole across the once-cloudless afternoon sky. The squall was blowing off the land. It moved with theatrical speed, drawing a murky curtain over the brightness of the day, and accelerated the already gusty winds. Black clouds overtook the blue sky and raked the water's surface with precipitation, something between liquid and solid, bits of hail, sleet, that biting hybrid called *snain*. In the distance, thunder boomed like a kettle drum. Arseneault had paddled for two hours through the wind and sea spray. He had been submerged in the bay for another thirty minutes. His skin was icy and his body heat had started to drop. He was cold beyond all reckoning. Suddenly, he began to clamber onto the wobbly deck of Kek's kayak.

"Get down!" Kek shouted.

Arseneault slid back into the bay. "We've got to get to shore!" he pleaded. "I'm too cold!"

"There's no way," Kek said. "Not here."

Kek's paddling had been futile. Pushed by the wind and the flood tide, the two young men had drifted past the mouth of Chance Harbour. To their right, increasingly close, rose the raw stone walls of Cranberry Head—this was the shoreline that Arseneault hoped to reach. The waves beat against the cliffs, bounced back, collided with the next surge, and stirred up a wild and spasming sea. There was no place to land, no way to get up the steep rock face without being crushed against its broken edges by the storm.

EIGHTEEN

The Science

Every winter, in ice-bound communities around the world, brave or foolish souls hurl their near-naked bodies into frigid oceans or holes cut into frozen lakes as a test of their hardiness. They call these baptisms polar bear swims. And every year, one or two never make it back to shore. Their deaths are likely the result of cold shock, or what experts also call sudden drowning syndrome. Abrupt immersion into water 15°C or less triggers a deep, involuntary inhalation of air. For some people, this unexpected reaction can spell the end. *Gasp. Gulp. Swallow. Choke.* Lungs empty of buoyant air and swell with water. Victims who aren't wearing a life jacket disappear beneath the surface and die of asphyxiation.

René Arseneault, like Mark Campbell and Shawn Amirault, would have experienced cold shock as soon as his kayak tipped. His body would have quadrupled its breathing rate, panting involuntarily like a sheepdog in a heat wave. After five minutes, this heightened respiration usually drops to near-normal, but the initial reaction can still cause small muscle spasms. To compound the predicament, the ability to hold a breath in cold water drops roughly in half, so that reaching the surface with a closed mouth becomes especially difficult. By shooting the body back above water as fast as possible, a life jacket protects as much from the threat of cold shock as it does from the longer-term danger of fatigue and drowning. But even a life jacket may not be enough to save someone from the effect of cold shock. In older victims or those with wonky tickers, the spike in heart rate and blood pressure (caused by a severe adrenaline rush) can knock the heart's natural rhythm out of whack. If such an arrhythmia isn't corrected, the misfiring blood pump can lead to ventricular fibrillation, cardiac arrest, and death. All in the first few minutes of taking a dunk.

While we've known for centuries that hotness is the sign of life and that death announces its arrival with an icy-fingered touch, the precise workings of our internal furnace puzzled early philosophers and scientists. According to Plato, the heart held in its chambers an innate internal fire. Galen, the Roman medical authority, proposed that the brain controlled our breathing as a kind of thermostat so that cool air from the lungs could balance the heart's pilot light and avoid injury from the extremes of hot and cold. Renaissance thinkers conceived our bodily functions in even more mechanistic metaphors. René Descartes thought the heart was simply a vessel in which to heat the blood, like a boiling pot or fermentation still, so it could fuel the skin-covered robot that was a human. Other scientists speculated about the mix of ingredients in our blood that catalyzed this fermentation: water, salt, earth, a touch of sulfur, "spirit" (a mysterious ether that made stars bright and semen potent), and what one writer described as "nitrous little bodies."

Homo sapiens, we now understand, evolved as a tropical species, and the African savannah remains embedded in our DNA. In biology-speak, humans are both homothermic and endothermic—that is, our average body temperature of 37°C remains static (varying no more than two degrees in a normal day) and our internal heat largely arises from the metabolism of food. Our earliest forebears didn't have to worry about the cold because they lived in a thermoneutral zone, where air temperatures hovered between 28°C and 34°C. Throughout our subsequent history, by trial and much error, we have been forced to figure out ways to regulate the temperature of our increasingly hairless bodies through a microclimate of insulative clothing so that we could colonize chillier climates. The fact that cold kills was hardly a revelation to our Ice Age ancestors, despite their tropical roots. By then, that chill would have been bred into their imaginations, if not their genes.

Death from cold water has been a less obvious phenomenon, its effects hidden by the more immediate threat of drowning. For centuries, cold-water deaths were simply listed as "overcome by the sea." There was even institutional pressure against providing safety from ocean waters, let alone understanding the risks. Until 1815 and the end of the Napoleonic wars, the British Navy maintained its seafaring empire through the policy of impressment. "The press gangs went into the pubs every night, clubbed a few people, put them onboard the ship, and there they were for the rest of the commission of the ship," explained Dr. Chris Brooks, the head research scientist at Survival Systems, an international rescue-training company based in Dartmouth, Nova Scotia. "If they were given a life jacket or any flotation to survive if they sank, they could have used that to escape and swim ashore."

By the early twentieth century, life-jacket technology and regulations had improved, but the medical understanding of hypothermia remained mired in the Dark Ages. In 1912, the sinking of the *Titanic* transfixed newspaper readers. One survivor described unlucky passengers floating past, in life belts and calm water, face down and already dead. Another boat arrived on the scene within two hours but could do little for the hundreds of passengers who had succumbed to hypothermia in the near-freezing North Atlantic. In the rush to lay blame for the sinking of the "unsinkable" ocean liner, most of the 1489 victims were listed simply as "drowned." Much of the blasé attitude to hypothermia, according to Dr. Brooks, stemmed from a snobbish assumption that death at sea was an occupational hazard for the working-class seamen and fishermen who plied the northern waters—the cost of doing business as a maritime nation. "We still lose one hundred and forty thousand people in open-water deaths every year," said Dr. Brooks, who keeps a stuffed beaver in his office as a reminder that, for all our modern technology, Mother Nature knows best how to keep out the cold.

The Second World War changed that dismissive attitude. During the Battle of Britain, German and British pilots parachuted over the English Channel and the North Sea. Even with life jackets, survival rates were low. In 1941, British medical officer Edgar Pask allowed himself to be repeatedly chloroformed and then dropped in a swimming pool to discover how, with many of the designs of personal flotation devices, unconscious airmen likely drowned face-first in the ocean long before hypothermia set in. In Nazi Germany, scientists pushed their research program even further. "The Germans had a very good air-sea rescue service and they were going out for these people just as they'd hit the water—maybe forty minutes," said Dr. Brooks. "They were hauling them out quickly, and to their amazement, they were dying—and they didn't understand why." The desire to know more about hypothermia began nearly at the top. Heinrich Himmler, the notorious head of Hitler's SS, insisted that the Germans be first to crack the code of cold-water immersion. "The Nazis believed that they had to have this information in order to survive as a nation," wrote Dr. Robert S. Pozos, a biologist who studied the Nazi hypothermia trials. To learn about the effects of low oxygen and high altitude, medical scientists with the *Luftwaffe*, the German air force, had already employed their own pilots as test subjects. The airmen developed symptoms of high-altitude illness but none died. To understand hypothermia, Himmler and his scientists chose human subjects drawn from other quarters. In the summer of 1942, at the Dachau concentration camp, two sets of gruesome experiments began.

A cruel selection priority was devised: Jews, Gypsies, stateless persons, foreign Catholic priests, criminals, and political prisoners. A German technician later testified that close to three hundred subjects were used as human guinea pigs and ninety didn't survive. The precise death toll may never be known. In the first experiment, concentration camp detainees were immersed in a metal-lined vat filled with ice water between 2°C and 12°C. One group wore the *Luftwaffe's* flying outfits. Other subjects lay naked in the cold water. Another group was tested using prototypes of survival suits. Uniformed doctors measured skin and rectal temperatures and heart rates, and analyzed blood and urine samples. A second set of experiments compared methods of rewarming hypothermic prisoners. Shivering victims were immersed in hot baths, wrapped in blankets, held in a warm cradle, or rubbed vigorously. Doctors also forced naked female subjects to lie next to hypothermic victims and even have sex with them in attempts to reheat skin and core temperatures. The final report on the hypothermia experiments was submitted to Himmler in the fall of 1942, buried in a cave as the Third Reich collapsed, discovered by American troops and then analyzed by a U.S. doctor, Major Leo Alexander, after the war.

American military researchers, who lagged behind British and German scientists in the science of cold, relied on the Dachau data collated by Major Alexander to support their own postwar studies into the effects of hypothermia and its use to prolong life during open heart surgery. The Alexander report was also cited in major non-military investigations of temperature regulation. Hypothermia researchers could use the findings in the report without directly referencing the Nazi scientists. By the time the ethical question of whether or not to employ this ill-gotten information arose in the general scientific community, the Nazi data had already informed research projects in North America and beyond. Even if no scientist ever consults the Alexander report again, the foundation of our current understanding of hypothermia has been built with at least a few bricks taken from the terrible actions of the Dachau doctors. Every life we now save from cold-water immersion owes a small debt to the victims who perished in those infamous experiments.

While our bodies may be tropical in design and susceptible to heat loss, they have evolved a few defenses to slow the cold at least, a physiological Maginot Line against the blitzkrieg of hypothermia. The initial evasive maneuver is a phenomenon known as peripheral vasoconstriction. At the first touch of cold, our nerve endings emit an SOS, and capillaries near the skin's surface constrict until these small blood vessels clamp shut, preventing nearly all blood from returning to the extremities. Like an emergency-scene attendant making triage decisions, our body will ration heat toward the all-important organs rather than waste remaining warmth on what it considers expendable extras: skin, toes, fingers, nose, ears. In so doing, we create an insulating survival suit out of our own chilled, blood-thinned flesh, a barrier between the surrounding water or air and the deeper tissues at the body's core. Within five or ten minutes, skin temperature can plummet from the mid thirties to 10°C or less, until it stabilizes just above water temperature. Because of the insulating effect, the body's core temperature may actually rise half a degree. The reduced blood flow of the icy skin-suit can stave off serious drops in internal temperature for thirty minutes, and buy time to escape or be rescued.

After cold shock, the second stage of cold-water immersion, often called swimming failure, usually happens within this half-hour window, as muscles begin to cool. Until that point, hypothermia doesn't have enough time to set in. Your body simply can't lose heat that fast. Swimming failure operates by a cruel irony. In trying to save themselves, victims hasten their own deaths. Researchers have tracked the rapid decline of even the best swimmers in cold water. They've found that swimming can increase your rate of heat loss and muscle cooling by between thirty to forty percent compared with floating still. With each stroke, blood rushes to your arms, chest, and shoulders, where warmth is more quickly released from these conductive fleshy areas. The technique of even Olympic-caliber athletes deteriorates quickly as their muscles cool. In one test, swimmers wearing life vests averaged less than a kilometer in 14°C water before swimming failure set in and they couldn't continue. When you tumble into the ocean or a cold lake, the natural reaction is to keep moving: swim to the nearest shore, swim toward a disappearing boat, swim to keep generating body heat. Unless your destination is less than a kilometer away, such an instinct is often fatal. And forget about it, if you haven't put on a safety vest. "Swimming in cold water without a PFD [personal flotation device]," one leading researcher has argued, "is suicidal."

Hypothermia proper is the next and best known stage of cold-water immersion. Clinically defined, it is simply the decrease of the body's core temperature below its average of 37°C. Beyond this threshold, physicians and scientists grade the severity on a rough three-step scale, from mild (37°C to 35°C), to moderate (35°C to 30°C), to severe (less than 30°C). The divisions are not arbitrary. At each station of this chilly Via Dolorosa, the body and brain react to stall the decline in internal heat. Perhaps the body's most underappreciated cold-fighting strategy is the simple act of shivering. Often dismissed as a passive symptom of cold weather, shivering works well to maintain enough heat to survive prolonged exposure. The tiny and involuntary muscle contractions can generate almost five times the warmth of a body at rest. At temperatures above 20°C, shivering alone may be enough to offset heat loss. Many of the racers who launched kayaks onto the Bay of Fundy reached the stage of mild hypothermia, at which point intense shivering kicked in. For several paddlers, their core temperature drop had been serious enough that their shaking muscles wouldn't calm for an hour or longer after they got off the water, even once they changed into dry clothes, gulped soup and cocoa, and stood beneath a steaming shower.

In the end, hypothermia poses a deadly paradox. Victims of mild hypothermia will feel colder than their bodies really are because the skin temperature has dropped so abruptly. Protected by the ice-cool layer of blood-thinned skin, their core heat can sustain them for an hour or more, if they can keep a clear head. Too often, though, the shocking cold and the experience of violent shivering cause victims to panic, to try to swim for shore, to lose hope entirely. They often make bad decisions, and then these bad decisions are compounded by their bodies' inability to execute them. Hands become too numb to grip flotation devices or launch flares. Muscles are too weak to swim. Panic exacerbates the psychological trauma of the cold as the body declines through moderate hypothermia: skewed consciousness, faulty memory, anxiety, despair, even paranoia and hallucinations.

Even those who maintain their cool in the cold eventually cross a physiological border. Once a body's temperature dips below 30°C, all bets are off. Shivering has likely stopped. The victim is unconscious, or soon will be. The sluggish beat of the cold-numbed heart can be thrown out of its normal rhythm at any moment, disrupting and then stopping the necessary supply of blood-borne oxygen to the brain. Raising body temperature from this hypothermic precipice, even by trained medical personnel, is both slow and dangerous. The victim has entered a twilight world from which few return.

NINETEEN

The Survivor

M ost Fundy lobstermen, like Keith Mawhinney, didn't think much about kayaks or the people who paddled them. It's an attitude shared by many who work the world's oceans. "Commercial fishers tend to be scornful of kayakers," paddling pioneer John Dowd observed in *Sea Kayaking*, his influential guidebook, "and their advice is often full of gloom." Still, a few baymen appreciated the allure of a kayak—the intimate, contemplative perspective that a small boat provides on the waterways and wildlife of their home by the sea.

Mark Mawhinney, Keith's cousin, was one of the region's most avid part-time paddlers. He had lobstered and scalloped for thirty-one years, ever since he was seventeen. The morning of the race, however, he had left his boat, the *Quaco Duck*, berthed in Chance Harbour. Instead, he had borrowed a kayak from a young emergency-room doctor who lived near Trail's End and worked in the city. She liked Mawhinney and was happy to lend her neighbor a boat whenever the urge took him. He had occasionally considered buying a kayak of his own and had dropped by Bob Vlug's house a few times to inspect his stock. That morning, he chose one of the doctor's wider boats—he preferred not to perform a circus act getting into the narrower vessels—and paddled for a few hours on the west branch of the Musquash River. Even buffered by a fringe of forest, the wind was blowing hard by the time he got off the water. He knew the conditions would be that much rougher out on the bay. Around one in the afternoon, as he dropped off the kayak, Mawhinney could see people exchanging bikes for boats and launching from McLaughlins Cove.

The bayman kayaked to keep his weight down and to sightsee when he wasn't fishing. He figured he had explored almost every trickle of freshwater between Saint John and the American border. He didn't have much experience on the bay, though, not in a kayak at least, and reckoned he wouldn't dare be out on it today. He had heard about the race and its route, and knew the obstacles the racers couldn't see now but would soon face. The southwest wind, running with the flood tide, would collide with the ledges between Chance Harbour and Dipper Harbour—that all added up to one tricky stretch of water, even for a lobster boat. Once kayakers got past Reef Point, the wind-driven waves would strike against the tide's back eddy, and grow to two or three times the height of the breakers in the cove. "That there's hellish," he would have warned the racers. "Out there, there's an awful tide rip. It ain't no fit place to be."

While most captains knew to keep a good kilometer or so off Dry Ledge on such a day, few locals had as visceral a respect for the cold waters of the bay as Mawhinney. Almost twenty years ago, on the first of July, Mark and his younger brother John, aboard their forty-one-foot wooden boat the *Lorrie & Kathy II*, had been wrapping up the final day of the spring lobster season. Both men were bushed from hauling traps. They had stacked the stern high with empty cages, which wouldn't be dropped again until winter. With the last cage pulled, they headed for home. The Mawhinney brothers were navigating through rough waters off the shore of Partridge Island, a squib of lighthouse land (once a quarantine for typhus-infected potato famine refugees) joined to West Saint John by a causeway. Suddenly, something in the ship's structure—a wooden plank near the turbines perhaps, Mark couldn't be certain—broke loose.

The boat began to list. Waves crashed over the already weighted stern and water spilled across the deck, pressing it down even more. As though snatched by an unseen hand, the back of the boat disappeared beneath the waterline. Mark realized the vessel was about to capsize and dashed up the tilting deck into the wheelhouse. It was too late to radio for help, so he grabbed a pair of life vests as the foundering boat reached its tipping point. The bow lurched skyward and then plunged underwater like a rock, drawing Mawhinney down into the black cold. Water rushed into the wheelhouse and swirled around his waist. He grabbed a last breath, pulled back his arm, and punched the glass windows, slicing open his fist. He burst through the jagged opening and wriggled like a squid for the weak translucence above his head.

When he surfaced, the boat had vanished. All that remained were the flotsam of fishing gear and the plywood remnants from the shucking house, under which the two men kept dry when cleaning scallops. His brother, ten years his junior, was clinging to a board. Mark joined him on the floating perch. The wood was barely buoyant enough for them to raise their heads out of the water. Shore was too far to swim for, even if either brother had been a strong swimmer. Fishermen rarely were. Most simply went down with their vessels, as their rubber boots filled with water. The Mawhinney brothers only had one life jacket—the other had been torn from Mark's hand as he had escaped—and no way of signaling for help. The rest of the safety gear was at the bottom of the bay. As night fell, all they could do was hold on to the shucking house and pray that another boat would spot them floating in the dark.

Back in Chance Harbour, the Mawhinneys' mother noticed that her two sons were overdue. She phoned Saint John, where the Canadian Coast Guard operated a refueling base for tenders and kept a helicopter. (It would be another two decades before the government assigned a lifeboat to the city.) From the base, an official told her that he had seen a white lobster boat heading down the coast. "No," she said, "their boat is orange." The coast guard never dispatched a vessel to investigate.

John Mawhinney clung to the shucking house for three hours until his strength began to wane. Suddenly, he let go. He disappeared before his brother could do anything. He vanished into the dusky gloom and ocean depths, drawn away by the bay's powerful currents. His body would never be found.

On the edge of shock and despair, Mark Mawhinney somehow managed to hold on—and on and on. At times, his consciousness started to blur, and he felt his will to survive dissolve. His hands, his arms, his legs had become frozen stumps. It would be so easy to just let go. It would feel so free and so final. He fought back those thoughts and refocused his mind and restored his numb-fingered grip on his improvised life buoy. Through the dark, he thought he could discern the shadowy outline of land. And voices. He could swear he heard voices. Perhaps he was hallucinating. Perhaps this was how the end really sounded—angels calling to him from the rocks.

Finally, the tide tossed him up like driftwood onto Saints Rest Beach. He crawled up the pebbly shoreline. It was nearly three o'clock in the morning. He had weathered an astonishing eight hours in water no more than 14°C. But now he was deathly cold and could barely move. His heart felt like a fist of ice in his chest. Had he survived his odyssey in the bay only to die alone on the beach? He saw lights, heard voices again. "Help!" he croaked. A pair of friends had driven down to the beach in the middle of the night to hang out and listen to music. They were shocked to find the bedraggled lobster captain, soaked through and shivering, like some forlorn sea creature cast out of the bay. At the hospital, doctors told Mawhinney that his body temperature had plummeted to below 27°C, well beyond the threshold of severe hypothermia, on the verge of cardiac arrest. When his mother arrived, her surviving son was lying in a hospital bed, his sea-chilled skin the blue pallor of the summer sky. He recovered quickly and was released the next day. That winter, he was back lobstering.

Ever since the loss of his brother and their boat, ever since that long night in the bay, Mawhinney suffered poor circulation. His doctors warned that after such an extended immersion, one that would have killed most other men—one that should have killed him—his strained heart would be more susceptible to the effects of the cold. That was fine. He didn't plan on taking another dip. But he would keep fishing. And there wasn't much he could do if misfortune pulled his ticket a second time. "It's always the nature of going to sea," he often said. "There's a little risk involved."

M ark Mawhinney didn't think much more about kayaking or the race until 3:00 p.m., when he decided to stretch his legs. He looked and talked like most of the other Mawhinney men: thick as a beam across the shoulders and chest, with a wide squarish head, red faced from sea spray and sun, and an unhurried drawl. He was a bit more jovial than his cousin Keith, unafraid of sharing his gap-toothed smile. Mark lived with his mother in a bungalow across from the Chance Harbour wharf on Highway 790, marketed by city folks as the Fundy Coastal Drive. Because of his poor circulation, he liked to keep the blood churning in his legs with strolls in the woods near his house or along the rocky coastline. He parked his truck beyond the bridge over the Moose Creek estuary on Cemetery Loop Road and worked his way along the grass-lined trail past the headstones of the old graveyard. On days off, when he wasn't kayaking or fixing traps, he often explored this quiet, mostly uninhabited peninsula of scrubby forest and rocky beach, halfway between Chance Harbour and Dipper Harbour. The path opened up to an east-facing view of Lobster Cove. There, on a stretch of beach, he spotted a pair of kayakers pulled up on shore. Both looked miserable.

"How do we get back to the highway?" one asked.

Mawhinney pointed out the trail. The two men abandoned the boat and paddles and trudged off. By then, the blue sky had darkened and the wind huffed with new force. A thunderous crackle echoed through the clouds. All so sudden, too. It was a dirty day, more like a winter storm than a spring shower. Mawhinney continued toward the boggy bayside tip of the peninsula that overlooked Man Rock. Along a southwest beach near Round Meadow Cove, more kayakers had quit the race. Mawhinney spoke with another two pairs of competitors—three men and a woman, all in their late twenties to mid thirties. They also asked for directions back to the highway. One of the paddlers, soaked to the hide from spray and waves, complained bitterly about the cold. Another had gone ghost white, stutter-voiced, and seemed disoriented. Mawhinney noticed that the woman seemed to fare better, or at least moaned less, than the men. Mawhinney directed all four toward the highway.

Along the beach, Mawhinney recognized Bob Vlug standing with Malcolm Brett, his paddling partner. The two older men were contemplating their next move in the deteriorating weather. Vlug seemed to want to continue. Brett was having none of it, not in a lightning storm. Another kayak beached, and Sara Vlug and Jayme Frank emerged from the vessel. After guiding the Two Bobs to the highway, Frank and Vlug had launched back onto the bay. They had encountered the remaining safety kayak and told the two volunteers to beach and warm up. Not long after that, the squall had closed in faster than they had seen a storm run before. They knew it wasn't wise to be on the water when the lightning hit.

"Did you see any solo boats go by?" Sara asked her father. He hadn't.

That wasn't what the organizers wanted to hear. Sara had a rough idea of who was still out on the bay. She and Jayme Frank were most worried about the solo racers in the tippier kayaks. And they knew that at least two of them still hadn't been accounted for.

Mawhinney could hear the tension in their voices. "I'll go for help," he offered. He hustled down the trail, as fast as he could remember dashing since he was a school kid, past Lobster Cove and the graveyard, and leapt into his truck. He was back home within minutes. He called Fundy Marine Traffic, the communications hub in Saint John, and the operator relayed his emergency message to the coast guard. Then he rushed down to the wharf, untethered his boat, and negotiated the *Quaco Duck* around the breakwater. He knew that if anyone had gone overboard in these seas, they would be lucky to last half as long as he had. As he prepared to search the coast, he spotted the high bow of the *D.P. Clipper* plowing through the waves toward Chance Harbour. Mawhinney raised another of his cousins on the radio.

"Hey, Bobby," he asked, "did you see any kayakers out there?"

TWENTY

The Search

Constable Wayne Burke, musician and Mountie, watched from the vantage of his living room as the storm barreled toward the bay. He had just poured a cup of tea, a little after 3:30 p.m., when through the wide picture window, he saw a shadow fall upon the anchored lobster fleet, a stone's skip or two across the breadth of Dipper Harbour from his house. A towering shroud traveled swiftly from behind the inland hills until it had swept over his shoreline home, rattling the eaves and obscuring the windows with rain. Then the storm collided with the bay. The Fundy waters darkened and whitecaps bucked against the grain of the rising wind. Thunder coughed and echoed across the waves.

In twenty-five years with the Royal Canadian Mounted Police, mostly along the Atlantic coast, Constable Burke had witnessed his share of wild weather. This storm was far from the worst he had experienced. It was full of sound and fury, yes, but unlikely to signify much to seen-it-all locals. Still, he was struck by the velocity of its charge. A bright if breezy spring day had deteriorated with little warning into a maelstrom of wind and waves. The storm must have been a squall line—a wall of individual thunderstorms arrayed like blitzing linebackers. It looked like the Hollywood version in *White Squall*, Burke thought, the sailing-trip-gone-bad flick starring Jeff Bridges, with a tragic ending to make any mariner (or parent) squirm. The leading edge of a squall, known to meteorologists as a convection line, is a dangerous place to be caught. Along the fast-tracking vanguard, powerful vortices whip up unpredictable gusts of wind, even tornadoes and waterspouts. The Fundy squall was already churning the bay into a frantic chop.

That morning, Burke had checked the marine forecast and learned that a cold front descending from Quebec would deliver strong southwest winds. He knew about the small-craft warning, too. But the storm wasn't supposed to arrive until the evening. And the forecast had made no mention of a full-on squall. The storm had landed early and hit with greater than expected force. "Even with a good forecast," Constable Burke liked to tell people, "the ocean is one of the most unpredictable things God put on this good earth. It can turn on you like—" And he would snap his fingers for effect, the sound of a branch breaking underfoot. The bay had proven him right again.

He suspected (and hoped) the storm would blow itself out by the time he punched in for his five o'clock shift at the Lepreau District station. He hoped (and suspected) the lobstermen had all aimed for safer harbors at the first sign of the squall. Still, he wasn't surprised when his phone rang, around 4:20 p.m. It was the dispatcher from Lepreau. The 911 center in Fredericton had fielded Mark Mawhinney's emergency call. Kayakers were out on the bay, not far from Chance Harbour, ten kilometers east of his house, competing in a race. "Two may be missing," the dispatcher told him. Burke was needed to report to duty to coordinate the search efforts on the land, while the coast guard took to the sea. Looking out his window again, he could see the harbor-front property of Bob Vlug. Burke had a good idea where to begin.

Constable Burke looked every inch the Mountie: tall, broad shouldered, his dark hair tinged just perceptibly with steely gray, his body still trim and solid into his late forties. He sported one of the thick, stubby, throwback moustaches that seemed to be handed out to recruits along with their service pistols. He talked and acted nothing like the wired and wise-cracking street cops of prime-time TV, all angst and attitude. Instead, he worked methodically, listening first before leaping to judgment, with a quiet competence from years of training with one of the best-known police forces in the world.

Dispatches on his posting in New Brunswick usually kept him on land: traffic accidents on Highway 1, domestic disputes, the occasional B&E. Still, Constable Burke was as comfortable as many lobstermen out on the water. He had worked several postings in the outports of Newfoundland, where the ocean was colder and the seas even more unpredictable than the Bay of Fundy. He had been trained in water safety and later taught it there. On offshore patrols, he had often steered one of the force's twenty-seven-foot fast-rescue craft, or FRCs, rigid-hulled Zodiacs souped up with a pair of one-hundred-and-fifty-horsepower outboards—fifteen times the power of the race Zodiac. He had once been clocked doing sixty-two knots—a hundred and fifteen kilometers per hour—the boat skipping across the water like a polished stone, as much an airborne vehicle as a seaborne one. What impressed him about these boats was how they seemed to love the rough stuff, how their handling actually improved in choppy conditions. But even with an FRC, Burke wouldn't have wanted to head out on the bay on an afternoon like this one, not unless he absolutely had to.

During his tenure in Newfoundland, Burke had been one of the first RCMP officers to get called to help whenever a maritime situation arose. He had worked with search-and-rescue personnel in all his postings and knew the importance of throwing down the throttle in an emergency. If kayakers had gone missing or had fallen into the cold waters of the Bay of Fundy, rescuers would have an hour or two to reach them before the paddlers succumbed to hypothermia. They would have to act fast.

Two hundred kilometers away, the 911 message was patched through to the Joint Rescue Coordination Centre in Halifax, Nova Scotia. Coast guard officer Wendell Sperry, one of two maritime rescue coordinators on duty, jotted down the details: *A kayak race from Chance Hbr. to Dipper Hbr. 2 kayakers missing and unaccounted for.* The East Coast JRCC, one of three search-and-rescue command hubs in Canada, was housed on the sprawling Department of National Defence dockyards. A long picture window overlooked the harbor and the narrows—a bottleneck of water that funnels into Bedwell Basin, where huge convoys had mustered for the dangerous Atlantic crossing during World War Two.

Two minutes after the call, Corporal Sperry reached Mark Mawhinney on his VHF radio. The fisherman confirmed that the paddlers were in single kayaks, that he was going to search the bay in his own boat, and that he thought the race organizer's name was Bob Vlug. Sperry's partner was already on the phone with Fundy Traffic in Saint John and ordered an all-ships bulletin on VHF 16, the international channel for distress calls. Fundy Radio could broadcast a mayday signal (a boat in distress) or, in this case, a less urgent or less certain pan-pan call. Translation: *There's a vessel missing. We don't know where it is. Keep an eye out and report your positions.* Behind Sperry's chair stretched two wall-sized maps of the Canadian Maritimes and eastern Arctic. On one map, magnetic strips depicted all the armed forces aircraft and coast guard boats available for operations, from small Zodiacs to ships two hundred and fifty feet long. In a glance, Sperry could get an immediate read on his resources and calculate how to react to a mayday call or missing vessel using the digital tracking and communication tools connected to his computer and three desktop monitors.

Like chess masters, the rescue coordinators had to weigh the strengths, weaknesses, and positions of their pieces on the board: the swiftness of spotting planes; the agility of air force helicopters; the hands-on skills of wet-suited, drop-from-the-sky search-and-rescue technicians (known as SAR Techs or "angels in orange"); the all-weather readiness of the coast guard lifeboats. Then there were the pawns in a search-and-rescue operation: the Canadian Coast Guard

Auxiliary. Not as trained or mobile, but perhaps better positioned to act, these civilian volunteers could search in fishing boats or pleasure craft. Sperry could also press into service vessels run by the RCMP, regional and local police forces, fire departments, and enforcement vehicles from the Department of Fisheries and Oceans. Finally, any private boat in the vicinity—as big as a super-tanker, as small as a dinghy—could be ordered to aid a mission as a vessel of opportunity. Under international law, unless sea conditions put the boats at too much risk, their captains had to divert and help a search mission. Sperry had once commandeered the *Queen Mary 2* because the eight-hundred-million-dollar, hundred-and-fifty-thousand-ton luxury liner was closest to the scene. Often, several vessels would be tasked simultaneously. Unlike in a chess match, sacrificing one piece to save another was not an option.

Corporal Sperry was no mere desk jockey. Like all rescue coordinators, he had earned his chair in the JRCC through exemplary service on the water. He had worked aboard large coast guard vessels for sixteen years, nine of them as a navigation officer, and had completed two tours in the High Arctic. During the Halloween Gale of 1991—the infamous "perfect storm" of Hollywood myth making—he had stood on the ten-meter-high deck of the *CCGS Mary Hichens*, amid wind gusts of a hundred knots, and had looked up with widening eyes at wave crests that loomed another six meters above him. The afternoon squall of June 1, 2002, wasn't going to write its way into the history books. He had witnessed far worse.

Still, things moved quickly at the JRCC. Sperry gathered information over the crackling radio connection with Mark Mawhinney. Orders were dispatched to the crew of the *Courtenay Bay*, a coast guard cutter stationed in the shadow of Saint John's Harbour Bridge. The four-person crew of the fifty-two-foot rescue vessel remained on twenty-four-hour standby—ready to suit up, dash from quarters, untie their lines, and be off the dock in half an hour. Ten minutes after the call from the JRCC, the lifeboat was on its way.

Back in Dipper Harbour, Constable Burke only had to drive his squad car a hundred meters down the road to reach the Vlugs' house. He knew the family well, as neighbors if not friends. In the two years since he had moved to New Brunswick, Constable Burke had become a familiar face around the coastal villages of Chance Harbour, Dipper Harbour, and Maces Bay, and even as far as Saint John—although perhaps more for the festival concerts and fundraisers at which he performed. Strumming guitar and singing traditional and original Celtic songs, Burke moonlighted as a folk musician in a band called the Mizzen Men. It was one of the rare opportunities for the cop to step from behind the badge.

The Vlugs had been organizing kayak tours for longer than Burke had lived in Dipper, and he usually saw a dozen kayaks arranged along the front lawn or stacked on a trailer for transport to the next trip. Today, the boats had been dropped in random disarray between the beach and the Vlugs' yard. In the near distance, a few kayakers hauled one out of the water and dragged it up to the house. The driveway and adjoining road were filled with cars and trucks that Burke didn't recognize. People in nylon warm-up pants and fleece jackets came and went through the front and back doors and the renovated barn.

Inside the main house, he found a scene of confusion. The rooms were crammed with people, many huddled under blankets and towels and trying to tame their shivering. Some were chatting, laughing even. Others looked more concerned. The appearance of a Mountie in uniform didn't improve the mood. Deanna Vlug greeted her neighbor and explained the situation. The last stage of the race had been taking place on the bay when the storm had blown through. Several racers—at least two, she thought—were still missing. Burke returned to his car and patched through to the coast guard.

Motoring out of Saint John Harbour at sixteen knots, the crew of the *Courtenay Bay* knew how tricky it would be to spot a pair of kayakers in the water, especially with strong winds stirring up the sea clutter. Amid the obscuring waves and chop, a crew could be almost on top of a small boat before they saw it. Two weeks earlier, the *Courtenay Bay* had been called out to rescue another pair of kayakers. The paddlers had been overturned by high winds and strong currents, a few kilometers off Saints Rest Beach. A third friend had struggled to shore and called 911. That afternoon, enough other boats had been in the vicinity of Saint John's busy harbor—police and fire department launches, plus tugboats from the Irving refinery—that the capsized paddlers were quickly spotted, plucked from the bay by the coast guard, rushed to shore, and treated for hypothermia.

Kayak calls were uncommon, though. The East Coast JRCC and coast guard didn't search as often for paddlers as their colleagues on the West Coast, where the sport had blossomed—and with it, an increase in rescue operations for overdue or capsized kayaks. "We call them 'sea coffins,'" a maritime rescue coordinator in Victoria, British Columbia, told me. "We think they should have handles on the sides to help the pallbearers." He was only half joking. Sea kayaks can venture into coves and shallows that motorized rescue boats can't reach. "When you're searching for them," he said, "you have to search every little nook and cranny." Around British Columbia's Gulf Islands or Vancouver's English Bay, dozens of kayaks might be out on a summer afternoon. Sorting the lost from the found can be frustrating. While expedition paddlers will pack a VHF radio, satellite phone, or flares for emergencies on overnight trips, day trippers and kayak renters often don't bother.

If there is one safety device that coast guard trackers wished kayakers and other mariners would carry, it's an emergency personal indicating radio beacon or EPIRB. With a flip of a switch, a digital EPIRB beams out a signal at 406 megahertz, the frequency reserved by law for distress calls, which will be picked up by a quartet of search-and-rescue satellites. The distress call is relayed to and decoded by a mission control center, and then the geographical information and name of the registered user is sent, around the world if necessary, to the closest rescue coordination center. Early EPIRBs were as bulky as old German hand grenades, expensive, and plagued by false alarms. Digital versions are slim as cell phones, have dropped in price, and aren't nearly as buggy. "They've saved a lot of lives over the years," the West Coast rescue coordinator assured me. "We get there real quick."

EPIRBs are mandatory equipment on commercial boats and on aircraft (where they are called emergency locator transmitters or ELTs). Hikers, hunters, mountain climbers, backcountry skiers, or anyone venturing into serious wilderness can purchase similar satellite protection with a pocket-sized personal locator beacon or PLB. Such high-tech help has prompted philosophical debates among outdoor adventurers. Are we really in the wild if help is a flick of a switch away? Don't gadgets diminish the experience of the outdoors, or at least reduce our responsibility to know what we're doing when we step out the front door? And should taxpayers foot the bill for expensive search-and-rescue operations every time a city slicker with a cell phone or a locator beacon gets lost in the woods? Most of the controversy is moot. Few recreational boaters or wilderness wanderers ever invest in an emergency beacon. Maybe it's just the expense, although paddlers are willing to sink thousands into state-of-the-art kayaks. Maybe it's the belief that accidents only happen to other people. Or maybe it feels too strange to buy a device that you'll only ever use if something very, very bad occurs.

Certainly, slim profit margins and meager budgets don't allow most outfitters or race organizers to equip vessels with EPIRBs or even cheaper VHF radios. None of the race kayaks or even the rescue boats in the Fundy challenge carried anything more than a whistle for signaling. There were still other ways for the coast guard to track down a missing vessel. If the rescuers knew where the kayaks had last been seen or had capsized, Corporal Sperry and his JRCC colleagues could boot up a computer program that could calculate from the tidal currents, wind, and type of vessel precisely where the lost racers might have drifted to. Without this information, the search team had little to go on.

It would have been better if the lifeboat was already on-site. The *Courtenay Bay* had been stationed in Saint John for less than two years, and the coast guard often sent out the cutter, at the request of organizers, to watch over community events and regattas on the bay, such as dory races at the Fundy Fishermen's Festival in Dipper Harbour. These missions were good training for the crew and good PR for the new boat. Coast guard officials couldn't promise anything, of course. Should an emergency call come through, the lifeboat would have to leave the scene immediately. It could act as a backup at best. Neither the *Courtenay Bay*'s crew nor the JRCC in Halifax, however, had been contacted about the Fundy Multi-Sport Race or knew anything about the event—the route that it covered, how many participants would be on the water. When it reached Chance Harbour, the Courtenay Bay would simply have to sweep the general area and hope for the best.

At 4:45 p.m., the maritime coordinators in JRCC Halifax called the race organizers. A new voice picked up. "I think the missing kayakers may have been found," the person told them. "Let me check and see." "Maybe" didn't cut it at the JRCC. Three minutes after the ambiguous reply, the air rescue coordinator from the Canadian Forces redirected a CP-140 Aurora aircraft already en route from a previous assignment. Its new mission: get to Dipper Harbour quickly. Deploying the Aurora was the kind of improvised call that rescue coordinators made on a daily basis. The air coordinator could have chosen instead to send out a CC-130 Hercules, a four-propped troop carrier that would have offered better aerial spotting plus the ability to drop SAR Tech rescue swimmers by parachute if the missing kayakers were spotted in the water. However, a Hercules would need to be scrambled from the air base in Greenwood, Nova Scotia, a hundred and ten kilometers across the bay from Chance Harbour. Both aircraft could be tasked, but then two large, fast planes would be sharing a tight airspace. That would raise the risk of collision. Instead, the Aurora could sweep the scene and provide eyes from the sky until the *Courtenay Bay* powered up the coast from Saint John. If the Aurora ran low on fuel and hadn't located the missing kayakers, the JRCC could launch a Hercules to take its place in the sky. That option was unlikely—a fully fueled Aurora could fly for seventeen hours over a range of eight thousand kilometers.

The JRCC coordinator called the organizer's number again at 4:57 p.m. Still no firm news about the missing kayakers. Four minutes later, the coordinator radioed the pilot of the Aurora, which had an ETA on the rescue scene of nine minutes, and issued search instructions: *Stick close to shore. Do a run between Chance and Dipper harbors. See if you can spot any targets and identify them.* As the Aurora approached the New Brunswick coastline, it decelerated from nearly seven hundred and fifty kilometers an hour to two hundred and sixty and dipped to a search altitude of about three hundred and fifty meters over the bay. Originally built for anti-submarine warfare, the Aurora and its dozen crew members were well equipped for any surveillance operation. Drug running, fish poaching, human trafficking, oil spills, missing boaters—anything above or below the ocean's surface could be detected with its panoply of radar, acoustic sensors, infrared camera, magnetic-anomaly detector, night-vision goggles, gyrostabilized binoculars, and plain old human eyesight. The roar of its four turbo-prop engines reverberated overhead, a mechanical thunder unmistakable to those on the shore, as the plane combed the coastline.

By 5:30, the Aurora still hadn't spotted any paddle craft on the bay. The radio operator overheard chatter from a VHF channel and relayed it back to the JRCC in Halifax. *One kayaker had been located.* One was still missing. The operator picked up a name and a cell phone number and forwarded both to the JRCC. A fishing vessel, called the *D.P. Clipper*, may have been involved in a rescue. Seven minutes later, the JRCC patched through to the captain of the *D.P. Clipper*. He confirmed that the missing kayakers had been located and brought to shore. Constable Burke was heading to Chance Harbour to meet this vessel of opportunity. With the lost kayakers off the water, the need to continue the search seemed to be over. The JRCC coordinator told both the *Courtenay Bay*, yet to reach the scene, and the circling Aurora aircraft to disengage operations—to "stand down" in rescue lingo. The cutter turned back for Saint John. The plane was diverted to a new incident. Neither vessel had much of chance to perform a role in the operation. Still, the missing persons had, apparently, been found. The search work of Canada's full-time rescue professionals was done.

TWENTY-ONE

The Wharf

Like many of the baymen, Edward Jacques had been up before
dawn to chase lobsters. During fishing season, he kept the scanner
of the VHF radio in his trailer home dialed to the marine weather
channel. He often booted up his computer, too, and compared the
radio forecast with the Environment Canada website. On his kitchen
wall, beside his Fishermen's Friend clock, he had tacked a tide table
so he could reckon the effect of the currents. He figured he wouldn't
be hauling traps all day, not with a weather warning and a sou'west
wind predicted for the afternoon.

Jacques had fished since he was twelve but didn't own a boat.
Instead, the small, spry fifty-three-year-old worked as a sternsman—
at one time for Keith Mawhinney, now aboard the *High Sierra*, a forty-
footer captained by his next-door neighbor. That Saturday, the two
men set out early and fished for a good six hours, off Manawagonish
Island, near Irving Nature Park. Around one in the afternoon, the

wind picked up as predicted, whitecaps formed on the crests, and they decided to head home before the seas got too dirty. As they passed Cranberry Head, a little before three, they were surprised to spot kayakers heading away from the shelter of Chance Harbour. As the squall broke overheard, they docked, unloaded lobsters for the buyer, and washed down the *High Sierra*. Done for the day, Jacques wandered up the wharf road to the eighty-four-square-meter trailer home he shared with his wife.

Cindy Jacques was a commanding presence, ten years younger than her husband but twice as broad and doubly voluble, too, with a laugh as loud as a foghorn and a temper that boiled as fast as a brass kettle. Edward had barely enough time to say hello to her and strip out of his fishing gear before someone knocked at their door. Cindy flung it open to find a tall, handsome man in his early twenties standing on the steps of their trailer in dripping wet athletic gear. He didn't look like a Jehovah's Witness or a charity case, although he was a bit wild-eyed.

"I need to borrow your phone," he insisted. "It's an emergency."

The racer had been one of the last of the solo kayakers on the water. Near Reef Point, he had heard a safety whistle cut through the roar of wind and breakers. He had doubled back toward the distress call, but he couldn't spot the other kayaker or kayakers. He couldn't see much over the waves. The solo racer had paddled into the shelter of Chance Harbour, tied his kayak to the pontoon wharf, and dashed up the ramp toward the nearby trailer home. He used the Jacques' phone to call the Vlugs' house in Dipper Harbour. Then, wrapped in a blanket, he waited for his sister to arrive from the finish line with dry clothes.

The Jacques' afternoon was about to get even stranger. Soon their cramped kitchen would become an impromptu command center for a rescue operation that the couple only dimly understood. More kayakers would appear and so would fishermen and the local fire-rescue crew. People would demand their phone again and make calls, coming and going through their squeaky screen door. Cindy would hustle up and down the hill to the wharf, carrying blankets, until she was breathless and on the edge of a heart attack. She would drape another young fellow, plucked from the bay like a lobster, in a pair of dry shorts and one of her billowy XXL T-shirts. Then her husband would chat to the shivering racer to keep the boy from lapsing into shock on their kitchen floor until an ambulance could ferry him to the hospital. Edward and Cindy Jacques would host more unexpected visitors than over the twelve days of Christmas, and it would be hours before they could sit down again, have a smoke, and wonder what the hell had just happened.

Sara Vlug and Jayme Frank were among the first people to occupy the Jacques' trailer. After beaching their kayak near Man Rock, where they had met Sara's father and Mark Mawhinney, they had jogged along the shore, looking for missing racers. The sound of a siren had quickened their pace into a sprint toward the highway. In the trailer, they checked on the solo racer, who was a friend of theirs. Five minutes later, a fisherman knocked and announced that another boat had brought a kayaker to the wharf. Frank left to investigate. Vlug remained.

"Are you one of the organizers?" Edward Jacques asked. He knew Vlug's father but didn't recognize the daughter.

"No," said Vlug, "I'm a volunteer."

"Well, whoever is running this race is an idiot!" said Jacques. "They need their eyes checked and their arses kicked. The marine forecast told us what was gonna happen this afternoon."

"I'm just one of the volunteers," repeated Vlug.

Vlug borrowed the phone and dialed her parents' house. Someone who had been checking off names at the finish line answered. Vlug asked if Boon Kek was there. He wasn't. What about René Arseneault? The volunteer shouted his name above the hubbub of the crowded house. Another person replied, "Oh, yes, René's here." Okay, thought Vlug, that was one missing racer accounted for. One more to go. Suddenly, another knock at the trailer. A second fisherman had come up to tell Sara that Jayme wanted her down at the wharf—*now*.

The *D.P. Clipper* and its crew had been out on the bay for nearly ten hours that day. Around six in the morning, as dawn illuminated the fog banks to the south, Captain Bob Mawhinney—brother of Keith, cousin to Mark—had raised anchor and steered the boat from its spring berth in Chance Harbour. He usually moored up the coast in Dipper Harbour, minutes from the seaside bungalow where he lived with his wife and three teenaged kids and knew the Vlug family as neighbors. But starting even twelve kilometers closer to his traps offered extra time to catch more lobsters. And Bob Mawhinney was very good at catching lobsters. He could draw on five generations of family knowledge of these coastal waters. His willingness to head out earlier and stay out later than others and in wilder weather, too, had made Mawhinney, now forty-eight years old, one of the most successful baymen. Two years earlier, he had leveraged his profits and a new bank loan to buy the *Clipper*, forty-five feet long and twenty-one feet across, the biggest boat in the region's lobster fleet. He hoped to recoup his investment with a few more good seasons.

An hour and a half after setting out from Chance Harbour, Mawhinney and his crew of three—his sons, Andrew and Peter, and his first mate of nine years, Wayne Nicholls—had arrived northeast of where the Bay of Fundy meets the Saint John River. Mawhinney and his crew had checked the two hundred and fifty traps they had baited with herring the day before. In the past week, they had worked eighty hours on the boat's deck, but their catch had been meager: a few buckets of smaller lobsters, barely legal, not the long, plump crustaceans he preferred to bring to market. Still, it was too early in the season to expect more or to worry about the haul yet. The water would warm. The lobsters would come.

Around eleven that morning, the southwest breeze had picked up. By one o'clock, the bay had turned choppy. Two hours later, Mawhinney headed for home early. There wasn't much point in getting pitched around for the sake of a few undersized lobsters. He usually took Saturday nights off anyway. And always Sundays, so his family could attend the Fundamental Baptist church in the city. Mawhinney kept his boat as close as he dared to the shoreline between Saint John and Chance Harbour. The flood tide was running in the middle of the bay. Along the shoreline, though, there was an hour or two when a captain could find slack water, even an ebb flow, and not fight the strong tidal currents. They were halfway home when the sky blackened, clouds mustered from land and onto the bay, and thunder echoed off the waves. A heavy rain beat against the wheelhouse, and the crew held steady as the *D.P. Clipper* pitched from side to side. Lightning split the horizon. The squall lasted thirty minutes, maybe less, before spinning out to sea around 4:00 p.m. It would be a clear run to home from here, Mawhinney thought, as the rain let up.

That was when he spotted the kayaker.

Boon Kek and René Arseneault had drifted past the entrance of Chance Harbour and nearly all hope of rescue. They were drawing nearer, twenty-five meters or so, to the serrated edge of Cranberry Head and the haystacking waves that rebounded off its rock face. Arseneault's voice began to slur. Kek could no longer discern the outline of his companion's words. Then Arseneault's grip loosened on the bowline and his limp body slid deeper under the water with each wave.

Kek dropped his paddle across his spray skirt and grabbed Arseneault by his life jacket. With both hands, he pulled Arseneault to the side of the boat and kept him from folding into the water. Kek had to lean in the opposite direction to avoid tipping. The two men, one drifting in and out of consciousness, maintained this precarious embrace. Now Kek had no way to control the kayak. They were at the mercy of the wind and the tide and the erupting water. The broken cliffs loomed closer. Twenty meters. Fifteen. Ten.

Finally, Kek spotted a boat in the distance and freed a hand to begin waving. The vessel seemed to be heading toward them.

"Hang on," he urged his helpless companion. "There's a boat coming." Kek thought he heard a mumbled reply.

The lobster boat pulled up beside the kayak, and Bob Mawhinney took stock of the situation. He wheeled the vessel around, so that the two men could be lifted onto the hydraulic tailgate off the stern.

The waterline was still a meter and a half below this fold-down ramp, so his first mate and his sons timed their efforts with the rise and fall of the waves. It was like trying to shake hands with a bungee jumper. With each swell, the crew reached for Arseneault as Kek held on to him tightly—too tightly.

"You've got to let go!" Mawhinney shouted.

"He'll drift away!" Kek replied.

The crew waited for the right moment again and pulled René Arseneault into the *D.P. Clipper*. His eyes stared blankly and his arms remained fixed in the air, as though still hugging the bow of the kayak. Then they grabbed Kek and dragged him aboard. He insisted that they snag his kayak, too. Quickly, the crew covered the two competitors in rain gear and extra jackets, and Wayne Nicholls embraced the cold body of René Arseneault.

"How is he?" Kek asked.

"Don't worry—we've called an ambulance," said Nicholls. "Take care of yourself."

"I'm all right."

"No, you're not," said Nicholls.

Kek was too focused on Arseneault to notice his own shivering body. "I was just talking to him," he said.

"You were?" said Bob Mawhinney.

Arseneault was unconscious. The captain had taken a course in CPR years ago, but his certification had lapsed. Instead Mawhinney leaned in and pressed two fingers against the boy's neck and found the carotid artery, exactly how his doctor had shown him to do to monitor his own high blood pressure. He thought he felt movement, a thrush beneath the cold, pallid skin, but he couldn't locate a steady beat. It was impossible to be sure, with the deep murmur of the boat's engine underfoot and the rattling of the wind against the hull and their fishing gear. He had to get them to shore.

Kek slumped against the gunwale of the boat, and felt its 535-horsepower engine engage and the vessel begin to charge through the waves. His body shuddered as the adrenaline drained from it and he realized how cold he had become. It didn't matter. They had made it. They were almost home. They had survived.

Around 4:30 p.m., Jayme Frank reached the wharf at Chance Harbour and pounded down the metal stairs of the floating dock toward the *D.P. Clipper.* There he saw, with relief, a kayak on the deck and Boon Kek huddled in the boat, cold but safe. In the wheelhouse, Bob Mawhinney was on his cell phone with the coast guard.

"I'm so sorry," Boon told him. "I lost the kayak."

"Are you kidding?" Frank replied. "It's right there."

"No," said Kek and pointed to a pile of rainwear and fishing gear near the wheelhouse. A pair of shoes and bare calves projected out. Frank lifted away the coverings and exclaimed, "René!" Still in his life jacket, René Arseneault stared back at Frank with blank eyes. "He's in shock," said Wayne Nicholls. Frank feared the young racer's condition was worse than that. Arseneault didn't seem to be breathing. The race organizer dropped to his knees and began CPR and artificial resuscitation. The minutes felt like hours.

"You can stop," a fisherman said, tapping his shoulder. "I think he's breathing." Frank knew that the rise and fall of the young man's chest was only his own breath inflating the lungs. He kept up his efforts until he heard Vlug's voice on the wharf. "Sara, get down here!" he shouted.

Vlug looked over the edge and was startled by the scene below—her boyfriend on his knees, blowing into a sprawled kayaker. She rushed onto the boat to help Jayme. Elaine Small, an off-duty nurse who lived in Maces Bay, descended from the wharf and boarded the *D.P. Clipper,* too. Bob Mawhinney, her brother-in-law, had called from the boat, and she had sped to the scene.

"I can't find a pulse!" Vlug yelled. The three first responders tried again and detected a faint beat. Just as quickly it disappeared. Nurse Small performed the chest compressions of CPR while Frank took over the artificial resuscitation and blew again into the cold lips of the racer.

"I tried to help him," muttered Boon Kek, wrapped in a blanket. "I tried to help …"

They kept up their efforts for fifteen minutes until members of the Musquash Fire Department reached the docks. The fire-rescue crew took over resuscitation efforts with a hand-pumped air bag to inflate

Arseneault's lungs with oxygen. A siren echoed over the hills. The local ambulance was occupied with the injured cyclist, so another vehicle had to be dispatched from Saint John. Half an hour after the *D.P. Clipper* had reached Chance Harbour, the new ambulance wheeled up to the wharf and two attendants shuttled a gurney down the stairs to the pontoon dock. By then, a small crowd had coalesced around the *D.P. Clipper*: racers, volunteers, fire-rescue crew, curious locals. A klatch of lobstermen looked out at the subsiding storm, then down at the plastic kayaks scattered across the dock.

"I'd just as soon stack 'em up," one declared, "and put an axe through 'em all."

TWENTY-TWO

The Family

A little after two that afternoon, Jean-Guy Arseneault fielded a call from André. "René finished fourth in the bike race," his eldest son said. "I watched him get into the kayak."

In his green Chevy pickup, Jean-Guy drove across town and down Highway 1 to Dipper Harbour. At the wharf, a few lobstermen were jawing, fueling their boats, and checking their cages. Jean-Guy asked about the race. One of the baymen suggested he check at the Vlugs' house, across the harbor, where colored kayaks were on the beach and lined up near a large house. He parked beside the property. Not long after he arrived, the electrical storm rolled over Dipper Harbour. Cold rain and pebbles of hail rebounded off his truck's windshield. When the storm passed, Jean-Guy got out to look for René. He saw exhausted racers sitting on the grass. A pair of mountain bikers arrived at the house. "They've pulled everyone off the water," the cyclists said. "They're finishing the race on bikes because of the storm."

Jean-Guy was confused. He thought that René had launched onto the bay. He should have been done by now. Why was it taking so long? Jean-Guy had seen a few kayakers arrive but not for some time now. Maybe René had finished early and caught a lift to Rothesay. Jean-Guy borrowed a cell phone from a woman, a mother of six boys who had been anxiously waiting for her husband to complete the race, too, and called the house on Dobbin Street. Nobody answered. By 5:30 p.m., after Jean-Guy had waited more than two hours, René still hadn't appeared at Dipper Harbour. No kayaks were arriving anymore. Jean-Guy walked up to the house.

"Has anybody seen my son?" he asked the young woman who answered the door. "His name is René."

Her face turned white. "Yeah," she said. "I'm gonna get somebody else." She disappeared into the crowd.

A minute later, another young woman, her red hair sea-damp and tousled by the wind, stepped out of the house.

"Mr. Arseneault?" said Sara Vlug. "There's been an accident. You need to go to the hospital."

The day of the race, Jacqueline Arseneault had worked in the front yard of her two-story house in Rothesay, as she liked to do most spring and summer weekends. She took pride in her garden full of roses and hostas. With each new season, though, the digging and the pulling proved harder on her wrists. The joints and tendons ached from carpal tunnel syndrome, brought on by long hours of data entry at her job. Even with the pain, her garden was a relief from a week at the offices of Irving Oil. Later in the afternoon, the breezy air took on an extra chill. The wind whistled through her trees and the summer sky went slate gray. Thunder echoed down the Kennebecasis Valley. And then the black clouds unleashed sheets of rain.

Jacqueline knew she ought to head inside. Instead, driven by an inner voice, she kept working. She uprooted tall weeds from her flower beds as the rain pelted her shoulders and back and soaked through her light shirt and shorts. For half an hour, she remained oblivious to the crackling downpour. By the time the storm blew itself out, her clothes hung heavy on her wet skin. Only then did Jacqueline head inside. She stood in her quiet house, water pooling around her shoes, and was filled with a premonition that something, somewhere had gone wrong. She shook off the thought, changed into dry clothes, and fixed a quick dinner. Around 5:30 p.m., she tidied up the kitchen and drew a warm bath. The running faucet drowned the gong of the doorbell. The phone's ring caught her attention, but she ignored it. The phone rang again, and rang and rang. Finally, she walked into the kitchen and picked up the receiver.

"We're in your yard," a man's voice announced. "It's the Rothesay police."

Jacqueline rushed to her door. Something, she guessed, had happened to one of her boys. Constable Norman Mackay—he had worked in the area for years—and a second officer stood outside. Their caps remained on their heads. This detail of etiquette, Jacqueline knew, justified all her fears. The officers, she realized, had come bearing the worst possible news.

"You have a son, René?" Constable Mackay asked. "He was in a race today?"

"What's going on?" Jacqueline replied.

Constable Mackay held out a hand to steady her before he spoke.

That afternoon, André Arseneault had gone to the university to set up the broadcast for the national fencing championships. Two hours before the first match, he and two other camera operators uncoiled cables from the mobile unit van and tested the cameras' live feeds. A little before 7:00 p.m., a tap on his shoulder interrupted his work.

"Are you André Arseneault?" A stranger held a piece of paper with his name on it. "You need to go see your father at the hospital."

Saint John Regional Hospital sat on the edge of the campus, minutes from the university's gymnasium. André entered Admissions. The nurses directed him down the hallway. When he rounded a corner, he saw his father and felt a pang of relief. He had feared his dad had been in a road accident on his way to Dipper Harbour. André recognized the two people sitting next to Jean-Guy: Sara and Jayme, the organizers of the Fundy Race. They all rose, and André immediately understood that something had happened to his brother.

Time splintered for Jacqueline Arseneault. It exploded into crystal shards across her living room carpet and pierced her skin. To escape its bite, she raced back and forth in the narrow hallway, pinballing off the walls. In the living room, she was startled to find Constable Mackay still standing there, firm as a post. Jacqueline wanted to ball up her fists and strike him across the chin, if only to prove that he was real, that this fractured moment was more than a bad dream. Words leapt from her throat in an animal-like howl.

"I *hate* you!" she shouted at the officer. "I *hate* you!"

"We need to call someone," he said. "Who can we call?"

Jacqueline calmed enough to ask the officers to phone one of her sisters. She could feel the walls of her home tumbling in on her. Her mind went blank. She was driven to the hospital and arrived around 7:00 p.m. As she walked through the sliding doors, she recognized Father Michael LeBlanc, her pastor from Our Lady of Perpetual Help. His presence in the waiting room extinguished her faint hope that this might be a case of mistaken identity. Father LeBlanc had performed the last rites of the Catholic service over René's body. Jacqueline waited numbly in a chair. Finally, doctors led her into the emergency room. Constable Burke of the RCMP was already there.

And then she saw René.

Her son lay on a stainless steel gurney. A long sheet of thin paper covered the lower half of his naked body. His wet clothes had been stripped away. His eyes, always flickering with mischief, were taped shut. Jacqueline placed her left hand across his chest and touched his forehead with her right hand. His skin was still cold, so very cold. Simply holding him drained her own warmth. A hint of azure tainted his usually sun-browned skin.

Jacqueline remembered René's first day on earth, more than twenty-two years ago. He had been born, three weeks before Christmas, a "blue baby." Not enough oxygen had pumped through the tiny child's new blood, but he had recovered from that first shock of life and had grown to be a man. He had fought his way into the world as her blue boy, she thought, and now he was leaving the same way.

Someone helped Jacqueline, sobbing again, into a wheelchair and rolled her out of the emergency room. After that final vision of her son, she would remember little else from this most terrible of days.

PART FOUR
The Reckoning

The extreme sports movement continues to gather momentum. This penchant for recreational risk-taking may be the defining characteristic of an entire generation of young people. Many believe that it will change the face of recreation forever and become a fertile source of litigation.

—David Horton, "Extreme Sports and the Assumption of Risk"

From the beach I see rising
winds across water.
Glass ponies of the sea ride
toward land, then turn back
into the waves.

—Stephen Stamp, "Glass Ponies of the Sea"
(in memory of Darryl Smith and Gareth Lineen)

TWENTY-THREE

The Wake

Word of René Arseneault's death passed quickly across the city of Saint John and beyond. As evening fell, at the Vlugs' house in Dipper Harbour a few stragglers from the race remained, still warming up or waiting for taxi rides back to parked cars. Over the last few hours, a pall had muted the gathering, with rumors of an injured cyclist, roll calls for missing racers, the roar of a rescue plane overhead, and then stories that a kayaker had been rushed by ambulance to hospital. Then the shocker: Someone had died. A person they had all stood beside, maybe even joked with, was no longer alive. Quietly, the last participants took their leave. The Vlug family had enough on their hands right now. The house emptied and, for the first time that day, fell quiet.

That evening, back from the hospital, Constable Burke typed and faxed a news release that named the deceased: "Mr. Arseneault was participating in a kayak race," it read, "when an incoming thunder storm suddenly caused high seas on the Bay of Fundy. Arseneault's kayak overturned as a result of his extreme fatigue, and he was unable to get back inside." The fax mentioned Boon Kek only as a "fellow racer" who had held on to Arseneault for "the better part of the hour." (The organizers and the Arseneault family would protect Kek's anonymity, and his name would not appear in any news reports for nearly a year.) The RCMP release noted that an investigation was ongoing.

The news crackled across the radio waves that night. The next day, local TV stations broadcast reports of the accident. Soon participants had to explain to worried, even angry wives and parents, husbands and children, what had gone on at the fatal race. They were never in danger, they assured their families. Not in any real danger, they told themselves. The wife of one middle-aged racer refused to speak to her husband for several weeks. Another forty-year-old racer was one of only three solo kayakers to finish, but his ten-year-old son was unimpressed by his father's second-place prize. "Great, dad," said the youngster, "you risked your life for a headband!" A mother hadn't even known that her seventeen-year-old son planned to compete. He and his high school buddy had never kayaked before, and they got cold and disoriented halfway to Dipper Harbour. That was where the patrol kayak found them stalled in the storm—the boys had stopped paddling without even realizing it—and ordered them off the water. The young racer's mother was appalled by his account of the chaotic race. Her son thought it was the greatest adventure.

On Monday morning, the front page of the *Telegraph-Journal* announced to the city: "Kayaker Capsizes in Bay. Tragedy: Rothesay Man Killed by Hypothermia." In an interview, Sara Vlug described Arseneault as a frequent visitor to her parents' store. "I wish I could go back twenty-four hours and talk to him," she said, before starting to cry. "We consider him a friend." Bob Mawhinney, captain of the *D.P. Clipper*, was frank in his assessment: "It's not a place to have that race in the first place." Arseneault's obituary ran in the same edition, and readers were struck by the accompanying headshot. His high-school graduation portrait appeared next to the photo of a retired brigadier general who had passed away at age ninety-one—one man at the natural end of a long and eventful life, the other just entering the bloom of his own ambitions.

The increasingly critical tone of media inquiries annoyed the organizers. When another reporter approached Sara Vlug, she declined to comment. "We're not saying anything else because the more we release, the bigger the story gets," she told him. That didn't stop the story from spreading. Her quote appeared in a longer newswire article picked up by papers across the country. The article looked beyond the stormy conditions as an explanation for the accident. Joe Kennedy, one of the last racers Arseneault had encountered on the water, claimed to the reporter that the incident "was just a matter of somebody who didn't have the experience or the strength to be out in those conditions." The article also outlined larger issues that would shadow the race for years. "Arseneault's death raises concerns not only about the safety of sea kayaking," the reporter suggested, "but also of extreme races which push athletes to the limits of their endurance." Adventure racing, long an obscure sport, was about to be judged in the court of public opinion. Even the less extreme pastime of sea kayaking would be dragged before a skeptical jury.

On Tuesday, June 4, another front-page story in the *Telegraph-Journal* (headlined "Tricky Conditions Forecast Long Before Fatal Kayaking Leg") wondered if the storm that allegedly led to Arseneault's death was as unavoidable as had been previously suggested. A meteorologist at the Maritime Weather Centre in Halifax confirmed that the marine forecast had called for large waves on the bay and southwesterly winds of up to twenty-five knots by early afternoon. The organizers declined to tell the reporter whether they had checked the weather forecast beforehand. "I'm too emotionally drained," said Vlug, when pressed for an interview. Nine days after the Fundy race, the paper's editors published a commentary about the incident, titled "Weighing In on Extreme Sports." The facts of Arseneault's death "cannot be isolated from the broader circumstances" of how, in the editors' words, this "grueling test of stamina" was organized and overseen. The list of key questions identified by the editorial would become the focus of informal debate, government review, and legal wrangling. Why was the paddling stage held last, when participants were at their most fatigued and prone to the cold? ("The only way you could add more factors for hypothermia," one racer later told me, "was if you had people chug beer before they got into their boats.") Was a single motorized vessel enough of a safety net? What other first-aid measures were at the ready? Did organizers and racers know about the marine forecast? Why wasn't René Arseneault pulled from the bay after the Zodiac operators rescued him the first time? And how did organizers assess the racers' readiness to navigate the Bay of Fundy?

The editorial also acknowledged a complex concept relevant to all organized adventures, outdoor races, and guided expeditions—the issue of shared responsibility. "Endurance athletes, even at the recreational level, must always bear considerable responsibility for their own safety," emphasized the editors. Participants must know their limits, listen to their bodies, and recognize when to avoid unnecessary dangers. In races, organizers also share responsibility for the safety of paying participants and clients, no matter what legal disclaimers are embedded in signed waivers. "We urge an independent and rigorous examination of the safety precautions—or lack thereof—of this adventure race," concluded the editorial. "This is an increasingly popular sport. Let's hold this particular event up to scrutiny, lest its sad outcome be repeated. An inquest would be just the tool." Finally, the editors opened the discussion to their readers and printed beneath the article a clip-out questionnaire: "What can be done to help extreme sports become safer," it asked, "given a competitor's desire to be pushed to the limit?" Over the next week, readers would send in their own opinions about what went wrong and why.

While the organizers were no longer speaking to the media, they did communicate about the race with the participants. On June 19, they sent an email message, signed "Jayme & Sara" and titled "Post Race Update," from the Eastern Outdoors internet address to a list of racers and volunteers. "By now I am sure everyone knows about the horrible tragedy that occurred during the race on June 1st. We would just like to thank all of you for your tremendous support during these difficult times," the message began. "The many cards and emails we have received have been a great help in trying to deal with this from an organizer's point of view. Something went terribly wrong that day and we may never know the entire truth. Our hearts and thoughts go out to the Arseneault family during this difficult time. We would also like to apologize for not holding an awards ceremony and the confusion following the race."

They listed the finishers and asked participants for feedback, positive or negative, about the race. "If we are able to continue organizing races we wish to do so to the best of our ability. We would like to know how we could make this race better while at the same time offering a sense of adventure and staying away from the 'triathlon mindset.'" They concluded: "We would like to thank all the teams that competed in this year's race and hope to see you all racing again sometime soon."

Bob Carreau, the elder of the two Tallywhackers, was still troubled by his experiences on the bay. Back home in Bathurst, he responded to the organizers' message. "As a racer/participant I accept partial responsibility for knowing when I'm in over my head and stopping or turning back," he wrote. "However, I share this responsibility with the race organizers." He described his own background on the race committee of the Baffin Island ultramarathon. He wrote about the need to sort fit, well-equipped runners from ambitious, naive newbies, to be prepared to delay the race or even cancel it if the weather turned sour. "This wasn't the Eco-Challenge," he continued. "Yes, I want to be challenged. No, I don't want to be catered to or involved in some bogus 'armchair' adventure race where I get a certificate and a T-shirt that I can show the boys at work on Monday. But I need to know that the participants have thought out as much of the 'what-if' scenarios as possible.

"We were a 'team' out there that day. I was on the same 'team' as you. A team that makes these events possible (either as an organizer, supporter, or participant). If I had decided not to go into the water or had turned around, then maybe others would have decided the same thing. Part of this tragedy was the fault of the participants—the 'do or die' mentality. Knowing this, you need to have someone (third-party independent) that can make an unbiased decision at any point in the event to alter or terminate the race."

He never got a reply.

On the Tuesday and Wednesday after the race, Brenan's Funeral Home in Saint John held a wake and viewing. A steady procession of friends, family members, and participants, including the two organizers, offered condolences to the Arseneault family. René's body lay in an open casket, his red motorcycle jacket and helmet beside it. Boon Kek arrived with his two friends from the race and waited to enter the viewing room. "Bring him here," said Jacqueline Arseneault, when she learned that the last person to see her son alive was in the lineup. The night of the race, Kek had been taken to the hospital in the ambulance with the injured biker, and had been told of René's death by Jean-Guy Arseneault, but Jacqueline had been too distraught to notice him. Now he stepped out of the line and met with the family. "Thank you ... thank you so much for what you tried to do for my son," Jacqueline managed to say between fits of sobbing.

Next to her stood Denis Arseneault, René's other older brother, who had been studying business in Halifax when he received word of the tragedy. Thinner, shorter, less muscular, and more angular than René, he was the bookish good student rather than the outgoing athlete. Denis nevertheless shared René's dark brown eyes and thick eyebrows, the same wide-lipped smile, the same young Acadian handsomeness. Kek was struck by how much the brothers looked alike. That, more than anything else, finally drove home the reality of what had happened a few short days ago.

Other participants found it hard to chase away memories of the Fundy challenge. One racer attended the wake and recognized Arseneault—she had chatted with him at the start line, about the weather of all things—and couldn't sleep for weeks afterward, until her friends urged her to seek counseling. During the storm, another kayaker had discerned what sounded like a safety whistle, but her boyfriend and race partner hadn't heard the whistle, and they had been too focused on keeping their own kayak upright to perform a search. Still, she was haunted by the prospect that it might have been Kek and Arseneault calling for help.

Five days after the race, Constable Mackay led another procession of mourners into Our Lady of Perpetual Help, a Catholic church in Rothesay, where René Arseneault had once been an altar boy. So many people attended the noontime funeral that the overflow had to be accommodated in an adjacent hall and the sounds of the readings and remembrances piped into the room. Again, Arseneault's motorcycle gear hung at the front of the church. Father LeBlanc, who had performed last rites, told the congregation that the young man had run the "marathon of life" and that now he would live for eternity in heaven.

Chris McCully, René's best friend, ascended the dais to deliver the eulogy. "How hard could it be to talk about a person who talked so much and talked so violently with his hands and so loudly?" he began and described René as often laughing, always joking, and never sitting still. A competitive rower and coach, McCully shared René's love of sports. "He was hard to keep up to," he admitted, "as an athlete and a friend." Finally, McCully finished with a censored version of the drinking toast that all their buddies would raise, on a Saturday night in Saint John or during their spring break in Cuba. "Here's to you and here's to me, the best of friends we'll ever be," he recited, fighting back tears. "But if we ever disagree—" McCully excised the expletive that René would raucously add "—here's to you and here's to me!" The church filled with applause.

Later that summer, a handful of René's friends ran in the annual Marathon by the Sea, the race for which he had also been training. None was an especially keen runner, but they trained and then jogged or walked wearing T-shirts embossed with the message: "In Memory of R.A." Jacqueline Arseneault met them at the finish line. She was so proud of these young men and women. She knew René wouldn't have wanted anybody wasting tears on him. He would have preferred this moment instead, a circle of his friends pushing their bodies hard and sharing a laugh. She could imagine her son, like one of the handcrafted angels she collected, looking down upon them all and teasing, "Okay, you guys did okay, but I did better!" He was that competitive. It was funny and sad at the same time to think about, but he would probably have taken pride in being the first in his family to get to heaven, too.

In the months that followed, Jacqueline Arseneault stopped dreaming. Her back would stiffen at the wail of a siren or even the ring of her phone. Her head would pivot at the sight of a red motorbike streaming down the highway—she saw them everywhere. She lost the carefree bounce to her gait, her easy laugh. Therapy helped a little, but it couldn't chase away all the fears, nor the prospect of losing another son. "Mom, you have to let me out of the bubble," begged Guy, her youngest, when she stayed up late for him to come home. Guy, she knew, was in a bubble of his own. He never even mentioned his dead brother by name.

After the funeral, as the numbness wore off, the Arseneault family wished they had known more about the Fundy race, wished they had understood better the dangers that their son would face. Still, Jacqueline and Jean-Guy had few delusions that they could have said or done anything to stop René from competing. They had never been able to slow him down before—not on the baseball diamond or on his motorbike, not training for a marathon or even in the middle of one of his voluble rants. He was headstrong, determined, competitive to the end. "It could have been marbles and he still would have played to win," his parents admitted. "René would not have quit."

TWENTY-FOUR

The Controversy

In the weeks afterward, at other events and on internet message boards, organizers and adventure racers dissected the facts and rumors about the incident and waited for fallout from the Fundy death. Some argued that the Fundy Multi-Sport Race shouldn't be considered an adventure race proper, but rather an off-road triathlon. The event allowed solo competitors and required no orienteering by compass, whereas teamwork and wilderness navigation had always been cornerstones of the sport. But most people realized that such nuances of taxonomy would be lost on the general public, investigating officials, and, especially, insurance companies. Organizers of all outdoor activities had already experienced dramatic spikes in their premiums (tripling in some cases, despite no claims filed) as the insurance industry tried to recoup its post–September 11 payouts. A wrongful-death suit or bad publicity from the incident could jack up premiums to the few insurers still willing to underwrite guided adventures and events. That would be enough to push many businesses into bankruptcy. Most insiders agreed, though, that it had only been a matter of time before someone died at an adventure race.

There had been close calls before. In 1995, at the first Eco-Challenge, a hypothermic competitor needed to be airlifted by helicopter after overnighting in a watery canyon in Utah. At one Raid Gauloises, a racer caught a virus from bat guano that kept him on a respirator for nearly a month. In 1997, at ESPN's X-venture Race in Baja, Mexico, dozens of racers keeled over with heat stroke in temperatures so withering that the rubber in their shoes had begun to melt, while a Swedish kayak champion had to be airlifted to San Diego after she fell into a brain-boiling hyperthermic coma. Following this near-death fiasco, ESPN ditched the event; adventure racing was too extreme even for the X Games. At the 2000 Eco-Challenge in Borneo, a cyclist punctured a lung on a branch. One racer had a leech removed from his eyeball; another, from his penis. Eighty participants came down with high fever, chills, and other symptoms of leptospirosis, a bacterial infection picked up while swimming through a jungle river. And only two months before the Fundy challenge, a twenty-seven-year-old woman had died of a heart attack at the end of a four-day race in Argentina.

With the new media attention, organizers became especially cautious about safety. Frontier Adventure Racing, a Toronto-based company, produced one of North America's most popular series of events, and Dave Zietsma, the founder, was a top-ranked Eco-Challenge veteran. Less than two months after the Fundy Multi-Sport Race, he had planned to hold a thirty-six-hour race along the Bay of Fundy. Jayme Frank and Sara Vlug of Eastern Outdoors were to act as the local co-organizers, a first for Zietsma's company, which was exploring franchising possibilities. On June 19, Zietsma sent team captains an email and explained that the "events of June 1st have brought us to reconsider the protocol for the kayak portion of the race." Safety measures would include a minimum of three rescue boats, a shortened kayak leg, disqualification of teams that ventured more than a hundred meters from shore, and the requirement that, if bad weather arose, all teams had to beach and radio race officials. He

supplied a list of mandatory gear that contained a conspicuous difference from the Fundy Multi-Sport Race, one that he had decided
before the tragedy. All kayakers had to wear wetsuits. Why didn't every
cold-water race insist on wetsuits? "The issue is extra cost for
competitors," said Zietsma. "I look at it like you just can't do without
it." He found a company that would rent suits cheaply.

Zietsma knew accidents can happen quickly in the outdoors. Two
years before the Fundy event, at a thirty-six-hour race in Fernie,
British Columbia, Kyle Turk, a media relations staffer for Frontier
Adventure Racing, had veered off a road in his truck during the event
and drowned in a river. (Technically, Turk was the first person to die
at an adventure race in North America, but because he was an
employee rather than a participant, the accident drew little media
attention.) Zietsma realized that it was impossible to make any
adventure race one hundred percent safe without removing every
ounce of adventure. Ultimately, he felt that the tabloid headline that
dogged the sport—"Is Adventure Racing Safe?"—was the wrong
question. "Adventure racing is never going to be as safe as a running
race or triathlon. It has inherent risks," he said. "Let's stop talking
about whether it's safe or not safe. Let's ask, 'Is it a quality event?' And
to me, a quality adventure race matches the competitors' preparedness
with the challenges of the race course."

There was no how-to manual for hosting an adventure race. Most
new organizers learned through trial and hopefully not too serious
error. South of the border, a sanctioning body called the United States
Adventure Racing Association had formed. Canadian organizers were
discussing a similar group of their own. The challenge was in the sheer
variety of events and races. How do you design rules to fit them all?
Most of the major races, such as the Eco-Challenge and the Raid
Gauloises, could afford elaborate emergency protocols and dozens of
medical technicians. Single-day introductory events existed in a
grayer area of self-regulation. "Unfortunately, anyone can hang out a
shingle and put on a race," complained another experienced race
organizer. "No one has the intent of doing anything that's unsafe, but
a) in many cases they just don't know. It's one thing to do a number
of races; it's completely another to organize one. And b) in many cases

they just don't have the resources to hire medical personnel or a support staff or vehicles or work through contingency plans."

As many organizers and participants pointed out, the triathlon had gone through its own growing pains, and accidents still happened at these controlled races. Runners got bone splints or burnout. Cyclists crashed and snapped wrists and clavicles. The swimming sections posed the greatest danger. In the mass start, hundreds of competitors would charge into a lake or an ocean, like a commotion of harbor seals on a herring break. The shock of the cold water. A foot to the face. Goggles knocked askew. A breath snatched at the wrong moment and a gulp of water instead. Faster swimmers surging over you. A distant safety vessel. It wasn't hard to imagine an unfortunate swimmer going under and unnoticed, the body found the next day. Eventually triathlon organizers united to create standards and founded, in 1989, the International Triathlon Union, a sanctioning body to ensure safety at races around the world. Head counts, rescue boats, lifeguards, and temperature guidelines now ensure that everyone who dives into the water at the start of a race comes out on the other side.

Of course, just because a sport has a sanctioning federation doesn't ensure that every organizer will make the right decisions. A week after the Fundy race, the inaugural Utah Ironman attracted fifteen hundred competitors. Amid the confusion of an accidental start cue, a fifty-three-year-old triathlon veteran drowned in the windswept waves of what locals had already dubbed a "killer lake." Nevertheless, triathlons had matured to the point that, despite the occasional headline-grabbing accident, no one considered these endurance races so extreme any more. Adventure racing, on the other hand, was still on the wild frontier of unusual and unregulated outdoor sports.

The fallout from any outdoor accident can be so loud and messy that legislators often feel they must wade into the wilderness and enact safety measures. Several other adrenaline sports have passed through the cycle of tragedy, reflection, and regulation, often with a lawsuit or two to lubricate the learning process. In the 1970s, whitewater rafting came into vogue for everyone from corporate team-building motivators to church youth groups. With a guide at the oars, a raft ride down a fast-moving river requires little training or endurance. During the industry's early years, regulation was erratic. Standards, if they existed, varied throughout North America and Europe. Some states and provinces didn't even require rafters to wear life jackets, let alone helmets or wetsuits. In 1979, the death of three rafters in British Columbia convinced the Canadian government to introduce non-mandatory standards and licensing. That didn't prevent more accidents. During a seven-week span of summer in 1987, twelve more people drowned in the province in four separate accidents. In the most widely publicized incident, five American advertising executives died on a company-sponsored trip when their raft overturned in the middle of the infamous White Mile, a set of class-five rapids—the most dangerous still navigable—on the Chilko River. (The tragedy would inspire a 1994 made-for-TV movie starring Alan Alda.) None of the paddlers was wearing a wetsuit in the frigid waters, and no backup raft or safety boat was available to rescue the capsized clients. One of the families successfully sued the sponsoring company. The rash of deaths focused public concern on the under-regulated sport. Federal and provincial authorities strengthened rafting standards and enforced stricter rules for operators.

Some people prefer to get their whitewater thrills without the safety of a rubber boat. Canyoning (known as ghyll running in the United Kingdom and kloofing in South Africa) invites participants to trek, climb, rappel, and swim through watery gorges that are prone to flash floods. In 1993, the drowning deaths in Utah of two leaders from a Mormon scout troop and a subsequent lawsuit focused attention on the dangers of fast water rushing through narrow slits in rock. Six years later, twenty-one young travelers were swept to their deaths when a thunderstorm sent rainwater surging through a canyon in the Interlaken region of Switzerland. Three directors and three guides from the adventure company were found guilty of negligent manslaughter for not ensuring proper safety measures or attending to weather reports. After the tragedy, Switzerland adopted a code of conduct for extreme sports outfitters and developed courses to educate guides.

Backcountry skiers venture beyond the relative safety of groomed ski resorts to seek the same gravity-assisted rush as rafters and canyoneers. The euphoria comes with a trade-off—the risk of avalanche. A single step on an unstable slope or a loud noise can be all it takes for several layers of snowpack to shear away and accelerate down a mountain, as awe-striking a natural force as any river at full bore. Most backcountry skiers enter avalanche terrain armed with beacons (wallet-sized electronic devices used to detect buried skiers), search probes, and shovels. Even with these precautions, fatalities are not uncommon. Between 1984 and 2003, about half of the two hundred and thirty people who died in avalanches in Canada were backcountry skiers. On November 13, 1998, Michel Trudeau, son of former prime minister Pierre Trudeau, was swept down a mountainside by an avalanche and drowned in Kokanee Lake in British Columbia. Four winters later, seven teenaged students from Strathcona-Tweedsmuir, an elite private school in Alberta, died under a kilometer-long snow slide near Rogers Pass, not far from where seven other skiers had been killed two weeks earlier. By that season's end, twenty-nine people had perished on Canadian slopes.

The high profile of the Michel Trudeau and Rogers Pass accidents directed public scrutiny to the risks involved in backcountry skiing and adventure-education programs. Ross Cloutier, a risk-analysis consultant and the founder of the adventure programs department at Thompson Rivers University, in British Columbia, wrote two post-avalanche studies of the school-trip incident. He argued for a federally funded national avalanche center. He also expressed concerns about whether parents had been informed enough about the dangers of the ski trip and about Parks Canada's laissez-faire attitude to allowing school groups into avalanche terrain.

Cloutier, however, is no proponent of nanny-state regulation. He has led a climbing expedition to Mount Everest, founded a heli-skiing company, taught search and rescue, and supports the general aims of adventure education. He has also argued for "no rescue" wilderness zones, roadless terrain where experienced outdoor travelers could escape the digital grid and be left entirely on their own, even if they get into trouble. Cloutier has long argued that there is a difference between genuine wilderness adventure and the kinds of guided trips and extreme sporting events that have become so popular. "No matter how you attempt to package it, outdoor experience without the risk of harm is sport or guided tourism, not adventure," he noted. "Fear, as a result of risk and danger, is also part of the adventure experience.... Adventure only occurs where there is the risk of death."

In the wake of any fatality, outdoor professionals such as Cloutier often flinch as politicians and other outsiders take noisy notice of their adventurous interests. The uninformed attention often means poorly conceived regulations, more layers of red tape—exactly what people who venture into the wild hope to escape in the first place. John Dowd, the sea-kayaking pioneer, warned about this creeping bureaucracy in a plea for personal responsibility appended to a recent edition of his popular guidebook. "In North America, entire industries are populated by folks who need to be needed, including the medical and legal professions, the police, the coast guard, search and rescue, regulating bureaucracies, and many others." All these agencies, he granted, perform vital services. However, when we rely on their aid, we implicitly agree to live by their rules. "This rule-making infrastructure frequently becomes so mind-numbing that it leads individuals to feel increasingly powerless. To counter this alienation, many people turn to outdoor adventure." But what happens when the urge to adventure gets hemmed in by the law?

Canoeists and kayakers have long sung the creed of self-reliance. Paddling magazines publish accounts of trips gone bad for readers to learn from. The morning of the Fundy race, the Saint John newspaper had run a review of a novel that speculated on the most famous paddling accident in Canadian history: the mysterious death in 1917 of painter Tom Thomson in Canoe Lake. An avid paddler, Thomson often navigated deep into the network of the lakes and hardwood forests of Ontario's Algonquin Park. He canoed and portaged and found inspiration for his sketches and landscape paintings in the park's seasonal transformation. "The artist was a magnificent paddler and strong swimmer," noted the book's reviewer. "But he died after what appeared to be a solo canoeing mishap in calm weather, quite near an island, on a lake he knew like one of his canvases. His upturned canoe was found eight days earlier. His paddle remains missing." Accident, suicide, or even murder—the true cause of Thomson's death has fascinated history buffs and canoeing aficionados for nearly a century.

In post–Tom Thomson Canada, the paddling accident that generated the most controversy was the 1978 canoe fiasco in Lake Timiskaming. The northern lake divides Ontario and Quebec, and forms a narrow, deep, and cold 117-kilometer extension of the Ottawa River that eventually spills into James Bay. A three-week trip had been organized by St. John's School, a Christian boys' academy based near Toronto. Barely into the first day, the four trip leaders led their twenty-seven charges, aged eleven to thirteen, on an ill-advised crossing of the lake in top-heavy and untested twenty-two-foot expedition canoes. All four vessels tipped over from the rough conditions or during the rescue attempts. Some boys made it to shore in the leading canoes. Others tried to climb, unsuccessfully, back into the flooded vessels. Many huddled in their life jackets in the frigid water, uncertain of what to do next, as warmth leaked out of their small bodies. Several managed to swim to safety, although that effort proved too much for a few of them. The next morning, the bodies of twelve boys and one trip leader were found floating in the lake or curled up on shore. The catastrophic trip became a *cause célèbre* in Canadian and international newspapers and on TV for weeks.

Like Outward Bound, the school administrators of St. John's had designed a curriculum on building character through physically punishing ordeals in the outdoors. They had also cultivated close relationships with the parents who had sent their young sons to the institution in the belief that the public educational system failed to develop such qualities in students. This parent–teacher intimacy shielded the school and the trip leaders from criticism over the deaths, despite close calls on previous expeditions. An inquest pointed out obvious lapses in judgment: improper route planning, poor emergency preparation, no paddling practice on the new canoes, no easy way to get out of the cold water. "These factors," author, educator, and expert canoeist James Raffan noted in his book about the tragedy, "had repeatedly led to the same kind of accidents." Just no deaths—until then. In the end, no criminal charges were laid, no civil lawsuits filed. The fatal trip would remain a cautionary tale for paddlers and guides, but it would never set a legal precedent for assigning blame in a death by misadventure.

After the Fundy race, at least one person was unsurprised to learn about another paddling death in Canada. For more than a dozen years, Tim Ingram, the self-deputized Ralph Nader of canoeing and sea kayaking, had led a rancorous and often lonely campaign against the dangers of boats that—without the proper safety tools—he considered unsafe on any sea. For his controversial opinions, he had fallen from grace among North America's paddling establishment and had founded his own protestant movement. On his combative website and public internet forums, in a self-published book and relentless letter-writing campaigns, he warned of the risks of kayaking and the conspiracy of silence surrounding paddling deaths. What frustrated Ingram most about the fatal toll on the world's waterways was that a solution existed, one that could save hundreds of lives every year—if only the right people would listen.

Ingram had grown up in Ontario and summered at YMCA-run camps, where he had learned how to swim and canoe. Counselors had demonstrated to the boys how to roll up their gear, sleeping bags, and matches especially, in a plastic groundsheet and stuff the waterproofed bundle into a canoe pack. Squeezed between the gunwales, the packs added buoyancy, a lesson in hydrophysics that stuck with Ingram. Nor did he forget the time that he and his campmates, fifteen years old, swamped their canoes, struggled to shore, and had to ask a cottager to phone their lodge. It took a few days until they felt right again after several hours in the cold water—and that had been in August. He could only imagine how his body might react to a longer immersion in even colder water.

In 1984, while working as a family therapist, he built a log home near Georgian Bay. It seemed the perfect time and place to take up kayaking, and so he bought a small river craft. As a boy, he had helped his dad build a cabin cruiser and always enjoyed tinkering with boats. To learn more about kayaks, he immersed himself in the literature of ancient and modern vessels. He studied the Inuit's seal-skin designs and the folding kayaks mass-marketed by Johann Klepper. Throughout the early to mid 1900s, the German tailor's versatile wooden-framed and canvas-covered *Klepperboot* sparked an explosion of interest in the sport (among casual day paddlers, ambitious adventurers, and later World War Two commandos) that the modern renaissance in sea kayaking has yet to match. In 1928, Franz Romer, a twenty-nine-year-old war veteran, paddled a Klepper for the first kayak crossing of the Atlantic Ocean: six thousand four hundred kilometers and fifty-eight straight days from the Canary Islands to the Virgin Islands. (After a pit stop, he paddled north from Puerto Rico toward New York City, missed a hurricane warning by an hour, and was never heard from again.)

Armed with new knowledge, Ingram designed, patented, and started selling a line of his own folding kayaks. Modern folding kayaks nearly all use inflated air bags, held within the skeleton frame and fabric skin, to keep the canvas taut while the boat is being put together and to provide flotation in case of a puncture. The concept was based on the seal-skin float, called an *avataq*, that the Inuit used as a buoy on their harpoons and to stabilize their boats in rough seas. Ingram had read about other kayak adventurers who had made trans-oceanic crossings, such as Ed Gillet's sixty-four-day Pacific odyssey from California to Hawaii. All these long-distance paddlers had used wide kayaks with stabilizing floats—sponsons was the nautical term. The earliest sponsons were air-filled chambers or wedges of cork attached along the upper sides of canoes. Ingram wondered if he could retrofit plastic or fiberglass kayaks with removable sponsons. In half an hour, he sketched and then cut a crude prototype out of plastic tubing. He called his sponsons Sea Wings.

He needed a test site. In 1987, a late-summer storm blew across Parry Sound, not far from his house. Ingram readied his kayak, buckled the sponsons around its hull, and launched into the teeth of the gale. "It was like paddling an armchair," he recalled. "The problem of being surprised and capsized by a breaking wave didn't exist." He kayaked past the coast guard station and watched as the cutter rushed to rescue bigger yet less sea-worthy boats. His improvised sponsons were a success—or at least would be once other paddlers learned about them. Over the next two years, he refined the design and received a U.S. patent. In 1992, a canoe company agreed to manufacture and include sponsons with several boats. Ingram's creations were a meter long, fifteen centimeters in diameter, weighed half a kilogram each, and attached around a canoe or kayak's hull with a pair of buckled straps. They could be inflated in under a minute by blowing into a plastic tube, although Ingram planned to install carbon dioxide cartridges for nearly instant inflation in an emergency. Filled with air, the sponsons looked like a pair of giant hot-dog buns barnacled to a kayak or canoe. New paddlers could use them to stabilize a boat or deploy them if the weather turned ugly. After a capsize, the Sea Wings transformed a flooded kayak or canoe into a nearly untippable life raft, so that paddlers could escape the threat of hypothermia by quickly getting out of the water and back into their boats.

He advertised his invention in magazines and at trade shows. He showed pictures of his seven—and ten-year-old daughters using the Sea Wings to paddle a flooded boat to shore. In 1992, the Geological Survey of Canada sent a scientist out to map the floor of the Beaufort Sea in one of Ingram's folding kayaks armed with sponsons. "The great advantage of the Sea Wing," observed John Dowd in his best-selling guidebook *Sea Kayaking*, "is that it leaves the kayaker in a more stable position than before the capsize." Other reviewers agreed, including the U.S. Army Special Forces, whose waterborne troops gave the Sea Wings a thumbs up after a field test in 1994. The sponsons were especially useful, they found, to keep kayaks from tipping over when broached by side-striking waves.

An incident in Lyme Bay, off the coast of England, confirmed for Ingram the need for better safety equipment, especially when novice paddlers take to the seas. In March 1993, a group of eight high school–aged students and their teacher joined two guides for a ten-kilometer, half-day kayak trip on the North Atlantic. The neophyte paddlers and their teacher quickly got into trouble in the waves, and all of them tipped. The guides didn't have flares. Six hours after the group's expected return time, rescuers in a lifeboat and a helicopter finally retrieved the missing paddlers. By then, four students had succumbed to hypothermia. The deaths sparked calls for retribution and reform in the United Kingdom. The manager of the outfitting company was charged with four counts of manslaughter, tried, and sentenced to two years in prison. In 1995, the government passed the Activity Centres Act to remedy safety standards among the growing number of outfitters.

Ingram believed that kayak and canoe operators in North America deserved similar legal scrutiny. On the cold lakes and oceans of Canada, the real risk of canoes and kayaks was not just drowning but hypothermia. So-called life jackets often only kept capsized paddlers afloat long enough to die from the cold. Ingram claimed that the common self-rescue techniques and tools taught to sea kayakers (the Greenland roll, the paddle float, the hand pump) were difficult to perform or useless in the rough waves likely to cause a capsize. They might be fun to practice in a heated pool, and instructors made money by selling lessons. However, capsized paddlers needed a surefire way to make their boats more stable.

Ingram grew frustrated by the slow sales—two hundred in a good year—of his Sea Wings. The paddle float, his competitor in the safety market, had been introduced to kayakers in the early 1980s. By the time Ingram developed his sponsons, the inexpensive floats had become standard issue with almost all boats. Most kayakers have trained with a paddle float to perform an outrigger-style self-rescue. Few have ever tested a set of sponsons. In 1994, Ingram accused the editors of the major paddling magazines of ignoring his invention because of pressure from competing advertisers and paddling organizations, such as the American Canoe Association, which benefited from selling instruction (rather than safety tools) to new paddlers. He discontinued his marketing efforts in those publications. The advent of the internet let Ingram take his campaign for paddling safety to a global audience. For the next decade, he incited heated debates on paddling newsgroups and websites, until the sites shut down, splintered, or banned him entirely. His opponents argued that new paddlers should learn how to read the seas and to roll when necessary, or stay clear of difficult waters. Skeptics said that his Sea Wings were like training wheels—good for beginners, but nothing that a serious adult paddler would ever need. Ingram accused his critics of being dupes of the kayaking industry and what he called its "drowning business plan." "Canoes and kayaks are the most dangerous watercraft in the world," he argued, citing statistics from the U.S. Department of Transportation. "Almost all canoe and kayak deaths are due to hypothermia-induced drowning."

Sponson Guy, as the obsessive Ingram became known, did an end-run around the paddling establishment and directly lobbied government regulators. He wrote letters and emails to the U.S. and Canadian coast guards, law enforcement officers on both sides of the border, as well as the attorneys general of various American states. In his fiery missives, he accused paddlers' organizations and publications of deceiving clients with Enron-style tactics, of behaving like a sadistic death cult, and worse. Depending on his political mood, he compared them to George W. Bush or the Nazis. To build a case, he clipped accident reports and posted hypothermia stats and email correspondence on his website and then corralled this material into a self-published book—one part research, two parts tirade—and didn't hide his bias in its title: *Canoe and Kayak Scam Kills 1000 Americans.* "The Puritans of the canoe and kayak industry seem to think great suffering is necessary to sell canoes and kayaks," he wrote. "This idea not only kills more than one hundred people a year in the U.S. but does not sell the sport effectively, like a more rational, safety-based marketing approach."

The American Canoe Association claimed that Ingram only wanted to sell more sponsons and threatened a libel suit if he didn't tone down his attacks. The controversy divided otherwise placid paddlers. Ingram's cause wasn't helped by his caustic remarks and old internet photographs of the bearded, wild-eyed kayak maker hunched atop a Sea-Winged boat like a lakeside Unabomber. His actual character didn't square with his online infamy, however. In person, the now–clean-shaven Ingram was a mild-mannered social worker with a passion for the outdoors and a tinkerer's need to fix problems. Let loose on a computer keyboard, though, he transformed into a one-man rhetorical wrecking machine. Even his supporters wondered if sponsons might reach more paddlers—and save more lives—if he would let his invention do the talking instead.

Finally, Sponson Guy had a breakthrough. Ingram's lobbying got the attention of the U.S. Coast Guard, an organization that had largely left kayakers to their own devices. Researchers interviewed paddlers, examined kayak-safety literature, and published a twenty-six-page report titled *The Efficacy of Sponsons on Canoes and Kayaks.* Ingram was delighted, if not surprised, when its conclusions endorsed his invention. "While sponsons are not widely used in the recreational boating community," read the executive summary, "in several applications—with proper training and setup—they can be an effective safety enhancement measure." Ingram's excitement didn't last. He was shocked to learn that, despite its findings, the U.S. Coast Guard had no plans to mandate sponson use. There wasn't the political will, officials told him. For every kayaker who liked sponsons, there were two or three who didn't. Paddlers balked at sponsons for reasons that ranged from the philosophical (one shouldn't rely on technology that might fail), to the economic (they cost three times as much as paddle floats), to the superficial (they looked silly).

In justifying inaction, the report also cited at length the theory of risk homeostasis. Gerald Wilde, a psychology professor at Queen's University in Kingston, Ontario, had pioneered the idea, and his concept had been reiterated in influential editorials published in several major paddling magazines. Wilde floated the notion, based on statistical studies, especially of traffic fatalities, that "in any activity, people accept a certain level of subjectively estimated risk to their health, safety and other things they value, in exchange for the benefits they hope to receive from the activity." More controversially, he claimed that regardless of safety precautions we all have a "target risk"—a set measure of danger with which we're comfortable. When regulators mandate seatbelts for cars or speed laws, drivers will unconsciously adjust their behavior—chatting on a cell phone, running a yellow light, or tailgating—to maintain the same target-risk level. From his statistical analyses, Wilde argued that educating people about the benefits of cautious decision making and the costs of risky behavior works far better to lower target-risk levels (and to reduce accident rates) than legislating new safety measures and devices.

The coast guard was happy to promote sponsons, preach kayak safety, and then let paddlers decide for themselves. "You have a good product, if you would try to market it the right way," a U.S. official told Ingram. The disappointed sponson maker wasn't convinced. In an angry reply, he compared the official's boss to the murderous Taliban. The U.S. Coast Guard promptly cut off all communication with the safety gadfly.

Despite his setbacks, Tim Ingram continued to document paddling deaths around the world and to build his case against the canoe and kayak industry. A father and son in Minnesota. Two Girl Guides on Lake Huron. Three boys on a lake north of Winnipeg. René Arseneault in the Bay of Fundy. Two hundred deaths a year on the waterways of North America. All of them, in his mind, preventable. All of them, therefore, tantamount to murder.

TWENTY-FIVE

The Investigation

On the Monday morning after the race, Dr. Marek Godlewski stepped into the morgue at the Saint John Regional Hospital and removed the body of René Gabriel Arseneault from its steel cabinet. Then the Polish-born pathologist studied the clinical file for context to the case. The young man had been picked up by ambulance in a code blue state—non-responsive and in need of resuscitation. The attendants had stripped the wet clothes from the victim and applied instant hot packs to his armpits and groin. Before racing back to Saint John, siren screaming, they had hooked Arseneault to a cardiac monitor—there was activity, but it was weak—and then fired a shock through his chest with the defibrillator paddles. Twelve minutes after the first charge, they had shocked the heart again. A few minutes later, via a tube snaked down the windpipe, they had delivered two milligrams of epinephrine, the naturally produced hormone better known as adrenaline, to encourage the heart to regain its beat. The attendants had performed chest compressions to drive the drug through his body.

Thirty-one minutes after leaving the wharf, at 5:36 p.m., the ambulance had pulled into the covered bay of Saint John Regional Hospital. The head ambulance attendant had inserted a catheter and a continuous bladder irrigation system, attached to a pair of two-liter bags of warm fluid, which could cycle through the body and heat the young man's deeply chilled internal organs. Then René Arseneault, strapped to the rolling gurney, had been rushed into the emergency room. He had arrived with a core temperature of 28.9°C, more than eight degrees below average for the human body and beyond the threshold for severe hypothermia. At 6:00 p.m., after failing to get a regular heart rhythm, the emergency room staff ceased resuscitation efforts. They had rewarmed the victim's body above 30°C—you're not dead, according to physicians, until you're warm and dead—and made the final pronouncement. The apparent cause: hypothermia.

Dr. Godlewski's task was to confirm or contradict this theory. An examination of the body revealed no sign of trauma, no suspect welts or bruising. Results from a toxicology test allowed Godlewski to cross out another possible cause. The blood tests were negative for drugs or alcohol. Arseneault had remained faithful to his teetotaling while training for the race. The final ambiguity to unknot was the tricky question of whether a victim found immersed in cold water died from drowning or hypothermia. One symptom of drowning is foam in the airways and lungs—pulmonary edema froth—from swallowing water. Foam doesn't appear, however, in about fifteen percent of people who drown. These "dry drownings" occur when people fall into the water, run out of air, and the larynx muscles constrict to keep water from spilling into the lungs. Sometimes cold shock alone can set off a laryngeal spasm. So powerful that it shuts off airflow entirely, and the victim asphyxiates without once tasting water. Dr. Godlewski could find no evidence of froth in the airway, and while the young man might have suffered a dry drowning, it seemed unlikely based on the clinical file, especially the steep decline in body temperature. The pathologist agreed: René Arseneault had succumbed to hypothermia.

What had he felt as his brain and body slowly shut down in the cold waters of the bay? When precisely had his heart quit? And how could his fatal descent into hypothermia have been avoided? These were more complicated, more controversial questions beyond the scope of the autopsy lab.

The evening of the race, as soon as he had heard from the hospital that someone had died, Constable Wayne Burke had turned over the remaining search operations to another RCMP officer and driven to Saint John to secure the body. If there was to be an autopsy, coroner's inquest, or criminal investigation, he had to be certain that the body hadn't been tampered with. Once he had delivered the body to the morgue, he could begin to piece together how René Arseneault had died—and whether the RCMP should pursue charges. Throughout the investigation, Burke conferred with his superiors, who agreed that he needed to provide enough clues to answer a difficult question. Should the organizers be charged with criminal negligence?

He put aside all other cases. That night, he took a statement from Boon Kek, who was still in shock. Over the next few days, Burke interviewed the Arseneault family, Bob Mawhinney, and others involved in the race and the rescue. Burke had always drilled into his water-training students that their first task every morning, before pulling on their pants, was to call for the day's marine forecast. That was the next piece of evidence he tracked down. The forecast for that afternoon, he was told, was twenty-knot winds or greater. The thunderstorm may have been an early-arriving fluke, but the winds were always anticipated. It had been his own policy as a sailor never to go out in anything blowier than twenty knots. Past that point, sailing became more work than fun.

Burke had spoken briefly with Sara Vlug and Jayme Frank at the wharf in Chance Harbour, after the ambulance had departed. He invited them now to his RCMP office in Maces Bay. When they arrived, however, the two organizers declined to talk about the incident on their lawyer's advice.

Criminal negligence is an uncommon and serious charge. Most cases stem from motor vehicle accidents and drunken mishaps, not outdoor races. In Canada, guilty verdicts in fatal incidents can lead to life sentences. Because of the punishment, the bar of proof is high and rests on two concepts. People accused must be shown to have had a duty to act in a manner in which they failed to act, to respond in the way a "reasonably prudent" citizen could be expected to behave, and their action or inaction must have led to the injury or death. Most of all, the accused must have demonstrated by their negligent behavior not simply oversights or lapses in good judgment, but "wanton and reckless disregard for the lives and safety" of the people around them. That is tough to prove in all but exceptional cases. Three days after the accident, Constable Burke and his RCMP superiors decided that the people who participate in triathlons and adventure races, such as the Fundy event, understand they are taking risks. There was no way the Crown prosecutor could pursue a successful criminal negligence trial.

Constable Burke filed his notes but figured he hadn't heard the end of the case. There would likely be an inquest or a civil suit, where the standards for establishing the burden of proof would be lower. He might have to testify at both. In nearly twenty-five years on the force, he had seen countless deaths, all different—accidents and homicides and suicides, the young and the old. He had learned how to tune out the emotional nuances of the experience, to focus on the facts instead. This one, though, would stick in his memory, not just because he was close to retirement, or because marine deaths were rare for Mounties to tackle. His two eldest sons were a year or two younger than the Arseneault boy. In his interviews, he had discovered what a fine young man René had been. He tried to imagine what his parents must be going through, tried to see the world through the glaze of their loss. He couldn't. Nobody, he figured, could get over it.

"Those people should not have been on the water, based on the forecast alone," Burke would admit, three years later, after he had retired to Prince Edward Island and a quieter life of golf and guitar playing. "There's no way they should have been on the water, it's as simple as that."

In March of 2003, *explore* magazine published my feature article about the race. One month later, the New Brunswick coroner's office announced it would hold an inquest into the Fundy Multi-Sport Race. News outlets throughout the Maritimes and across the country used the inquest as another opportunity to ruminate about the safety of adventure sports, although at least one paper wondered what the fuss was all about. "Had irony not died, peacefully in its sleep of course," wrote the opinion-page editors of the *Ottawa Citizen*, "it might be odd to see a nation wracked by obesity panicking at extremely risky sports that are, judging by the results, inexplicably safe."

Saint John seemed an unusual host city for a critical examination of wilderness competitions. Outside observers were surprised that the small, conservative port city even had an adventure race, let alone would become the site of the first legal inquisition into the safety of the sport. The trend in outdoor recreation and organized adventures was far more conspicuous in wealthy West Coast metropolises such as Vancouver, Seattle, or San Francisco, and mountain towns in the Canadian and American Rockies. Saint John, as sober as its name suggested, was about as far from these outdoor meccas (as well as the Hollywood hype machine that marketed extreme sports to the masses) as you could get without falling off the edge of the continent. Here, collars remained proudly blue and the air carried an acid tang from the pulp mill where many locals worked. Citizens looked skeptically at fads imported by out-of-town yuppies, especially anything that involved wearing spandex. For all its civic attempts to gussy up the harbor front as the Fundy City, Saint John still came across as a no-nonsense company town with one steel-toed boot back in the Industrial Age.

On an afternoon's recess midway through the inquest, I jogged around historic uptown and then stretched against the red-brick building where I had rented a room. A hulking local in his late forties, throttling a cigarette between nicotine-stained knuckles, had been perched on a stoop across the street since I'd arrived. As he watched my post-jog contortions, he exhaled a stream of smoke and spoke for the first time: "You're just gonna die like the rest of us." That was Saint John for you.

The inquest would be a public airing of the coroner's investigation, a year of interviews with racers, organizers, fishermen, emergency personnel, and other experts. Twenty-five witnesses would be called over four June days. At the opening session, family members, reporters, a pair of kayak guides, and other curious citizens filed into a high-ceilinged courtroom. Jayme Frank and Sara Vlug were both in attendance, huddled with their legal counsel. Jean-Guy and Jacqueline Arseneault, as well as several of her ten sisters and other relatives, sat on the pew-like benches on the opposite side of the courtroom. Sunshine beamed through the tall windows as a lawn mower droned outside.

Heather Harrison, the presiding coroner, explained to the five-person jury and the half-full courtroom the purpose of the inquest. The goal was to determine the facts surrounding the death of René Arseneault and to forge recommendations that might prevent injuries or deaths in similar circumstances. Testimony at the inquest could not be used in future legal proceedings. "A coroner's inquest is not a trial," explained Harrison. "Coroners are not judges, and this is not a court assembled to hear evidence and determine blame or guilt. This inquest is a fact-finding not a fault-finding process." She cautioned the jury to disregard rumors or news reports about the events of June 1, 2002. They should attend instead to the stories to be told over the next four days. James McAvity, a middle-aged lawyer with a confident, chatty courtroom manner, was the legal counsel for the coroner and would prompt memories from each witness.

André Arseneault took the stand first. He described dropping his brother off and returning with his video camera. A TV monitor was wheeled into the middle of the courtroom, so he could replay the twenty-two minutes of raw footage he had shot. His mother left the room before the tape was shown. Jacqueline had never watched the final images of René. She wasn't sure if she would ever want to. From his seat, Jean-Guy stared at the TV but let his eyes drop when his son appeared on the screen and his excited voice filled the courtroom. For several seconds, André's camera lens focused on the sandy trail of his brother's boot prints leading to the water's edge.

The two organizers were called up next, first Jayme Frank, then Sara Vlug. A photo of the couple would appear the next morning on the front page of the local newspaper. In it, they looked oddly relaxed—smiling, in matching sunglasses—as they walked to the courthouse. Their mood at the inquest was more somber. Frank sat in the witness stand, wearing a white shirt and tie. In a quiet voice, he recalled the lead-up to the race, his actions over the course of the day, and the aftermath.

"How did the various people in various places communicate with each other?" asked McAvity.

"We didn't have any communication," Frank admitted. "There is no cell service in Dipper Harbour, so we didn't have that luxury."

What about VHF radios? Too expensive, Frank replied, for a race of that size.

After more than an hour on the stand, Frank described finding Arseneault on the fishing boat, blowing into the boy's mouth, and performing CPR. His calm voice began to quaver. Tears sprang to his eyes. Hunched in her seat, Sara Vlug was also red-faced and weeping.

James McAvity asked: Did the organizers contact the RCMP, the coast guard, St. John Ambulance, or the volunteer fire department?

"No," replied Frank.

Finally, McAvity let the organizer share thoughts about the concept of shared responsibility, a theme that would recur throughout the inquest.

Frank said that when he had first gotten interested in adventure racing, he had trained in sea kayaking and mountain biking. Several times as a racer he made judgment calls about whether to continue through a precarious section of a race. Once, his team pulled up on an island in the middle of a paddling stage because of rough conditions. Another time, they stopped at a rock-climbing stage because they felt the rope section wasn't safe for the less-experienced teams trailing them. It was all part of the blend of physical effort and mental judgment that defined adventure racing—that defines adventure.

"Some people consider it an extreme sport," Frank admitted. "Competitors go in knowing that there are risks involved. They accept that the organizers have taken a certain amount of precaution to present a safe race course. And the racers take their responsibility, saying, 'Well, I'm going out there. I'm competing. I'm going to push myself as hard as I can in this extreme event.' That's the way most people go at it. You're not sure of exactly what you are going to encounter, and sometimes that may be something very spectacular and sometimes it might be something fairly dangerous."

Sara Vlug took the stand and gave her own account of the day, from her pre-race overview to her thoughts one year after the event. She remembered talking to René at the start line and then snapping a photo of him during the running stage. In hindsight, she admitted, mandatory wetsuits would have been a good idea, as would VHF radios for organizers and the safety boat operators. And what about the Zodiac?

"In the past two races, we'd only ever had the one Zodiac," said Vlug. "And that had worked in the past. It had been enough for safety. It had done the proper job in rescuing anyone that needed to be rescued, so going on past experience we felt that this was adequate safety."

McAvity asked her, too, about the issue of shared responsibility. Like her boyfriend, Vlug described a moment from one of their earliest adventure races. They were competing in Virginia. It had rained for five days straight, and they were less than thirty kilometers from the finish—a short mountain-bike stage to go. Both were thoroughly soaked, though, and on the verge of hypothermia. They stopped at a nearby house and asked to use the phone, knowing it meant disqualification. "That was the end of our race and we regretted it," she recalled, "but we can *say* we regretted it."

"It is the organizers' responsibility to have some degree of safety, but it is a shared responsibility," she continued. "It is up to us to provide a certain safety net, but safety nets often have holes in them—and that's pretty obvious."

McAvity asked Vlug for any final thoughts.

"We didn't organize a race this year," she told the courtroom, "and Jayme and I will no longer be organizing races, pretty much because of what happened. We feel we are better racers than organizers and to leave the organizing up to the people who may be better at it than we are."

Over the next three and half days, the jury would hear the story of the race told from different perspectives. Several of the racers had been invited: Mark Campbell, Shawn Amirault, Robin Lang, Peter Hancock, Bob Carreau, Joe Kennedy. The operators of the tandem safety kayak and the Zodiac offered versions of events. Representatives from the Canadian Coast Guard and Canadian Forces outlined the futile efforts of the Joint Rescue Coordination Centre to help with the search. "The only thing that was remarkable—and I'm not sure that it affected in any way the outcome of our search-and-rescue operations—was just the confusion and lack of continuity of a contact with the race organizers," said the coast guard's supervisor for marine search and rescue. "Every time we called, there was somebody different answering the phone, answering machines, that sort of information."

Joe Kennedy, the wildlife biologist, had been one of the last people to see Arseneault alive. Not long after he and his partner had passed the struggling solo paddler, they had decided to land on a beach and pull on warmer clothes before returning to the bay and finishing the race. Kennedy used a metaphor to explain his own take on shared responsibility. "I view an adventure race as the same as if you were planning a highway," he said. "Highway builders can lay out a route and they have to be responsible to ensure the route is safe, but they still can't guarantee that participants—the drivers—are going to be traveling that route safely. You have to be responsible to respond to specific conditions and take actions to protect yourself—be it slowing down on a snowy highway or recognizing bad weather conditions in kayaking."

Peter Hancock had been one of the most vocal critics of the race. The problem, he suggested, was that the organizers were such skilled athletes and kayakers that they seemed to have lost the sense of what it was like to be a beginner—and yet most of the participants in their race were newcomers to serious ocean paddling. "If you had staged this event with a bunch of keen adventure racers, they probably would have had super kayaks, they would have been experienced, they would have had wetsuits or drysuits," he had told me. "God knows, you would have had more support services—at least safety boats that were sturdy enough to stand up to the weather. It would have been a different event. Instead it was a really low-level event with a cheesy little safety boat and participants who were just a bunch of hackers. Everyone was completely ill-suited for kayaking in those conditions." The father of two included himself among the clueless hackers who shouldn't have been on the bay that afternoon.

After the race, Hancock had been bothered by how the media coverage made it sound like Arseneault had been the unlucky victim of a "perfect storm." "There was this perception that suddenly this gale came out of nowhere, and until then it was perfectly safe and everyone was surprised," he said, "and that was not the case." There had been a strong southwest wind on the drive from Bathurst the day before. They had heard a forecast for more of the same. On the bike route, he remembered pedaling into a headwind. And by the time Hancock reached the beach, the surf conditions were rough. Perhaps people thought the weather turned nasty because of how ugly the sea conditions became once they hit the exposed bay and the turmoil of Dry Ledge. And the fast-moving squall line, with its thunder and sheets of rain, added an exclamation mark to the challenges of the day. "It became a convenient thing for some people to fall back on," said Hancock. "You know, 'We can't predict the weather.' It's like the guys on Everest: 'Weather came out of nowhere and we just got caught unaware.' That's not at all what happened. The water was really rough, it was freezing cold, and you had a bunch of hackers out there. And I believe the hackers and the organizers—everyone—should have had the good sense not to go on the water."

At the end of Bob Carreau's testimony, the voice of the father of four wavered as he summed up the feelings of many in attendance. "That's what it is—it's a game, eh," he said. "Nobody's supposed to die. We're supposed to push ourselves. You know, maybe you're gonna fall off your bike and bang your head. But nobody's supposed to die."

The most anticipated moment of the inquest came as Boon Kek took the stand and spoke quietly into the recording microphone. The entire courtroom leaned forward in their seats to catch every word as he described his personal background, his efforts in the race, and the last hour of René Arseneault's life. Until then, his name had been kept out of the newspapers, and Kek had only ever spoken about that endless hour on the bay to a few people: Constable Burke, Jayme Frank and Sara Vlug, a trauma counselor, and, later, to me. His friends understood the rough outline of what had happened but they didn't press the reticent psychology student for details. He had not told his parents. His answers were short, factual, without speculation. He detailed his desperate drift across the mouth of Chance Harbour with Arseneault clinging to the bow of his kayak, and then, for a moment, the flow of his narrative became caught on a particular memory.

"There was once when he tried to climb on top of my kayak and I shouted at him to get down," Kek said. "And I still feel bad for doing so because all he … well, he wanted to get warm. But I shouted at his only attempt at it. What was going through my mind was that if he flipped us both…." His voice trailed off.

When asked by McAvity if he had anything else to add, Kek declined. At the next recess, a small scrum of TV, radio, and newspaper reporters were waiting for him on the courthouse steps.

Bob Mawhinney, captain of the *D.P. Clipper*, and Wayne Nicholls, his first mate, cut out early from a day of lobstering for an appearance at the inquest. Like Peter Hancock, Mawhinney had been troubled by what he had seen. "It didn't need to happen. It could have—and probably should have—been avoided," he had told me. "There's a lot of precautions they could have taken." More rescue craft. Mandatory wetsuits. VHF radios. Numbers on the kayaks. Boats are all required to carry flares, he explained. After their four-year expiry date, the old flares still work fine but need to be replaced to comply with regulations. Even a box of expired hand flares, distributed among the racers, might have been a cheap backup option if their emergency whistles couldn't be heard. "If Boon had a hand flare, that young fellow would've been rescued—someone would have seen it from Chance Harbour."

For the coroner and jury, Mawhinney described finding the two young men in the bay, rushing them to shore, trying to warm them up, and coordinating rescue efforts with the coast guard. And then he repeated his concerns about the race. "It's like me going out fishing in a canoe: I wouldn't do it," he said. "I heard that the Zodiac was twelve, thirteen feet"—in fact, it was smaller—"that's not adequate. People in two kayaks as watch boats. What are you going to do when you get two kayakers in the water? Are they gonna be able to get them out of the water? Inadequate, I would say. Definitely inadequate."

Mawhinney had been taught that if you respect the bay, it would respect you back—to a point. He could appreciate—again, to a point—the urge to explore this quiet coastline in a kayak. "Summertime, it's beautiful there, definitely is," he agreed. "But you have to pay heed. Conditions change in a half hour. Conditions were probably fine when they left the beach, I don't doubt that in the least. But just this week, we're coming home by the same area, and I said, 'Look, look at that, Wayne. Same conditions.' In the harbor, flat calm almost. Got out around the corner, and the sea's building up so. At particular times it's not a perfect area, no, with the ledges and tide rips and tide. But if I was a kayaker and wanted to go on a beautiful, scenic paddle, there's no better place."

Not every question found a satisfying answer. Several witnesses had described the safety Zodiac—its rescue of Mark Campbell, its struggles in the sea conditions, its failure to return to the bay. Jason Stanley, the former employee of Eastern Outdoors, told the courtroom that both he and Owen Vlug, the Zodiac's other occupant, had felt too cold and scared to set out again. Jayme Frank and Sara Vlug described a similar conversation with the two young men. Owen Vlug, however, testified that he had been willing to go back on the water and look for racers, but he couldn't do it alone, once Stanley had refused.

"Without a second person, you couldn't get off the beach," explained Vlug, when pressed by McAvity.

"Did you want to go back out?"

"Did I want to? I would have gone back out."

"Did you *want* to go back out?" the lawyer repeated.

"No," said Owen Vlug. "I *had* to go back out. That was the job."

"There were no other people to take his place."

"No, there wasn't."

The two people who did leave from McLaughlins Cove to search for missing racers, after the kayak section had been canceled, never appeared at the inquest. Bob Vlug, the sponsor of the event, and his race partner, Malcolm Brett, declined the coroner's requests to give testimony.

Finally, Dr. Marek Godlewski, the regional pathologist, described the stages in René Arseneault's slow death from hypothermia. Once in the water, his hypothalamus—the brain's thermostat—would have reacted by constricting warm blood from reaching his body's cooling skin and by amping up heat production at the cellular level. When neither of those mechanisms staunched the loss of heat and his core temperature began to drop, Arseneault's shivering response would have kicked in. As his temperature fell to 32°C, the metabolism of his brain would have slowed and brought on cold narcolepsy. A clouding of consciousness, a slurring of speech, even hallucinations—who knows what visions came to him in the last moments of his life. Finally, anywhere below 30°C, he would have blacked out entirely. Circulation, breathing, the beating of the heart—all would have diminished. Less oxygen could reach his brain. The rhythm of his frozen heart would begin to stumble, skipping beats, losing coordination, until it slipped into what cardiologists call ventricular fibrillation—a helpless spasming of the heart's muscles that one medical textbook compared metaphorically to a writhing sack of worms. Death would come quickly, admitted Dr. Godlewski, unless the heart's beat could be restored with CPR, medication, or a defibrillator. After even a few minutes without a pulse, Arseneault's brain would have been irreversibly damaged.

The jury retired before noon on the fourth day to consider recommendations. "You may not express any conclusion of civil or criminal responsibility," the coroner reminded the five jurors, "and you are prohibited from naming any person or persons responsible for any act or omission that may have contributed to the death of René Arseneault." Three hours later, they returned from the recess. The jury's forewoman read the findings aloud. They confirmed that Arseneault had met his death as a result of hypothermia from accidental prolonged exposure in the Bay of Fundy—hardly a surprise. They offered nine specific recommendations: that participants in ocean kayak races demonstrate an acceptable level of experience; that organizers notify authorities about events beforehand; that an adequate communication system be available at races; that marine weather forecasts be given to participants; that every racer wear a checklisted race number; that flares be supplied with each kayak; that strong consideration be given to wearing wetsuits for kayak sections of races; that waterproof skirts be strongly considered, too; and, finally, that "there should be more awareness of a shared responsibility between the organizers and participants." The coroner thanked the jury and added one recommendation of her own: that a list of race participants be readily available to emergency personnel.

The recommendations were only that—non-binding suggestions to be distributed to government agencies, media outlets, and relevant organizations. There was no umbrella agency in Canada to oversee the sport, but the inquest had learned that discussions were under way among race organizers to start one. The recommendations would be followed up by this group. In 2005, two years after the inquest, the Canadian Adventure Racing Association was founded and soon developed a set of safety guidelines for race organizers. The same year, the Lifesaving Society published the *Preparation Guide for Boating Event*, which expanded on many of the inquest's recommendations and singled out "triathlon events involving a water portion" and "kayaking on the Bay of Fundy" as activities in need of careful oversight.

As the inquest dispersed, a pocket of newspaper reporters and TV journalists huddled around the Arseneault family on the steps of the courthouse. Jacqueline praised the work of the jury. "These are not costly measures," she said. "We just hope that any other participants or kayakers be aware of the dangers and educate themselves. And think about the fact that this could be your son or brother." She looked relaxed for the first time in months. "I'm satisfied," she announced to the reporters. "A closure has come over me in a sense."

TWENTY-SIX

The Last Breath

O nce I had obtained security clearance, Dr. Peter Tikuisis led me
across the grounds and through the hallways of Defence
Research and Development Canada, a military science complex
north of Toronto, near the old Downsview airport. For sixty-seven
years, the DRDC (founded by Sir Frederick Banting, the discoverer
of insulin, and previously known as the Defence and Civil Institute of
Environmental Medicine) has been a global leader in sleuthing out
how extreme environments affect the human body and brain. In
immersion tanks, swimming pools, and environmental simulators,
researchers once submitted thousands of soldiers, sailors, and airmen
to frigid dunks and miserable chills. Many of the world's top cold
researchers (including Dr. Chris Brooks of Survival Systems) had
worked at or collaborated with the institute's scientists. Today, the
facility's cold-weather and cold-water labs have largely been
shuttered, sold for parts, or mothballed as legacy projects. The

Department of National Defence has more pressing research needs, and the armed forces' top brass now feel they have learned everything they need to know about equipping their soldiers to fight a cold war.

"For any question they might have," said Dr. Tikuisis, a senior scientist at the DRDC, with a measure of pride, "we could probably give them a ninety-five percent solution."

One of the most useful tools to emerge from these chilly experiments can be housed on a single computer. Dr. Tikuisis sat me down in front of one and booted up the software. On the screen, a graphical window appeared that looked like any database, a system to track courier packages perhaps or a warehouse's inventory. The sequence of fields, clickable buttons, and pull-down menus asked for personal details—age, gender, height, weight, body fat, even "garment ensemble"—that read, at first, like an online dating service. That impression was dispelled by the remaining rows: fatigue, immersion, wetness, relative humidity, wind speed, air temperature, water temperature, sea state. Hidden behind this interface were years of data culled from incident reports, inquests, and scientific studies, all joined by complex mathematical algorithms that Dr. Tikuisis and his colleagues had meticulously compiled. In a few key strokes, the Cold Exposure Survival Model could calculate how hypothermia will affect anyone exposed to cold water or air.

Did it work? "It's done a decent job," admitted Dr. Tikuisis.

He didn't have to be so modest. The CESM delivers such accurate survival estimates that the Department of National Defence sold the software, through a private company, to agencies around the world. The American, French, and Australian coast guards all use it. After Danish search-and-rescue teams had underestimated the survival time of a victim during a boating accident, a subsequent inquiry discovered that the Canadian-made CESM could have provided a more accurate prediction. The program is now bundled into standard search-and-rescue software packages and remains the best tool anywhere to predict what our bodies will do when exposed to the cold.

Dr. Tikuisis typed in numbers from a few case studies, clicked the run model button, and showed me the results. In the program's group mode, the CESM can estimate how many people aboard a capsized vessel or downed aircraft will survive for how long. (The computer model had been inspired in part by the crash landing of a Canadian Forces plane on Ellesmere Island in 1991, after which five personnel died of hypothermia, so the software was designed to consider both land and sea emergencies.) In the individual mode, it accepts data for a single person and then calculates two key markers: functional time and survival time. The first number suggests how long it will be before a person's core temperature drops below 34°C, when muscles become numb, speech slurred, and thinking slowed, and the victim is essentially rendered helpless to cooperate in a rescue effort. Survival time, a higher number, ticks down the hours and minutes that search-and-rescuers have to find a missing person before the body's temperature dips to 28°C. Past that point, the victim will be mentally and physically incapacitated, and most likely unconscious. Unless there is an intervention, Dr. Tikuisis added, the person will soon die.

"So that brings us to your case ..."

Three years after the inquest, I had first heard about Dr. Tikuisis's computer program. Before then, I had read research papers and textbook chapters that graphed survival times for hypothermia, with water temperature along one axis and hours of predicted life down another. Experts acknowledged these tables were rough estimates at best. Actual times of death differed significantly depending on age, body mass, clothing, fatigue—variables the CESM corrected for—as well as more complex factors that the software could not capture, such as whether victims were good shiverers or fast coolers, and deaths from cold shock or swimming failure. Even my most pessimistic readings of these graphs, however, suggested that death by hypothermia after an hour's immersion in 9°C water, for a young man in good health with no previous heart conditions, was highly unlikely. Not impossible. Just on the far end of the probability curve.

At the inquest, the pathologist had outlined the basics of death by exposure in his autopsy. No hypothermia experts had been called to testify, however, and the issue of precisely how Arseneault had died had been glossed over. An opportunity had been missed to understand better the complex dangers of cold-water immersion.

Dr. Tikuisis entered Arseneault's age (twenty-two), weight (one-hundred-seventy pounds), height (five foot eight), and other information into the computer. Then we added the climatological data from the Bay of Fundy for June 1, 2002, as recorded by Environment Canada and then reported at the inquest: water temperature (9°C), air temperature (11°C), average wind speed (thirty kilometers per hour), and sea state (definitely "heavy"). We ran the program.

The first results surprised us, even despite my earlier readings of the hypothermia charts and records. According to the CESM, Arseneault should have had a functional time of more than two and half hours and a survival time of nearly five hours, far longer than the hour or so he had drifted in the water before being picked up. We adjusted the variables again. Boon Kek had said that Arseneault looked fatigued, after nearly six hours of running, cycling, and paddling, so we selected "exhausted" rather than "tired." We dropped the body mass index to twelve percent, knowing how lean and fit the young man was. We tweaked the variables to consider how cold he must have been already—from launching through the surf, from the crashing waves, from the leaky spray skirt, from his initial capsize— even before his kayak went over for a second time. Still, the lowest result the CESM spat out was a functional time of an hour and fifteen minutes. That was close to the point at which Arseneault had become slurry and then semi-conscious, and Boon Kek had to grab hold of his life vest. The survival time, though, was more than three hours. According to the computer, Arseneault should not have been dead. Not after a single hour in the bay. Not in his condition.

"This person did not die from hypothermia," said Dr. Tikuisis.

So why hadn't René Arseneault made it home alive?

An hour after my first meeting with Dr. John Hayward, the retired biology professor already wanted to stick a thermometer into my brain to measure how my gray matter reacted to an ice-cream headache. He promised he would perform the same procedure on his own noggin. He had never done anything to his human guinea pigs, he explained, that he hadn't first tested on his own willing flesh. Officially, Dr. Hayward had hung up his lab coat fifteen years ago.

However, he still had a few questions that he wanted to answer—and he still had the experimental equipment in the shed behind his log home in Saanich, British Columbia. As one of the world's leading experts in cold-water immersion, the emeritus professor at the University of Victoria had cracked many of hypothermia's major mysteries. And yet he never felt satisfied that the dangers of cold water and the proper treatment for hypothermia had reached a wide enough audience. Every day, people died—unnecessarily, in his view—with their heads still out of the water.

Dr. Hayward hadn't planned to spend his career making students cold. As a Ph.D. researcher at the University of British Columbia, and a post-doc at the University of Alberta and Harvard Medical School, he had focused his lab work on the role of brown fat in the hibernation of bats. Three years into his tenure at the University of Victoria, a colleague who taught physiology in the department of physical education approached him with a tragic case study. A friend of the phys-ed professor was said to have drowned in the channel of Pacific Ocean between Vancouver Island and Washington State. The puzzle: his friend had been wearing a life jacket. (Dr. Hayward rarely used the term "life jacket" anymore, because if a safety device didn't remove victims from cold water, it didn't deserve the name.) The two men discovered there was little academic literature about cold-water immersion. "Even at that stage in North America," recalled Hayward, "there was no real understanding of hypothermia." A foundation of knowledge had been laid during World War Two (including the contentious Dachau data) and followed up by a few American and British scientists. Still, an understanding of what happened to a body as it cooled remained largely a blank slate.

The University of Victoria pair were joined by another phys-ed professor who was curious about the physiology of swimming. Without funding for an environmental laboratory, the trio of scientists arranged passage aboard coast guard research boats and dropped subjects overboard into the Strait of Juan de Fuca. They were allowed to cool volunteers down to 35°C, the lowest temperature any ethics committee would agree to. The three colleagues always took the first dip. Dr. Hayward pushed his body into mild hypothermia more than a hundred times (while tall and lean, he proved to be a "good shiverer"), and his wife would sometimes join the team to fill the quota of test subjects. Once word of the experiments spread across campus, they rarely lacked undergraduate guinea pigs. (That the experiments often involved a fifteen-centimeter rectal thermometer may have surprised some students.)

"Even though it was a miserable thing to be in the Strait of Juan de Fuca for an hour, it was an adventure in their lives—and even better, an adventure at university," said Dr. Hayward. "They could see it was going to have benefits. They ended up 'enjoying' it for the cause."

The researchers probed the effects of hypothermia from every angle. They tested the metabolic response of the human body and learned the importance of shivering. They compared how gender, age, waves, and body mass affect temperature loss. They gauged the effectiveness of twenty-three different survival suits and evaluated the success rates of various resuscitation methods. Over the years, Dr. Hayward published dozens of academic papers, penned safety brochures and textbook chapters, lectured to the RCMP and Canadian Coast Guard, and testified at coroners' inquests and public-safety meetings across Canada (including after the Lake Timiskaming tragedy). His reputation extended around the world.

Dr. Hayward wanted more than answers. He wanted solutions. He designed and patented devices to stave off or treat hypothermia. Most famously, he tweaked the design of a floater suit to create a light, affordable, fashionable (at least for 1975) sailor's jacket that didn't need to be stowed away like the heavier suits used by commercial mariners. "We were trying to find ways for the Average Joe to wear the same thing to the hockey game and then go out on the water with it on," explained Dr. Hayward. In an emergency, a reflective hood covered a person's head, the jacket kept body heat from escaping at the neck, underarms, and sides, and a neoprene flap insulated the groin by transforming into a pair of thermal shorts, which looked like a yodeler's knickers. The Thermofloat jacket doubled potential survival times for hypothermia victims, and the Canadian Coast Guard fielded testimonials from people who said it had saved their lives. Profits from the jacket earned more than all other university patents combined.

Not every one of Dr. Hayward's inventions made such a splash. At his kitchen table, he pulled from the back pocket of a PFD a neatly folded device called the Sea-Seat. The square meter of polyurethane-coated nylon could be inflated with sixty puffs into an improvised life raft, like a harem cushion with a button center. Capsized paddlers could ride the waves on it, while bilging out a flooded kayak or awaiting a rescue. It would have certainly made a difference to Boon Kek or René Arseneault. When it was released in 1986, Dr. Hayward's Sea-Seat received positive reviews in kayaking publications, and yet—like Tim Ingram's Sea Wings—the safety device never received federal government approval and never took off among sailors or paddlers.

Dr. Hayward collaborated frequently in the past with Dr. Gordon Giesbrecht, a phys-ed professor at the University of Manitoba and now the leading cold researcher in Canada, perhaps the world. Dr. Giesbrecht was a part-time polar explorer whose media savvy and unorthodox methods (injecting his body with ice water, for instance) had earned him the nickname of Professor Popsicle. In 2006, the two men published a paper in the *Wilderness and Environmental Medicine Journal* that Dr. Hayward thought I might find interesting. Ethics committees still only allowed most cold researchers to chill subjects to 35°C, the border of mild hypothermia. Therefore, little could be known about what really happens to the human body when it hits 30°C and below. Dr. Hayward has long known of one tragic episode that still haunts the university where he did most of his research. The accident could supply a nearly complete portrait of the descent into hypothermia for a young athlete—from the physical exertions of racing, through the first shock of the cold, to the brink of death and beyond.

On January 15, 1988, around four in the afternoon, varsity rowers from the University of Victoria launched several boats. They were part of an elite program that often produced Olympic-caliber male and female athletes (eventually including several gold medalists). Elk Lake, the team's training area, is a fat smile of freshwater three kilometers long. At its widest, the lake stretches a kilometer and a half across, from the forested western edge to its eastern shore, which rubs shoulders with the main highway into the city. Visitors arriving from the airport or the ferry terminal can often spot university or national crews sculling across the lake. That afternoon, rowing coach Lorna Ferguson fired up the outboard on her fourteen-foot aluminum launch and then escorted three groups of rowers for a short practice. Two sixty-foot shells, the *Doug White* and the *Howard Petch*, each held eight well-muscled rowers and a jockey-sized coxswain. The third, smaller boat was rowed by a crew of two.

Rowers practice in Victoria year-round, as winter air temperatures rarely dip below freezing. That afternoon, the thermometer hovered near 7°C, and the wind added a chop to the lake. The two larger shells began to buck in the rough water. Coach Ferguson ordered the nine-person crews back across the lake to the boathouse, and then checked on the smaller boat. The two rowers were already close to shore, so she returned to help her other crews. The coach found the *Doug White* halfway across Elk Lake. The other sixty-foot shell was nowhere to be seen. It was nearly 5:00 p.m., darkness was falling, and the storm was sharpening its teeth. Winds of thirty kilometers per hour, with gusts hitting eighty, kicked up standing waves and slowed even the progress of the motorized launch. The narrow, lightweight body of a rowing scull is far more easily tipped than even a single-person sea kayak. Crews learn to row in synchronicity to maintain the precarious center of gravity. A sudden shift in weight or a miscue with an oar (what rowers call "catching a crab") can send the whole team sprawling into the water. And the boats aren't designed for rough conditions.

The waves had proven too tricky for the crew of the *Howard Petch*. Coach Ferguson discovered the student athletes in the water, circling the swamped shell. She pulled all nine shivering rowers into her own small boat, aimed for shore, and almost made it. The heavily weighted launch filled with water, swamped, and overturned as the rowers jumped out and swam to land. From a nearby house, they called the police. It had been nearly half an hour since coach Ferguson had seen the crew of the *Doug White* rowing in the direction of the boathouse. They must have made it there by now.

They hadn't. Like the rowers in the *Howard Petch*, the waves and wind had flipped the *Doug White* and pitched its crew into the 4°C water, colder than the Bay of Fundy in June. (At dawn the next morning, Dr. Hayward took the temperature of the lake, not far from his own log house.) Typical for rowing practice, life jackets had neither been worn nor stored on the boat, not that a racing shell had much space for carry-on luggage. The nine rowers were dressed only in training garb: T-shirts, sweatpants, sweaters, toques, light jackets. There was no way they could right the scull, empty the boat of water, and get back into it. Instead, as meter-high waves doused their heads, they spread out along the boat's length and held on to the hull and oars. They shouted into the dusk for help. On shore, eight minutes after first calling the authorities, their coach heard their cries and realized that the other boat had gone over, too. She immediately alerted the police of the emergency.

The rowers held on to the overturned shell and tried to keep from losing track of each other in the gloaming dusk. "We believed that by just hanging on to the boat and kicking lightly," one athlete would recall, "that we would stay warm without sinking the boat." The cold water soon numbed their fingers and sapped their strength, and their kicking likely quickened the loss of heat through swimming failure. Several times, rowers became separated from the boat and teammates swam to retrieve them. At 5:36 p.m., fire department rescuers launched a Zodiac and scoured the area where the *Doug White* had last been spotted. In the dark, they could see little more than wind-whipped whitecaps. Even on the small lake, the rescuers wouldn't find the rowers for another thirty minutes, not until 6:00 p.m., nearly an hour after the crew had capsized. Just as the rescue boat arrived, nineteen-year-old Gareth Lineen could hold on no longer and disappeared from the overturned shell. (Nine days later, Navy divers would pull his body from Elk Lake.) The rescuers struggled to get the remaining rowers into the Zodiac. Another fourteen-foot aluminum rescue boat arrived and helped to retrieve the crew members. All the rowers were nearly incapacitated by the cold. Three were on the verge of unconsciousness. They were rushed to shore, still thirteen minutes away, and in that time—exposed to the wind and cold air—the three most hypothermic rowers (who were also the leanest and smallest) stopped shivering and lost consciousness. They were taken by ambulance to a nearby hospital and treated with a variety of rewarming methods. All three young men had dropped in core temperature to 28°C or less; one measured as low as 23.4°C. Two of the rowers were rewarmed back to consciousness and recovered fully. Despite working on him for more than two hours, emergency room physicians could not restore a pulse to nineteen-year-old Darryl Smith.

The death of two young varsity athletes shocked the city and the campus. Rowing was supposed to be strenuous but never dangerous. The fatal accident occurred not on a wild remote river or open ocean, but on a small suburban lake. One survivor remembered the flash of car headlights along the adjacent highway, as he and his teammates clung to the boat in the dark. Safe ground had looked so close. In the end, for two of the nine rowers, the line between survival and death had been the slimmest of divides. A four-day inquest heard testimony from forty-two witnesses and delivered eighteen safety recommendations to the university's rowing program and the city's emergency services. These suggestions included designing a personal flotation device that could be used by rowers and providing better training in the treatment of hypothermia.

Eighteen years after the incident, Hayward and Giesbrecht tried to understand why some of the rowers had succumbed more swiftly than others. They published their conclusions in a paper titled "Problems and Complications with Cold-Water Rescue." Body size, as they predicted, had made a difference in the Elk Lake incident. Most of the heavier rowers fared better and didn't lapse into unconsciousness. Lineen, who lost his grip of the boat and drowned as help arrived, seemed to be an exception. He was one of the largest of the crew. Still, as both researchers knew, while body fat might insulate the core, skin temperature is what determines such neuromuscular factors as hand strength and dexterity. Cold can quickly make even the biggest victim ham-fisted and fumble-thumbed, with lethal results.

Lineen's death might have been an example of what researchers call "circum-rescue collapse." The phrase refers to the once-puzzling phenomenon of seemingly alert victims suddenly dying immediately before, during, or after a rescue. Dr. Chris Brooks had told me how German rescuers during the Second World War had reached downed pilots and U-boat sailors in the cold waters of the North Atlantic and found some of them alive and conscious. However, many of these survivors died after being pulled from the water, sometimes even hours later. One theory now speculates that knowing rescuers are near can have a psychosomatic effect on a victim. The brain relaxes and decreases the body's sympathetic tone, the mechanism that controls our fight-or-flight response. Adrenaline secretions drop off and, with them, heart rate and blood pressure. In severely cold victims, this relaxation may be enough to cause an already cold-slowed heart to lapse into an irregular rhythm or stop entirely. Simply hearing the words, "Hold on, someone's coming!" might be enough to kill you.

The eight remaining rowers had been conscious when they were pulled from the water. During the thirteen-minute boat ride to shore, three more fell unconscious. Dr. Hayward realized it was a textbook instance of "post-rescue collapse," part of the same phenomenon that had befuddled German rescuers during the war. Even after hypothermic victims are pulled from the water and treated with blankets and heat sources, the colder shell of external tissue will continue to conduct heat away from their bodies' cores. Over the next half hour or so, internal temperatures can decline another degree or two before starting to rewarm. Scientists call this effect "after-drop."

"Your best chance is to get warm moist air into the roof of the mouth and the brain-stem," explained Dr. Hayward, who had invented several portable devices that allowed emergency first responders to do just that. "The hypothalamus is the first place to stop after-drop. When it gets cold, everything else gets cold."

Fortunately for two of the hypothermic rowers, they were rushed via heated ambulance to a hospital within twenty minutes. One rower had regained consciousness by then and recovered fully after a brief spell of amnesia. His teammate arrived with a body temperature of 25°C, so low that his heart's rhythm, already slowed to forty beats per minute, could be stopped by the slightest disturbance. Emergency staff wedged heat packs around his neck, armpits, and groin, filled his airway and lungs with 43°C air, and started a gastric lavage and bladder irrigation to cycle warm fluids deep into his body. After eighty minutes, he had warmed back up to 30°C. Twenty minutes later, he was awake and talking.

Darryl Smith wasn't so lucky. When pulled from the water, he not only lost consciousness but also his pulse. CPR and electrical defibrillation by paramedics couldn't restore it. Emergency-room doctors added heat packs, warm blankets, hot-air inhalation, and warm saline solution shot directly into his jugular vein. They worked to restore a heart beat for more than two hours, as Smith's body temperature rose from a low of 23.4°C until nearly 32°C. Only then did they give up.

What makes Smith's death so tragic is that the act of getting rescued likely stopped his heart. As the rowers floated in the 4°C water, their bodies would have been subject to what's called "hydrostatic squeeze." The subtle pressure of the lake water applied an equal force against their bodies (and their circulatory systems) from toes to neck. Their cooling blood still grew more viscous and harder to pump, while the vessels and muscles supporting their arteries became less supple and elastic. If they had been on land, the rowers' blood pressures would have dropped precipitously. But in the water, hydrostatic squeeze helped to coax blood back toward their cores. (It works in the same way as an anti-G suit, another Canadian invention, which keeps a jet fighter pilot from passing out during high-G turns by squeezing the blood that pools in the legs up to the heart.) When rescuers arrived and lifted the rowers vertically into the safety boat, however, the hypothermic students lost the benefit of the water's hydrostatic squeeze. The abrupt press of gravity caused a massive drop in blood pressure—in one case, enough for the heart's pacemaker to lose its beat. René Arseneault would have been in the same situation. His blood pressure would have been balanced by the hydrostatic pressure of the Bay of Fundy until he was lifted vertically into the lobster boat.

In World War Two, *Wehrmacht* rescuers learned to use floating nets, ringed with Champagne corks taken from occupied France, to draw victims out of the North Sea and English Channel in a horizontal position. It worked. More downed pilots survived. Coast guard lifeboatmen and Navy rescue swimmers around the world are now trained to perform cold-water extractions with the same care. The *Courtenay Bay* and other coast guard cutters come equipped with a winching mechanism for these situations. Rescuers can position the boat beside a victim, lower a hinged carpet of open-faced black plastic squares (it looks like a giant bathtub mat), and then slide the floating victim, conscious or otherwise, into this cradle. The supine person can then be lifted and rolled horizontally onto the deck of the boat to avoid the rough handling or sudden drop in blood pressure that can cause cardiac arrest. Had the *Courtenay Bay* been able to reach the two missing kayakers in time, coast guard personnel would have deployed this winch-and-pulley system to take René Arseneault aboard. It might have been enough to save his life.

Even if they had known about the phenomenon of post-rescue collapse, Bob Mawhinney and his crew had little option but to haul both boys onto the stern of the *D.P. Clipper* by their arms and life jackets, their feet hanging in the water. Elaine Small, the nurse on the scene, had later told her brother-in-law that Arseneault was in all likelihood dead by the time Mawhinney's boat reached the wharf. She was probably right. Like Darryl Smith, René Arseneault had seemed close to safety when the lobster boat arrived to end his ordeal, and yet he didn't survive his own rescue. Doctors Hayward, Tikuisis, and Brooks all agreed. His death seemed a classic case of post-rescue collapse.

That final breath, of course, came only at the end of a long sequence of actions and inactions, decisions and miscues—each minor on its own perhaps—that eventually added up to the fatal sum. If any one of these variables had been different, Arseneault might still be alive. What if he had chosen to race with a friend in a stable tandem kayak? What if the paddling section had been first rather than last? What if the organizers—or the racers—had paid heed to the marine weather forecast for that afternoon? What if the kayaks had been equipped with race numbers, flares, spray skirts that didn't leak, Tim Ingram's Sea Wings, or Dr. Hayward's Sea-Seat? What if Arseneault hadn't been so driven to finish at all costs, especially after capsizing once already? What if there had been more safety boats? What if the

Canadian Coast Guard, the RCMP, the Musquash fire crew, or even the local fishing fleet had been alerted to the race *before* it had started to go wrong? And what if we didn't believe—hadn't been duped by reality TV and the merchants of extreme—that real adventure can be safely bought and sold off the shelf? That we can have the profound transformation of a true wilderness experience without any of the risks?

Those were speculations the family and friends of René Arseneault didn't like to consider. The answers weren't easy and didn't change anything. The simple fact remained: A young man had headed out that morning, his body electric with the prospect of physical challenge, the kind of competitive obstacles he had sought since he was a restless young boy and that he had always overcome. He had found a new antagonist out on the Bay of Fundy, and it had been a greater force than he had ever reckoned. He had fought hard to continue, to finish the race, but the wind and the waves and the fatal tide had proven too much. He had grown frustrated and tired and worried and wanted to quit—something few who knew him could imagine him ever admitting. Finally, clinging to a stranger amid a furious sea, all he had hoped for was to get home again.

TWENTY-SEVEN

The Trials

In the end, the answers from the inquest were not enough. The closure that Jacqueline Arseneault had felt at the end of the coroner's investigation proved to be fleeting. She wanted more. She wanted an apology. She wanted to hear the organizers admit that they had messed up. She wanted recompense for her family's pain. She wanted, most of all, justice for her son.

On May 21, 2004, the Arseneault family submitted a notice of claim in the Court of Queen's Bench of New Brunswick, ten days before the statute of limitations was to expire for a civil suit arising from the Fundy race. The claim launched legal proceedings against Sara Vlug, Jayme Frank, and Bob and Deanna Vlug, as well as Eastern Outdoors and the other corporate titles under which the Vlug family did business. In it, the Arseneaults asked that their family be reimbursed for damages suffered from loss of companionship, guidance, care, and valuable services, as well as for grief and funeral expenses. They also asked for punitive damages. The claim argued that Jayme Frank and the Vlugs, as organizers and sponsors of the race, owed a duty of care to all the participants and failed that duty through negligence in the conduct of the competition. The legal suit cataloged a long list of alleged failures: a failure to provide reasonable training and instruction for the sea-kayaking stage; a failure to explain to René the risks to which he would be exposed; a failure to stop the race and bring the competitors back to shore once the dangerous sea conditions were apparent; a failure to notify emergency authorities about the race; a failure to provide a communication system; a failure to let racers know the day's marine forecast; a failure to assign numbers to participants that would correspond to a list; a failure to equip each kayak with a flare or other warning device; a failure to demand that participants wear wetsuits; a failure to supply sufficient and appropriate rescue boats. "The Defendants' negligence was so extreme and cumulative," stated the Arseneaults' claim, "that it constitutes gross negligence under the law."

Negligence—including gross and criminal negligence—is a tricky legal concept that falls within the general purview of tort law. From the Latin root for "crooked," a tort refers simply to a civil wrong other than a breach of contract. Tort law focuses on compensation for fault-based accidents, injuries, and deaths. It is a major worry for outdoor guides, event organizers, wilderness educators, and anyone else who stewards clients into unpredictable natural environments. To avoid expensive lawsuits from accidents in the field, almost every outfitter in North America insists that clients first read and sign a liability waiver. In such a release, a person contracts away any right to legal redress from the operator in the case of accidental injury or death, even if it was caused by negligence. (Waivers are neither valid nor used outside of Canada, the United States, and Australia.)

All the competitors at the Fundy race had read, or at least scanned, and signed a one-page document titled "Participant Agreement, Release, and Acknowledgement of Risk." Few could remember the details of this waiver. In the past, most had scribbled their names beneath dozens of nearly identical pages of fine print. Many believed—wrongly—that waivers aren't worth the paper they're printed on, and that outfitters use the legal mumbo-jumbo to scare off frivolous lawsuits from clumsy competitors. In fact, well-composed liability releases have held up as defenses against negligence (though not criminal negligence) in North American courts, but not without some controversy. Increasingly, however, courts have applied a stricter interpretation of the law. Waivers must be clearly and specifically written, brought to the attention of participants, and signed after careful consideration rather than in the heat of the moment before a trip or a race. And they don't apply to anyone under the age of eighteen, not even if parents or guardians signed the waiver.

After 1996, the definitive judgment seemed to have been handed down in a lawsuit against Canadian Mountain Holidays, a British Columbia heli-skiing company. The case worked its way up to a six-month trial at the Supreme Court of British Columbia after an avalanche accident in 1991. Nine clients died, and the widow of a wealthy Mexican businessman sued for negligence. Despite her husband's limited English, the presiding judge ruled that he had every opportunity to understand the waiver he had signed and that, since there was no evidence of gross negligence, it should stand as legally binding. If this precedent held, the waiver used at the Fundy race should protect the organizers from a lawsuit, too.

The Arseneaults' lawyers, however, had found a potential loophole in the waiver defense. In 2001, the Canadian government had passed the Marine Liability Act. The legislation was aimed at large cargo vessels, cruise ships, and other commercial operators, yet the act was worded such that kayak and canoe outfitters might fall within its definitions. The act limited the amount that a company could be sued for loss of life or injury to a client aboard one of its vessels (at a maximum of approximately three hundred thousand dollars). The act also ruled that boat owners could no longer use waivers. Even before the Fundy tragedy, outfitters and outdoor educators had been in a panic about the Marine Liability Act. For adventure sports, the loss of waiver protection could mean another spike in insurance premiums. Insurers might balk entirely at underwriting outdoor activities without this legal safety net. The Fundy Multi-Sport Race case would likely be one of the first tests of the new act. The legal teams on both sides hunkered down to puzzle over precedents and the ramifications of the new law.

The Vlug family's lawyers delayed responding to the statement of claim for nearly two years until February 13, 2006. During that period, Bob Vlug had dissolved two of the companies that he owned and that had been named in the original suit, Fundy Yachts Sales and Charters and Eastern Outdoors (2002) Inc. In their statement of defense, the Vlugs and Jayme Frank denied most of the allegations in the original lawsuit. They argued that René had assumed all risks associated with the event and that, as organizers, they had "met or exceeded any duty of care on them with respect to reasonable precautions taken for the safety of the participants."

As rumors about the lawsuit circulated, participants, adventure racers, and local residents were divided in their opinions. Friends of the organizers and colleagues on the adventure-racing circuit were disappointed that the Arseneault family would turn to the courts to seek retribution for an accident that some observers considered largely the result of René's own impetuousness. (Several even suggested to me that Arseneault might have been accidentally smothered by the raingear and life jackets used to warm him on the *D.P. Clipper*.)

There were few precedents on which to decide the suit, and those that existed didn't fully reflect the Fundy race. How much risk do you assume when you sign up for an adventure, even one organized and advertised for beginners? What duty of care do organizers of such a race have to the participants, and how does it differ from teachers taking students on an outing or a hired guide leading a kayak tour? A judge or jury would have to apply Solomonic wisdom to determine contributory negligence—precisely how much René Arseneault was at fault for his own death. The last hours of his life would be parsed under a legal microscope until a judge could split a percentage of blame between the dead racer and the living organizers. This ratio would then be used to apportion any monetary award. Different courts could interpret the precedents and ratios of blame in strikingly different ways. And there had never been a civil suit against an adventure race's organizer. Nobody dared guess the outcome of the Fundy Multi-Sport Race case. It would be several years before the lawsuit worked its way through the courts. Any decision was likely to be appealed. Both families dug in for what could be a long and expensive legal siege.

Two years after filing the lawsuit, Jacqueline Arseneault began to worry that it was sapping energy and money better spent on her three remaining sons. With the focus on monetary awards and legal details, she feared her family might lose sight of why they were suing the organizers in René's name. "It takes over your life," she told friends. "It becomes an obsession. You're not functioning. You're in limbo." By the fall of 2006, more than four years after her son's death, Jacqueline considered abandoning the suit. Then, one afternoon, she walked into the grocery store where René had worked. A table had been set up to raise money for kids who couldn't afford sports fees and equipment. René, she thought, would have admired such an athletic-minded charity. Behind the booth was a familiar face, Constable Norman Mackay, the Rothesay police officer who had delivered the terrible news and who had led the funeral procession. They exchanged a few pleasantries and then talked about the race.

"That should have never happened," the constable told her, shaking his head. "It should never have happened."

That encounter restored her faith in the slow progress of the lawsuit. She talked again with Jean-Guy, her ex-husband, who had only grown more angry and determined since the inquest. She asked if they ought to continue the lawsuit. "I'll go to my grave, Jacquie, but I'm not giving up," he said. "I don't care how long it takes and how much money it takes." The Arseneaults asked their lawyer why there had been so many delays, why they didn't hear from his office for months at a stretch. Was the incident going to be forgotten and nothing learned from it? Had René's file been buried in a cabinet, abandoned for more promising cases? Their lawyer assured them that justice, while slow, would be served. "There isn't a week that goes by that I don't think about his file," he said. "It sits right here on my desk." They saw the folder. It was as fat as a phonebook with documents. They agreed to press on.

By then, the other Arseneault boys were finding their ways in their lives. Denis had graduated from university and moved to Toronto, where he was pursuing a successful marketing career. Guy, the youngest, rarely mentioned René's name. At first, he had seemed evasive and moody—not exactly unusual for a teenager—but Jacqueline worried he was into booze and drugs, that he didn't want to face up to the loss of his brother. After graduation, Guy moved to Fredericton and met a young woman who helped him find focus again. He still never spoke about his brother to his mom, but he had begun to tell his girlfriend stories from his boyhood and talk proudly about all that René had taught him.

André still worked as a producer for the local cable channel. He had moved out of his mother's basement and bought a house in nearby Quispamsis with his girlfriend. He had always seemed the most settled of the boys, so his turn toward the domestic didn't surprise his mother. One day, Jacqueline dropped by André's new house while he and his girlfriend were running errands. She opened the shed in the backyard, and her breath caught in her throat. There, stacked along the wall, were a pair of plastic kayaks. She had told all her sons that she never wanted them to go kayaking, not after what happened to René, that she wanted nothing to do with the sport or the bay. As she stood there, a truck rolled into the driveway. André sheepishly approached her.

"I'm sorry, mom, I meant to tell you before," he said. "We just got them. We only take them on the river and lakes. Never on the bay, I promise."

In early 2007, the two lawyers that had been handling the Arseneaults' case brought on board one of Saint John's oldest and largest firms to help with the research and litigation. The original legal team could find no previous cases that might serve as a guidepost for any future case. Because the organizers seemed disinclined to settle, the case was likely to go to court. If it did, any decision would set a precedent for similar events in New Brunswick and across Canada. As a new judgment on a new sport, it could even extend its influence beyond the borders, to the United States, Britain, and other countries that rely on common tort law principles in their own courts' decisions. Lawyers would have to build a case from the ground up. It could be another year, likely longer, before the Fundy Multi-Sport Race case appeared before a judge, let alone received a decision.

"It does not seem like five years to me," said Jacqueline Arseneault, reflecting on the last time she saw her son alive. "It feels, some days, like yesterday. We've always said we're prepared to go all the way with this. And we will go all the way with this. Jean-Guy calls it 'blood money,' but I choose not to look at it like that. I don't want people to think we're putting a price tag on my son. You cannot put a price tag on a child's life. I just hope that the system does its work."

TWENTY-EIGHT

The Aftermath

The Arseneaults weren't the only family whose lives were knocked askew by the events of June 1, 2002. In the year between the race and the inquest, Jayme Frank and Sara Vlug, the two young organizers, continued to compete as a team. After the inquest, they broke up. The strain of the tragedy and the renewed attention brought by the investigation proved too much for them as a couple. In many ways, Frank had borne the brunt of the official scrutiny for the accident. He was the one who had checked the weather report, who had gauged the sea conditions, who had helped launch kayaks and safety vessels from McLaughlins Cove, and who had made the final call—too late—to abbreviate the paddling stage. Bob Vlug, Sara's father, had been livid that inexperienced paddlers, in his store's kayaks, had been allowed to head out in such dubious conditions.

Even after their break-up, Vlug and Frank completed a few more races together as a team. Eventually, Frank left his job as a marine biologist in New Brunswick, moved to Toronto, and dropped out of the sport. The few times I had talked with him (on the phone, after the inquest), the soft-spoken Frank had seemed willing, if not eager, to discuss his experiences. But it had never been the right time—not according to Sara, not according to their lawyer. Then he simply wanted to move on with his life. It wouldn't be that easy. He would remain joined to the Vlugs and the Arseneaults, for the next few years at least, by the limbo of the lawsuit. His memories of the race would follow him forever.

Sara Vlug stayed in Dipper Harbour, where she worked as a kayak guide, as a part-time fitness instructor, and as a math and phys-ed teacher at Fundy Shores School. She could be spotted at track meets in the city urging on her small protégés. As promised, Vlug never organized another race, and the sport went into decline in Saint John. One of the last races in the area met with its own controversy when competitors (including Vlug, Jim Currie, and several other racers from the Fundy challenge) were sent into the woods on the first day of moose-hunting season. Vlug remained one of the most sought-after female adventure racers in the country and continued to compete with a variety of new teammates. In February 2005, she traveled to the Extreme Adventure Hidalgo, the biggest race in Mexico, where she had finished fifth a year earlier. On day two, racers dove into Laguna de Atezca, a water-filled volcanic crater, for a kilometer-long swim as a prelude to twelve hours of trekking, biking, and kayaking. Most villagers avoided the lake. It was cursed, they believed, by a malevolent sea witch who snatched young men as they swam and spat back their bloated corpses three days later. The results of the race didn't cure their superstition. One Mexican competitor failed to exit the swimming stage with his team. His body was pulled from the lake.

The sport had suffered another casualty. In the three years since the Fundy tragedy, adventure racing had been plagued by several high-profile fatalities. In 2003, at the Raid Gauloises in Kyrgyzstan, Dominique Robert, a forty-seven-year-old mountain guide and former Eco-Challenge champion from France, drowned when her canoe was pinned by overhanging tree branches in a fast-flowing river. The next year, at the Primal Quest in Washington State, Australian racer Nigel Aylott died after a loose rock struck his head while his team was descending a steep gully. "I do not race to risk my life or watch my friends die," said one top competitor who had narrowly dodged the same rockfall. "That is just a price that is too high in exchange for winning an adventure race."

By then, Mark Burnett had closed shop on the Eco-Challenge. After the 2002 event in Fiji, without any official announcement, he pulled the plug on the world's most popular adventure race. Those who knew the former commando said that safety concerns factored into his decision. Two weeks after Fiji, a Brazilian competitor who had ingested a worm during the race fell sick, nearly died, and remained in a coma for several months. As an organizer, Burnett had always been scrupulous about emergency measures. In the 1996 Eco-Challenge, he disqualified one team for entering a mountain stage without their mandatory sleeping bags. "You will not survive," he scolded the disappointed racers. Even with backup plans, a fatal injury seemed only a matter of time. Veteran racers already complained that Burnett's Eco-Challenge had lost its original vision of wilderness adventure by awarding coveted spots to inexperienced teams of Playboy bunnies, Hollywood movie stars, and reality-TV contestants, and then focusing coverage on these celebrity "athletes." A death at a race (especially of a playmate) would vindicate critics of *Survivor* and other productions by the man who once boasted that "bug-eating and backstabbing are the stuff of great entertainment." It would confirm their complaints that Burnett's brand of reality TV nursed sofa-bound sadists on the milk of human misfortune.

The sport had grown fast, perhaps too fast—from only three races in North America in 1995 to more than six hundred a decade later. Smaller single-day races flourished, especially urban treasure hunts modeled after the reality-TV hit *The Amazing Race*. But these competitions removed almost every hint of risk and adventure. They offered instead an experience somewhere between a 10K fun run and an Easter egg hunt. Around the world, there were fewer genuinely extreme events for top competitors such as Sara Vlug who longed to test their endurance and navigation skills against the call of the wild.

"Adventure racing is dead," many racers and organizers lamented, "or at least dying."

Mark Campbell once again found himself near the heart of the controversy. After the 2002 Fundy race, where he had been the first to capsize, the Canadian Forces network manager qualified for what would be the final Eco-Challenge. The Fiji race didn't end well for him either. On day six, his team was tramping along a riverbed through the jungle when a slick rock sent the burly racer sprawling. He opened a wound above his eye and that was it: game over. The next morning, a helicopter winched Campbell to safety, and he took consolation by posing for a photograph beside Mark Burnett, near the finish line that he never got to cross. Two years later, Campbell was at the Primal Quest when Nigel Aylott was killed. He had also been at the British Columbia race at which the media relations rep had drowned in 2000. Some friends wondered if he competed under a curse. He shrugged. It was just a matter of odds—if you run enough races, you'll be there when things go wrong. Mostly, things went right. For his inspirational efforts, Campbell was named the first civilian employee sponsored by the Canadian Forces' Army Elite Athlete Program. In 2007, he completed his sixteenth Ironman triathlon.

In Bathurst, New Brunswick, the Tallywhackers and their friends continued to bike and run and do triathlons and backpacking trips, although none was keen to try another adventure race—the Fundy event was the craziest thing they had experienced. Soon, new job opportunities drew all of them, except Peter Hancock, away from Bathurst. Their camaraderie had been forged in adventure, and so every year they tried to reunite for an outdoor get-together. They were a few years older, and a step or two slower, but they still pushed themselves as hard as ever—or almost as hard. On a cycling trip in Quebec, they were zipping down a winding asphalt hill when another rider in their group took the turn too fast and pinwheeled over his handlebars. He was taken away by ambulance with a cracked vertebra that could have paralyzed him or worse. It was another reminder, as if they needed one, of the risks that lay behind their own Type-T personalities.

And then there was Jason Stanley.

At the Fundy race, the Eastern Outdoors employee had weathered the rough ride in the safety Zodiac, the rescue of the injured cyclist, and even a dressing down from the fire-rescue crew for the lack of organization. As night fell, Stanley approached a cottage and borrowed a phone. When it rang in Dipper Harbour, Deanna Vlug picked it up. "Did you hear what happened?" she asked. "René died." Alone again, Stanley walked back to the beach and sat down on a rock, stunned by the news. Back home the next morning, all he wanted to do was stay in bed. That was what he did for the next week and a half. He regretted not attending the wake or the funeral, but he could only muster the energy to attend the three-hour counseling session, where he was told not to blame himself for Arseneault's death. That wasn't easy. It took him weeks to let his parents know exactly what had happened that day.

When he didn't show up to work, Sara Vlug called him at home. "Are you coming back?" she asked. Stanley didn't want to get in a kayak or go out on the bay—not now, not ever. He needed the paycheck, though, for tuition. The Vlugs agreed to let Stanley help out in the retail store rather than insist he return to the water as a guide. On Stanley's first shift back at Eastern Outdoors, Bob Vlug confronted his employee. "If you had stayed in the safety boat," he said, "you guys could have picked up René and he'd be fine."

Stanley started shaking, walked to the back of the store, sat down, and cried. Within a month, he had found a new job and had left Eastern Outdoors. He never wanted to see any of the organizers again, especially after the inquest, at which Owen Vlug had also insinuated that Stanley had abandoned his duty. Even with more counseling, Stanley felt a mix of anger and guilt and shame whenever he thought about the race. "It was a real tragedy," he told me, five years later, his voice cracking at the memory, "knowing René and what great a person he was and what a great athlete he was."

Malcolm Brett had been in the kayak with Bob Vlug that had run a sweep to look for missing paddlers. His wife, also at the race, had taught René as a boy. The loss of a child, he knew, was more than any parent could bear. It seemed obvious in hindsight that kayakers in trouble might drift east, away from the race route. But when he and Vlug had headed out, the true urgency of the situation hadn't been clear. "It's so logical now the way the wind was," Brett admitted, three years after the inquest. "The tide and the wind would have been acting together to push them backwards. At the time it never occurred to me to look for them behind Cranberry Head. I'd like to think that I'd have the smarts to do it another time, but you never know until you're there." John Brett, his son, had helped Arseneault set off in a solo kayak and had been shocked to learn of his acquaintance's death. Following the race, the forestry student and his father had discussed at length what went wrong that afternoon. "I was pretty disgusted by the whole thing," said John Brett. "It's almost like they let shit happen and then tried to deal with it."

As the sponsor and equipment provider, Eastern Outdoors was tarred by the negative coverage of the ill-fated race. Bob Vlug's business operations had already been financially tenuous. In 1998, he and his wife had pleaded guilty for failing to file income tax returns. Their lawyer asked for clemency because the couple had no taxable income during the years they hadn't filed. In 2004, just two weeks after the Arseneault family filed their lawsuit, the Vlugs announced they would be closing their retail store in Saint John. In the months leading up to the Fundy race, residents of Dipper Harbour and Chance Harbour had often seen Bob Vlug jogging and biking along the coast highway. After that day, he seemed to retreat back into his seaside house. "There wasn't a fellow here that wasn't angry," said one bayman about the sentiment toward the Vlugs after the race.

Bob Mawhinney, captain of the *D.P. Clipper*, admitted that locals were tough on the Vlugs, who were his nearest neighbors. But everyone in Dipper Harbour knew the bay was dangerous enough without sending newcomers onto its waters. The Mawhinneys and the other baymen returned to its depths and shoals, season after season, to fish for lobster and scallops. A few didn't come back. In November of 2003, *Pedro's Girl* sank east of Saint John. The captain and one crew member made it to shore and were treated for hypothermia, but a third man drowned. Three months later, the *Lo Da Kash* and its crew of four disappeared en route from Campobello

Island, near the American border, to Maces Bay, up the road from Dipper Harbour. The *Courtenay Bay*, two other coast guard boats, and three aircraft scoured the bay but could find no evidence of the fishing vessel amid the winter mists. A body washed ashore a week later and led searchers to the sunken lobster boat, two hundred meters from land, with a pair of drowned crew members still inside. The captain had been a Dipper Harbour man. His body was never recovered. A memorial stone, shaped like a lighthouse and etched with an image of the *Lo Da Kash*, now overlooks the bay on the bluffs at New River Beach. "For every life lost in the Fundy seas," it reads, "this monument stands for thee."

Anyone who was at the Fundy Multi-Sport Race always asks me one question: "How is Boon doing?" Despite his odyssey on the Bay of Fundy, Boon Kek never lost his passion for outdoor adventure, the reason he had come to Canada in the first place. Two months after the race, he went kayaking again, with friends watching over him, on the calmer waters of the Saint John River. And he felt … nothing. No memories from that afternoon on the bay came flooding back when he slid into a kayak cockpit again. Nothing more than the pleasure of being out on the water on a summer day. He never entered another adventure race, but he continued his triathlon training. After graduation, he stayed in Canada and met a local girl, found work in a running shop and then at the university campus in Saint John, helping foreign students adjust to life in a new country. In 2005, he traveled to British Columbia and completed his first Ironman, finishing the course in just under thirteen hours—and well under the seventeen-hour cut-off mark.

As the years passed, Kek never shook the belief that he could have, should have, acted differently. During his national service in Singapore, paratroopers were taught to do whatever it took to help their fellow soldiers. Kek understood that lesson in the abstract but felt he had failed the exam. It didn't matter that nobody else saw it that way. After the race, he had attended the three-hour counseling session with Jason Stanley, Sara Vlug, and Jayme Frank. He had been told that he had done all that he possibly could to save Arseneault, that he wasn't a trained rescuer, that to do more would have jeopardized his own life. The Arseneault family had submitted his name for a pair of bravery awards. He was a hero in their eyes. If Kek hadn't held on to René, Jacqueline and Jean-Guy Arseneault might never have known what had happened to their son or even had a body they could lay to rest—the Fundy tides don't give up their secrets easily. Kek shook his head at the notion that he was a hero. "I did what anyone would have done," he insisted. "Even though we all wanted to finish the race, part of that community is to help one another."

He had never panicked after Arseneault had capsized, after the storm had swept in, even after he had recognized they were being blown past the starting line and pulled off course. He had remained, if not calm, then at least clear-headed throughout that terrible hour. He had tried to save both boats. He had tried to save both boys. He had held on to Arseneault's limp body, balanced awkwardly in a kayak that was drifting toward certain destruction against Cranberry Head, and had retained the presence of mind to flag down Bob Mawhinney's lobster boat. That was what bothered him now—his conservativeness, the intense rationality of his upbringing in Singapore. From his psychology studies, he recognized the streak etched into his character. And yet there was little he could do about it. His mind circled back to the moment when René, unbearably cold, tried to drag himself aboard the remaining kayak—and Kek had ordered him off.

"I'm sure he was surprised by that," Kek admitted to me. "But in my mind, I thought that if he capsized my kayak, there's no way both of us could make it back. I was disappointed in myself. Maybe it was because I was taught to be so rational, so conservative, that it cost René. I notice these things in myself, but there wasn't anything I could do to help."

Kek didn't care for the legal debate about how to apportion blame between Arseneault and the organizers. Any shade of doubt trailed his own actions instead. He kept his survivor's guilt separated from the rest of his life, to be removed and considered whenever something reminded him of that day. He reflected on the race, not in anguish, but with the clarity of hindsight and a keen rationality that he wished he could occasionally shake. Kek knew he had done all the right things—everyone had told him so—and yet the rough arithmetic of his actions hadn't added up to the best result. He still couldn't believe that the race had gone so wrong, so fast. What if he had let Arseneault climb aboard his boat's deck, even for a minute, to escape the cold water? What if he had paddled for shore, even if a surf landing on the broken coast would have been reckless and likely fatal? What if he had ignored his rational good sense and gambled on a miracle?

"I definitely made a conscious reminder to myself," he told me, "that if something else ever happened like this, I would risk anything to help."

Return to the Bay

The night has fallen, and the tide ...
Now and again comes drifting home,
Across these aching barrens wide,
A sigh like driven wind or foam:
In grief the flood is bursting home.

—Bliss Carman, "Low Tide on Grand Pré"

On a Sunday morning in the summer of 2006, Boon Kek joined me to paddle the route of the kayaking section, from McLaughlins Cove to Dipper Harbour. He had been back on the bay only once before, a year after the race. Bob Mawhinney had invited him for a day of lobstering aboard the *D.P. Clipper*. The following year, Mawhinney had given me the same tour. I wanted to see the area again, this time from the vantage of a kayak. On previous visits, I had jogged the fifteen-kilometer trail through Irving Nature Park and cycled the forty-kilometer bike leg of the Fundy race. Now I needed to feel every inch of the paddling stage in my arms and shoulders. I hesitantly asked Kek if he wanted to come along. I wasn't sure how he would feel about returning to the site of the tragedy. He eagerly agreed.

I arranged for a guide and a wide tandem boat that Kek and I could share. The day broke clear and breezeless. The cove had undergone a few renovations since Kek had last stood on the foreshore. Winter storms had shuffled huge black boulders, slick with kelp, into new formations throughout the intertidal zone. With tides this high, you can never step onto the same beach twice. Our guide zipped up a wetsuit, and I wondered whether Kek and I should have brought along neoprene protection for ourselves.

We set off in ideal conditions. It took a few minutes to find our sea legs and then we synchronized our paddle strokes and glided across the water. The wooden poles of a herring weir projected from the shallows. As we approached the mouth of Chance Harbour, the beam of the automated beacon at Reef Point winked into the sun. To our left, we could see the high brown cliffs of Cranberry Head and the point where Kek and Arseneault had been lifted from the bay and into the *D.P. Clipper*. To our right stood the stacked rock wall of Chance Harbour's breakwater. The lobster boat had rushed the two lost kayakers for the safety of the floating dock behind its lee.

"Do you hear that?" our guide asked.

We could barely pick out the metallic clang of a bell buoy knocking in the breeze. The day of the race, the two buoys that marked the start and finish of the kayak section would have been sounding off like cathedral towers. And yet few people had heard the bells over the roar of wind and waves. We paddled mostly in silence, trailing our guide. The day was mild and the tide was slack enough that we could navigate between the mainland and Dry Ledge, its flat top lay exposed like a giant's skipping stone. The afternoon of the race, the wind and tide had fomented a clash of waves around these shallows that had driven paddlers offshore. Nobody would have risked the passage that we now took. It would have placed their kayaks, literally, between a rock and a hard place. As we headed through the gap, even at near-slack, we could feel a great force shifting beneath the hull of our plastic boat. A tidal current grabbed our vessel and lent our progress a nudge, as though we had stepped onto an electric walkway. Midway along the route, we beached for a snack on Lobster Cove. Here, other racers had abandoned their kayaks in desperate circumstances. Mark Mawhinney, the peripatetic fisherman, had happened upon teams who had abandoned the race amid the lightning squall. Not far from here, too, Jayme Frank and Sara Vlug had reunited with her father and realized that their sweep of the course had failed to collect the missing kayakers. Now, this same swathe of sand tempted us to catnap like Caribbean holiday makers. There were no ghosts on the Bay of Fundy for Boon Kek, no revelations waiting in its dark tides.

"It's different here," he told me. "It was such a different day then."

As we continued paddling, he barely recognized the bay. Today, we were carving across a paper-flat sea with little effort or disturbance. The glassy surface bore scant resemblance to the feverish waters that had confronted Kek and everyone else on June 1, 2002. Then, the bay had risen up in an undulating carpet of whitewater—wind stirred, tide turned, shoal disturbed. That constant, unpredictable motion had been as hard to read as a paperback novel on a rollercoaster.

At a dawdling pace, we reached the mouth of Dipper Harbour in less than two hours, far faster than all but the best kayakers at the Fundy race—and we had stopped for brownies along the way. As we rounded Campbells Point, we could spy the broad beach that fronted the Vlugs' property, empty of kayaks. We carried the boats up the concrete ramp beside the wharf. It was, we agreed, a perfect afternoon for a paddle. Scalloping season was under way, but the local fleet had anchored for a day of rest. On the water, we had only met a single solo kayaker as we had launched and later a solitary sailboat setting off from Dipper Harbour. Between the two harbors, we had enjoyed the stretch of coastline entirely to ourselves. On a summer weekend like this one, any other shore down the Pacific or Atlantic flank of North America would be teeming with pleasure-craft—sailed, motorized, or paddled. The Fundy coast, however, remains largely undiscovered by hobbyists and adventure tourists alike.

We drove back to Trail's End and relaxed with friends of our guide on a cottage deck that overlooked Chance Harbour. Lawn signs had popped up to protest encroaching salmon farms. During our kayak tour, we had passed one set of net-ringed corrals, built since the race. Another farm was proposed for a neighboring cove and would obscure its entire entrance. Our hosts lamented how the Fundy coast would be spoiled if more sites were approved. For now, though, we could admire the same million-dollar view the racers had seen as they had set off, an undisturbed panorama framed by the broken cliffs and wooded peaks of Cranberry Head and Reef Point. Someone had cooked a pan of the region's famous scallops, newly caught, spongy between our teeth and moist with the juices of the sea. Our guide described how he liked to scuba dive near here, shuck a scallop underwater, remove his regulator, and pop the mollusk into his mouth. You couldn't get more fresh than that. Maybe it would become a new sport: extreme scalloping. All we needed to complete the scene was a humpback whale breaching on the horizon. Then the postcard vision that had drawn Boon Kek halfway around the world, from his seaside home in Singapore to the Bay of Fundy, would be complete.

Conversation turned to the race that had departed from the nearby beach. Everyone had heard about it. Everyone had opinions about why the accident should have never happened. Our guide knew of my own long interest in the puzzle of that day, but I had only introduced Kek as a friend who was keen to join us for a day of kayaking. In fact, Kek understood better than anyone what had gone wrong that afternoon, what it felt like to be among the heaving waves and the lashing of the late-day storm, and yet he simply listened as the others talked. He was curious, he later admitted, about how the story had acquired a life all its own, passed from one person to the next, among lobstermen and guides and cottagers along this shore, exchanged between sea kayakers, racers, and other aspiring adventurers around the world. By then, the tragedy had hardened into legend, one more crag on a coastline already named for lost ships and ancient ghosts, a seascape storied with hope and despair. Boon Kek only wished he could rewrite the ending.

POSTSCRIPT

On Thanksgiving weekend of 2007, several months after I had submitted the manuscript for this book, newspaper readers and TV viewers across North America learned of another adventure-racing tragedy in Canadian waters. That Sunday morning, a group of eight "extreme athletes" had gathered for an ambitious day of physical activity: they planned to kayak five kilometers across Howe Sound, north of Vancouver, to Anvil Island, run up and down a small peak, paddle back across the sound to Porteau Cove, mountain bike sixty kilometers from Squamish to Whistler, chug halfway up the mountain, and then gather at a pub in the village to give thanks for another full summer of endurance endeavors and camaraderie. The exhausting wilderness itinerary wasn't part of any competitive event. It had been designed simply as a late-season training day for these friends, all of whom were accomplished outdoor athletes and adventure racers. Among them was Bob Faulkner, a legend in

Canada's racing community, a sixty-year-old former smoker turned ultra-Ironman who continued to compete in top-level international events (including seven Eco-Challenges) at an age when most of his peers were lounging in golf carts.

The holiday jaunt went awry, however, when the group launched four double kayaks from Anvil Island for the return journey to the British Columbia mainland. An October storm had steepened seas into two-meter breaking crests, while wind gusts of eighty-five kilometers per hour battered the boats during the crossing. In a tippier racing vessel, the two kayakers at the rear capsized in the rough conditions. The wind and currents separated Cheryl Beatty from Denis Fontaine, her common-law husband, and their boat. A tandem kayak retrieved Beatty and hauled her to Anvil Island, where one of her friends huddled against her hypothermic body while the other called for the coast guard from a nearby cabin.

Meanwhile Fontaine climbed across the overturned racing kayak and waited for the two remaining tandems to reach him. Deeply cold after a half hour in the 8°C water, he hauled himself into the center hatch of the boat containing Graham Tutti and Richard Juryn, so they could ferry him to shore. The two double kayaks were heading back together to Porteau Cove when the boat carrying Fontaine aimed instead for a closer spot of land. Bob Faulkner and his partner, out front in their kayak, continued toward the original take-out, where they phoned for help from their cars. Before the other friends could reach land, however, the open hatch in which Fontaine was perched filled with water and the top-heavy double kayak flipped, dumping all three occupants into the autumn-chilled Pacific. They decided to swim for shore. None of them made it. By the time coast guard vessels retrieved the trio of capsized kayakers, they had been immersed for an hour and a quarter: two of the men—forty-year-old Fontaine and Juryn, a fifty-year-old organizer of mountain bike races—succumbed to hypothermia or hypothermia-induced drowning. Thirty-five-year-old Tutti, a strong swimmer who had tried to tow Fontaine to safety, was briefly treated at a nearby hospital and released.

The headline-grabbing B.C. accident differed from the Fundy Multi-Sport Race tragedy in several key points. All eight friends were experienced amateur adventurers, rather than beginners, who lived on the West Coast, Canada's mecca of outdoor sports, and understood the dangers that lurked at the edge of their high-intensity hobbies. Several had just returned from an epic seventeen-day mountain bike expedition in Mongolia. That Sunday, they were training, rather than competing under the safety umbrella of an organized event, and had made the decision to set out into the gathering storm entirely on their own.

Still, the two incidents shared striking similarities. In both cases, a small-craft weather warning was in effect—and yet the competitive urge to finish the route trumped common sense. ("We should have turned back," Bob Faulkner told a reporter. "But this is our love. We were all experienced paddlers, and we were carried away by our own testosterone.") The Howe Sound kayakers were also under-equipped for rough ocean conditions; they wore life jackets and light athletic gear but not insulating wetsuits, and carried nothing more than paddle floats (no flares, VHF radio, or EPIRB, no Sea-Seat or sponsons) to call for help or remove victims from the cold in an emergency. And while survivors were able to phone 911 once on land, the prolonged exposure to the ocean waters proved too much for a pair of the paddlers. The shoreline was in sight and yet beyond their reach amid the turbulent sea.

In the weeks afterward, an outpouring of mourning for and memories of the popular middle-aged athletes filled newspapers and internet sites. For friends, family members, and other observers, the accident also cracked open the same questions raised by René Arseneault's death. What drives ordinary people to test their bodies against wind and waves on a morning when most of their neighbors would prefer to stay safely in bed? What physical rewards and psychological insights lay on that far shore to make the risks worth taking? And how do you ever measure the true price of adventure?

ACKNOWLEDGMENTS

In 2003, after my feature article about the Fundy Multi-Sport Race appeared in *explore* magazine, I realized there was a far deeper and more complex story still to be unearthed. I continued to interview participants, to gather research, and to piece together a complete chronology of events. To do justice to the tragedy in a book-length manuscript, I knew I needed to describe the race from the intimate perspective of the people who were there and from as many of these points of view as possible. I wanted to create a work of literary journalism that would drop readers onto the Bay of Fundy and force them to reckon with the same emotions and decisions faced by the organizers, the kayakers, and the rescuers. Reconstructing situations and conversations required that I interview dozens of people who competed as athletes or who were otherwise drawn into the orbit of the race. As I cross-referenced anecdotes and double-checked memories, participants told (and retold) their experiences to me. In many cases, I asked them to relive an episode they might have preferred to forget. All the scenes in *Fatal Tide* rely on these detailed personal interviews (as well as video footage, newspaper articles, inquest transcripts, Canadian Coast Guard reports, court documents, and other public records), and my book, in that sense, is a collaboration with everyone who was swept up by the events and the aftermath of the Fundy race.

I could not (and would not) have written this book without the cooperation of the Arseneault family—Jacqueline, Jean-Guy, André, Denis, and Guy—who opened their homes and their hearts to me at a time of great loss. René Arseneault's friends (Chris McCully, Matt Brooks, and, especially, Erin Dobson) also offered insight into his life and character, while Boon Kek was always willing to share his own recollections of that fateful day. Bob, Keith, Mark, Jean, and Debbie Mawhinney, Keith Nicholls, and Edward and Cindy Jacques explained their rescue efforts, the life of Fundy fishing families, and the mercurial nature of the bay. Logistically, writing a book about the East Coast while living on the West was a challenge, but my investigations were made easier by the hospitality I consistently enjoyed during my repeated visits to Saint John, Chance Harbour, Dipper Harbour, and other communities throughout New Brunswick and the Canadian Maritimes. Tourism New Brunswick and Tourism Saint John aided me with the logistics of one of these research trips. Gregory Thompson, Sandy Robertson, and Mike Bursey were particularly helpful in offering context about the region's history.

I tracked down and spoke with almost every racer who launched a boat onto the kayak section that afternoon, as well as other participants and witnesses of the Fundy race. While many do not appear in the book by name, all were vital in helping me to piece together a precise picture of what happened: Bob Carreau, Bob Leclair, Peter Hancock, Rob Hutchison, Marc Lejeune, Mark Campbell, Shawn Amirault, Jim Currie, Robin Lang, Trevor Maclean, Kevin Marks, Genevieve Macdonnell, Jan Trojanowski, Dana Henry, Paddy Thompson, Greg Backman, Chris Martin, Bruce Reid, Joe Kennedy, Jim Ketterling, Scott and Heather Purcell, Tim King, Michael Hallett,

Larry MacGillivray, Malcolm and John Brett, Shawn Bethune, Denise Hamel, Todd Price, Steve Adamson, Thesa Albert, Andrew Murphy, Frank McKinnon, Rodney Tolentino, Tanya Chisholm, Bill MacMackin, John Pike, and, especially, Jason Stanley.

Constable Wayne Burke of the RCMP (retired) and members of the Musquash Fire-Rescue Department (Wayne Pollock, Gilles Arseneault, Neil Galbraith, and Vanessa Dixon) outlined their investigations and rescue efforts. Background about search-and-rescue theory and practice was patiently shared with me by members of the Canadian and U.S. coast guards and Canadian Forces, including Andy Caines, Bob Donner, Luc LeBlanc, Sandra Inglis, Philip Cappel, Richard Kanehl, Jeff Nemrova, Marc Proulx, Sonia Connock, Wendell Sperry, Maurice Robert, Joe Doucette, and Don Duguay. Dr. Peter Ross, Dr. Debbie Weatherhead, Dr. Peter Tikuisis, and, especially, Dr. Chris Brooks and Dr. John Hayward articulated in lay terms the science and treatment of hypothermia. Dr. Fred Page at the St. Andrews Biological Station added to my general understanding of the Bay of Fundy, and Heather Harrison explained the workings of the New Brunswick coroner's office. Cynthia Thomson at the University of British Columbia, Ross Cloutier at Thompson Rivers University, Dr. Ron Pelot at Dalhousie University, Michael Pardy of SKILS, and Mike and Glenda Hanna of YouthSafe Outdoors all helped my research into the scientific, philosophical, and legal study of risk taking in the wilderness. Tim Ingram supplied detailed documentation of his campaign to improve paddling safety. I learned a great deal about adventure racing and other outdoor sports from Bob Miller, Kevin Hodder, Pat Chan, Jim Mandelli, Stacie Smith, Ron Tibert, Dave Zietsma, Steve Menzie, Dale O'Hara, Susan McKenzie, Geoff Langford, Wayne Leek, Hazen Simson, Kevin Wallace, John Jacoby, Richard and Elina Ussher, Paul Done, Aaron McConnell, Martin Dugard, Will Gadd, Colin Angus, Bob Faulkner, and, especially, Ian Adamson and John Yip, two athletes who continue to inspire me. Wanda Hughes of Go Fundy Events, Bruce Smith of Seascape Kayak Tours, and Kevin Sampson of Adventure High Inc. helped me to appreciate both the pleasures and perils of sea kayaking on the Bay of Fundy.

While I was at *explore* magazine, Charles Mandel first alerted me to the incident, James Little provided the editorial insights and Al Zikovitz the publishing forum for the original article, and Mark Schatzker set a high standard to try to match as a writer. At my new job in the Department of Writing at the University of Victoria, the university generously supplied two research grants and a semester of study leave. Valerie Tenning shuttled manuscripts across the country and Daniel Hogg contributed technical support for photos and maps. Library staff at UVic and the University of New Brunswick, Saint John, tracked down obscure articles and other essential secondary sources. The diligent work of the editors and reporters at the *Telegraph-Journal* in Saint John helped me to plumb the mood of their city before and after the race. I would have gotten lost in a thicket of research material without the organizational and fact-checking efforts of my two very able research assistants, Jessica Gillies and Aaron Shepard. Several other people also read drafts and steered the manuscript clear of errors in fact and expression. My deep thanks to John Yip, John Dowd, Marc Lejeune, Bruce Ramsay, Patrice Halley, Ron Manzer, Dr. Chris Brooks, and, especially, Ross Crockford. The keen eye of copy editor Madeline Koch saved the final draft from many embarrassments. Sam Hiyate, my literary agent at The Rights Factory, believed in the book from the earliest proposal—without his efforts, it likely would not have been written, let alone published. Diane Turbide at Penguin Canada was equally enthusiastic, and the completed version of the manuscript is far, far better for her editorial wisdom. I also owe a debt of gratitude to the Canada Council, which gave me an Explorations Grant early in my writing career that allowed me to discover I am a much better journalist than novelist.

Finally, even as the research for this book stole me away from my family, writing it taught me a great deal about taking risks, dreading loss, and the joys of coming home to the people I most love. In that way, the presence of my wife, Jenny, my son, A.J., and my daughter, Briar, appears on every page. I could have never done it without them.

The family of René Arseneault has set up an athletic scholarship fund in his name to be awarded to deserving youth who cannot otherwise afford sporting equipment and fees. Details about how to make donations can be found at www.fataltide.com.

Permissions were granted to use excerpts from the following books, essays, songs, and poems: *Homo Ludens* by Johan Huizinga, copyright 1950 by Roy Publishers, reprinted by permission of Beacon Press, Boston; *Inuit Kayaks in Canada* by E.Y. Arima, reprinted by permission of the Canadian Museum of Civilization; "Playing Symbolically with Death in Extreme Sports" by David Le Breton, reprinted by permission of SAGE Publications; "A Maritimer's Lament," courtesy of Wayne Burke; "Extreme Sports and the Assumption of Risk," courtesy of David Horton; "Glass Ponies of the Sea," courtesy of Stephen Stamp.

SELECTED BIBLIOGRAPHY

Adamson, Ian. *Runner's World Guide to Adventure Racing: How to Become a Successful Racer and Adventure Athlete.* Rodale, Emmaus, PA, 2004.

Adney, Edwin Tappan, and Howard I. Chapelle. *The Bark Canoes and Skin Boats of North America.* Smithsonian Institution Press, Washington DC, 1983.

Anderson, J.R.L. *The Ulysses Factor: The Exploring Instinct in Man.* Hodder and Stoughton, London, 1970.

Apter, Michael J. *Danger: Our Quest for Excitement.* Oneworld Publications, Oxford, UK, 2007.

Arima, E.Y., ed. *Contributions to Kayak Studies.* Canadian Museum of Civilization, Ottawa, 1991.

Arima, E.Y. *Inuit Kayaks in Canada: A Review of Historical Records and Construction.* National Museums of Canada, Ottawa, 1987.

Bartlett, Bruce. "Business Owners Violate Income Tax Act." *New Brunswick Telegraph-Journal.* March 24, 1998.

Barton, Daryl. "Release of Liability Forms: How Enforceable Are They in Outdoor Water Sports Activities?" *Michigan Bar Journal.* 82:8, August 1, 2003.

Begg, Kirsten. "Competitor Dies at Raid Gauloises." InsideTri.com. June 11, 2003.

Booth, Robert. "TV 'Survival King' Stayed in Hotels." *Sunday Times.* July 22, 2007.

Brooks, C.J. *Survival in Cold Waters: Staying Alive.* Transport Canada, Ottawa, 2003.

Brosseau, Danny. *Preparation Guide for Boating Event.* Lifesaving Society, Montreal, QC. 2005.

Brown, Chuck. "Survival of the Sneakiest? TV Castaways Pick a Millionaire Tonight." *New Brunswick Telegraph-Journal.* August 23, 2000.

Brown, Chuck. "Refloated Vessel Taken Ashore." *New Brunswick Telegraph-Journal.* September 30, 2004.

Brown, Ian. "When the Roof Rack Falls Off." *Globe and Mail.* September 9, 2006.

Broze, Matt, and George Gronseth. *Deep Trouble: True Stories and Their Lessons from Sea Kayaker Magazine.* Christopher Cunningham, ed. Ragged Mountain Press, Camden, ME, 1997.

Burnett, Mark. "What I've Learned." *Esquire.* Interviewed by Mike Sager. July 2001.

Burnett, Mark. *Jump In! Even If You Don't Know How to Swim.* Ballantine Books, New York, 2005.

Burton, Alan C., and Otto G. Edholm. *Man in a Cold Environment.* Edward Arnold Ltd., London, 1955.

Caissie, Michael, with John Chilibeck. "Police Rule Out Criminal Charges in Kayak Death." *New Brunswick Telegraph-Journal.* June 5, 2002.

Caldwell, Liz, and Barry Siff. *Adventure Racing: The Ultimate Guide.* Velo Press, Boulder, CO, 2001.

Canadian Red Cross. *What We Have Learned: 10 Years of Pertinent Facts about Drownings and Other Water-Related Injuries in Canada, 1991–2000.* Ottawa. <www.redcross.ca/article.asp?id=004625&tid=078> (December 2007).

Carter, Bill. "Survival of the Pushiest." *New York Times Magazine.* January 28, 2001.

Chilibeck, John. "A Race of Their Own: Two Fanatical Fitness and Nature Lovers Plan Their Own Eco-Adventure Race." *New Brunswick Telegraph-Journal.* April 17, 2000.

Cloutier, Ross, et al. *Legal Liability and Risk Management in Adventure Tourism.* Bhudak Consultants Ltd., Kamloops, BC, 2000.

Csíkszentmihályi, Mihály. *Flow: The Psychology of Optimal Experience.* HarperCollins, New York, 1990.

David, Grainger. "Hollywood Hitman Reality-TV Czar Mark Burnett Has Changed Television for Good—The Business Model, That Is." *Fortune.* August 23, 2004.

Delinsky, Barbara. *Does a Lobsterman Wear Pants?* Down East Books, Maine, 2005.

Department of National Defence. *RCC Halifax Case #0589.* Department of National Defence, Ottawa, June 1, 2002.

Díaz, Ralph. *Complete Folding Kayaker.* Second edition. Ragged Mountain Press, Camden, ME, 2003.

Dowd, John. *Sea Kayaking: A Manual for Long-Distance Touring.* Sixth edition. Greystone Books, Vancouver, 2004.

Dugard, Martin. *Surviving the Toughest Race on Earth.* Ragged Mountain Press, Camden, ME, 1998.

Duncan, Drew, and John J. Jackson. "Leaps of Faith: Risk, Negligence and Exculpatory Clauses for Dangerous Sports." *Policy Options*. March 1999.

Duxbury, Kenneth. *Seastate and Tides*. Stanford Maritime Limited, London, 1977.

Ebstein, R.P., and R.H. Belmaker. "Saga of an Adventure Gene: Novelty Seeking, Substance Abuse and the Dopamine D4 Receptor (D4DR) Exon III Repeat Polymorphism." *Molecular Psychiatry*. September 1997.

Eibel, Deborah. *Kayak Sickness: Selected Poems, 1958–1971*. Sono Nis Press, Port Clements, BC, 1972.

Elki, Toby. "The Seamy Underside of Reality." *Media Daily News*. February 24, 2006.

Fisher, Daniel. "Hypothermia for Fun and Profit." *Forbes*. November 1, 1999.

Fulbrook, Julian. *Outdoor Activities, Negligence, and the Law*. Ashgate, Aldershot, 2005.

Giesbrecht, Gordon G., and John S. Hayward. "Problems and Complications with Cold-Water Rescue." *Wilderness and Environmental Medicine Journal*. 17:1, 2006.

Grierson, Bruce. "*Really* Learn to Do an Eskimo Roll." *explore*. July/August 2005.

Hayward, John S., and Alan M. Steinman. "Cold Water Immersion." *Wilderness Medicine: Management of Wilderness and Environmental Emergencies*. Third edition. Mosby-Year Book Inc., St. Louis, MO, 1995.

Horton, David. "Extreme Sports and Assumption of Risk: A Blueprint." *University of San Francisco Law Review*. 38, 2004.

Hudson, Simon, ed. *Sport and Adventure Tourism*. Haworth Hospitality Press, Binghamton, NY, 2003.

Hughes, Alison. "The Extreme Test." *New Brunswick Telegraph-Journal*. August 3, 1999.

Huizinga, Johan. *Homo Ludens: A Study of the Play Element in Culture*. Beacon Press, Boston, 1955.

Hutchison, Derek. *Sea Canoeing*. Third edition. A&C Black, London, 1984.

Ingram, Tim. *Canoe and Kayak Scam Kills 1000 Americans*. 1st Books Library, Bloomington, IN, 2003.

Jack, S.J., and K.R. Ronan. "Sensation Seeking among High- and Low-Risk Sports Participants." *Personality and Individual Differences*. 25, 1998.

Jamison, Neal, et al., eds. *The Thrill of Victory, the Agony of My Feet: Tales from the World of Adventure Racing*. Breakaway Books, Halcottsville, NY, 2005.

Janes, Brad. "Tricky Trip: Four People, Two Kayaks and 11½ Hours on the Finicky Bay of Fundy—That Equals a Quest Fulfilled for Bob Vlug." *New Brunswick Telegraph-Journal*. August 25, 2000.

Kay, Joanne, and Suzanne Laberge. "The 'New' Corporate Habitus in Adventure Racing." *International Review for the Sociology of Sport*. 37:1, 2001.

Keatinge, W.R. *Survival in Cold Water: The Physiology and Treatment of Immersion Hypothermia and of Drowning*. Blackwell Scientific Publications, Oxford, 1969.

Kerr, Grant. "Kayaker Capsizes in Bay." *New Brunswick Telegraph-Journal*. June 3, 2002.

Kerr, Grant. "Danger 'Part of the Job.'" *New Brunswick Telegraph-Journal*. November 17, 2003.

Le Breton, David. "Playing Symbolically with Death in Extreme Sports." *Body & Society*. 6:1, 2000.

Leach, David. "After the Avalanches: Weighing In on Canada's Winter of Infamy." *explore*. Winter 2003.

Leach, David. "Death by Adventure: What Really Happened at the Fundy Multi-Sport Race?" *explore*. March 2003.

Leach, David. "Peak Performers." *Toro*. November 2006.

Leach, John. *Survival Psychology*. New York University Press, New York, 1994.

Levy, Buddy. "The Politics of Adventure Racing." *TV Guide*. September 29, 2001.

"Life Is a Risky Business." *Ottawa Citizen*. June 24, 2003.

Mann, Don, and Kara Schaad. *The Complete Guide to Adventure Racing: The Insider's Guide to the Greatest Sport on Earth*. Hatherleigh Press, New York, 2001.

Markman, Jon D. "The Last Adventurer." *Los Angeles Times*. August 24, 1990.

Markman, Jon D. "The Ultimate Race." *Los Angeles Times*. February 24, 1991.

McGuire, Peter. "Local Quartet Taking Adventure to the Extreme." *New Brunswick Telegraph-Journal*. May 21, 2001.

McKenzie, Susan. "One Canadian Finishes the World Championships." Canoe.ca. September 9, 2001.

Mendelsohn, Everett. *Heat and Life: The Development of the Animal Theory of Life*. Harvard University Press, Cambridge, MA, 1964.

Mickleburgh, Rod. "Season-Capping Kayak Adventure Kills Two as Storms Lash B.C. Coast." *Globe and Mail*. October 9, 2007.

Mickleburgh, Rod. "Shaken by Deaths, Extreme Athletes Vow to Press On." *Globe and Mail*. October 10, 2007.

Morris, Chris. "Fundy Death Raises Concerns about Safety of Kayaks and Endurance Races." Canadian Press. June 3, 2002.

Motavalli, Jim. "The Eco-Challenge Gets Challenged." *E Magazine*. July/August 1995.

Munsey, Christopher. "Frisky, But More Risky." *Monitor on Psychology*. July/August 2006.

Murphy, Austin. "The Agony of Victory." *SI Adventure*. July 7, 2003.

Pitts, Gordon. "An Empire Looks to the Future." *Globe and Mail*. March 26, 2005.

Potomac Management Group, Inc. *The Efficacy of Sponsons on Canoes and Kayaks*. United States Coast Guard, Washington DC, 2004. <www.uscgboating.org/SAFETY/efficacy.htm> (December 2007).

Pozos, Robert S. "Nazi Hypothermia Research: Should the Data Be Used?" *Military Medical Ethics*. Volume 2. Edmund D. Pelegrino et al., eds. Office of the Surgeon General, United States Army, Falls Church, VA, 2004.

Pozos, Robert S., and Lorentz E. Wittmers, eds. *The Nature and Treatment of Hypothermia*. Croom Helm Ltd., London, 1983.

Province of British Columbia. Findings and Recommendations as a Result of the Inquest into the Death of Darryl Smith and Gareth Aylmer Lineen. Coroner's Court of British Columbia, Sidney, BC, 1988.

Province of New Brunswick. An Inquest into the Death of René Gabriel Arseneault. Four volumes. Department of Justice, Saint John, NB, 2003.

Raffan, James. *Deep Waters: Is the Adventure Worth the Risk—the Lake Timiskaming Canoeing Tragedy.* HarperCollins, Toronto, 2002.

Robertson, G.A. The Mawhinneys of Maces Bay, NB. Unpublished manuscript, 2006.

Schulman, Neil. "Risk Homeostasis." *Wavelength.* April/May 2006.

"Sport's Safety in Question after Triathlon Death." Associated Press. June 11, 2002.

Smith, Alisa. "Meet Professor Popsicle." *Outside.* January 2003.

Stuart, Ryan. "Outwit, Outlast, Airlift: Canadian *Survivor* Wannabes Rescued by Chopper." *explore.* Winter 2004.

Supreme Court of British Columbia. *Kristine Louise Oddo Ochoa v. Canadian Mountain Holidays Inc., Jocelyn Lang and Dean Walton.* Vancouver, BC, September 25, 1996.

Swift, E.M. "Chilling Debut: The Discovery Channel World Championship Adventure Race Got Off to a Tragic Start." *SI Adventure.* September 17, 2001.

Thompson, Ethel. *The Tides of Discipline.* Print'N Press Ltd., St. Stephen, NB, 1978.

Transport Canada. *Sea Kayaking Safety Guide.* Ottawa, ON. 2003.

Trueman, Mac. "Fog Bound." *New Brunswick Telegraph-Journal.* June 1, 2002.

Wardell, Jane. "Geldof Sues over *Survivor* Copycat." Associated Press. September 27, 2002.

"Weighing In on Extreme Sports." *New Brunswick Telegraph-Journal.* June 10, 2002.

Wetzler, Brad. "Blood, Sweat, and Terrific Footage." *Outside.* April 2000.

Wilde, Gerald. *Target Risk 2: A New Psychology of Safety and Health.* PDE Publications, Toronto, 2001.

Wilkerson, James A., ed. *Hypothermia, Frostbite and Other Cold Injuries.* Mountaineers Books, Seattle, WA, 1986.

Wright, Harold E., and Rob Roy. *Saint John and the Fundy Region.* Neptune Publishing, Saint John, NB, 1987.

Wurdinger, Scott, and Tom Potter, eds. *Controversial Issues in Adventure Education.* Kendall/Hunt Publishing, Dubuque, IA, 1999.

Wyle, Francis E. *Tides and the Pull of the Moon.* Stephen Greene Press, Brattleboro, VT, 1979.

Zimmerly, David W. *Qajaq: Kayaks of Siberia and Alaska.* Division of State Museums, Juneau, AK, 1986.

Zuckerman, Marvin. "Are You a Risk Taker?" *Psychology Today.* November/December 2000.

Zuckerman, Marvin, and D. Michael Kuhlman. "Personality and Risk-Taking: Common Biosocial Factors." *Journal of Personality.* 68:6, December 2000.

Zweig, Paul. *The Adventurer: The Fate of Adventure in the Western World.* Akadine Press, New York, 1974.

PandoraHearts

Jun Mochizuki

CONTENTS

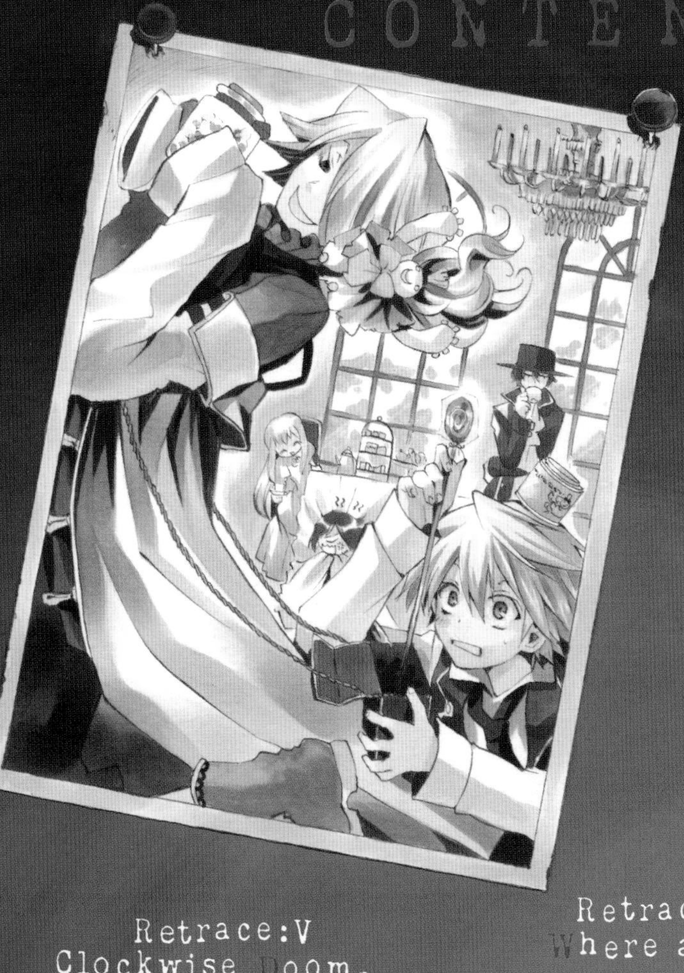

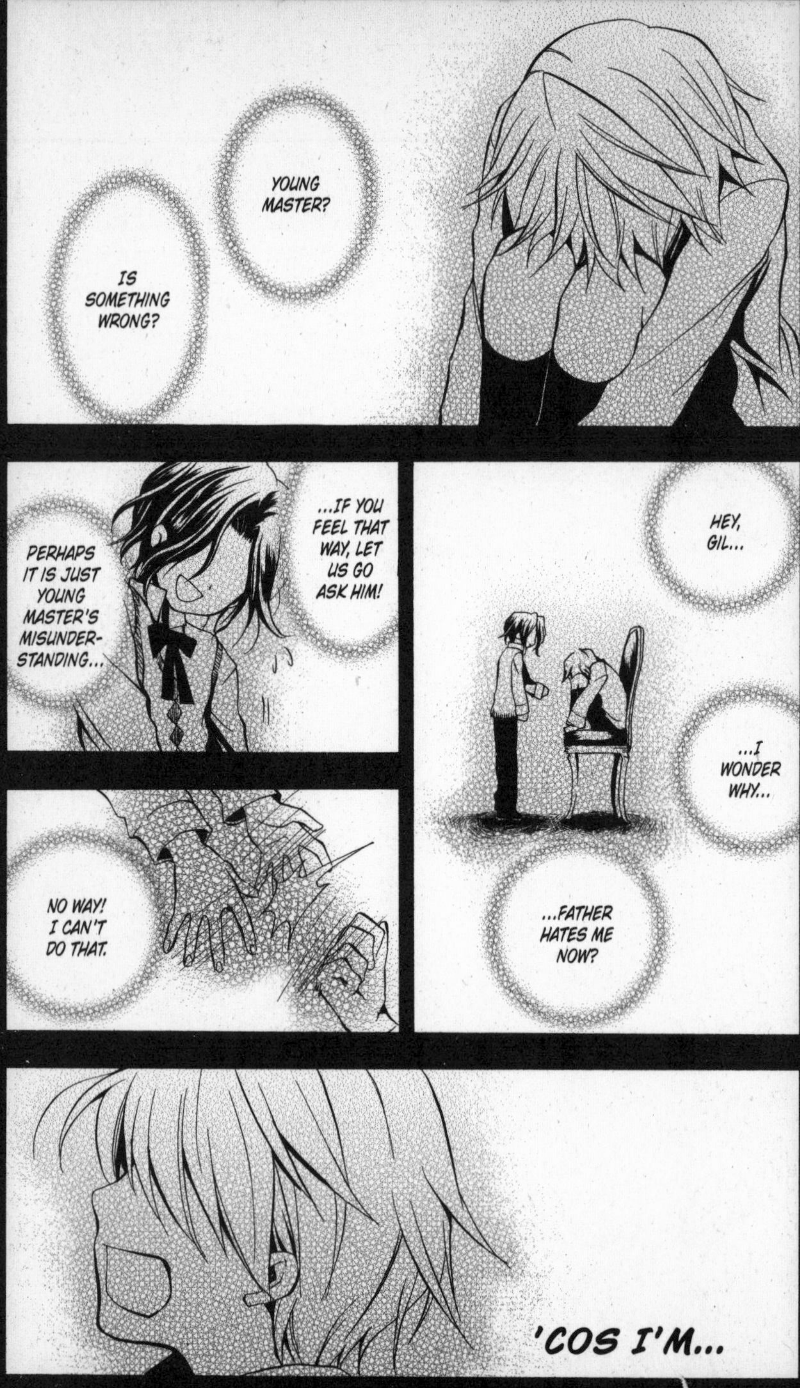
YOUNG MASTER?
IS SOMETHING WRONG?
HEY, GIL...
...I WONDER WHY...
...FATHER HATES ME NOW?
...IF YOU FEEL THAT WAY, LET US GO ASK HIM!
PERHAPS IT IS JUST YOUNG MASTER'S MISUNDER-STANDING...
NO WAY! I CAN'T DO THAT.
'COS I'M...

MASTER.

WON'T YOU BUY A FLOWER?

Retrace: V
Clockwise Doom

NAAAW. I DON'T.

I CAME TO LOOK FOR SOMEONE, BUT MY COMPANION GOT LOST, SOOO...

DOES MASTER LIVE IN THIS TOWN?

THANK YOU, MASTER!

WHO'S PAPA?

HEY!

...PAPA WENT LOOKING FOR HER! ♡

WELL, I'LL BE OFF THEN...

GEEZ, SUCH A TROUBLE-MAKER...

AH! ALICE! I'M SO GLAD HE FOUND YOU! ☆

AAH! HEY, WAIT!

NPUU (POUT)

ん゛゛゜

5

IF I TAKE THESE WITH ME, THEY'LL WITHER RIGHT AWAY.

EH...?

BUT IF YOU WEAR THEM...

MAN... WE ENDED UP WASTING PRECIOUS TIME, ALL 'COS ALICE GOT LOST.

WHAT ARE YOU SAYING!? I DIDN'T GET LOST!

SHE'S CUTE.♥

...THEY'LL KEEP BLOOMING IN MY HEART, ALONG WITH YOUR IMAGE, SEE?

あっハッ

AHA!

HA! HA!

WHAT HOST DID YOU STEAL THOSE LINES FROM?

DON (BAM)

トンッ

WHY, YOU...

YOU GUYS LEFT ME!! YOU'RE THE ONES AT FAULT!!

6

HEY... ...WE DIDN'T COME HERE FOR A PICNIC!

I CAN'T HELP IT! I'VE NEVER SEEN ANY OF THESE THINGS BEFORE.

DON'T TREAT ME LIKE A KID, SEAWEED HEAD!

IT'S EMBARRASSING. WHAT, ARE YOU A HICK OR SOMETHING!?

DON'T GAPE AT EVERY LITTLE THING WHILE YOU'RE WALKING!

...I THOUGHT WE MIGHT BE ABLE TO FIGURE OUT SOMETHING ABOUT ALICE'S MEMORIES THERE TOO.

SINCE I FOUND THIS WATCH THERE...

—TO THE MANSION WHERE YOUR COMING-OF-AGE CEREMONY WAS HELD?

YEAH.

OF COURSE YOU CAN.

CAN I GO...?

FUU (SIGH)

WELL... YOU TOLD ME TO "WORK FOR PANDORA," SO I THOUGHT YOU'D TAKE ME TO THEM.

I WOULD DEARLY LOVE TO...

...BUT WE WOULD NEED TO MAKE CONSIDERABLE ARRANGEMENTS BEFOREHAND...

SURI (RUB)

SURI

THAT HURT, YOU KNOW.

BESHI (CHOP)

...

NOW THEN.

WHYEVER ARE YOU SO SURPRISED?

BASA (FLAP)

KUH KEH KEH KEH KEH KEH! KEH KEH KEH!

LOOKS LIKE YOU'RE HAVING FUN.

I'LL GIVE YOU LOT PLENTY OF WORK TO DO!

DON'T WORRY!

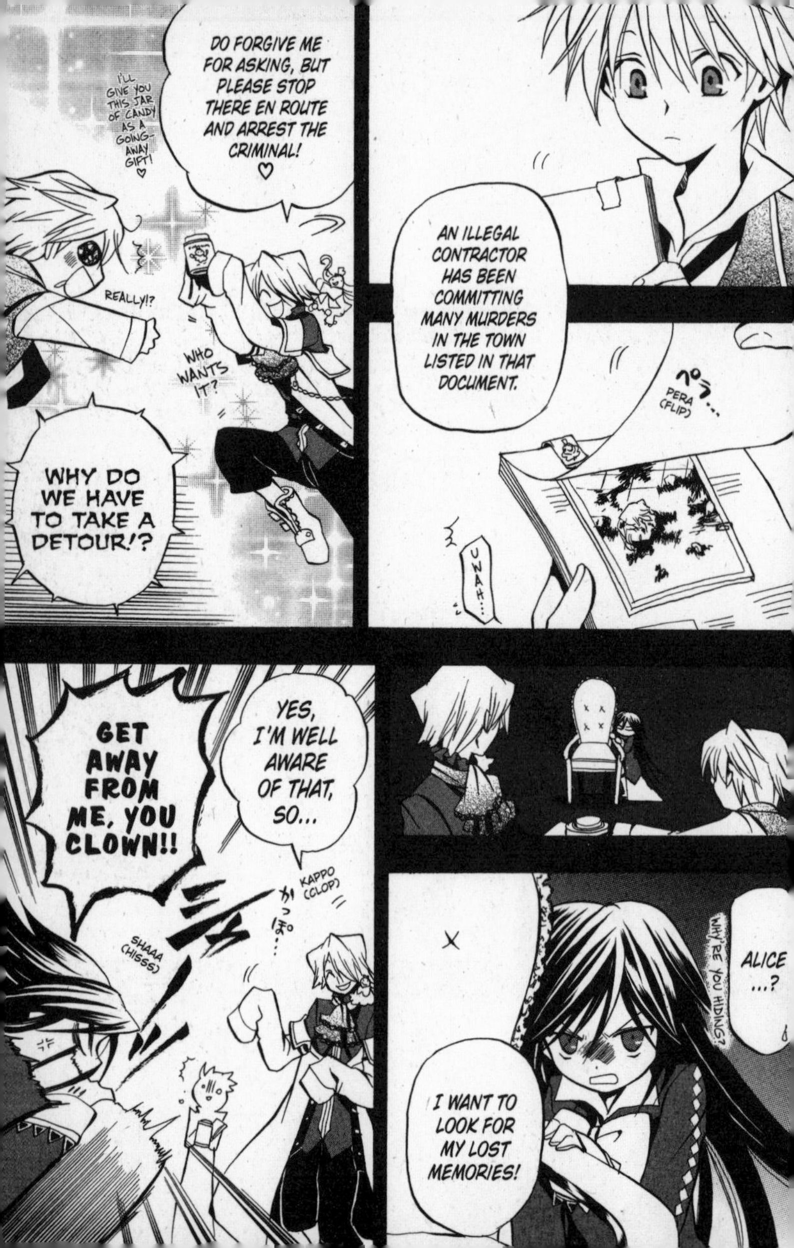
AN ILLEGAL CONTRACTOR HAS BEEN COMMITTING MANY MURDERS IN THE TOWN LISTED IN THAT DOCUMENT.
ぺら…
PERA (FLIP)
UWAH...
DO FORGIVE ME FOR ASKING, BUT PLEASE STOP THERE EN ROUTE AND ARREST THE CRIMINAL! ♡
I'LL GIVE YOU THIS JAR OF CANDY AS A GOING-AWAY GIFT! ♡
REALLY!?
WHO WANTS IT?
WHY DO WE HAVE TO TAKE A DETOUR!?
ALICE ...?
WHY'RE YOU HIDING?
I WANT TO LOOK FOR MY LOST MEMORIES!
YES, I'M WELL AWARE OF THAT, SO...
かっぽ…
KAPPO (CLOP)
GET AWAY FROM ME, YOU CLOWN!!
SHAAA (HISSS)

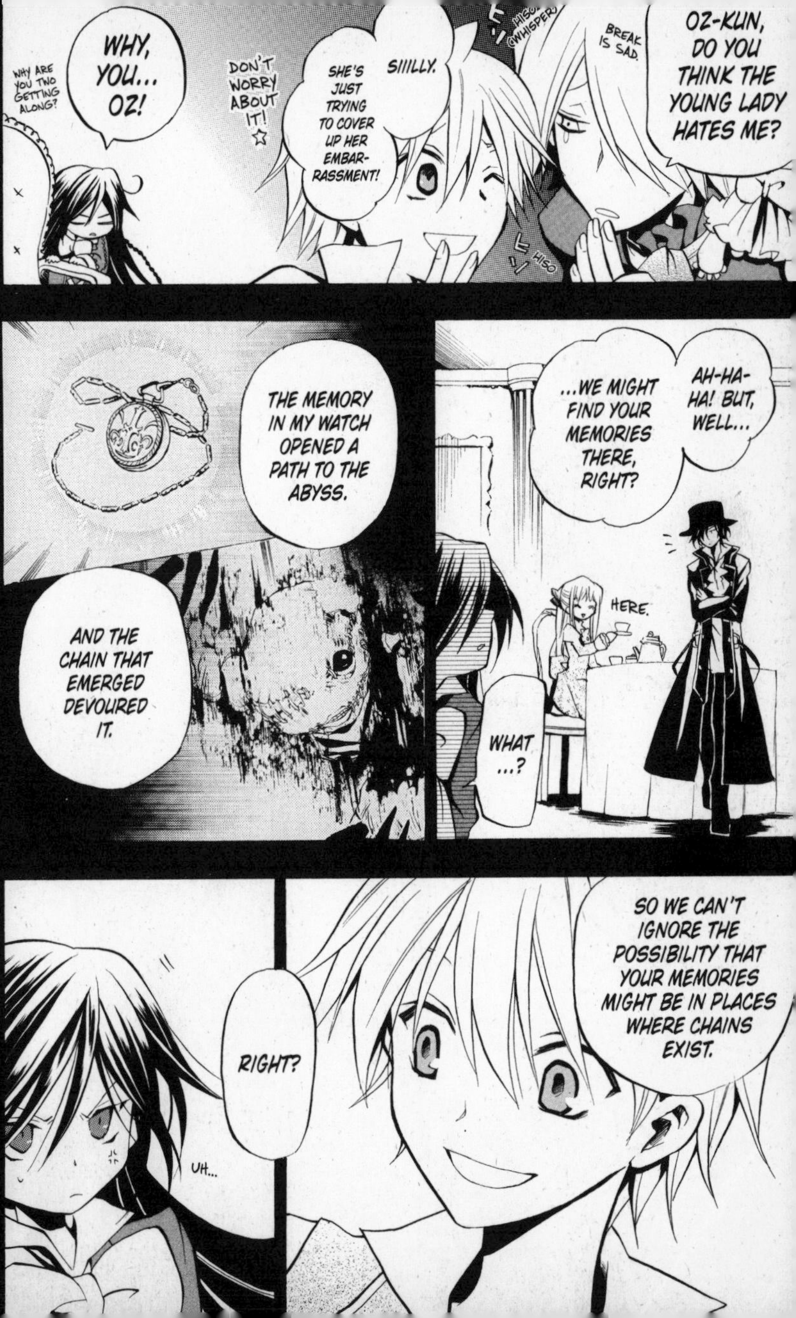
OZ-KUN, DO YOU THINK THE YOUNG LADY HATES ME?
BREAK IS SAD.
(WHISPER)
HISO
SIIILLY.
SHE'S JUST TRYING TO COVER UP HER EMBARRASSMENT!
DON'T WORRY ABOUT IT! ☆
WHY, YOU... OZ!
WHY ARE YOU TWO GETTING ALONG?
AH-HA-HA! BUT, WELL...
...WE MIGHT FIND YOUR MEMORIES THERE, RIGHT?
HERE.
WHAT ...?
THE MEMORY IN MY WATCH OPENED A PATH TO THE ABYSS.
AND THE CHAIN THAT EMERGED DEVOURED IT.
SO WE CAN'T IGNORE THE POSSIBILITY THAT YOUR MEMORIES MIGHT BE IN PLACES WHERE CHAINS EXIST.
RIGHT?
UH...

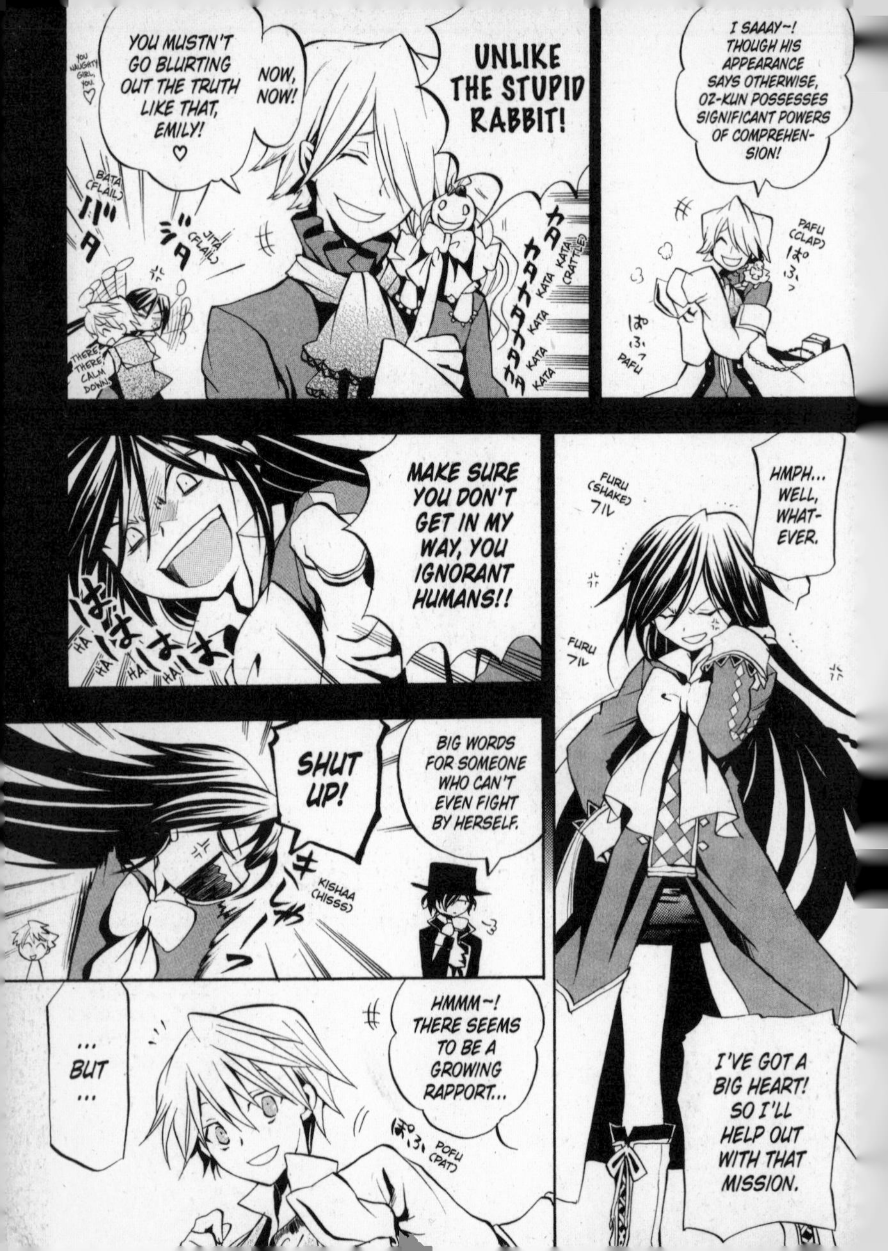
I SAAAY~! THOUGH HIS APPEARANCE SAYS OTHERWISE, OZ-KUN POSSESSES SIGNIFICANT POWERS OF COMPREHENSION!
PAFU (CLAP)
PAFU
UNLIKE THE STUPID RABBIT!
KATA KATA (RATTLE)
KATA KATA KATA KATA
NOW, NOW!
YOU MUSTN'T GO BLURTING OUT THE TRUTH LIKE THAT, EMILY! ♡
YOU NAUGHTY GIRL, YOU. ♡
BATA (FLAIL)
JITA (FLAIL)
THERE, THERE. CALM DOWN.
HMPH... WELL, WHATEVER.
FURU (SHAKE)
FURU
I'VE GOT A BIG HEART! SO I'LL HELP OUT WITH THAT MISSION.
MAKE SURE YOU DON'T GET IN MY WAY, YOU IGNORANT HUMANS!!
HA! HA! HA! HA!
BIG WORDS FOR SOMEONE WHO CAN'T EVEN FIGHT BY HERSELF.
SHUT UP!
KISHAA (HISSS)
HMMM~! THERE SEEMS TO BE A GROWING RAPPORT...
POFU (PAT)
... BUT ...

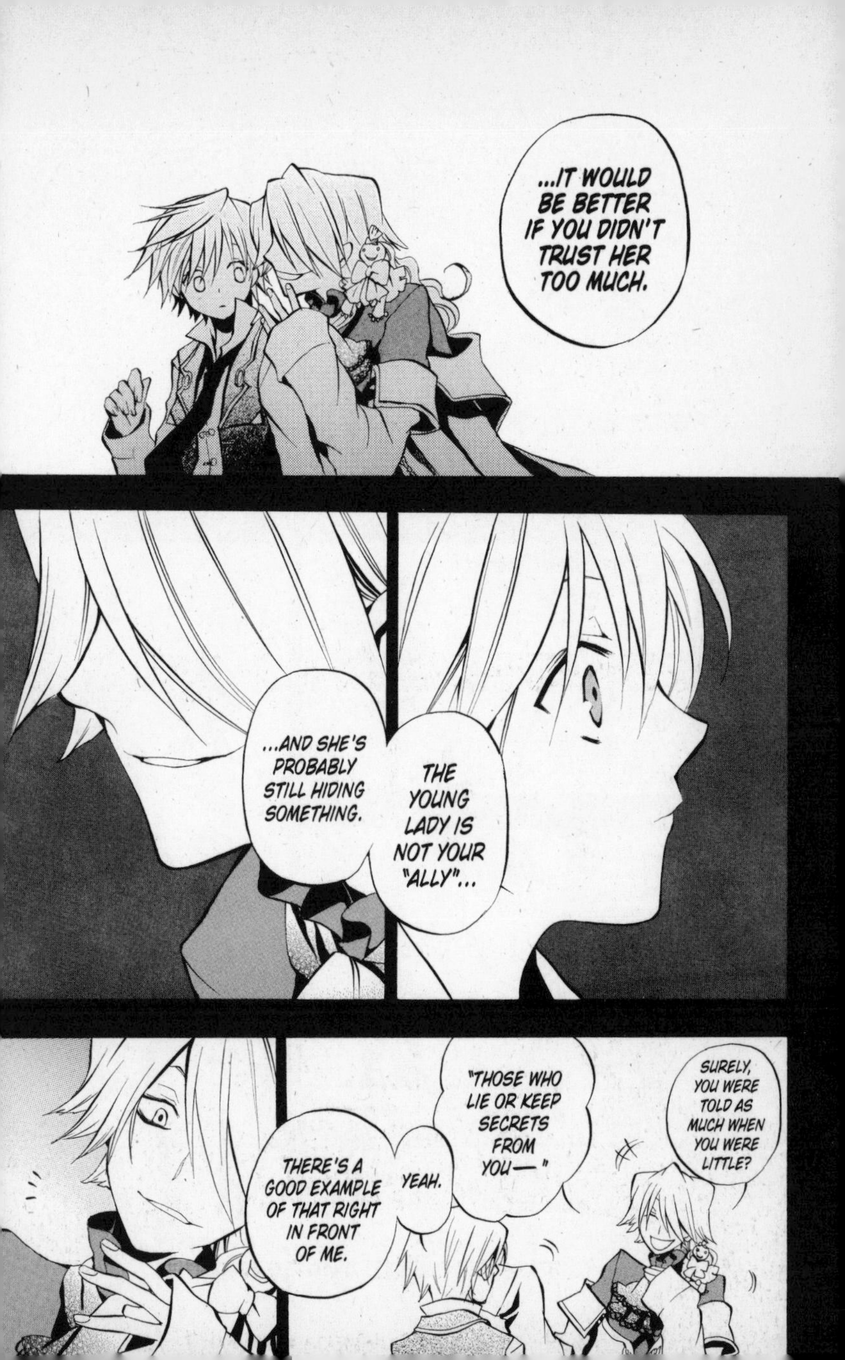
...IT WOULD BE BETTER IF YOU DIDN'T TRUST HER TOO MUCH.
THE YOUNG LADY IS NOT YOUR "ALLY"...
...AND SHE'S PROBABLY STILL HIDING SOMETHING.
SURELY, YOU WERE TOLD AS MUCH WHEN YOU WERE LITTLE?
"THOSE WHO LIE OR KEEP SECRETS FROM YOU—"
YEAH.
THERE'S A GOOD EXAMPLE OF THAT RIGHT IN FRONT OF ME.

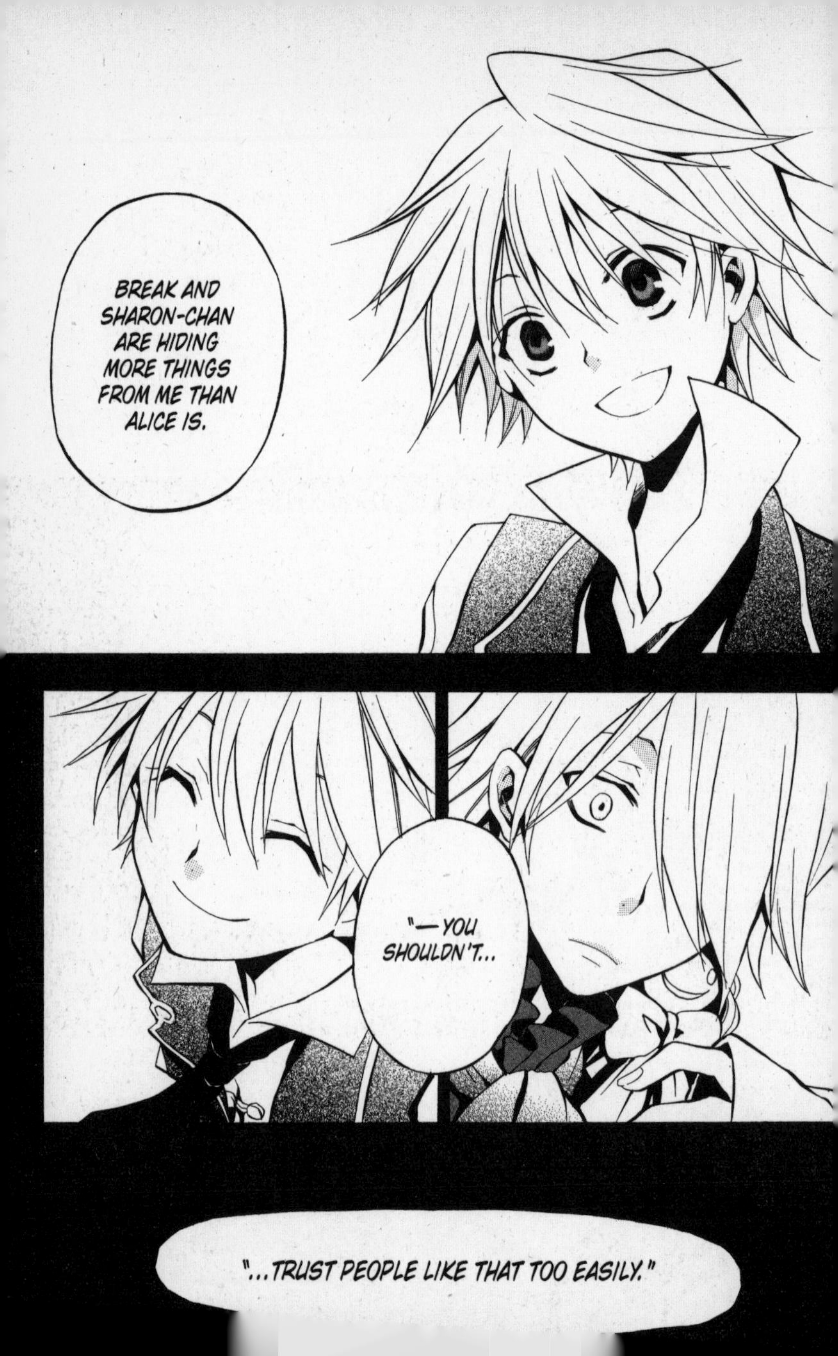
BREAK AND SHARON-CHAN ARE HIDING MORE THINGS FROM ME THAN ALICE IS.
"—YOU SHOULDN'T...
"...TRUST PEOPLE LIKE THAT TOO EASILY."

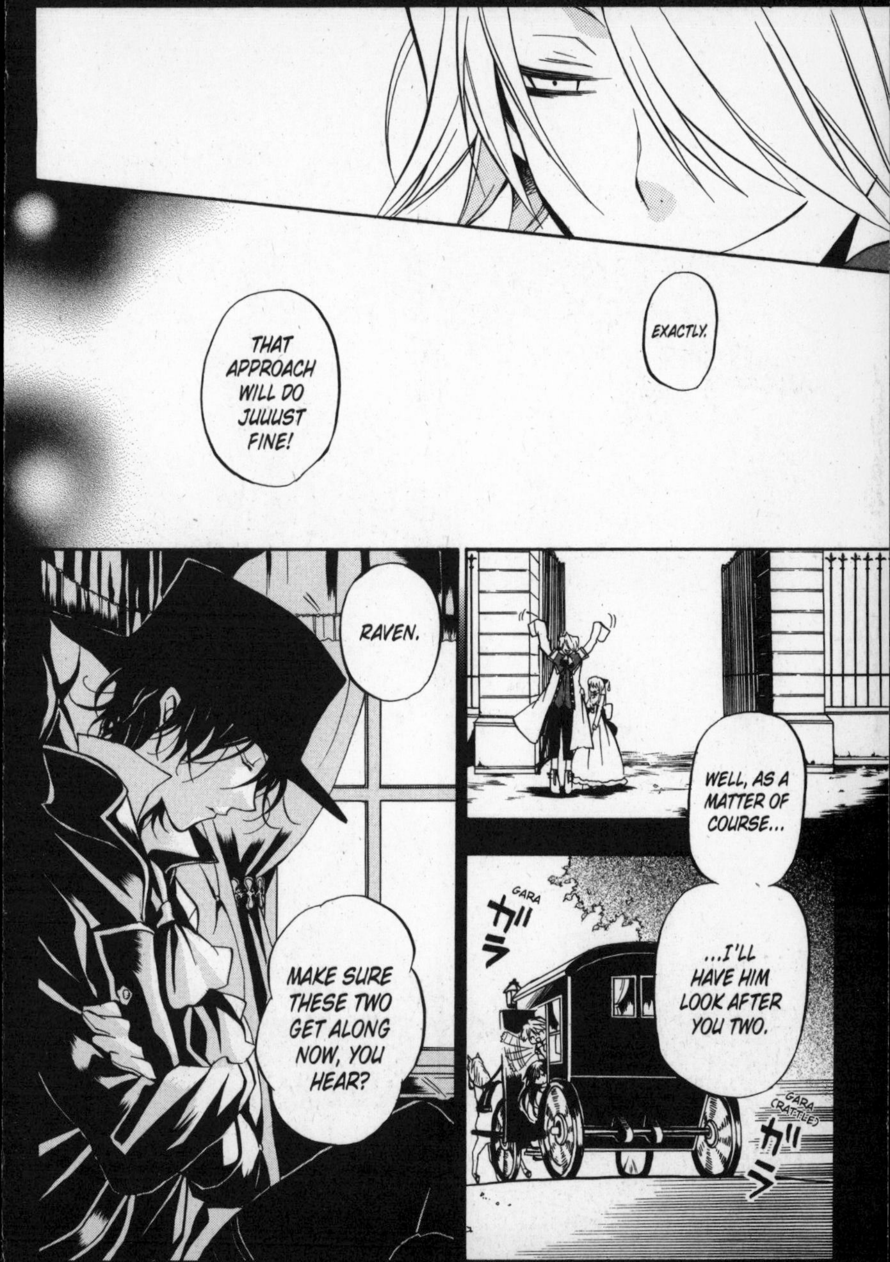
EXACTLY.
THAT APPROACH WILL DO JUUUST FINE!
WELL, AS A MATTER OF COURSE...
RAVEN.
...I'LL HAVE HIM LOOK AFTER YOU TWO.
GARA
MAKE SURE THESE TWO GET ALONG NOW, YOU HEAR?
GARA (RATTLE)

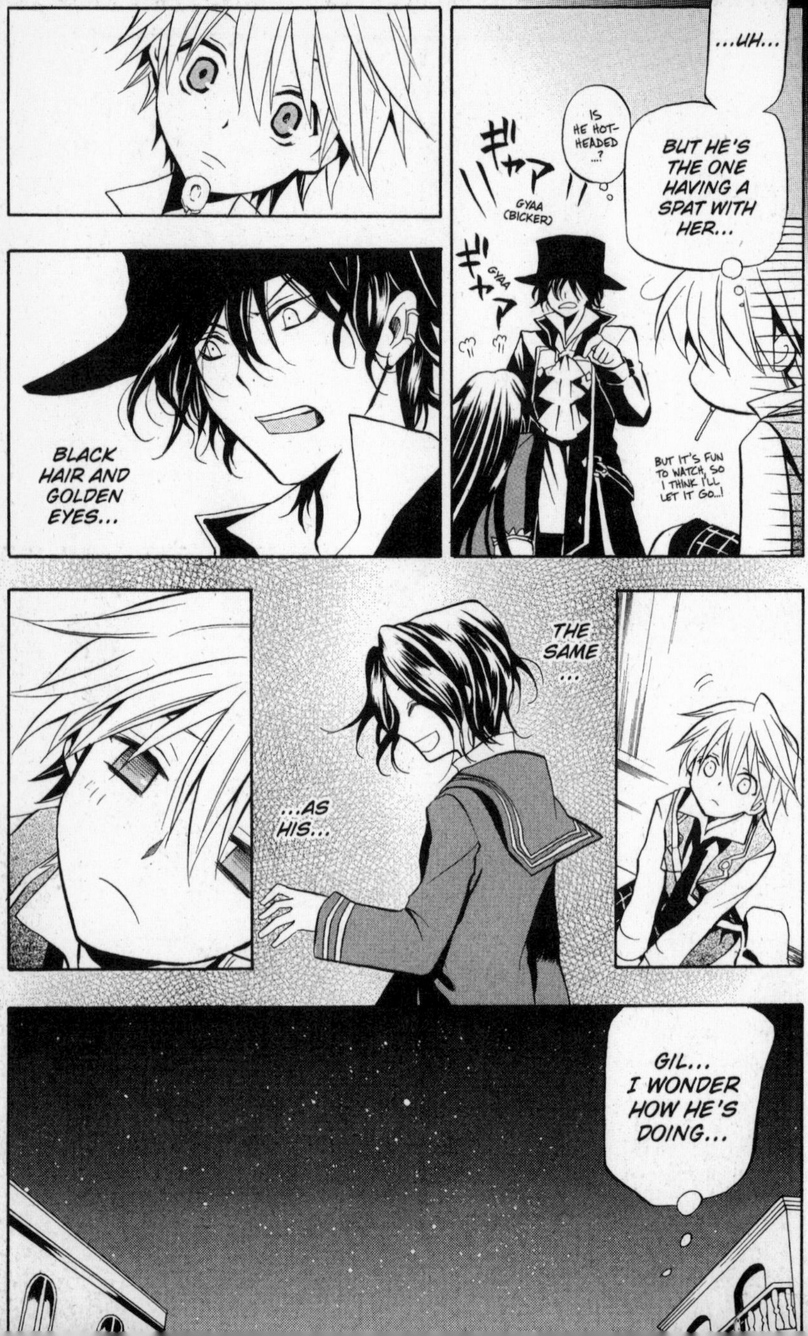
...UH...
BUT HE'S THE ONE HAVING A SPAT WITH HER...
IS HE HOT-HEADED ...?
ギャア
GYAA (BICKER)
ギャア
GYAA
BUT IT'S FUN TO WATCH, SO I THINK I'LL LET IT GO...!
BLACK HAIR AND GOLDEN EYES...
THE SAME ...
...AS HIS...
GIL... I WONDER HOW HE'S DOING...

WEREN'T WE GONNA LOOK FOR THE CONTRACTOR?

HEY.

....
...HEY, RAVEN?

I WANNA GET TO THE MANSION AS FAST AS POSSIBLE!!

IT'S LATE. WE'LL START WORKING TOMORROW.

WHY DO ILLEGAL CONTRACTORS TRY TO KILL PEOPLE?

GISHI (CREAK)

WHAT THE HELL!?

...WHAT ADVANTAGE DO THEY GET BY ENTERING INTO A CONTRACT WITH CHAINS?

WELL... I MEAN...

16

......

...SO IT'S NOT LIKE THEY FORCE THEMSELVES ON YOU.

EVEN ALICE WANTED MY CONSENT...

"YOU CAN CHANGE THE PAST."

THAT'S HOW CHAINS APPROACH PEOPLE.

...MANY... MANY TIMES...

...UNTIL THE INCUSE ON THEIR CHESTS COMPLETES ONE TURN.

I DON'T KNOW WHETHER THAT'S REALLY POSSIBLE.

BUT IN ORDER TO OBTAIN THAT POWER, CONTRACTORS MAKE THEIR CHAINS DEVOUR PEOPLE...

I DIDN'T NOTICE IT BECAUSE OF THE BANDAGES!

PUCHI (POP)

PUCHI

EH? FOR REAL !?

YOU'VE GOT ONE TOO.

IT APPEARS ON THE CHESTS OF ILLEGAL CONTRACTORS.

INCUSE ...?

AS TIME PASSES, THE HAND MOVES AND INSCRIBES MORE MARKS.

...IS A CLOCK THAT INDICATES THE TIME THAT REMAINS FOR A CONTRACTOR.

THE INCUSE ...

AND ...

...WHEN THE HAND RETURNS TO ITS ORIGINAL POSITION ...

18

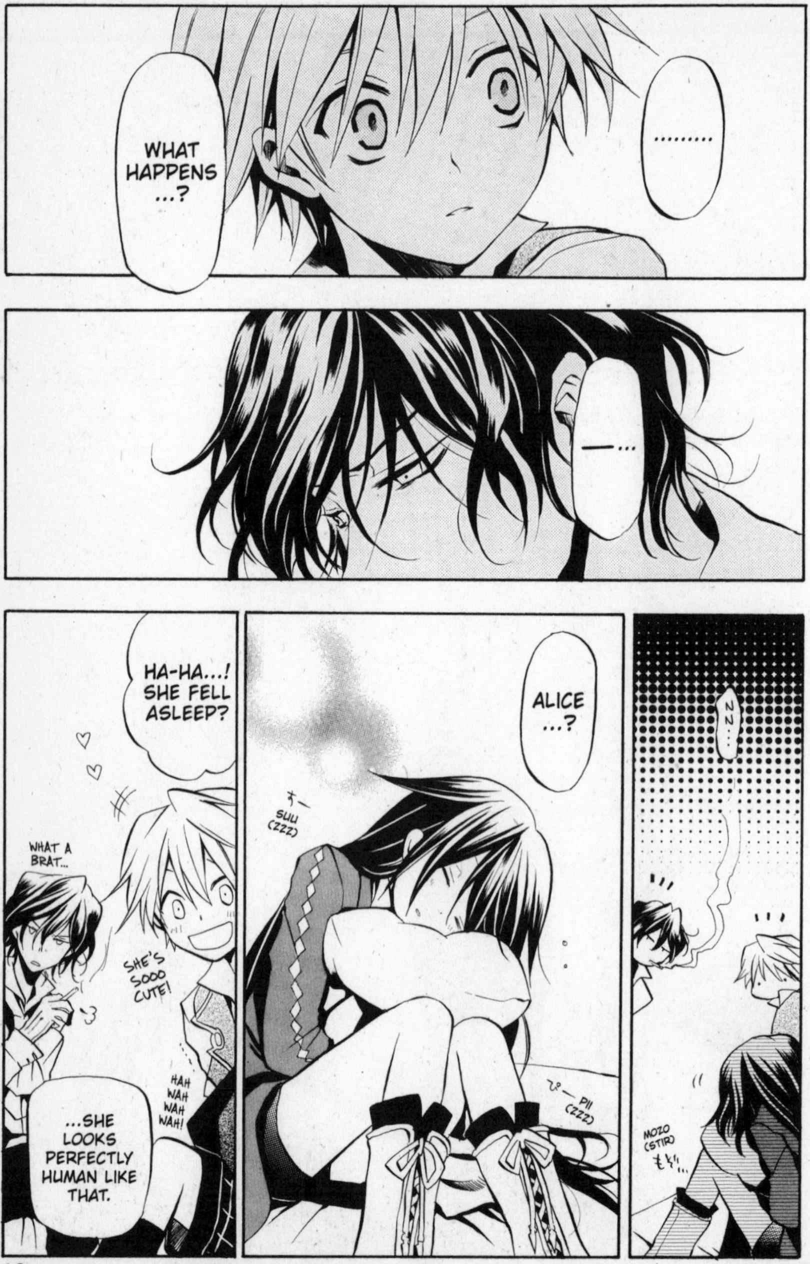
....
WHAT HAPPENS ...?
—...
NN...
MOZO (STIR)
ALICE ...?
SUU (ZZZ)
PII (ZZZ)
HA-HA...! SHE FELL ASLEEP?
SHE'S SOOO CUTE!
HAH WAH WAH WAH!
WHAT A BRAT...
...SHE LOOKS PERFECTLY HUMAN LIKE THAT.

ANYWAY, I'M GONNA GO ASK AROUND FOR INFORMATION.

ZURI (RUB)
ズリ…

YOU TWO START TOMORROW.

HUH? BUT YOU SAID WE'D INVESTIGATE TOMORROW...

...YEAH, YOU'RE RIGHT.

I WAS WAITING FOR HER TO FALL ASLEEP BECAUSE I FIGURED SHE'D INSIST ON COMING WITH ME.

EVEN THOUGH SHE WAS SO TIRED SHE FELL ASLEEP IN THE MIDDLE OF THE CONVERSATION.

YOU WANT TO GET TO THE MANSION AS FAST AS POSSIBLE, DON'T YOU?

I DON'T NEED TO SLEEP.

BUT RAVEN...

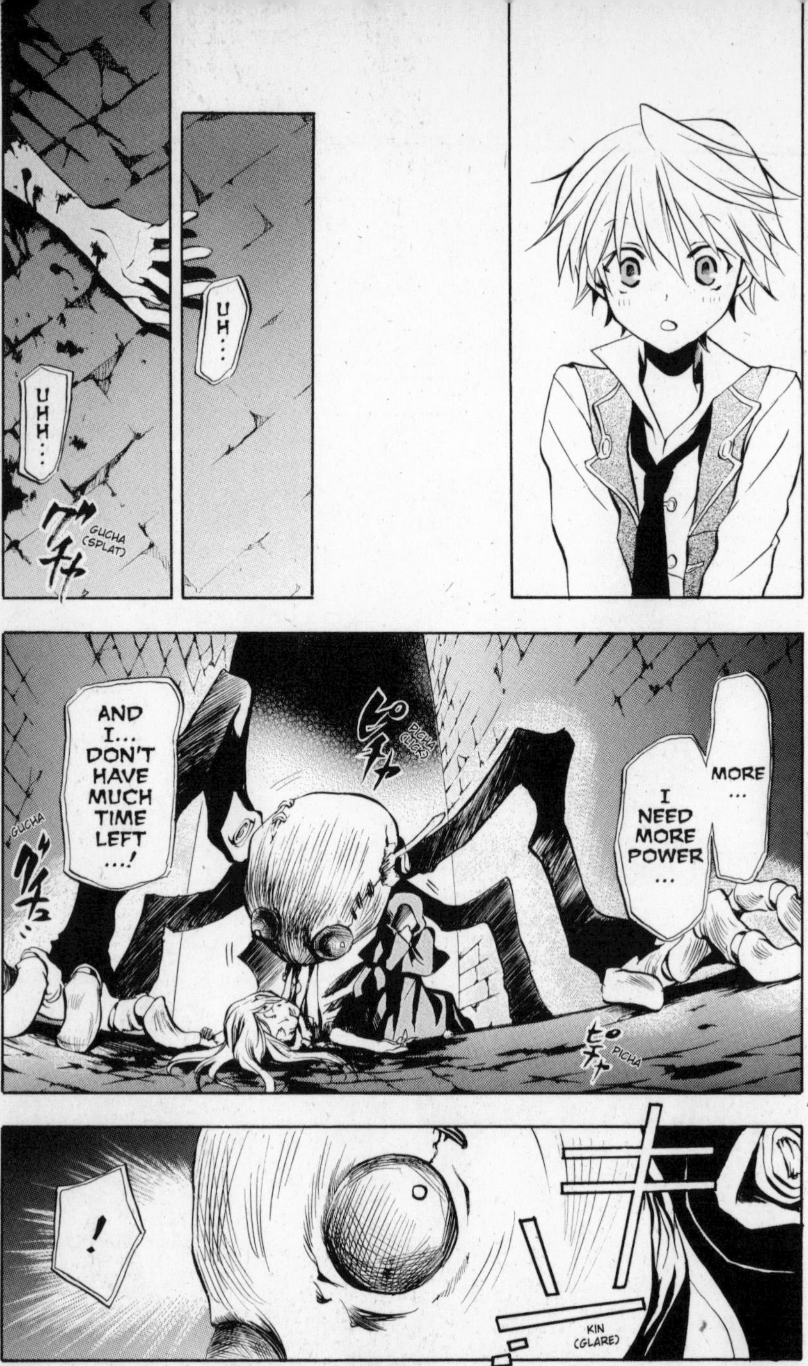
UH...
UHH...
GUCHA (SPLAT)
MORE... I NEED MORE POWER...
PICHA (CLICK)
AND I... DON'T HAVE MUCH TIME LEFT...!
GUCHA
PICHA
KIN (GLARE)
!

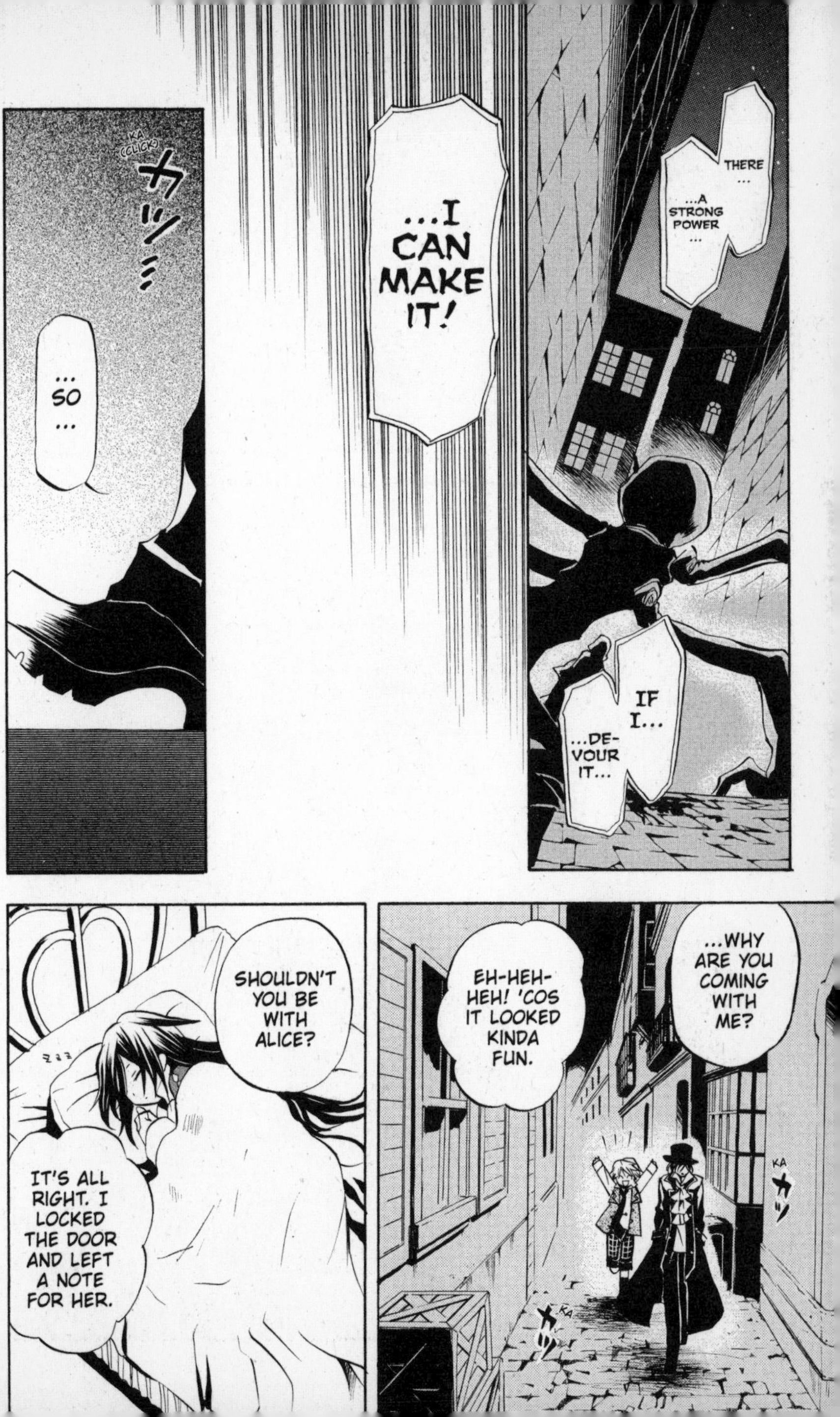
THERE ...
...A STRONG POWER ...
IF I...
...DE-VOUR IT...
...I CAN MAKE IT!
KA (CLICK)
カッ
... SO ...
...WHY ARE YOU COMING WITH ME?
EH-HEH-HEH! 'COS IT LOOKED KINDA FUN.
KA
カッ
KA
カッ
SHOULDN'T YOU BE WITH ALICE?
IT'S ALL RIGHT. I LOCKED THE DOOR AND LEFT A NOTE FOR HER.

HEH HEH HEH!

...WHAT IS IT? YOU'RE BEING CREEPY.

I'M GONNA KILL YOU...

"RAVEN NEEDS A LOOOONG POTTY BREAK, SO I'M GOING WITH HIM!" ♡

GU (DOINK)

WHAT DID YOU SAY!?

HERA (GRIN)

...I THINK RAVEN'S ACTUALLY A PRETTY GOOD GUY, LOOKS ASIDE!

HERA

WELL...

......

YOU LITTLE BRAT...

YOU WERE WORRYING ABOUT ALICE, EVEN THOUGH YOU KEPT COMPLAINING.

THAT WAS...

IT'S OKAY, IT'S OKAY! DON'T BE EMBAR-RASSED!

23

YOUR BODY NOW HARBORS THE POWERS OF AN ALIEN CHAIN...

YOU KEEP GETTING CAUGHT UP IN ALL THESE INEXPLICABLE THINGS.

HOW... CAN YOU BE SO CALM?

HOW CAN YOU LAUGH AS IF NOTHING'S HAPPENED?

GUESS YOU COULD SAY I'M GOOD AT ADAPTING.

ALICE SAID THE SAME SORT OF THING BEFORE...

HA HA ...!

I WANNA ENJOY THE PRESENT INSTEAD OF GRIEVING OVER THE PAST.

I CHOSE TO BE HERE WITH YOU GUYS...

...AND I'D LIKE TO FIND OUT JUST WHAT IT IS I'M BEING CAUGHT UP IN.

AND BE-SIDES...

KA Kツ (CLACK)

KA Kツ

KA Kツ

...I'M CURIOUS ABOUT WHAT EXACTLY ALICE IS TOO.

...IT BRINGS ME BACK TO THE PAST... AND IT KINDA MAKES ME WANT NOT TO LEAVE HER ALONE...

SO WHEN I SEE ALICE TRYING HER BEST TO LOOK FOR HER LOST MEMORIES...

ONCE...

...I LET SOMETHING IMPORTANT SLIP BY...

...WITHOUT TRYING TO FIND OUT THE TRUTH... 'COS I WAS SCARED OF GETTING HURT.

...AND I FIND HER DAZZLING.

...YOU'RE TRYING TO LEARN THE TRUTH NOW?

ISN'T THAT WHY...

IT'S HERE...

...OVER YONDER...

ズ
ZU
(SLITHER)

ズ
ZU

ズ
ZU

カ
KA
(CLICK)

カ
KA

YOU REGRET HAVING ONCE FEARED IT, RIGHT?

26

ZAWA
(FLASH)

THAT'S WHY YOU SAID...

..."I WANT TO KNOW WHAT THE BASKER-VILLES CALL MY SIN!"

WELL, THAT'S 'COS I'LL CAUSE MORE TROUBLE FOR EVERY-ONE IF I DON'T...

KA

...YOU'RE TRYING TO DISCOVER THE TRUTH NOW.

NO MATTER THE REASON...

KA

YOU'VE CHANGED *SINCE* THEN.

...EH ...?

DON
(BOOM)

!?

ARE
YOU
...?

...IS
OVER
THAT
WAY!

OUR
INN...

WHAT
WAS
THAT
!?

...
OHHH
...?

SHUUUU
(FWOOSH)

TAN
(TMP)

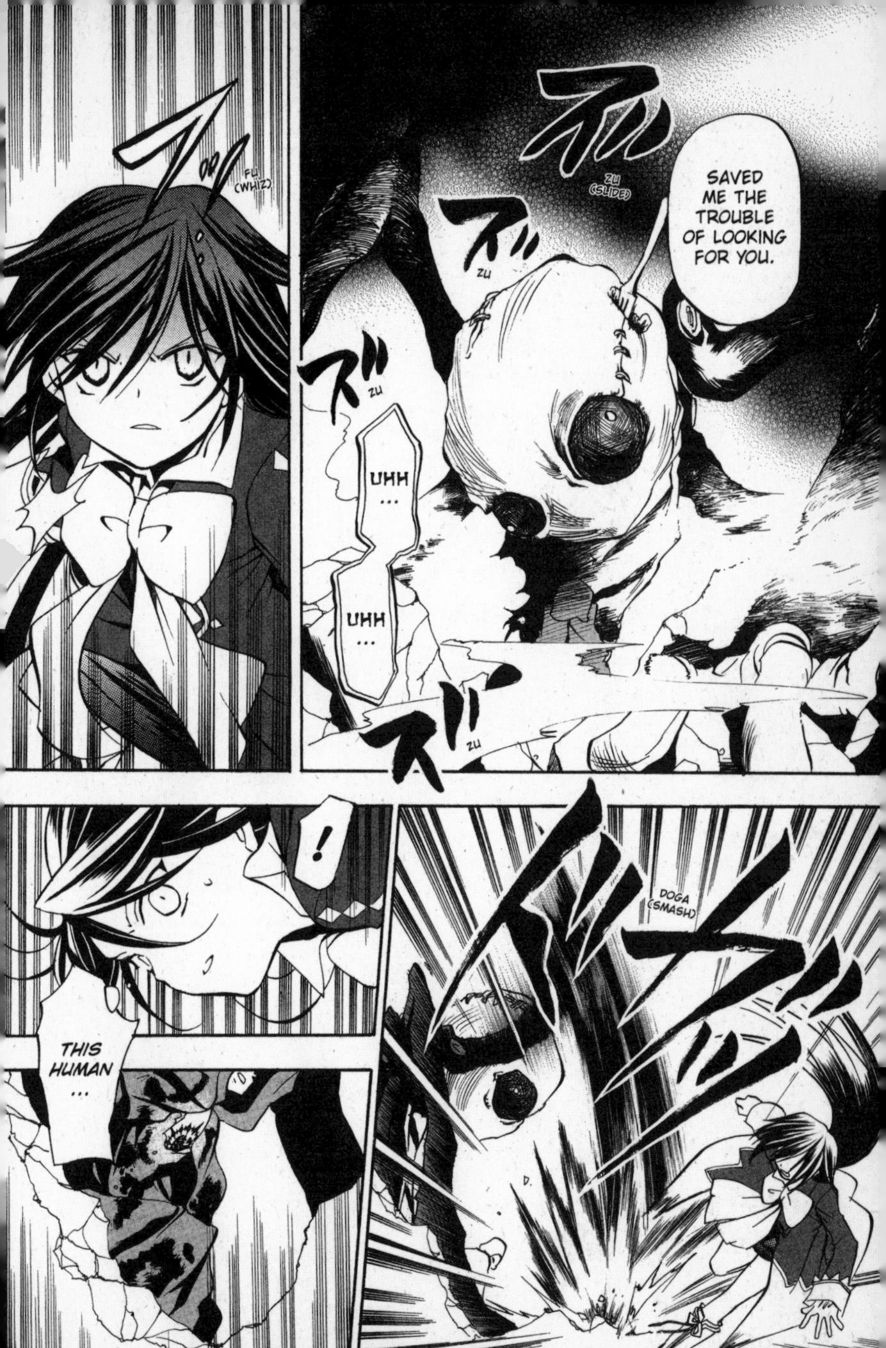
ZU (SLIDE)
SAVED ME THE TROUBLE OF LOOKING FOR YOU.
ZU
ZU
UHH... UHH...
ZU
FU (WHIZ)
DOGA (SMASH)
!
THIS HUMAN...

WHAT A HORRIBLE THING TO DO, BREAK.

THE HAND OF THE INCUSE...

...IS ALREADY...!?

OH DEAR. WERE YOU STILL AWAKE...

YOU INTENTIONALLY NEGLECTED TO GIVE THEM THIS PHOTO WITH THE INCUSE, HM?

...SHARON?

THIS...

NOW THEN, GAME OVER IS FAST APPROACH-ING FOR THE CON-TRACTOR.

I THOUGHT RAVEN WOULD BE TOO WORRIED ABOUT OZ-KUN TO ACCEPT THE JOB IF I DID.

NIKO (SMILE)

HAH!

HAH!

I WONDER IF THEY'VE FOUND ALICE YET...?

OZ!

ALICE.

I'M GLAD YOU'RE OKA—

OW!

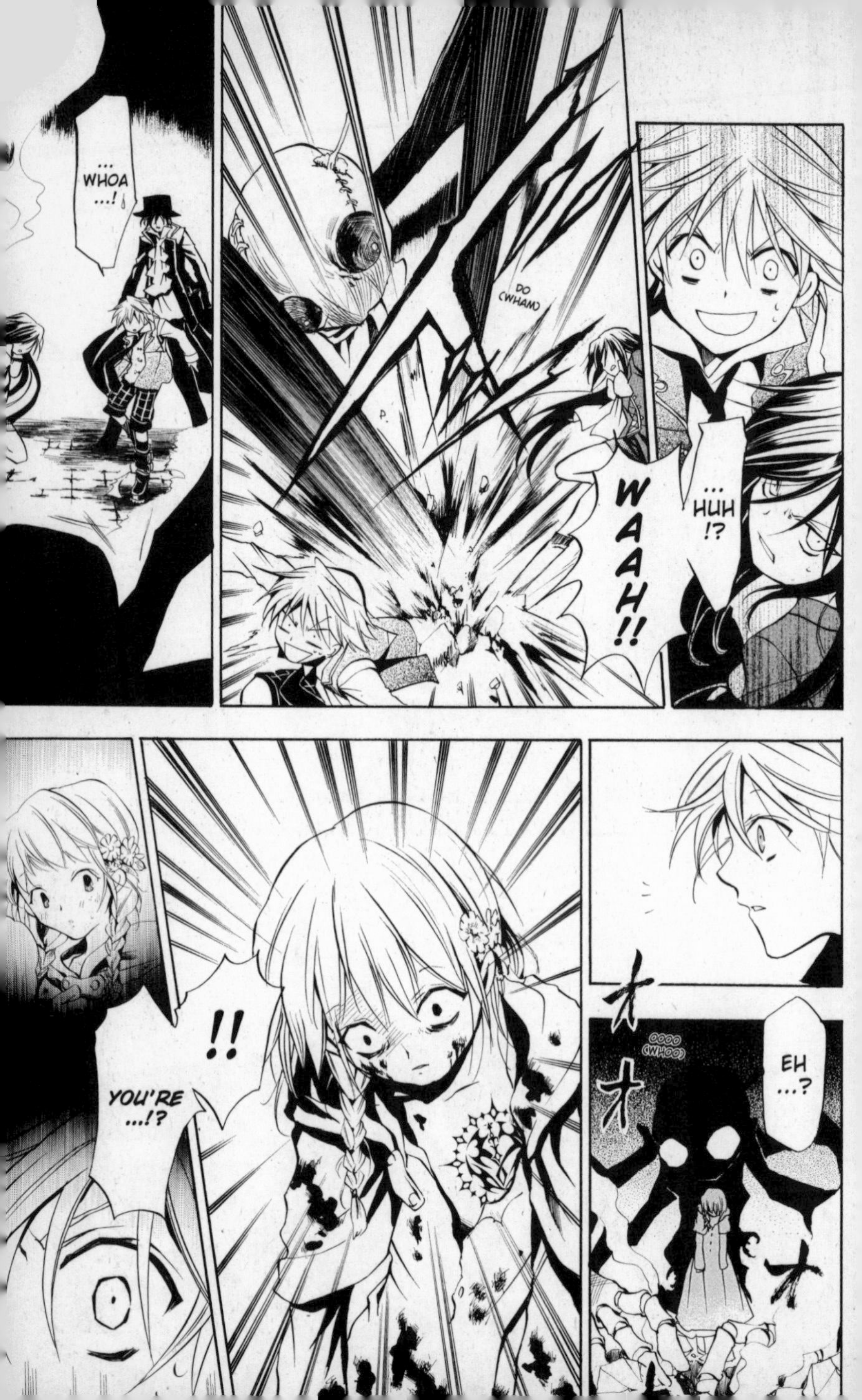
...HUH!?
WAAH!!
DO (WHAM)
...WHOA ...!
OOOO (WHOO)
EH ...?
!!
YOU'RE ...!?

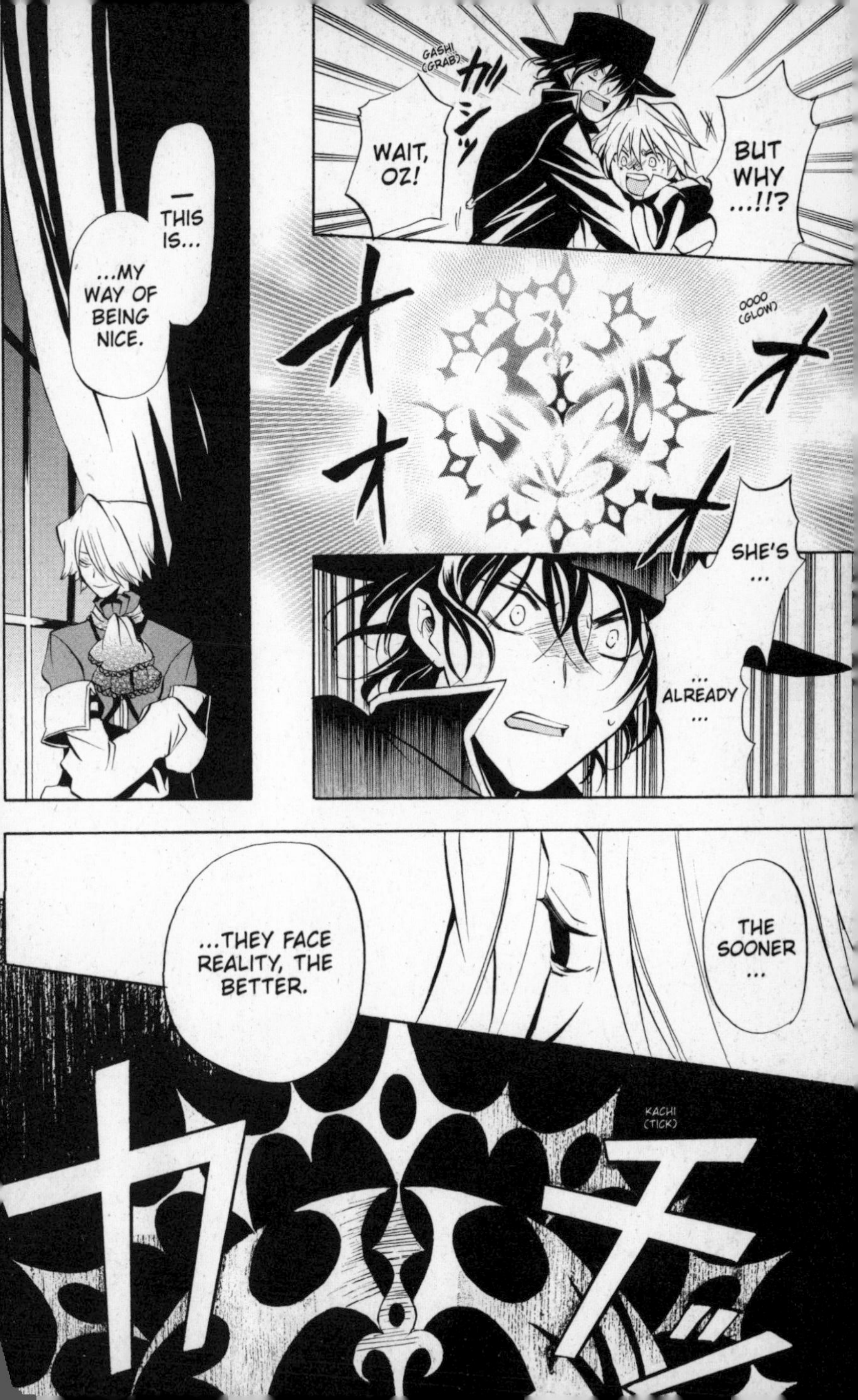
BUT WHY ...!!?
GASHI (GRAB)
WAIT, OZ!
OOOO (GLOW)
SHE'S ...
... ALREADY ...
— THIS IS...
...MY WAY OF BEING NICE.
THE SOONER ...
...THEY FACE REALITY, THE BETTER.
KACHI (TICK)

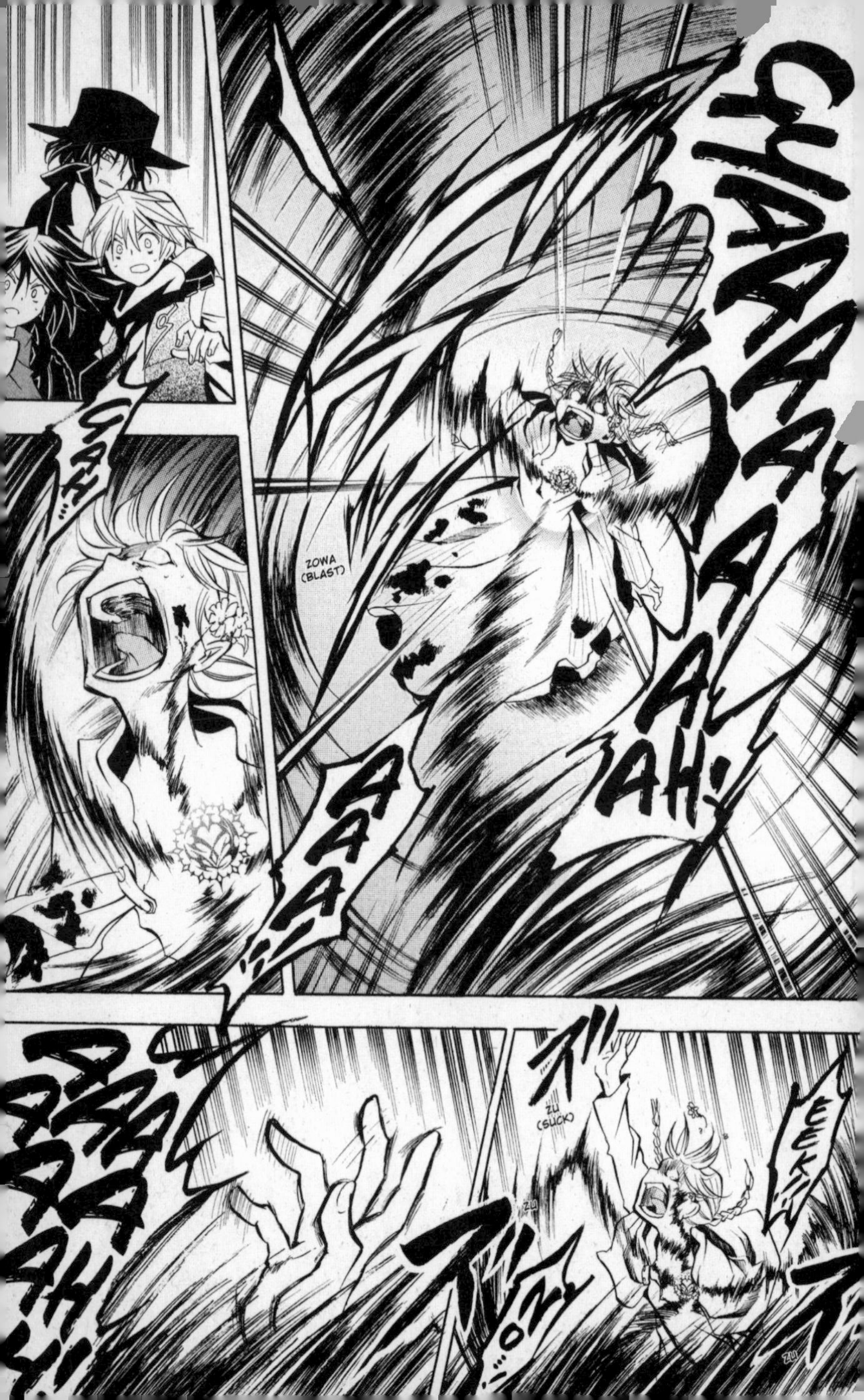
GYAAAAAAH!!
GAH...!
ZOWA (BLAST)
AAAA...!!
AAAAAAAAAH!!!
EEK!!
ZU (SUCK)
ZU
ZU

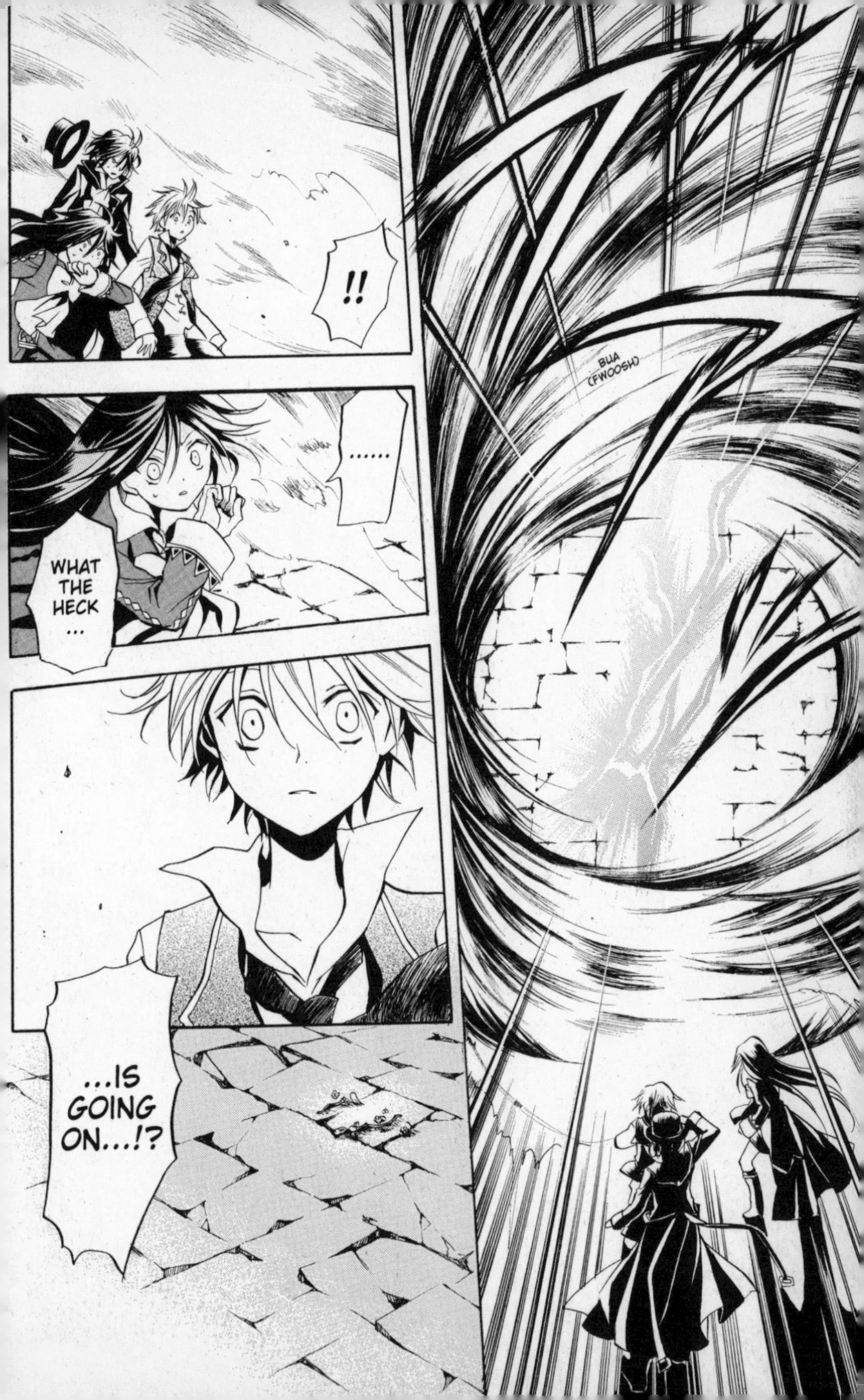
BUA
(FWOOSH)
!!
......
WHAT THE HECK ...
...IS GOING ON...!?

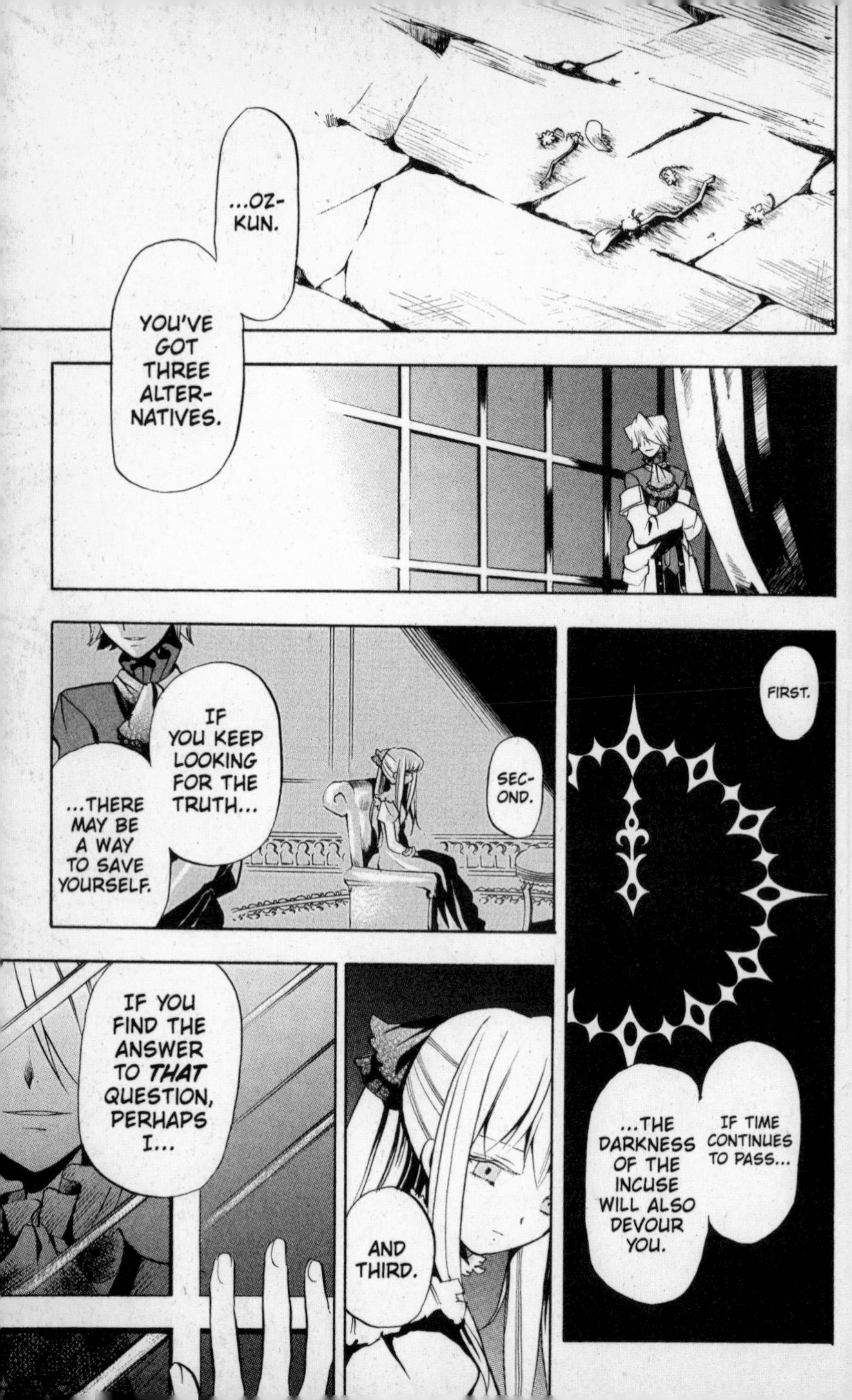
...OZ-KUN.
YOU'VE GOT THREE ALTERNATIVES.
FIRST.
IF TIME CONTINUES TO PASS...
...THE DARKNESS OF THE INCUSE WILL ALSO DEVOUR YOU.
SECOND.
IF YOU KEEP LOOKING FOR THE TRUTH...
...THERE MAY BE A WAY TO SAVE YOURSELF.
AND THIRD.
IF YOU FIND THE ANSWER TO *THAT* QUESTION, PERHAPS I...

...

REMEMBER THIS, OZ-KUN...

キリ
ギ
リ
... GYUU (CLENCH)

コツ...
KO (TAP)

THAT WHICH ULTIMATELY REMAINS...

...MAY NOT BE HOPE...!

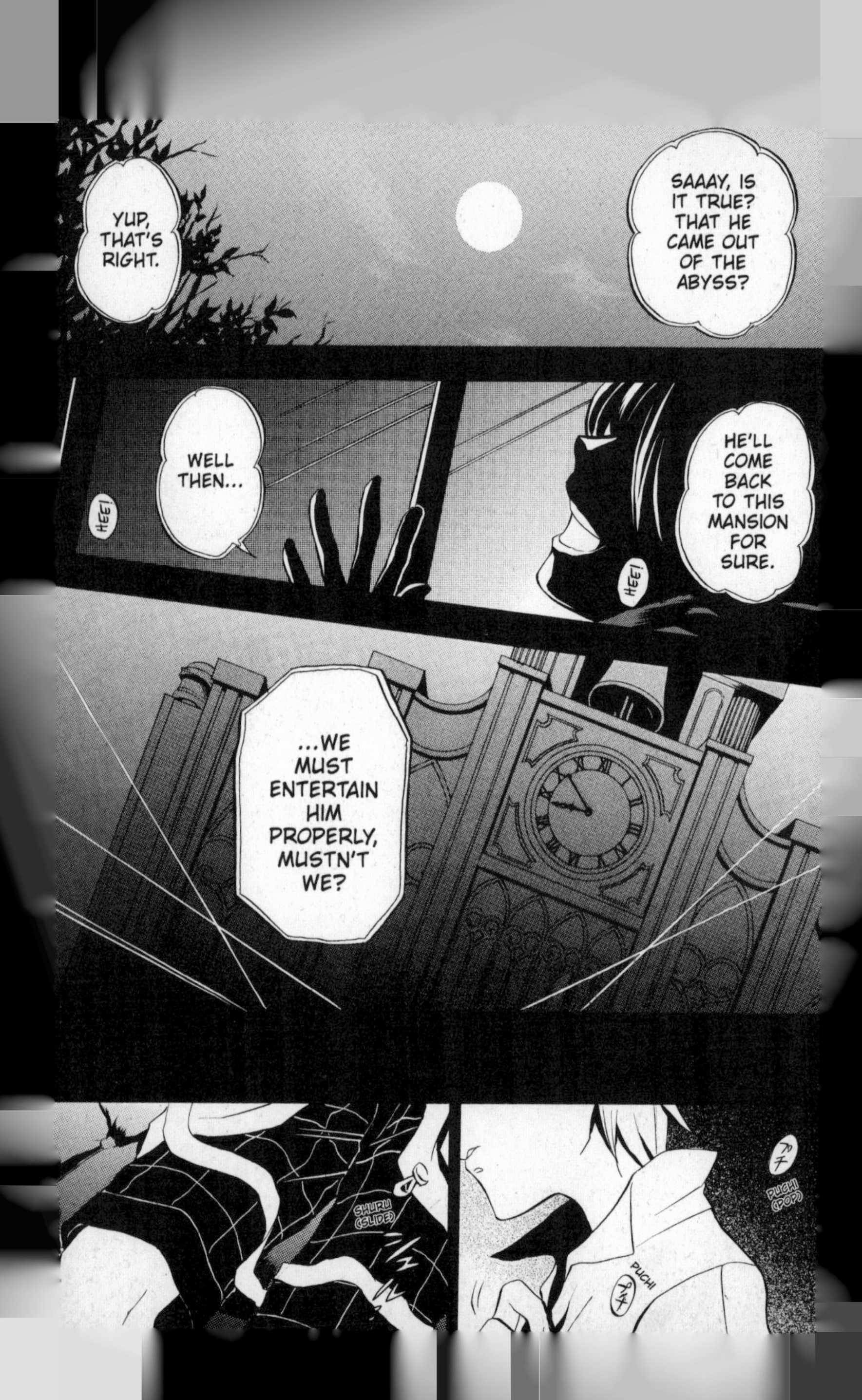
SAAAY, IS IT TRUE? THAT HE CAME OUT OF THE ABYSS?
YUP, THAT'S RIGHT.
HE'LL COME BACK TO THIS MANSION FOR SURE.
HEE!
WELL THEN...
HEE!
...WE MUST ENTERTAIN HIM PROPERLY, MUSTN'T WE?
PUCHI (POP)
PUCHI
SHURU (SLIDED)

THE INCUSE...

...INDICATES THE TIME THAT REMAINS, FOR A CONTRACTOR.

THE DARKNESS, WHICH SUCKED IN THE BRAT THAT TIME...

Retrace:Ⅵ
Where am I?

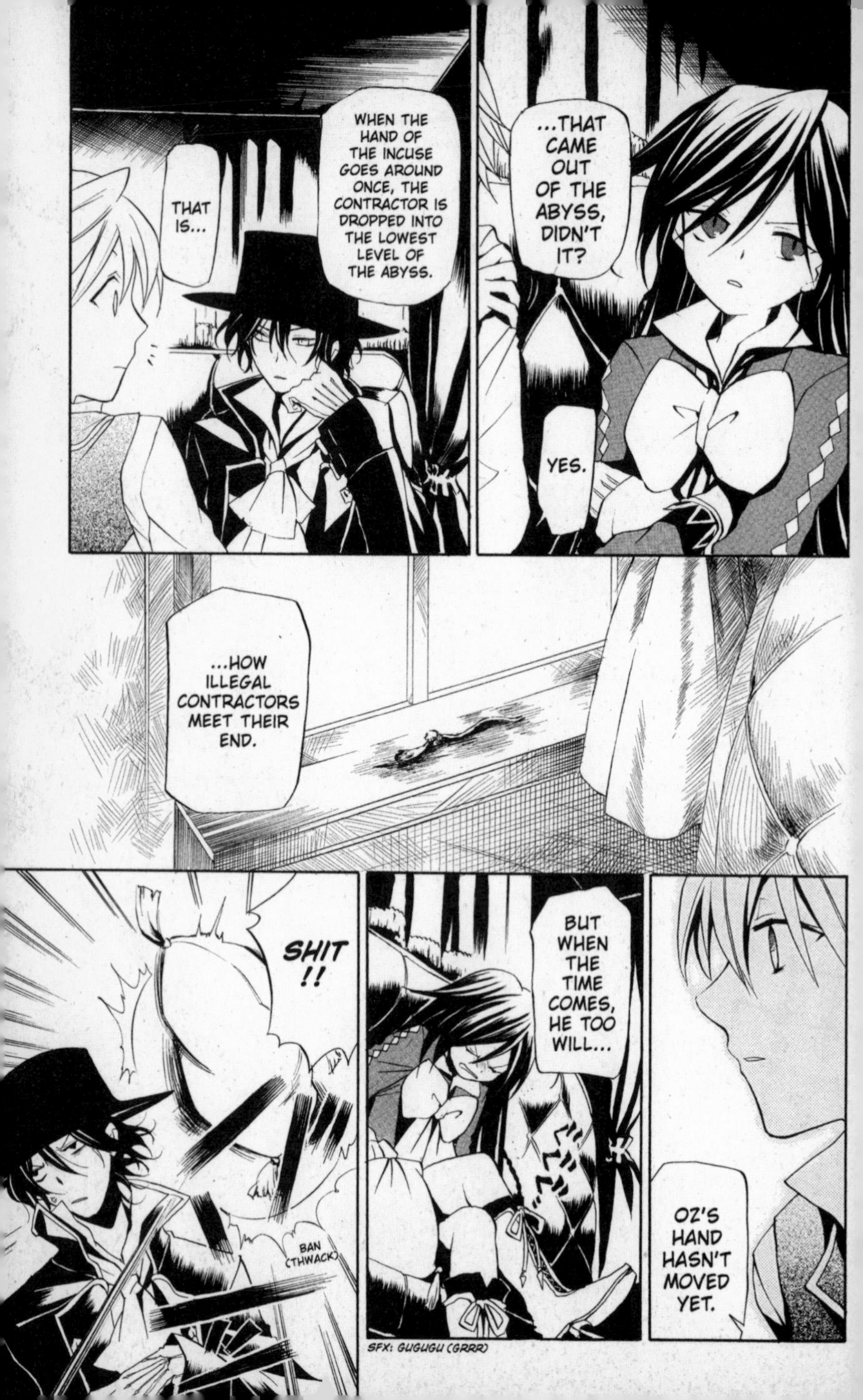
...THAT CAME OUT OF THE ABYSS, DIDN'T IT?
YES.
WHEN THE HAND OF THE INCUSE GOES AROUND ONCE, THE CONTRACTOR IS DROPPED INTO THE LOWEST LEVEL OF THE ABYSS.
THAT IS...
...HOW ILLEGAL CONTRACTORS MEET THEIR END.
OZ'S HAND HASN'T MOVED YET.
BUT WHEN THE TIME COMES, HE TOO WILL...
SHIT!!
BAN (THWACK)
SFX: GUGUGU (GRRR)

BECAUSE I THOUGHT YOU WOULD BE CONFUSED IF I TOLD YOU EVERYTHING AT ONCE.

I WAS GOING TO EXPLAIN IT LATER, OKAY?

FIRST OFF, WHY DIDN'T YOU TELL US ABOUT IT UNTIL NOW!?

ガラ GARA

ズ ガラ GARA (RATTLE)

ガラ GARA

...TO SEVER THE LINK BETWEEN THE CONTRACTOR AND THE CHAIN, I'D SAY.

...THE FASTEST WAY WOULD BE...

ISN'T THERE A WAY TO GET RID OF THE INCUSE?

....

YOU FOOL! YOU CAN'T...

THEN FIND A WAY TO NULLIFY THE CONTRACT.

ボス (CROSS)

ポカ (WHAP)

IN ANY CASE, WE NEED TO SEPARATE YOU AND OZ.

SO YOU JUST NEED TO DIE.

I THINK NOT!!!

HAH...

JAKA (CLACK)

...YOU STUPID RABBIT!

BUCHI (SNAP)

ZURU (SLIDE)

BAGO (WHOOMP)

...DO THAT!!

ZAWA (FWSH)

THEN FORGET ABOUT THE INCUSE AND FOCUS ON FINDING YOUR MEMORIES!!

DON'T BOSS ME AROUND WHEN YOU'RE JUST A SLAVE TO THAT CLOWN!!

DON (BANG)

AAH...

NN?

KI (GLARE)

OZ! YOU SAY SOMETHING TOO!!

....

...SOOO WHY DON'T YOU CONTINUE LOOKING FOR YOUR MEMORIES?

WELL, THERE'S NO USE RUSHING THINGS...

のほーん
NOHOOON (UNFAZED)

...SO WE CAN LEAVE THE INCUSE PROBLEM FOR THEM TO DEAL WITH.

WHAT I MEAN IS, BREAK SAID WE SHOULD FOCUS ON FINDING YOUR MEMORIES...

BYUUUUU (WHOOOOSH)

OWW!?

WERE MY WORDS TOO DIFFICULT FOR THE STUPID RABBIT? I DO APOLOGIZE.

IF THAT'S HOW IT IS, THEN SPIT IT OUT AT THE GET-GO, YOU SCUMBAG!

...WELL, SOMETHING LIKE THAT.

...RAVEN?

GURI (GRIND)
GURI

I'M GONNA FALL! I'M GONNA FALL, ALICE-SAN!!

NOOOOOOO!!

44

THANK YOU, MASTER!

...WHAT KIND OF PAST...

SO THEN...

HEY, RAVEN...

ホン
PON (PAT)

ポン
PON

AN ILLEGAL CONTRACTOR KILLS PEOPLE TO CHANGE THE PAST, RIGHT?

......

...WAS A LITTLE GIRL LIKE HER...

...TRYING TO CHANGE SO DESPERATELY, I WONDER...?

......

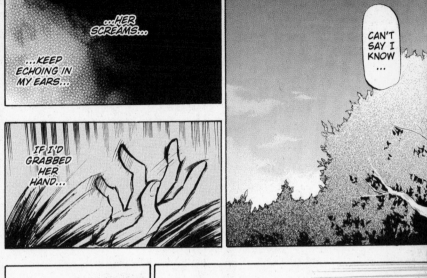

...HER SCREAMS...

...KEEP ECHOING IN MY EARS...

CAN'T SAY I KNOW...

IF I'D GRABBED HER HAND...

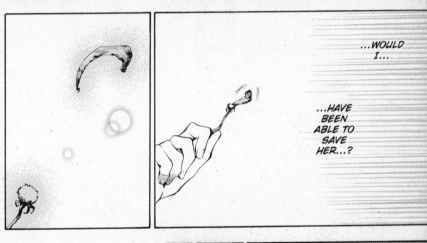

...WOULD I...

...HAVE BEEN ABLE TO SAVE HER...?

...WELCOME...

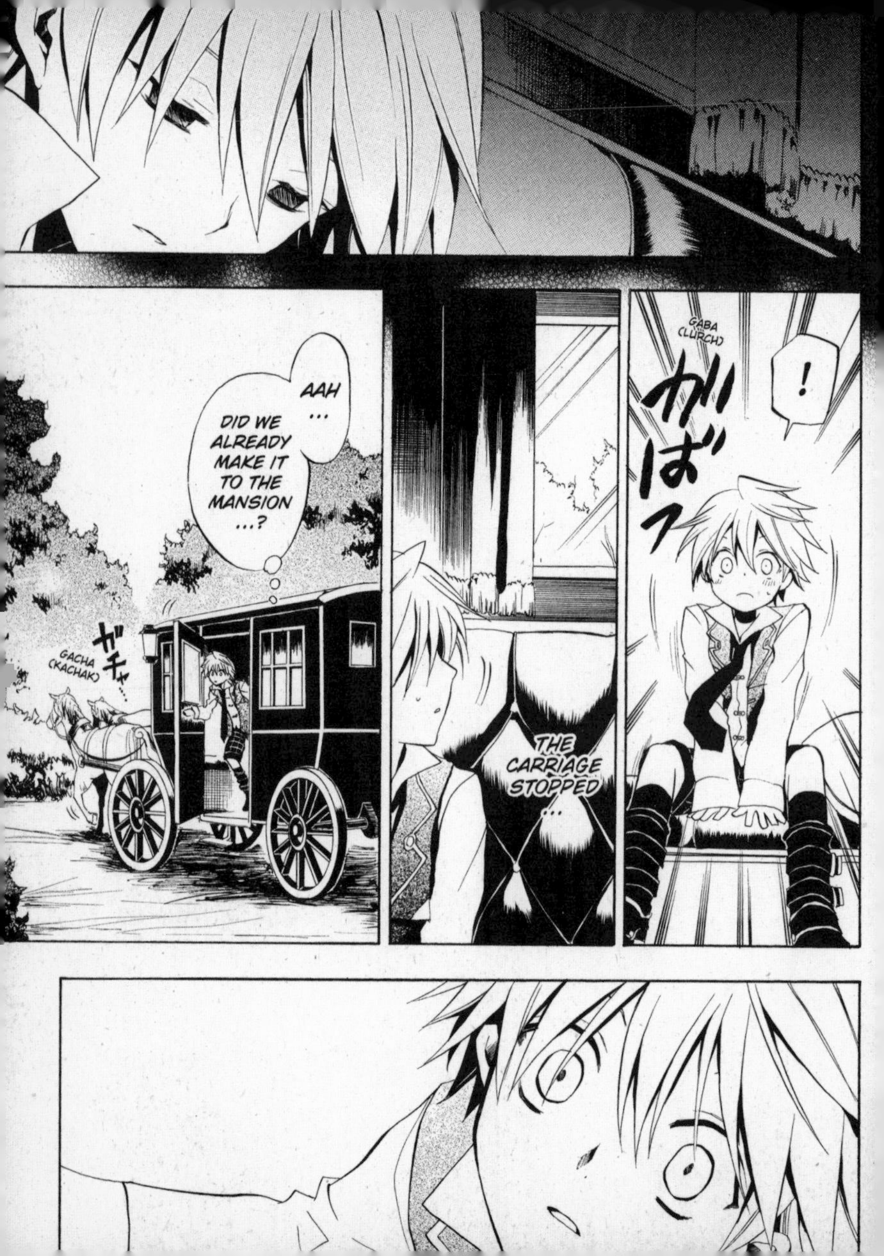
!
GABA (LURCH)
がばっ
THE CARRIAGE STOPPED ...
AAH ...
DID WE ALREADY MAKE IT TO THE MANSION ...?
GACHA (KACHAK)
ガチャ...

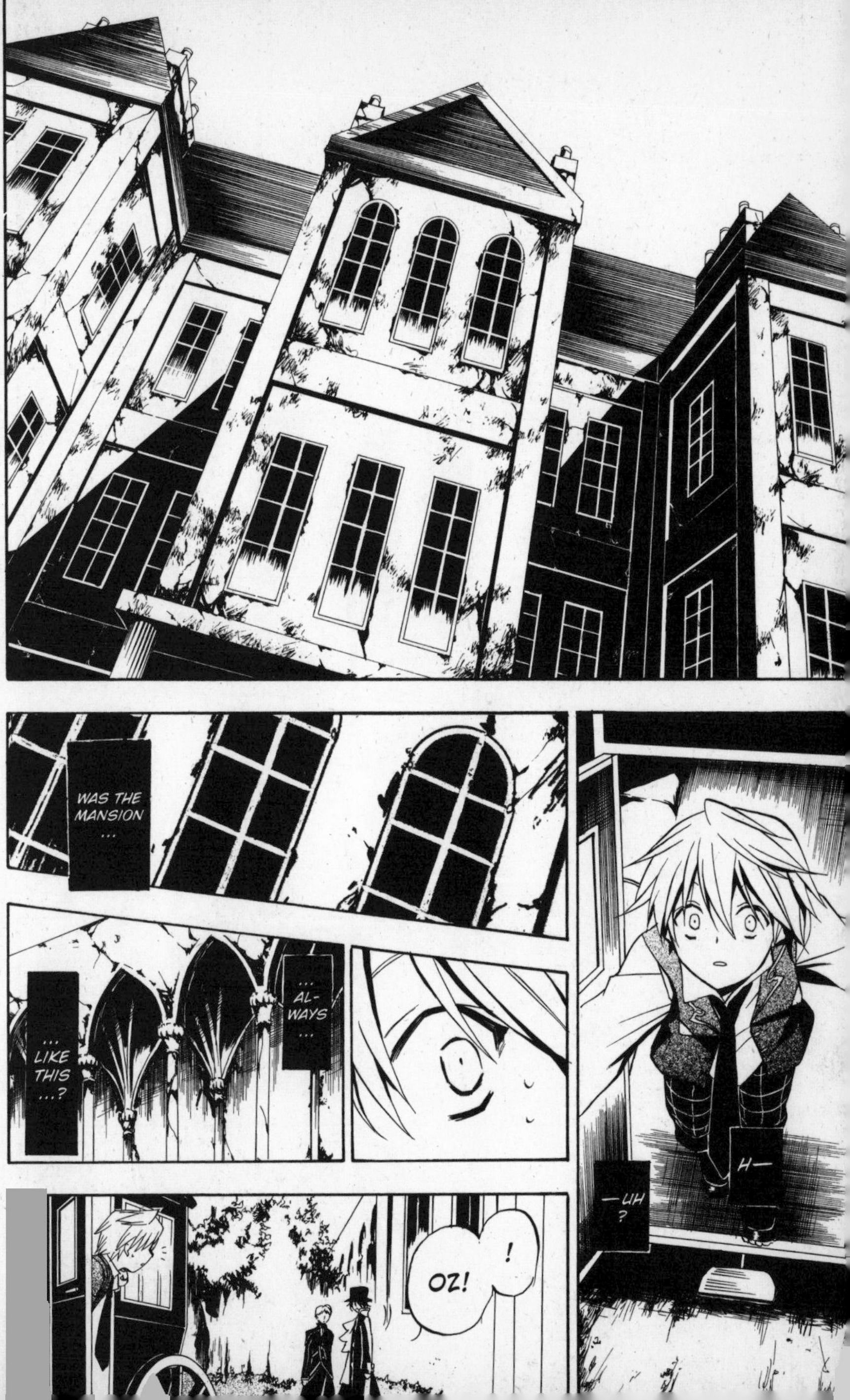
WAS THE MANSION ...
... AL-WAYS ...
... LIKE THIS ...?
H—
—UH ?
OZ!
!

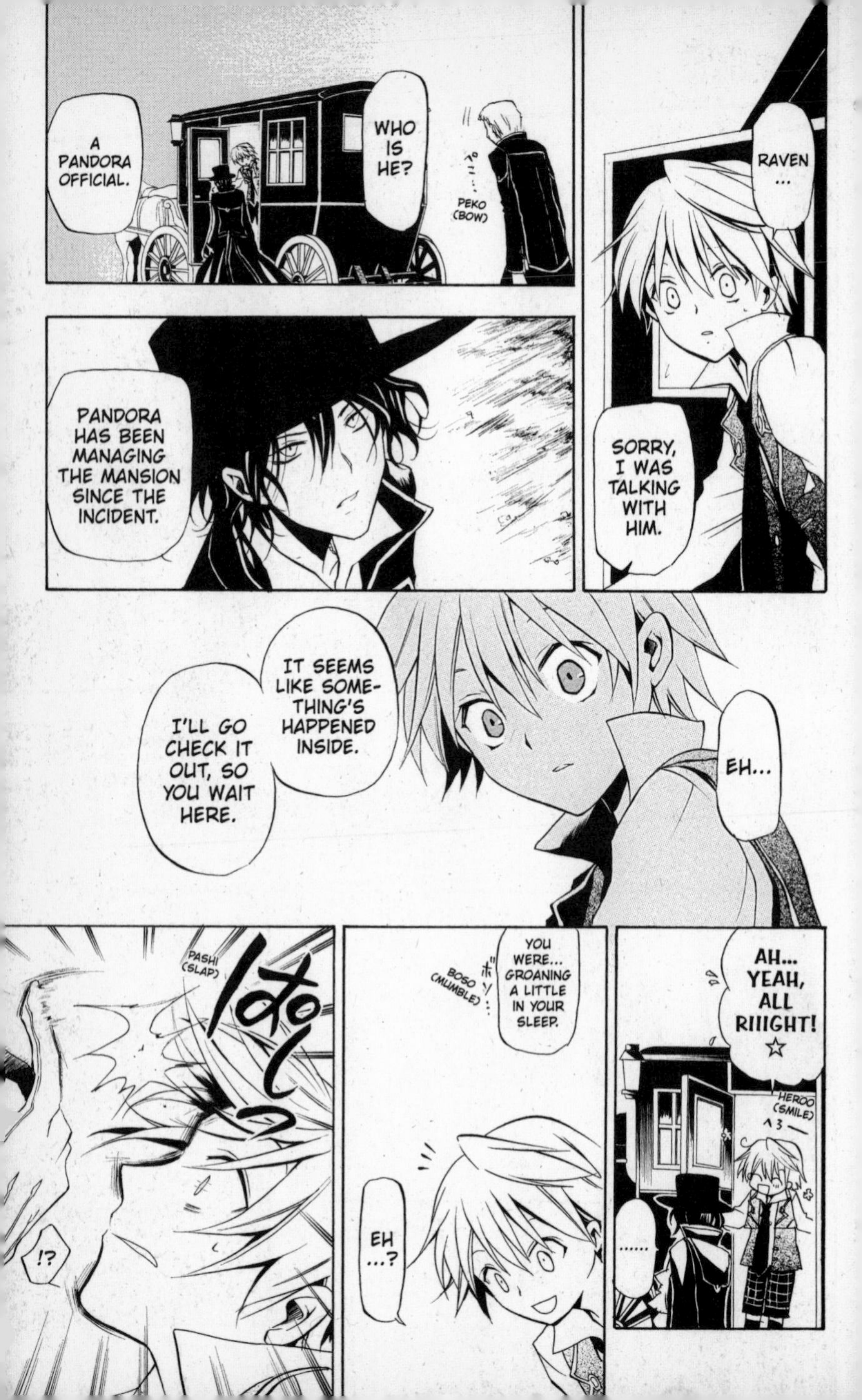
RAVEN ...
SORRY, I WAS TALKING WITH HIM.
WHO IS HE?
PEKO (BOW)
A PANDORA OFFICIAL.
PANDORA HAS BEEN MANAGING THE MANSION SINCE THE INCIDENT.
EH...
IT SEEMS LIKE SOME-THING'S HAPPENED INSIDE.
I'LL GO CHECK IT OUT, SO YOU WAIT HERE.
AH... YEAH, ALL RIIIGHT! ☆
HEROO (SMILE)
......
YOU WERE... GROANING A LITTLE IN YOUR SLEEP.
BOSO (MUMBLE)
EH ...?
PASHI (SLAP)
!?

NO ONE COULD'VE DONE ANY-THING... FOR THAT FLOWER GIRL.

DON'T THINK ABOUT IT TOO MUCH.

NOT I...

...NOR YOU...

...HE SURE SEEMS...

...A LOT LIKE GIL...

...SOME-HOW...

(PORI) (SCRATCH)

50

GIL... THE BLACK-HAIRED BRAT...?

AH. SORRY. DID I WAKE YOU UP?

......

MUNYA (SLEEPY)

MOZO (SQUIRM)

YUP, HE WAS AT THE PARTY...

SO... GIL'S...

...THE BRAT YOU CUT DOWN?

51

THAT'S HIM.

...YEAH.

...DOESN'T HAVE ANY MEMORIES FROM WHEN HE WAS LITTLE.

SEE, GIL...

IT WOULD BE NICE IF GIL WERE HERE.

?

SINCE YOU GUYS ARE SO ALIKE, HE MIGHT'VE BEEN A GOOD PERSON FOR YOU TO TALK TO, ALICE.

GUESS IT'S ALREADY BEEN ABOUT FIVE YEARS...

...SINCE UNCLE BROUGHT HIM TO US...?

MUKU (RISE)

HOHH...?

IT SURE BRINGS ME BACK.

52

—OZ.

COME HERE FOR A SEC.

HE'LL BE YOUR VALET FROM TODAY ON.

THIS BOY IS GILBERT.

HE COULD HARDLY REMEMBER ANYTHING BESIDES HIS NAME.

ONE DAY, OUT OF THE BLUE, WE FOUND HIM COLLAPSED IN THE GARDEN OF OUR MANOR.

...HE SEEMED TO BE REALLY AFRAID OF SOMETHING.

MAYBE THAT WAS WHY...

BIKU (FLINCH)

DON (BAM)

...YES...

SO YOU'RE...

...GONNA BECOME MY VALET, HUH!?

SO I...

SFX: MOJI (FIDGET) MOJI

...ALL RIGHT!

IF YOU DON'T, I'LL PUNISH YOU!

YES...

DONE!

SO YOU'LL DO WHATEVER I SAY, RIGHT?

YES...

OH, AND

...WILL YOU EAT MY VEGETABLES FOR ME!? I HATE THEM!

...YES.

SFX: HISO (WHISPER) HISO

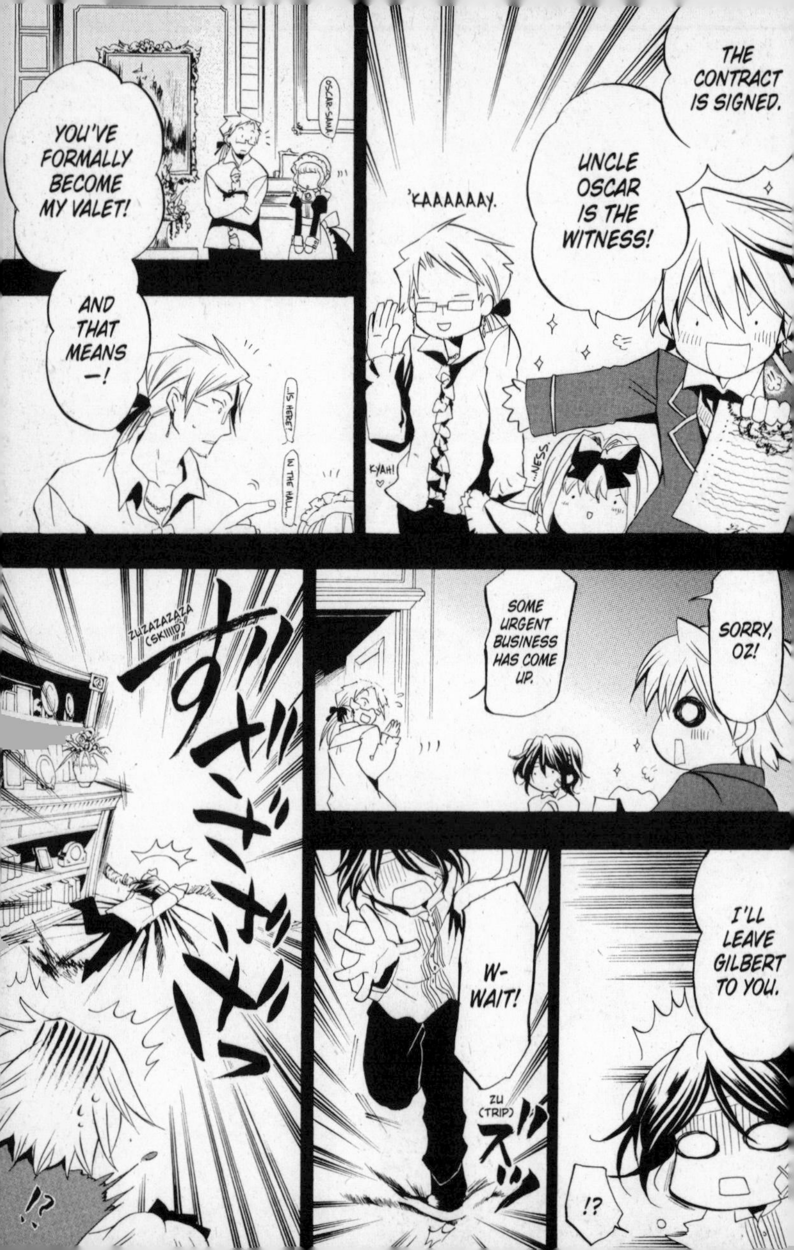
THE CONTRACT IS SIGNED.
UNCLE OSCAR IS THE WITNESS!
'KAAAAAAY.
KYAH!
...NESS.
YOU'VE FORMALLY BECOME MY VALET!
OSCAR-SAMA
AND THAT MEANS —!
...IS HERE?
IN THE HALL...
SORRY, OZ!
SOME URGENT BUSINESS HAS COME UP.
I'LL LEAVE GILBERT TO YOU.
!?
W-WAIT!
ZU (TRIP)
ZUZAZAZAZA (SKIIIID)
!?

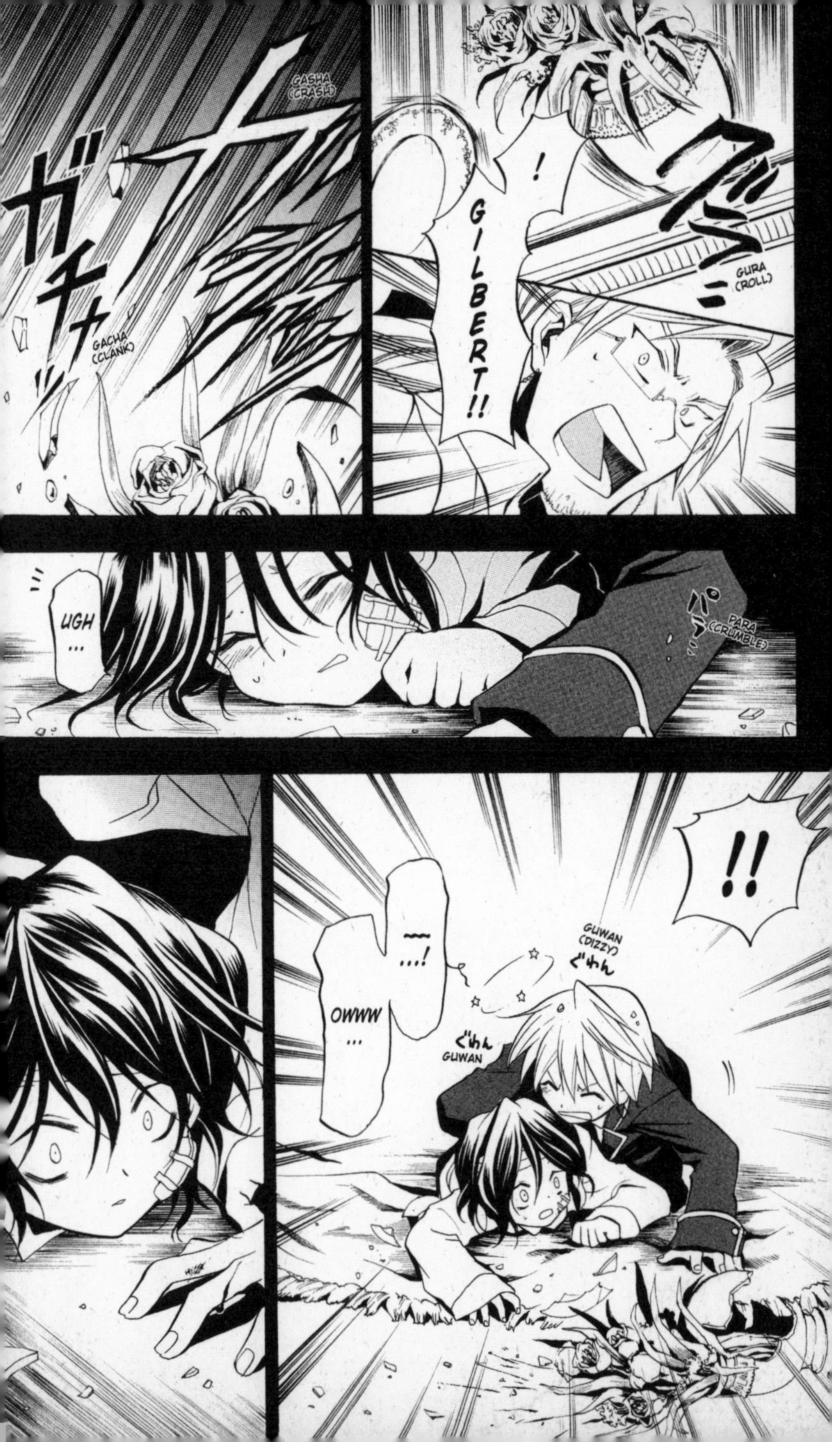

GURA (ROLL)
!
GILBERT!!
CASHA (CRASH)
GACHA (CLANK)
PARA (CRUMBLE)
UGH...
!!
GUWAN (DIZZY)
ぐわん
ぐわん
GUWAN
~~...!
OWWW...

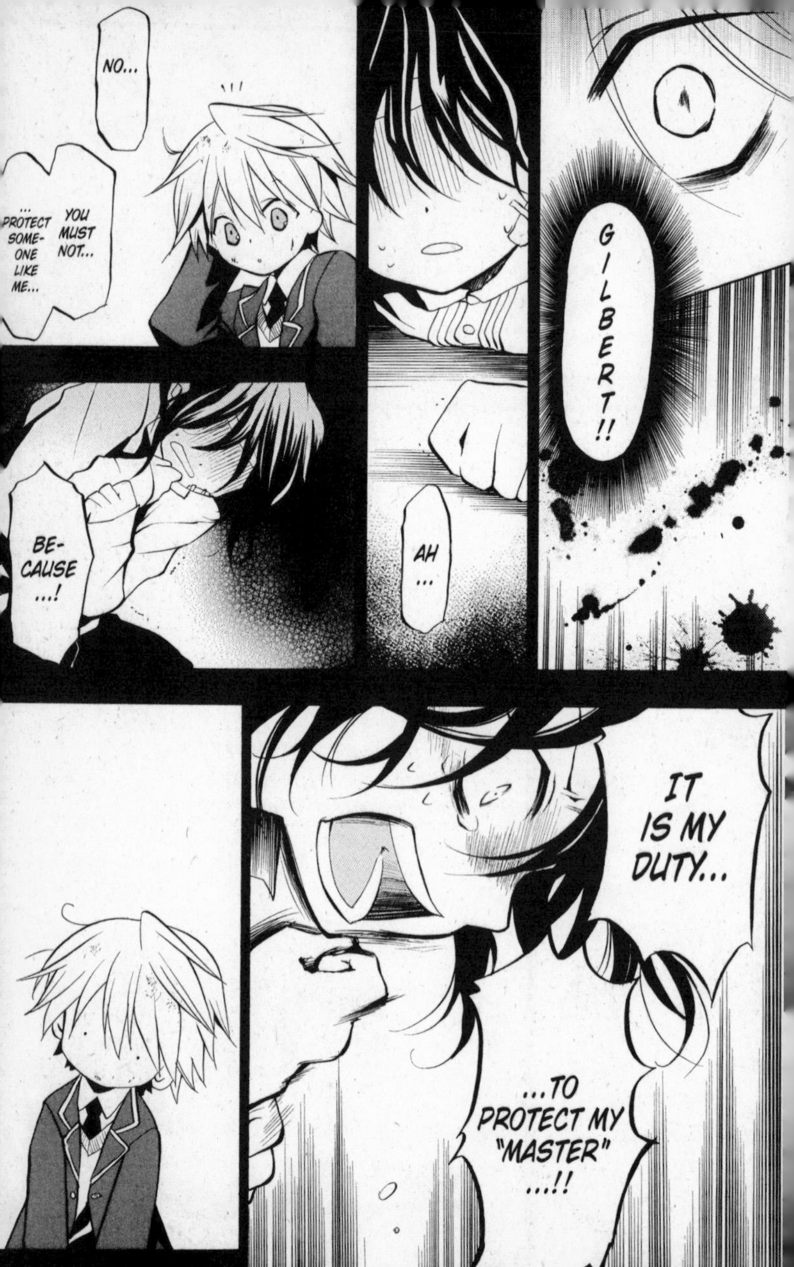
GILBERT!!
AH...
NO...
YOU MUST NOT...
...PROTECT SOME-ONE LIKE ME...
BE-CAUSE...!
IT IS MY DUTY...
...TO PROTECT MY "MASTER" ...!!

I WAS GOING TO SAY IT BEFORE, BUT...

I HAVE NO CLUE WHAT YOU MEAN!

WHAT'S THIS "MASTER" YOU'RE TALKING ABOUT?

...YOU'RE MY VALET NOW.

ZUGOU (WHACK)

PI!

EH-HEHH!

'COS THAT'S THE "LORD'S DUTY"!

AND THAT MEANS...

...FROM NOW ON, I'LL PROTECT YOU NO MATTER WHAT!

NICE TO MEET YOU, GILBERT!

I'M OZ VESSALIUS.

SFX: PYUU (SPURT)

......AFTER THAT, EVERY DAY WAS LOADS OF FUN!

BUN

NAH!

BUN (SWING)

...BUT HE'S A REEAALLY NICE GUY...

...AND HE WAS ALWAYS THERE FOR ME.

HE'S A SISSY...

...AND A CRY-BABY...

SFX: MOWAWAAAN (HAZY)

GYAAAAAAH!!

MEMORIES OF BULLYING GIL ☆

EEEK!!

UFU... UFU FU FU FU FU!

HOW DO I PUT IT...? HE SCREAMS IN SUCH A WONDERFUL WAY.

TO ME, HE'S...

...MORE IMPORTANT THAN ANY-ONE ELSE... HE'S MY PRECIOUS BEST FRIEND!

I'M SAYING YOU'RE TALKING NONSENSE.

FRIENDS OR WHAT-EVER...

...ARE JUST A BUNCH OF WEAKLINGS FLOCKING TOGETHER.

......

I HAVE NO IDEA...

...WHAT YOU'RE TALKING ABOUT.

EH?

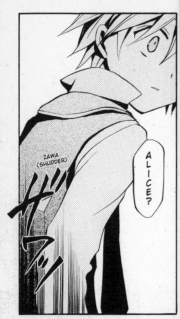

ZAWA
(SHUDDER)

ALICE?

I...

...DON'T
NEED
SUCH
THINGS.

!

ZOKU
(SHIVER)

THIS
PRES-
ENCE...

HUH
...?

ZAZA
(WSHH)

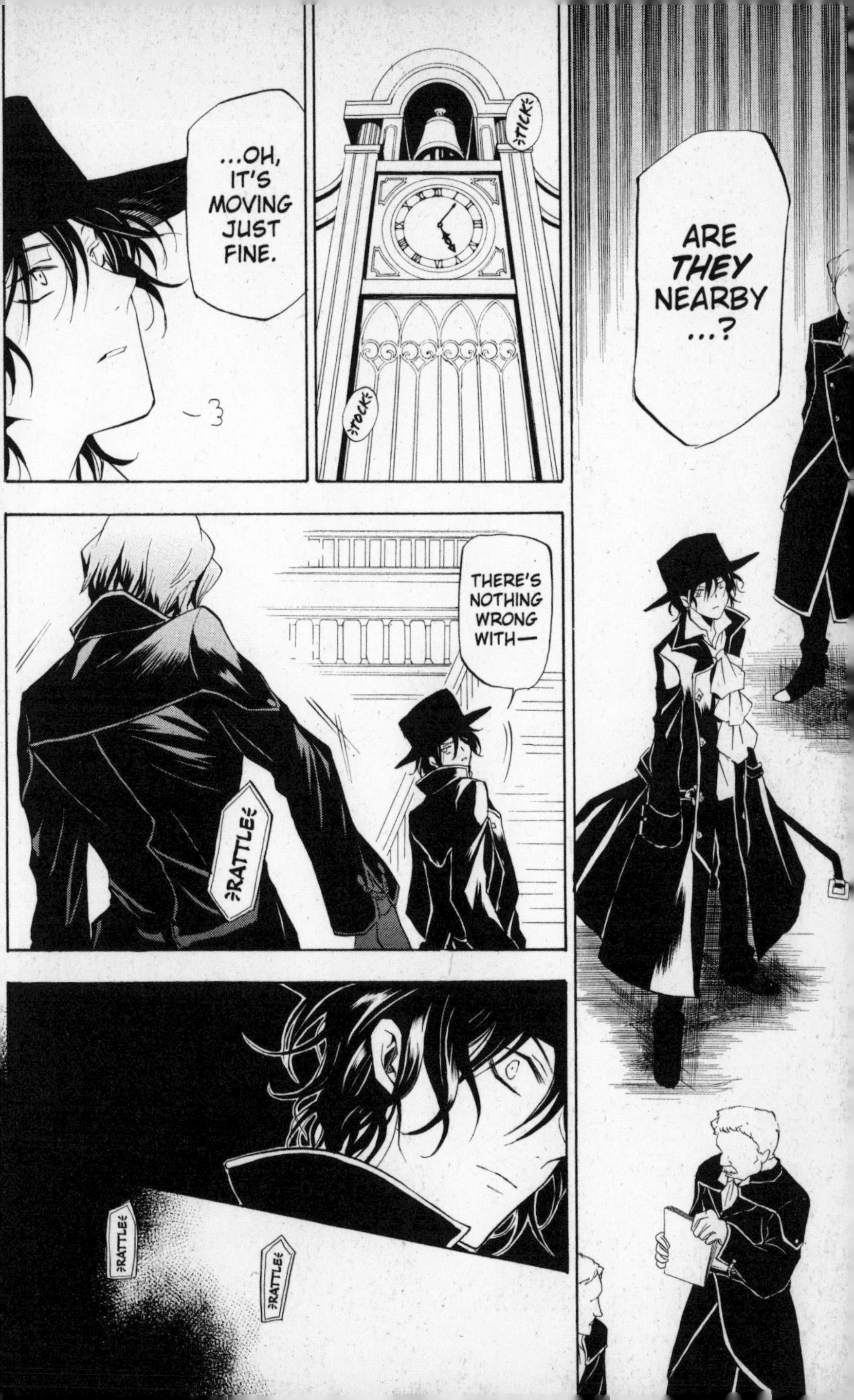
ARE THEY NEARBY ...?
TICK
TOCK
...OH, IT'S MOVING JUST FINE.
THERE'S NOTHING WRONG WITH—
RATTLE
RATTLE
RATTLE

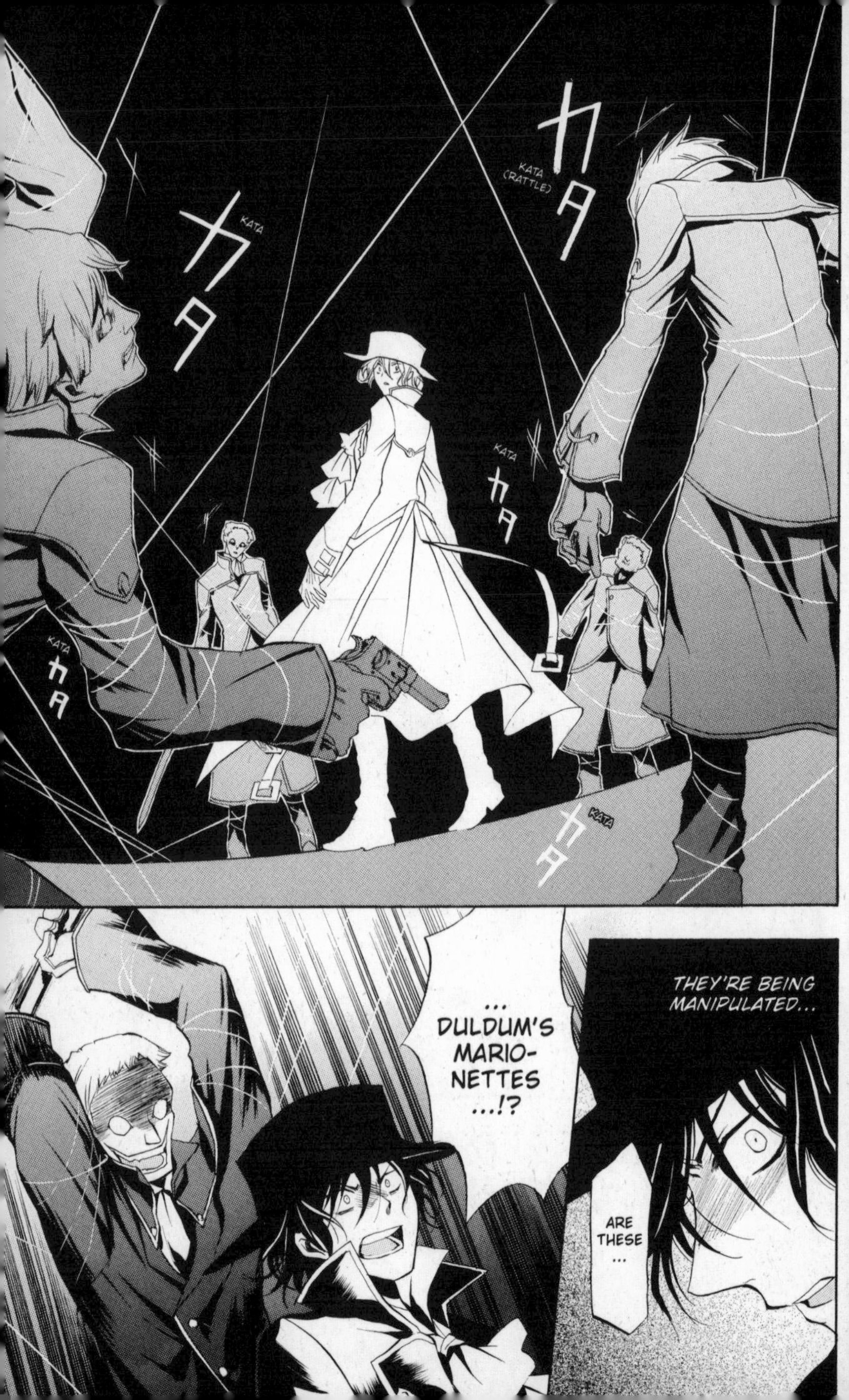
カタ
KATA (RATTLE)
カタ
KATA
カタ
KATA
カタ
KATA
カタ
KATA
THEY'RE BEING MANIPULATED...
ARE THESE ...
... DULDUM'S MARIO-NETTES ...!?

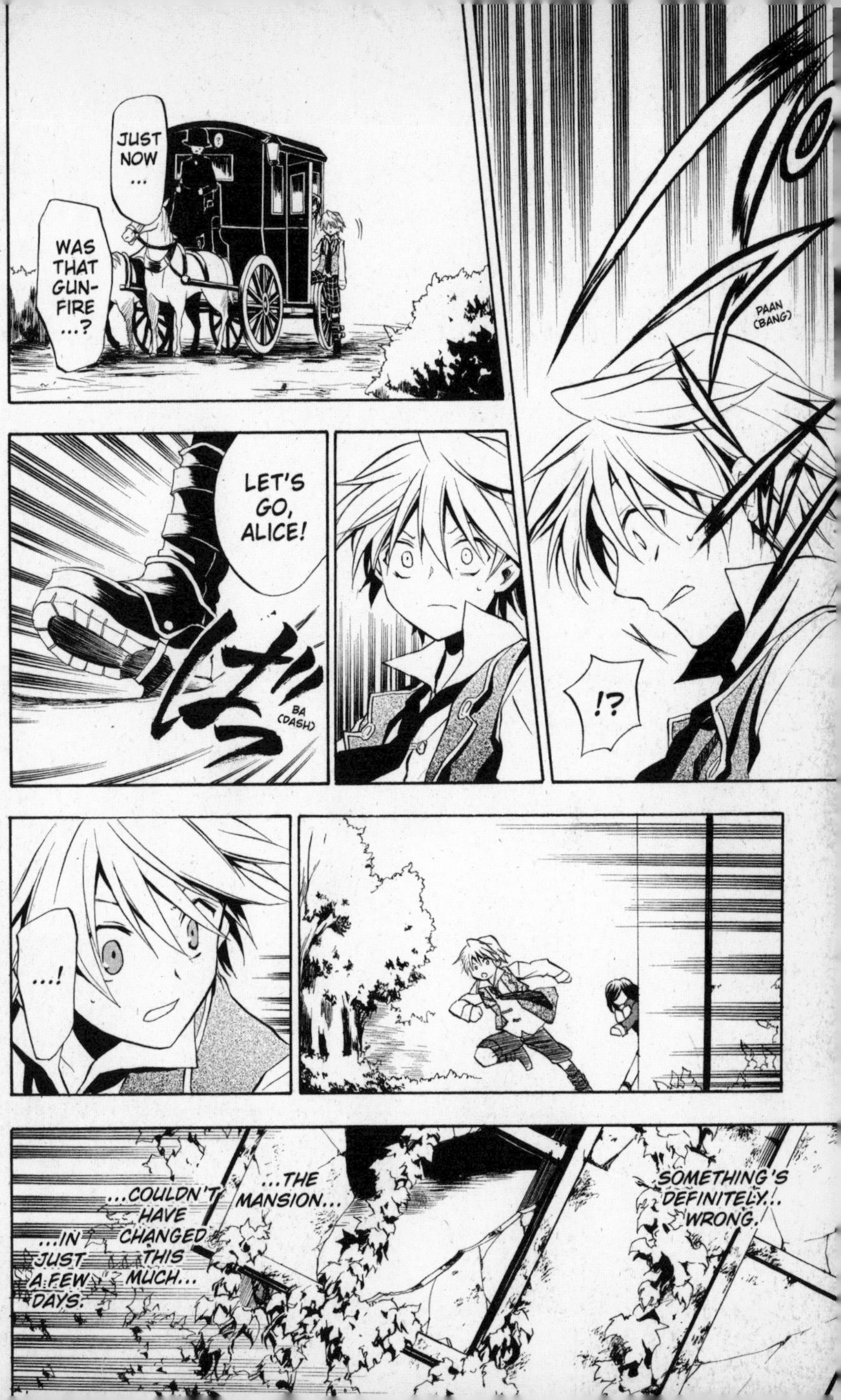

PAAN (BANG)
JUST NOW...
WAS THAT GUN-FIRE...?
!?
LET'S GO, ALICE!
BA (DASH)
...!
SOMETHING'S DEFINITELY... WRONG.
...THE MANSION...
...COULDN'T HAVE CHANGED THIS MUCH...
...IN JUST A FEW DAYS.

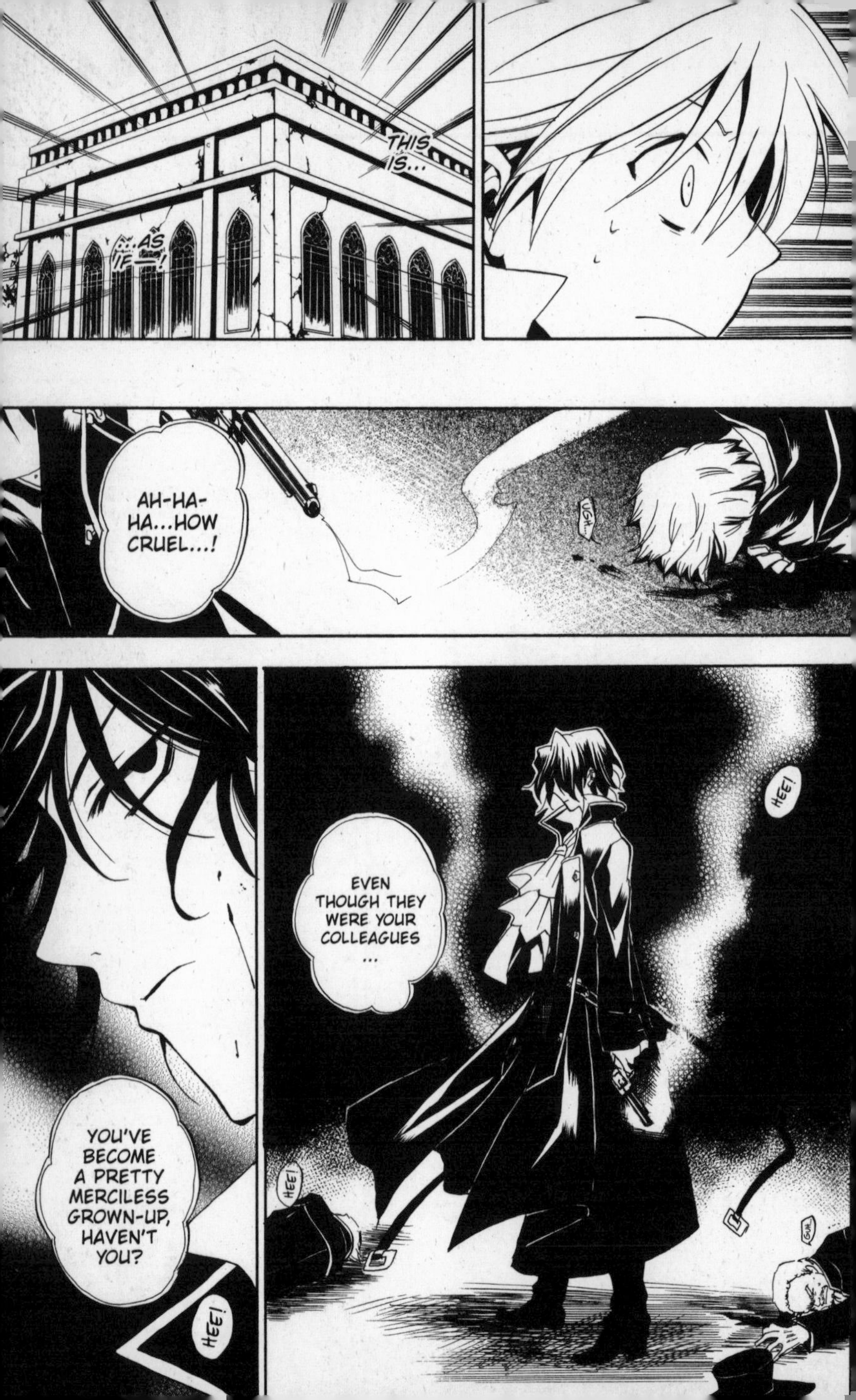
THIS IS...
...AS IF—!
UGH...
AH-HA-HA...HOW CRUEL...!
HEE!
EVEN THOUGH THEY WERE YOUR COLLEAGUES...
HEE!
GUH...
YOU'VE BECOME A PRETTY MERCILESS GROWN-UP, HAVEN'T YOU?
HEE!

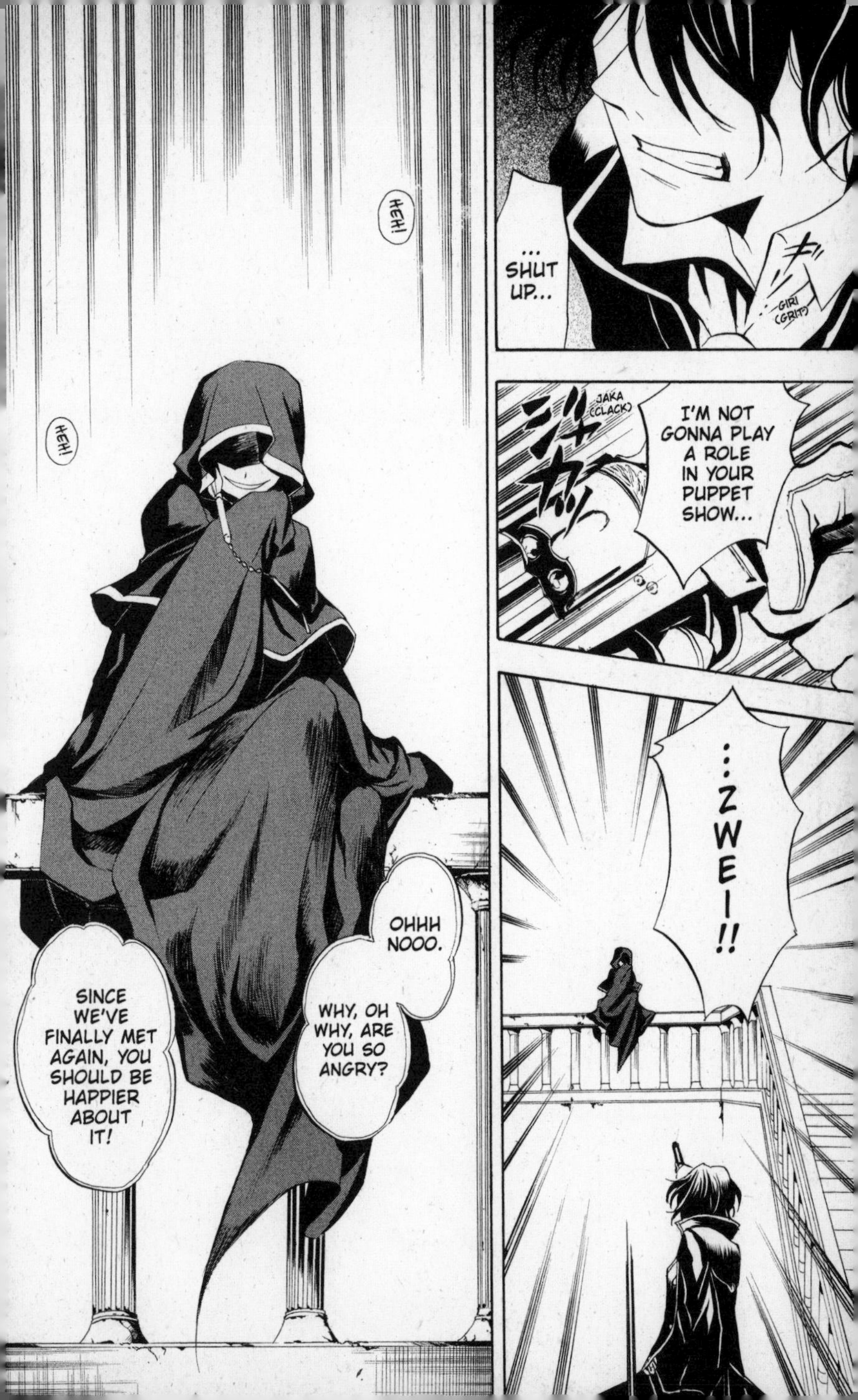

... SHUT UP...
GIRI (GRIT)
JAKA (CLACK)
I'M NOT GONNA PLAY A ROLE IN YOUR PUPPET SHOW...
...ZWEI!!
HEH!
HEH!
OHHH NOOO.
WHY, OH WHY, ARE YOU SO ANGRY?
SINCE WE'VE FINALLY MET AGAIN, YOU SHOULD BE HAPPIER ABOUT IT!

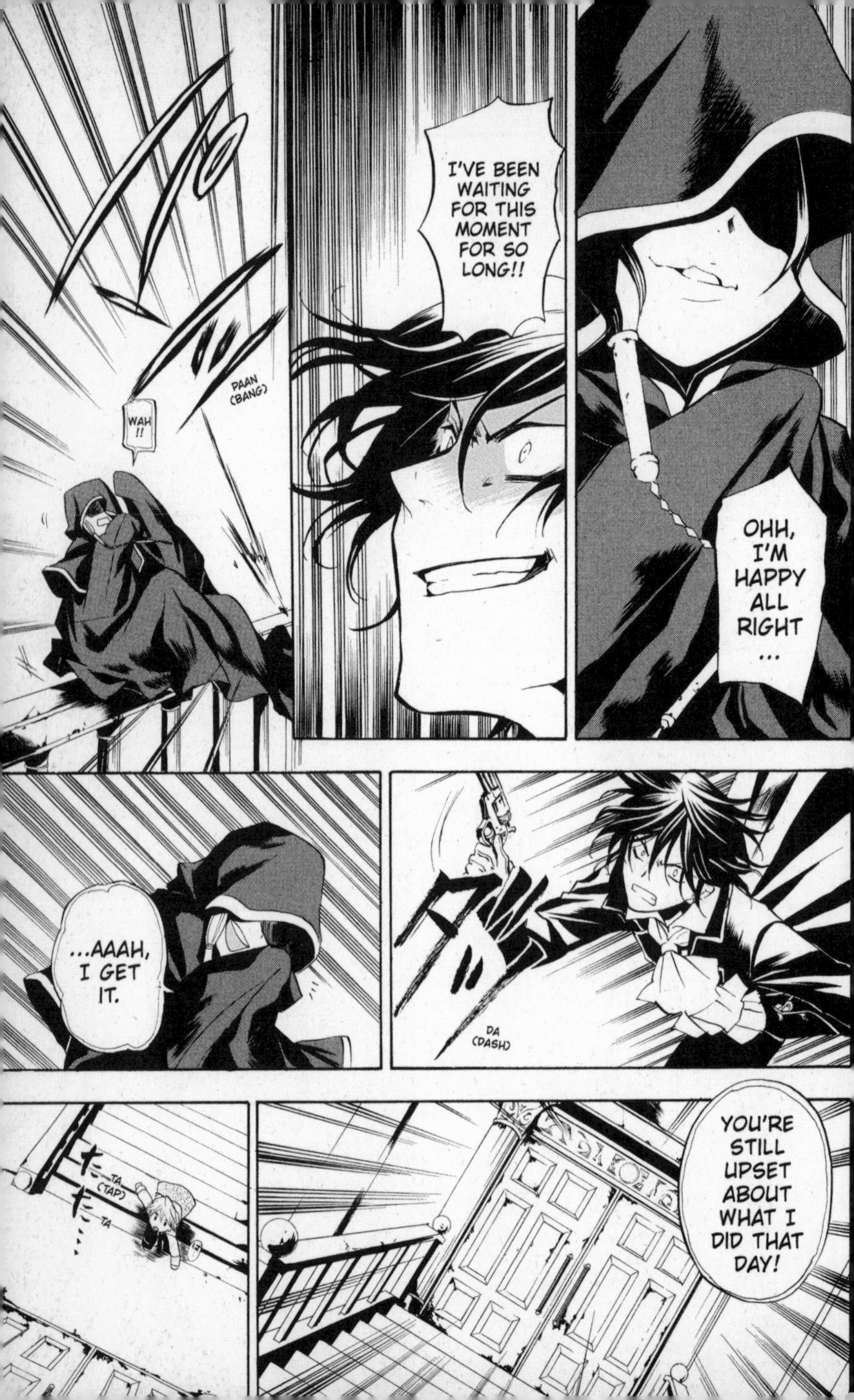
OHH, I'M HAPPY ALL RIGHT ...
I'VE BEEN WAITING FOR THIS MOMENT FOR SO LONG!!
PAAN (BANG)
WAH !!
DA (DASH)
...AAAH, I GET IT.
YOU'RE STILL UPSET ABOUT WHAT I DID THAT DAY!
TA (TAP)
TA

...USING YOUR BODY TO HURT YOUR YOUNG MASTER AT HIS COMING-OF-AGE CEREMONY, CAN YOU!!?

...YOU STILL CAN'T FOR-GIVE ME...

...FOR...

EH...?

......

HA HA!

YOU REALLY ARE SOOO SINGLE-MINDED...

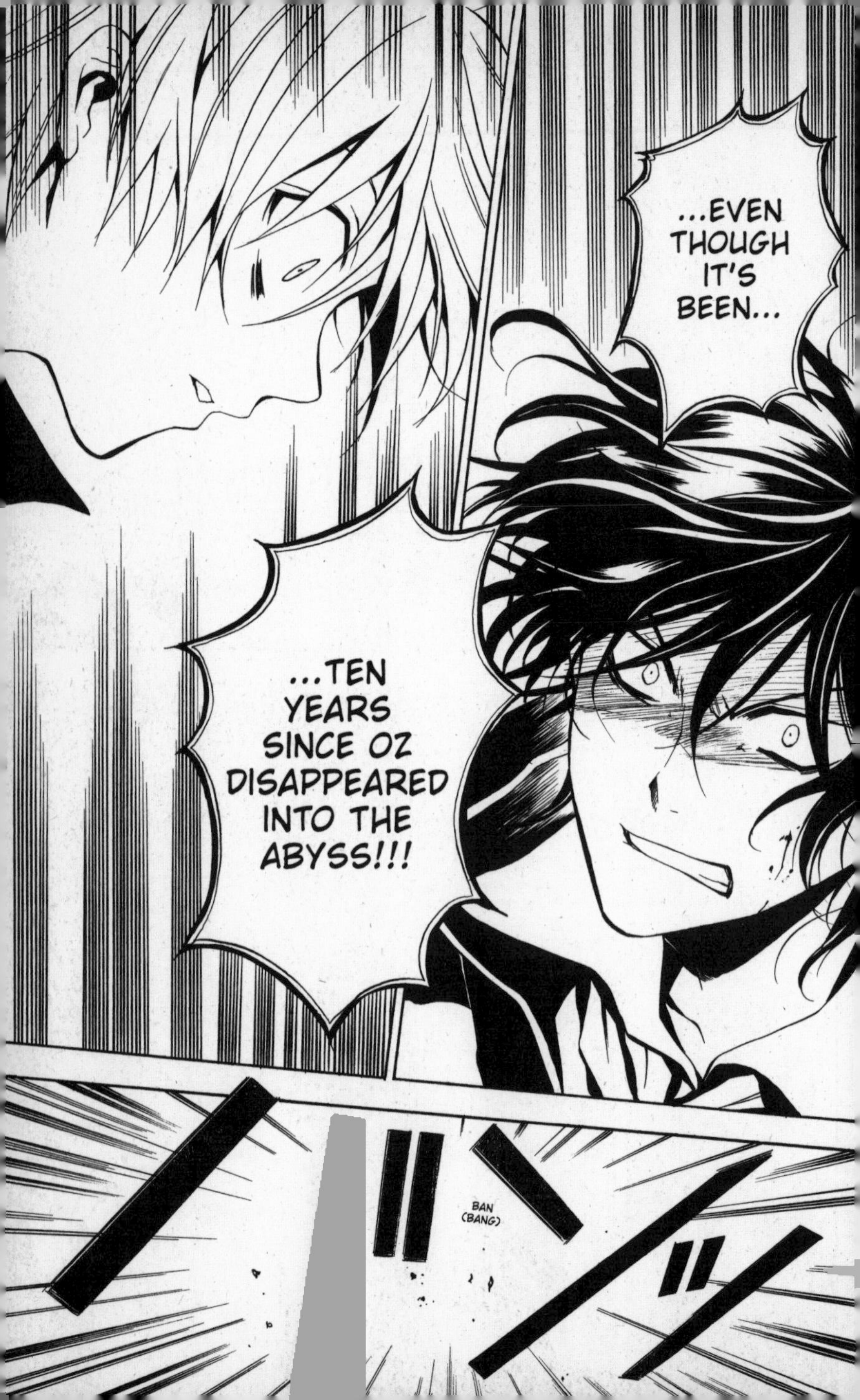
...EVEN THOUGH IT'S BEEN...
...TEN YEARS SINCE OZ DISAPPEARED INTO THE ABYSS!!!
BAN (BANG)

YOU FOOL!

DON'T COME HERE ...!!

NII (GRIND)

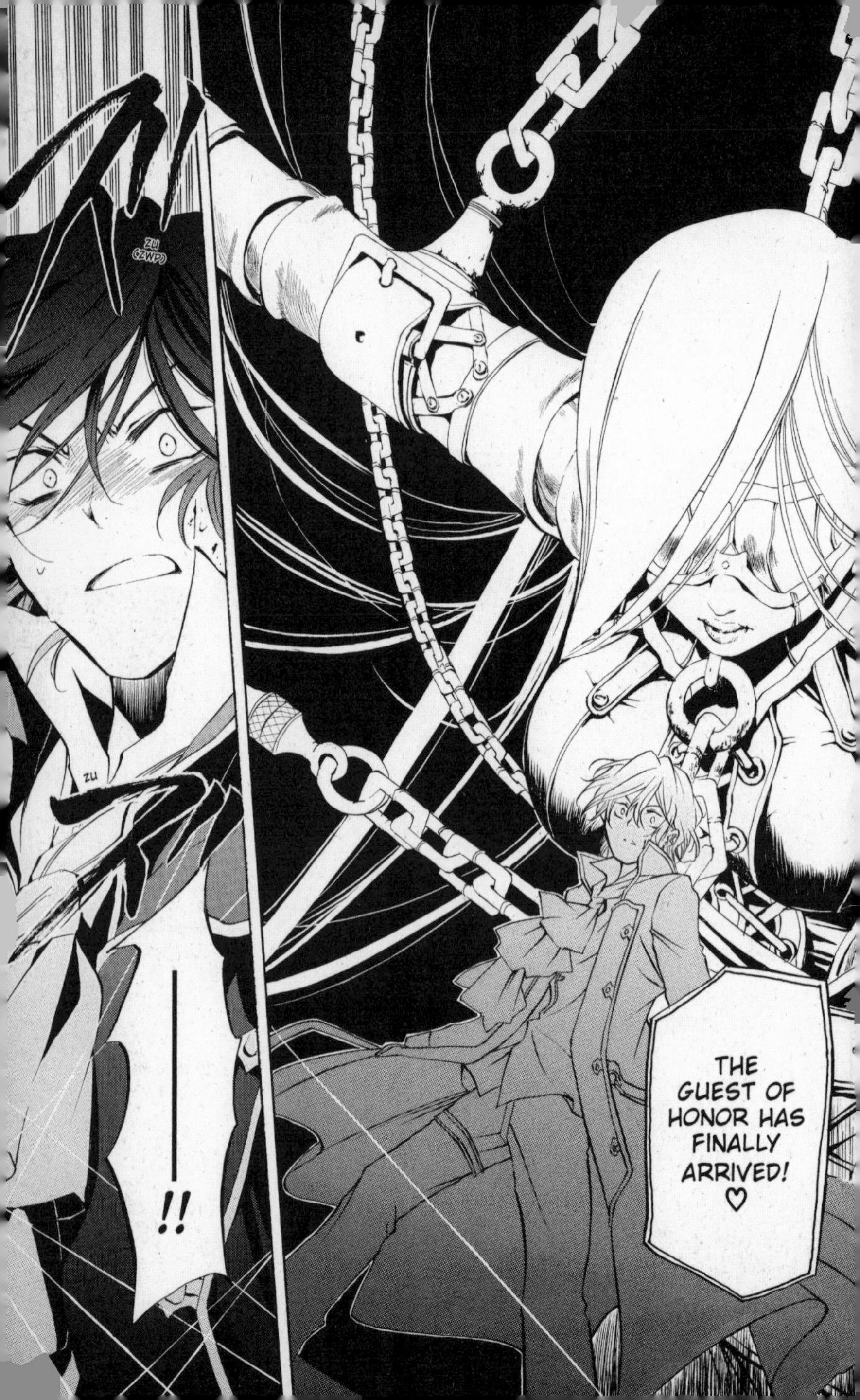
ZU (ZWP)
ZU
———!!
THE GUEST OF HONOR HAS FINALLY ARRIVED! ♡

STAY BACK, OZ!!

R—

ALLOW ME TO INTRODUCE YOU.

GUH...!

DARLING DULDUM HAS THIS TERRIBLY USEFUL ABILITY TO BIND AND MANIPULATE WITH ITS STRINGS.

THIS CHILD IS MY CHAIN...

...DULDUM.

...BECAUSE I HEARD YOU'D EMERGED FROM THE ABYSS AFTER TEN WHOLE YEARS!

...I'VE COME TO CELEBRATE...

YOU SEE, TODAY...

TEN YEARS ...?

WHAT'S HE SAYING?

......

NOW ...

...SHALL I BEGIN THE SPECIAL PERFORMANCE?

AND NEITHER HAS HE ...!

HEET

HEET

I MEAN ...

...BREAK AND SHARON-CHAN HAVEN'T CHANGED AT ALL.

...AND ONE OTHER ...

THE STARS OF THE SHOW ARE THIS BOY HERE...

...OZ VESSALIUS ...

THEN...

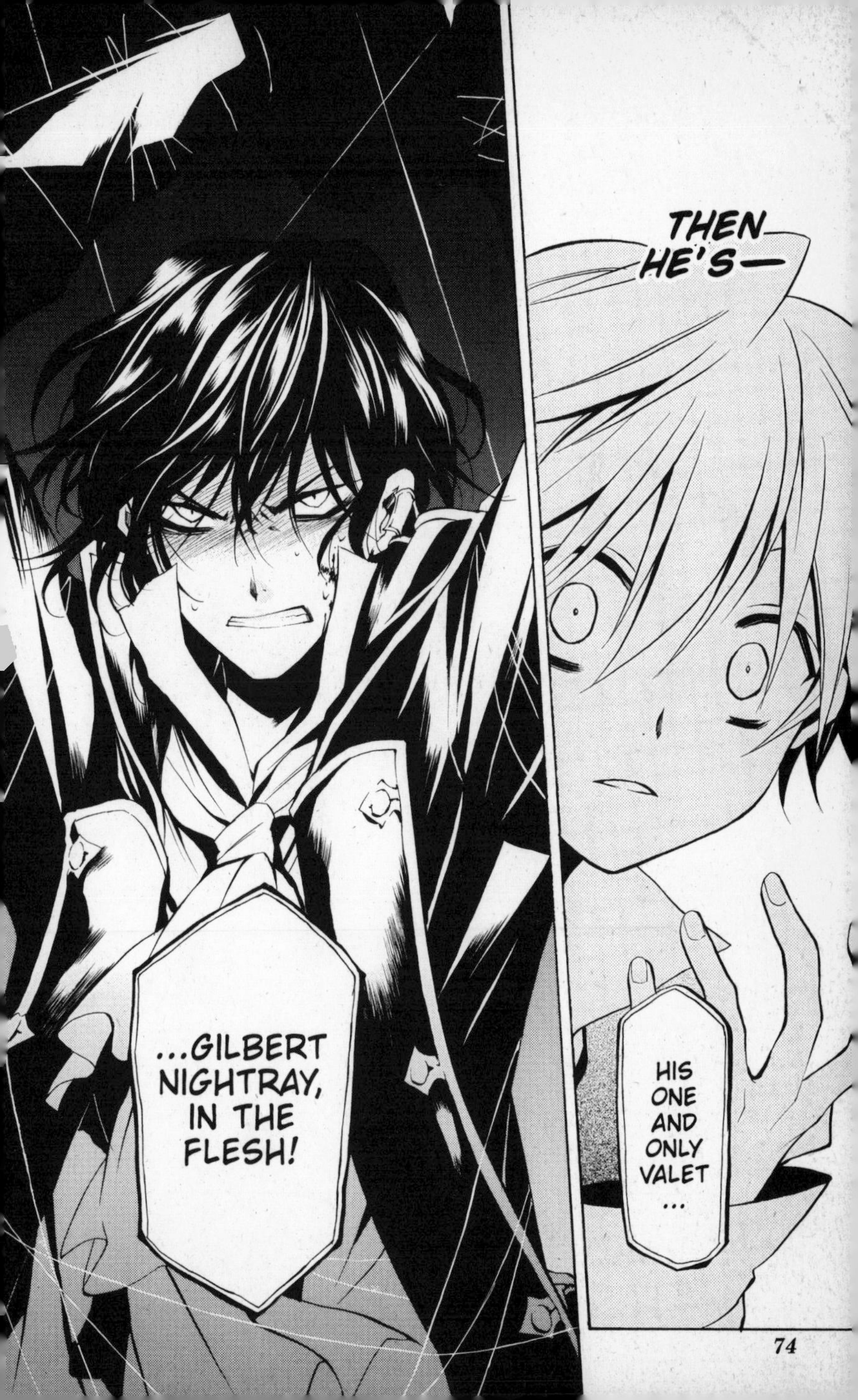
THEN HE'S—
HIS ONE AND ONLY VALET...
...GILBERT NIGHTRAY, IN THE FLESH!

Retrace:VII Reunion

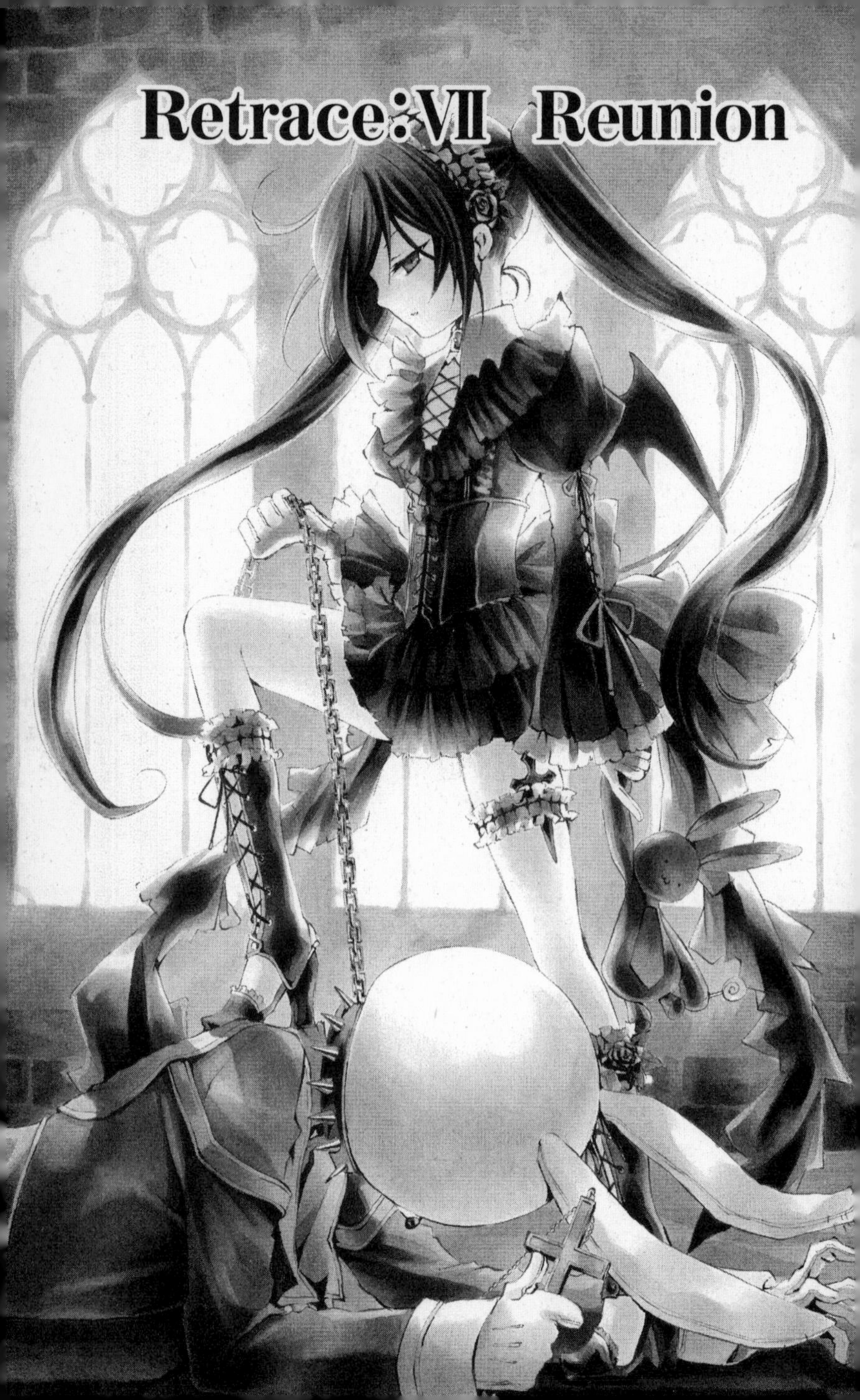

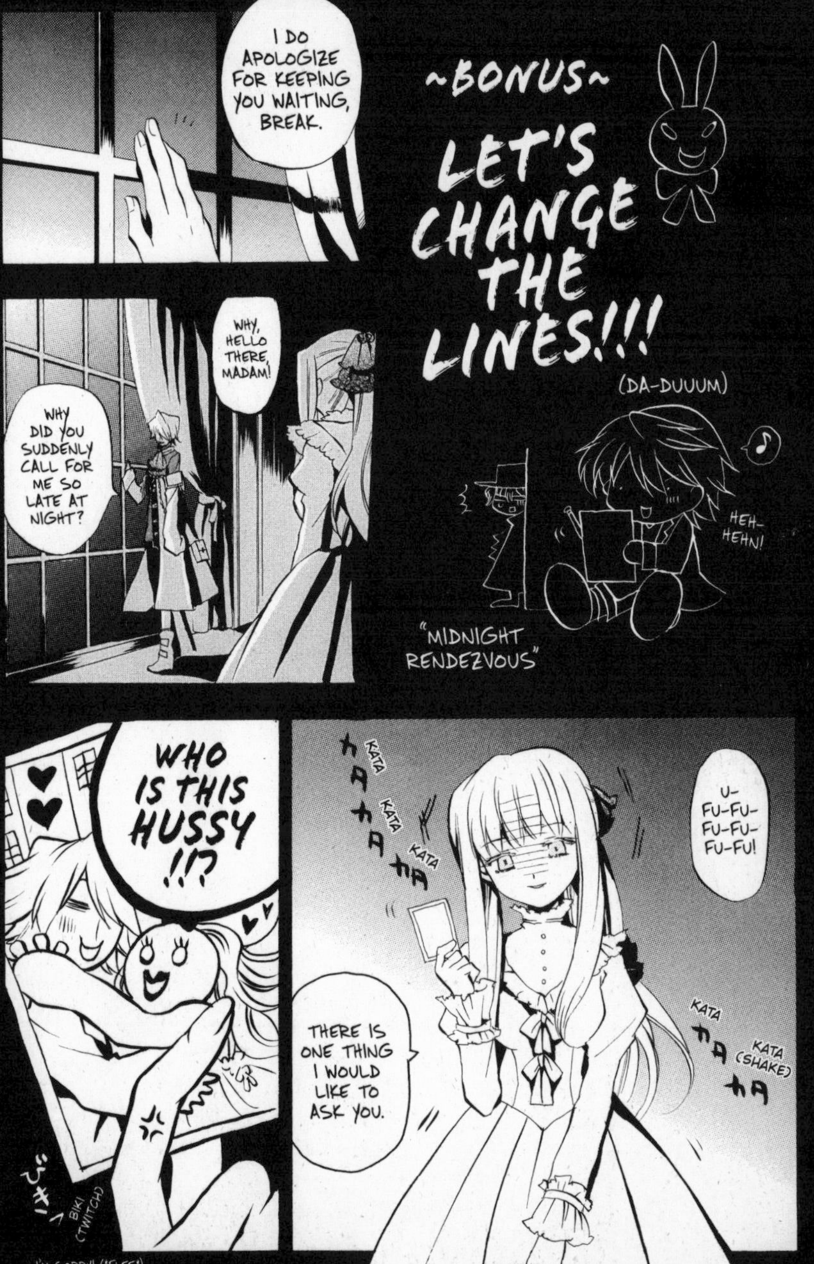
~BONUS~
LET'S CHANGE THE LINES!!!
(DA-DUUUM)
HEH-HEHN!
"MIDNIGHT RENDEZVOUS"
I DO APOLOGIZE FOR KEEPING YOU WAITING, BREAK.
WHY, HELLO THERE, MADAM!
WHY DID YOU SUDDENLY CALL FOR ME SO LATE AT NIGHT?
U-FU-FU-FU-FU-FU-FU!
KATA KATA KATA
THERE IS ONE THING I WOULD LIKE TO ASK YOU.
KATA KATA (SHAKE)
WHO IS THIS HUSSY!!?
BIKI (TWITCH)
......I'M SORRY! (*FLEE*)

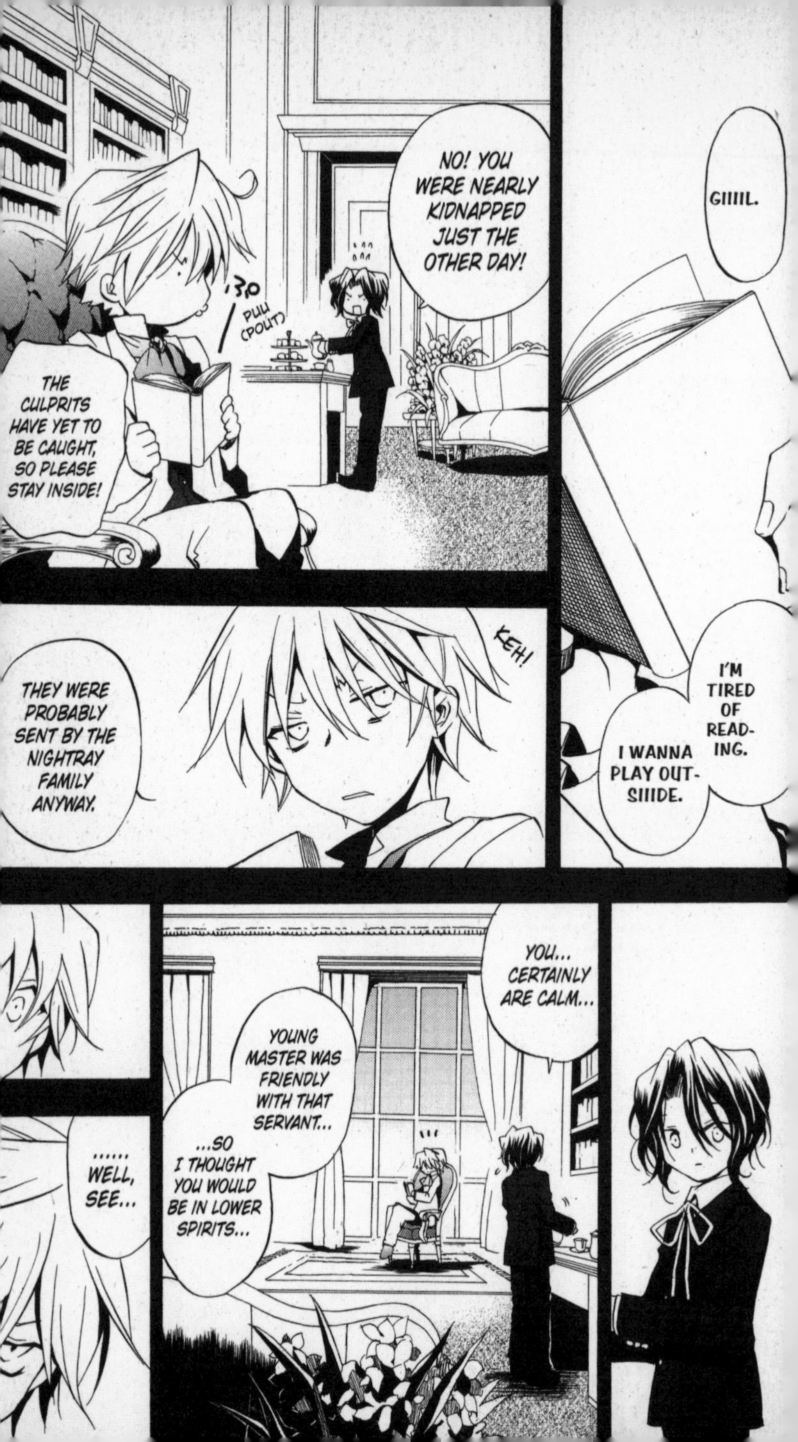
GIIIL.
I'M TIRED OF READ-ING.
I WANNA PLAY OUT-SIIIDE.
NO! YOU WERE NEARLY KIDNAPPED JUST THE OTHER DAY!
PUU (POUT)
THE CULPRITS HAVE YET TO BE CAUGHT, SO PLEASE STAY INSIDE!
KEH!
THEY WERE PROBABLY SENT BY THE NIGHTRAY FAMILY ANYWAY.
YOU... CERTAINLY ARE CALM...
YOUNG MASTER WAS FRIENDLY WITH THAT SERVANT...
...SO I THOUGHT YOU WOULD BE IN LOWER SPIRITS...
...... WELL, SEE...

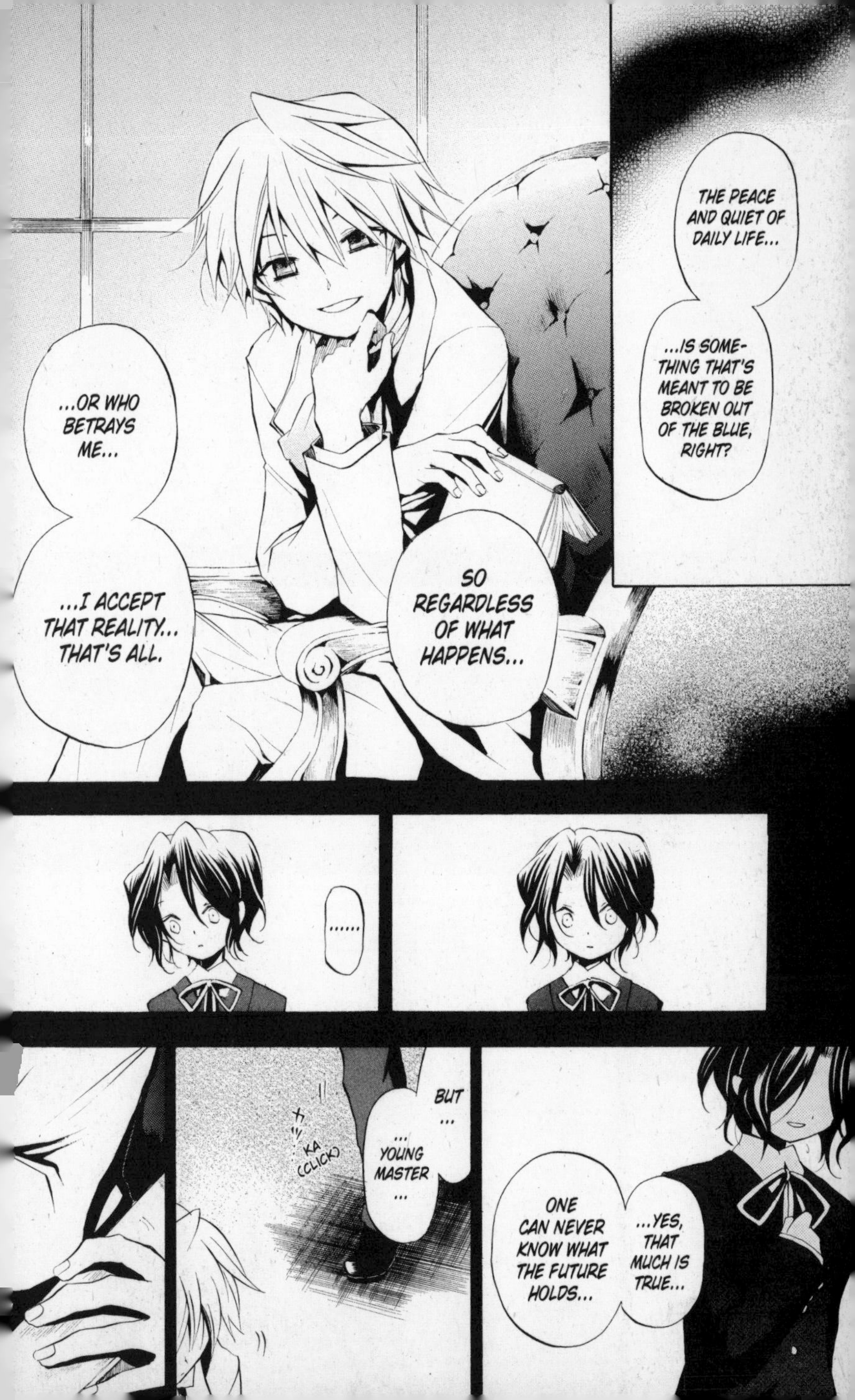
THE PEACE AND QUIET OF DAILY LIFE...
...IS SOME-THING THAT'S MEANT TO BE BROKEN OUT OF THE BLUE, RIGHT?
SO REGARDLESS OF WHAT HAPPENS...
...OR WHO BETRAYS ME...
...I ACCEPT THAT REALITY... THAT'S ALL.
......
...YES, THAT MUCH IS TRUE...
ONE CAN NEVER KNOW WHAT THE FUTURE HOLDS...
BUT...
...YOUNG MASTER...
KA (CLICK)

...I WILL BE WITH YOU NO MATTER WHAT TOMORROW MAY BRING.

I... KNOW THE DARKNESS IN YOUR HEART.

WE ARE...

...LINKED BY OUR SHADOWS, NOT BY OUR LIGHT.

AND YOU...

...KNOW THE WEAKNESSES IN MINE...

...NO MATTER HOW MUCH TIME PASSES...

...OR EVEN IF OUR SITUATIONS CHANGE...

SO...

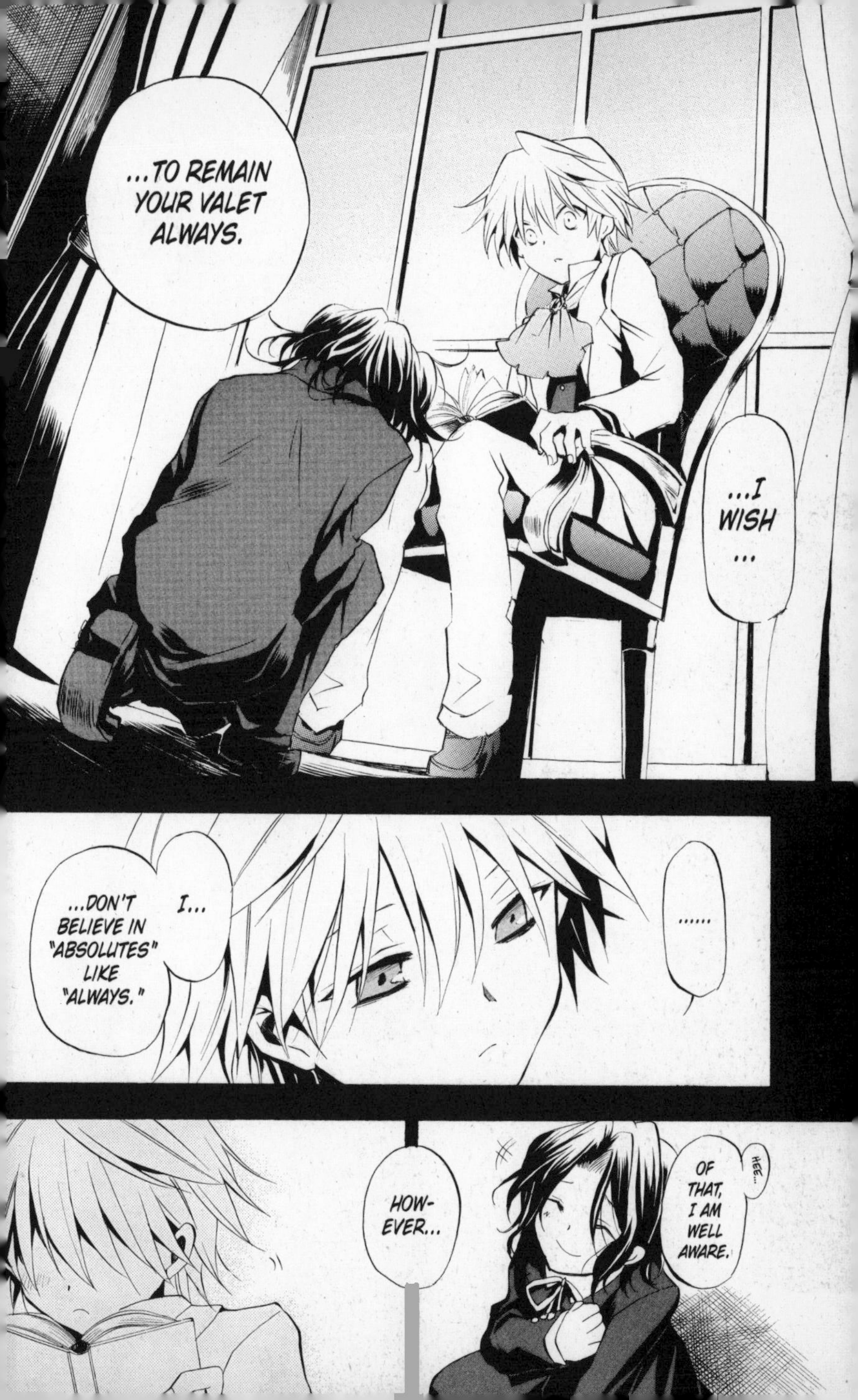
...I WISH...
...TO REMAIN YOUR VALET ALWAYS.
......
I...
...DON'T BELIEVE IN "ABSOLUTES" LIKE "ALWAYS."
HEE...
OF THAT, I AM WELL AWARE.
HOW-EVER...

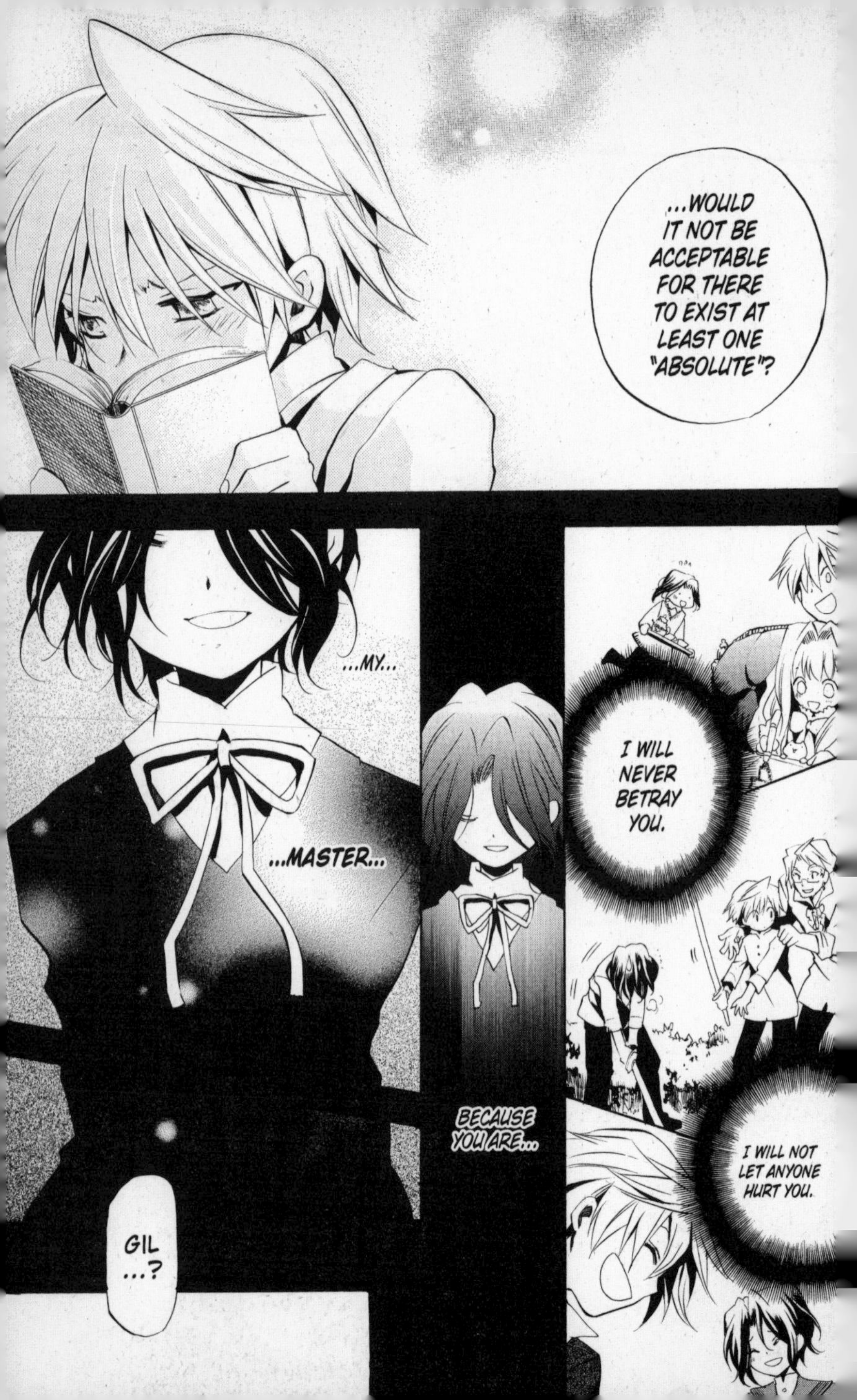
...WOULD IT NOT BE ACCEPTABLE FOR THERE TO EXIST AT LEAST ONE "ABSOLUTE"?
I WILL NEVER BETRAY YOU.
I WILL NOT LET ANYONE HURT YOU.
BECAUSE YOU ARE...
...MY...
...MASTER...
GIL ...?

GUI
(YANK)

!

IT'S QUITE A SHOCK, ISN'T IT?

HERE YOU ARE, BACK FROM THE ABYSS, ONLY TO FIND THAT TEN YEARS HAVE PASSED!

...GIL-BERT?

THAT'S ...

HEH.

EVEN IF YOU MANAGE TO ESCAPE...

... THERE'S NO GUARANTEE YOU'LL MAKE IT BACK TO YOUR TIME.

THE ABYSS IS A DIMENSION WHERE TIME IS OUT OF ORDER.

BUT DON'T YOU WOR-RY!

HEH...

I'M...

THAT'S WHY I CAME TO GET YOU.

...GOING TO DO YOU THE FAVOR OF DROPPING YOU INTO THE ABYSS AGAIN...!

!?

...THIS IS NOT GOOD, OZ...

HEH...

GIVE YOUNG MASTER A GOOD WORKING OVER...

...SO IT'S EASIER FOR ME TO TAKE HIM AWAY...

HEH...

...NOW THERE'S A GOOD BOY, GILBERT.

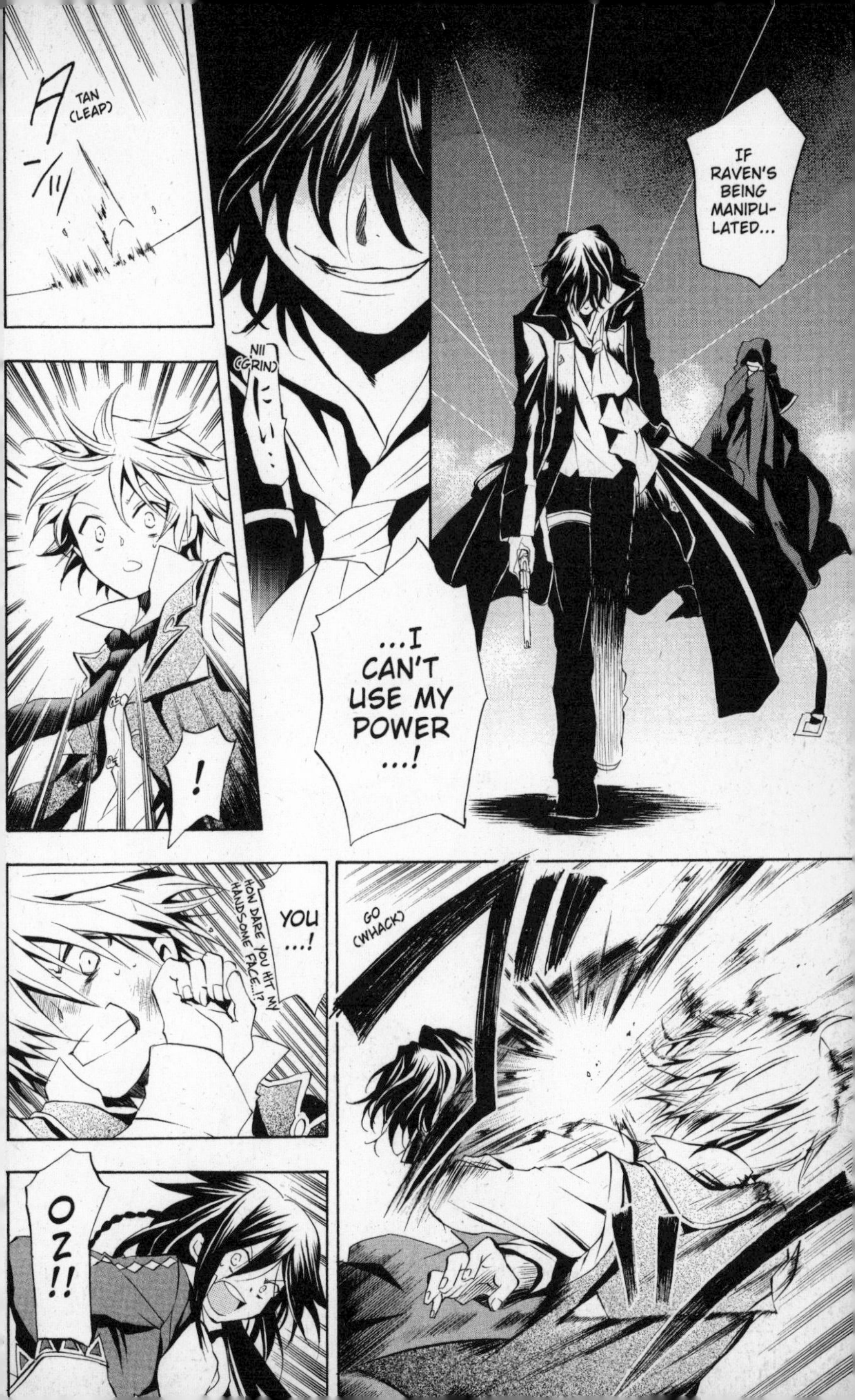

IF RAVEN'S BEING MANIPU-LATED...
...I CAN'T USE MY POWER ...!
NII (GRIN)
TAN (LEAP)
!
GO (WHACK)
YOU ...!
HOW DARE YOU HIT MY HANDSOME FACE...!?
OZ!!

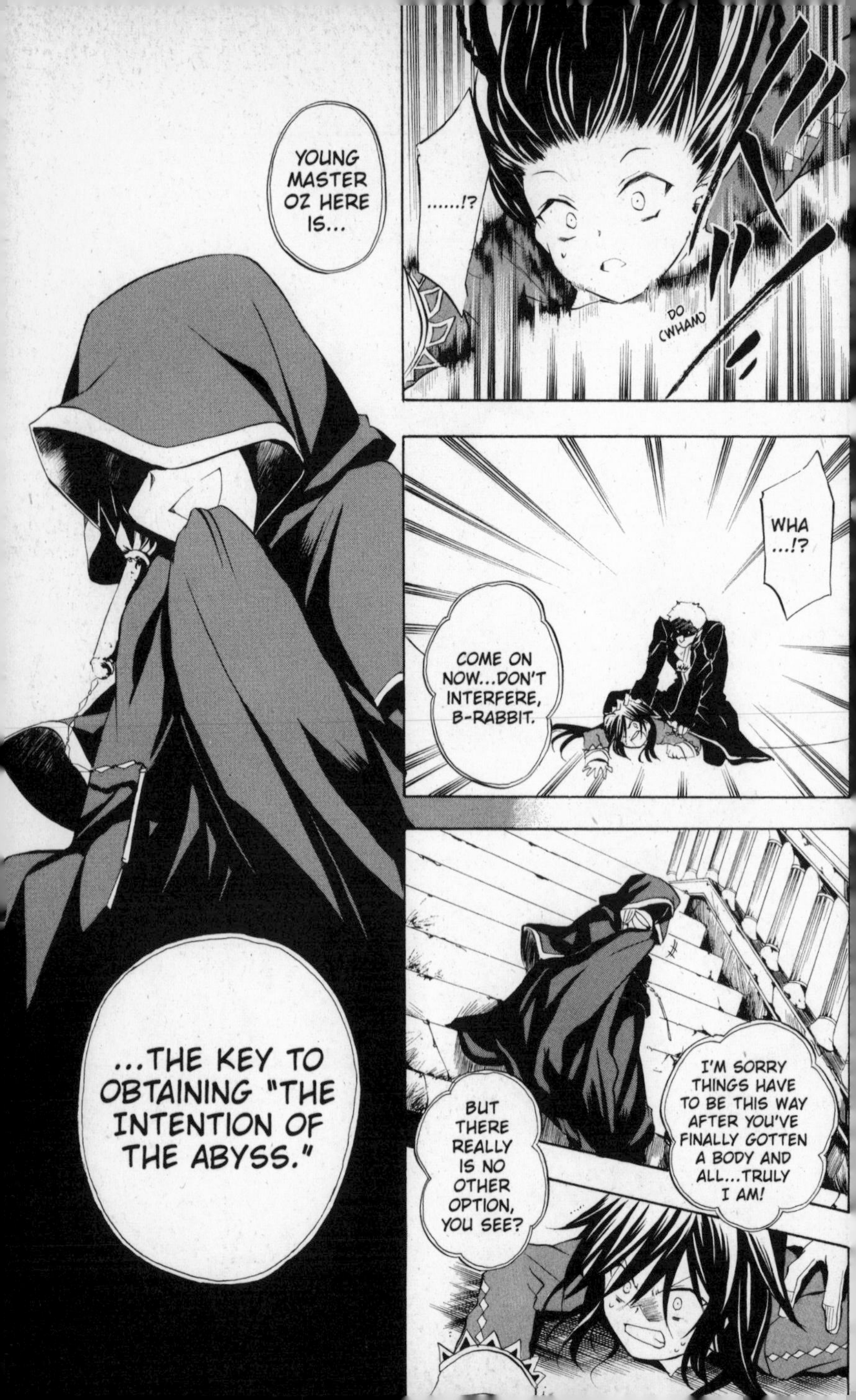

YOUNG MASTER OZ HERE IS...
......!?
DO (WHAM)
WHA ...!?
COME ON NOW...DON'T INTERFERE, B-RABBIT.
I'M SORRY THINGS HAVE TO BE THIS WAY AFTER YOU'VE FINALLY GOTTEN A BODY AND ALL...TRULY I AM!
BUT THERE REALLY IS NO OTHER OPTION, YOU SEE?
...THE KEY TO OBTAINING "THE INTENTION OF THE ABYSS."

AND·SO! ☆

FOR US BASKER-VILLES, HIS EXISTENCE POSES A GRAVE THREAT.

...TRUE, I THOUGHT RAVEN SEEMED LIKE GIL...

HAH...!

INTO THE ABYSS HE MUST GO!

...ARE ALL BECAUSE IT'S BEEN TEN YEARS SINCE THEN...!?

...AND THE MANSION LOOKING SO DIFFERENT...

BUT MY IMPRESSION OF HIM...

GU (GRAB)

!

BUT...

...I CAN'T JUST BELIEVE IT...!

LET ME GIVE YOU A TASTE...

...OF THE PAIN THAT... THAT I SUFFERED!!

JUST —!

DON (SLAM)

LET GO!!

(GA: GYANK)

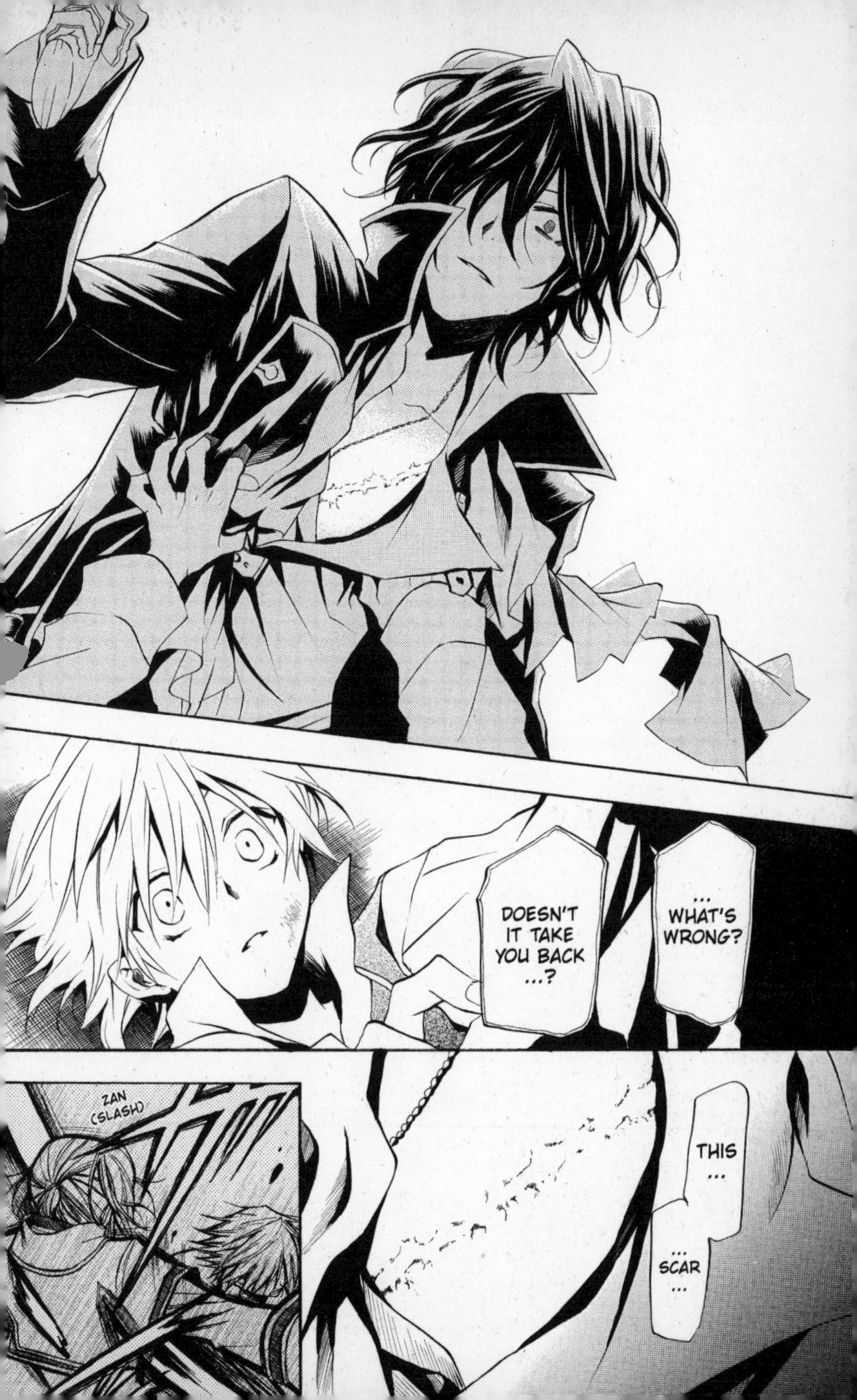
... WHAT'S WRONG?
DOESN'T IT TAKE YOU BACK ...?
THIS ...
... SCAR ...
ZAN (SLASH)

YOUNG
MASTER
—!!

YEAH
...

JA
(SHAK)

...ARE
GIL,
AREN'T
YOU...?

...YOU
REALLY
...

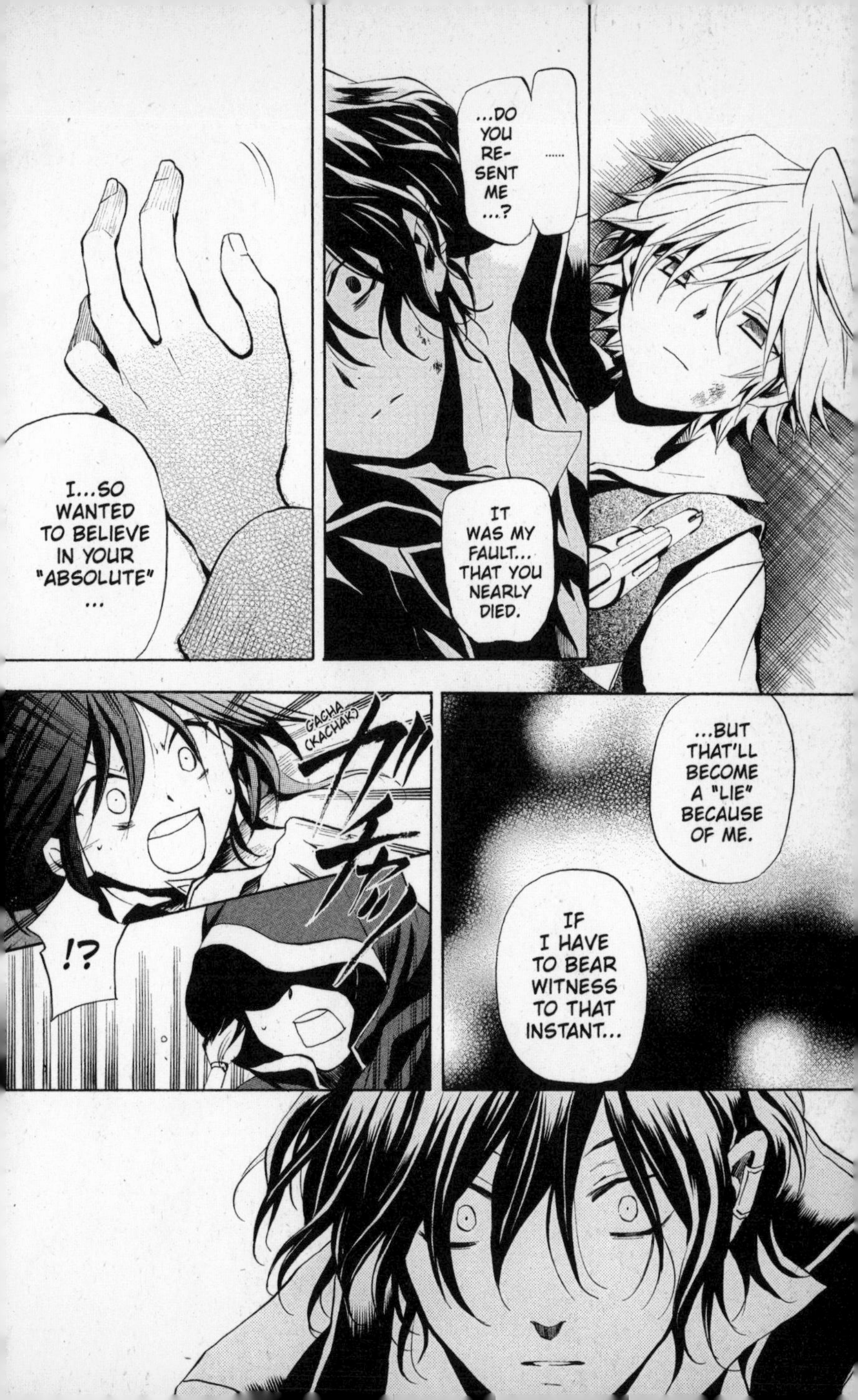
...DO YOU RE-SENT ME ...?
......
IT WAS MY FAULT... THAT YOU NEARLY DIED.
I...SO WANTED TO BELIEVE IN YOUR "ABSOLUTE" ...
...BUT THAT'LL BECOME A "LIE" BECAUSE OF ME.
IF I HAVE TO BEAR WITNESS TO THAT INSTANT...
GACHA (KACHAK)
!?

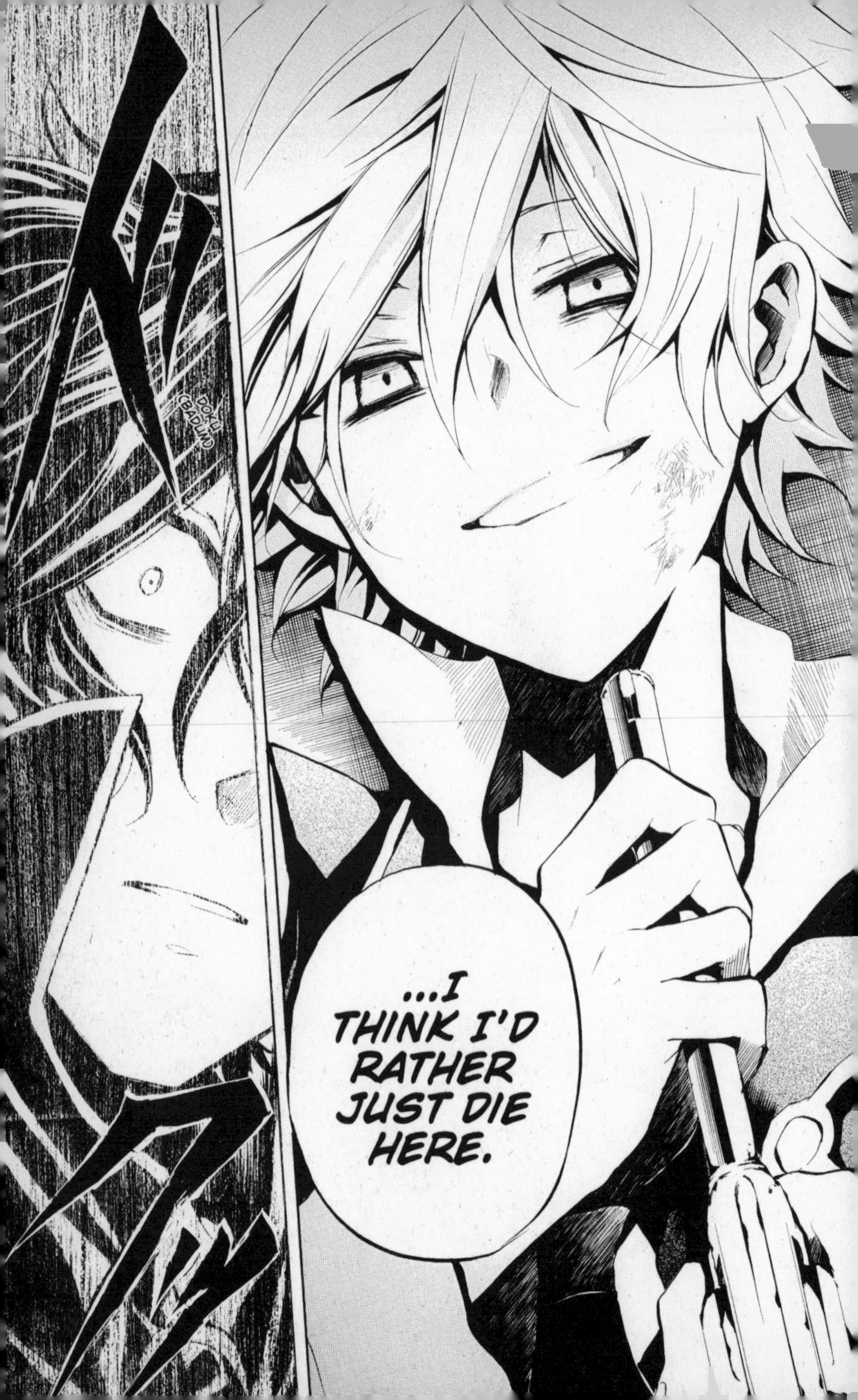
...I THINK I'D RATHER JUST DIE HERE.
DOKU (BADUM)

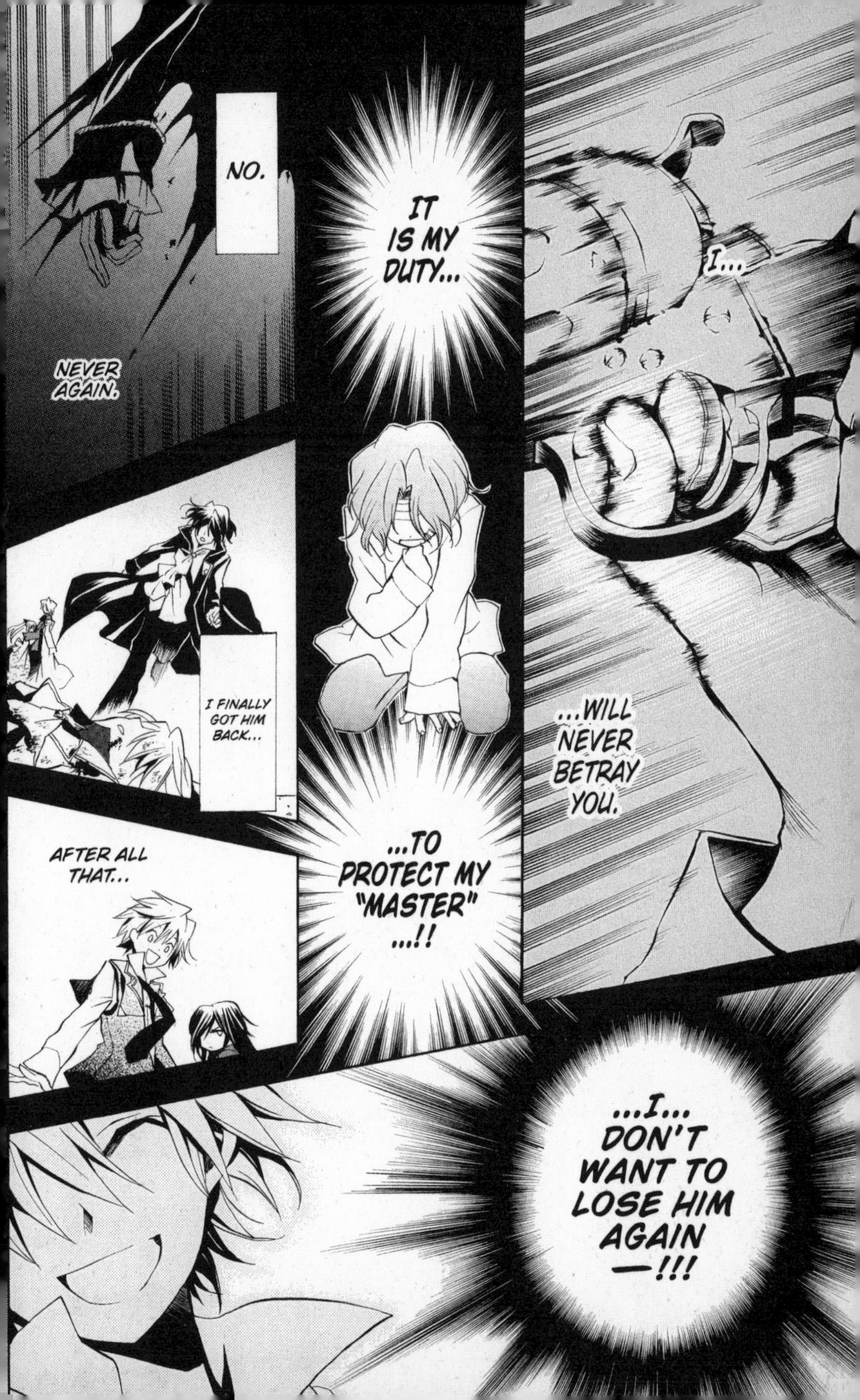
I...
...WILL NEVER BETRAY YOU.
IT IS MY DUTY...
...TO PROTECT MY "MASTER" ...!!
NO.
NEVER AGAIN.
I FINALLY GOT HIM BACK...
AFTER ALL THAT...
...I... DON'T WANT TO LOSE HIM AGAIN—!!!

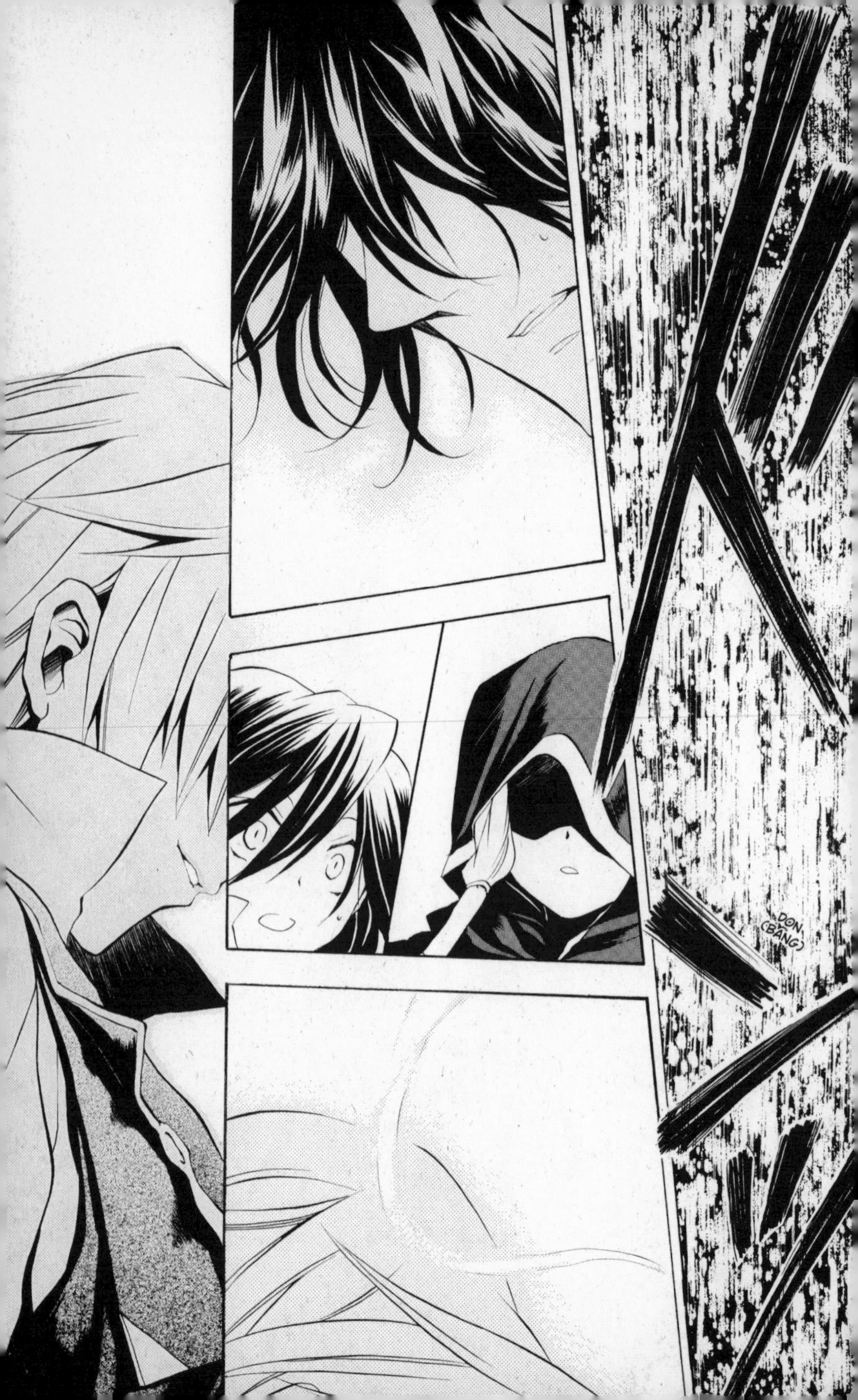
DON
(BANG)

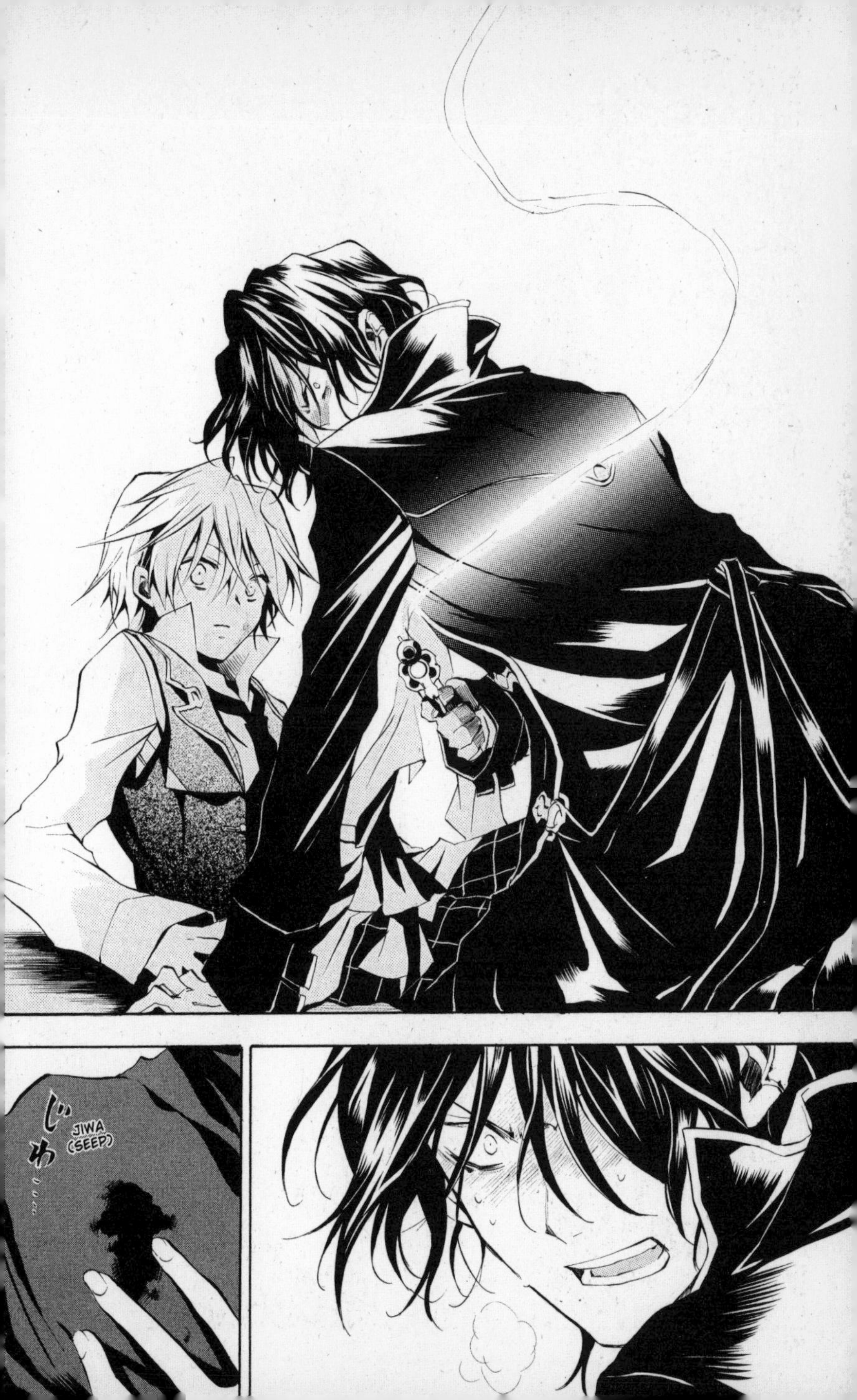
じわ……
JIWA (SEEP)

......

ヨロ
(STAGGER)

IT...
CAN'T
BE...

...DULDUM'S
STRINGS
...?

BOTA
(DRIP)

カチ
KACHI

YOU
TORE
OFF...

カチ
KACHI
(CLICK)

!

TAN
(LEAP)

......I HAVEN'T THE SLIGHTEST INTEREST IN A SCRIPT THAT'S GONE AWRY...

ギリ
GIRI
(GRIT)

HA-HA... I HATE TO SAY IT, BUT...

...IT'S TIME FOR THE CURTAIN TO FALL ON THIS SCENE!

PETA
(SIT)

LOOK FORWARD TO THE NEXT ACT...

...OZ VESSAL-IUS...!

ZURU (SLIDE)

......

KASHT...

ALICE, YOU'RE AH! ALL RIGHT? YOU'RE NOT HURT?

—WHAT WERE YOU THINK-ING?

HE REALLY IS GONE ...

I CAN'T SENSE HIM AT ALL ANY-MORE...

FLIIIII (PHEW)

TCH!

KA (CLICK)

...IS THAT SO...

......

IF I...!

I KNEW YOU WOULD.

IF I HADN'T BEEN ABLE TO STOP MYSELF —!

DO YOU REALLY... HAVE THAT MUCH OF A DEATH WISH...!?

THEN WHY!!?

PUFUU (PFFT)

NO WAY. OF COURSE NOT!

97

...YOU ABSO-LUTELY WOULD.

IF YOU TRULY ARE GIL, THEN...

...THE GILBERT YOU ONCE KNEW...!

I'M NO LONGER...

......

MY NAME IS...

...GILBERT NIGHT-RAY...

DO (THUD)!!!

GYU
(CLENCH)

THE GILBERT YOU SEE BEFORE YOU NOW...

...IS A MEMBER OF THAT NIGHTRAY DUKEDOM...!

...OF THE NIGHTRAYS... ANTAGONISTS TO THE HOUSE OF VESSALIUS—!

...DESERVE IT!!

I DON'T...

SO...

...DON'T TREAT ME LIKE YOU USED TO...

NIGHTRAY?

?

....

TA (DASH)

NOT AGAIN...

HAAH (SIGH)

.... NIGHT-RAY...

GABA (LEAP)

...WHAT YOU JUST SAID DOESN'T EXPLAIN ANYTHING!!

HEY...

....

WAIT, FOR-GET THAT...

SFX: SU (REACH)

...MORE IMPORTANT THAN ANY- ONE ELSE... HE'S MY PRECIOUS BEST FRIEND!

TO ME, HE'S...

I HAD ANY NUMBER OF OPPORTUNITIES...
...TO TALK TO HIM.

I KNEW THAT EVEN- TUALLY...

...HE WOULD LEARN THE TRUTH.

I'M PA- THE- TIC...

... RUNNING AWAY IN THAT SITU- ATION...

BUT EVEN SO, THE REASON...

...I COULDN'T TELL HIM WAS—

I OUGHT TO GO BACK RIGHT AWAY...

NOT TO MENTION THERE MIGHT STILL BE ENEMIES AROUND...

ZUUUN (GLOOM)

PARA (TINK)

AH HA HA !!

TWO DAYS AGO OR TEN YEARS LATER, THIS PLACE HASN'T CHANGED ONE BIT!

!?

GYOBI (JUMP)

WHOOOA!

THOUGHT YOU'D BE HERE! ☆

...TAKE CARE OF YOU.

HERE...

GIMME YOUR SCARF.

WH—!

WHAT DID YOU COME HERE FOR !?

HISSSS!

EH? WELL, TO...

BUT GOSH! THIS PLACE SURE BRINGS BACK MEMORIES, DOESN'T IT?

HA-HA-HA-HA!

WELL, YOU WERE TRYING TO PROTECT ME...

YOU FELL FLAT ON YOUR FACE. THAT WAS SOOOO LAME!

YAAAH!♥

ME, YOU, AND ADA WERE EXPLORING THE MANSION...

...WHEN WE STUMBLED IN HERE.

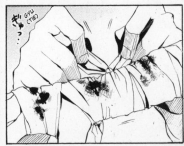

ギュ (TIE)

....

"BECAUSE I DIDN'T WANT YOU TO KNOW THAT I'D CHANGED."

B—

......

....

....

WHY... DIDN'T YOU TELL ME?

I...

...I THOUGHT —!

PFFT.

!?

AWWW YEAH, BULL'S EYE. THAT'S SOOO LIKE YOU. **TOTALLY LAME.**

WELL, THAT REALLY TICKS ME OFF, BUT...

THAT YOU'RE TALLER THAN ME NOW?

SO WHAT'S CHANGED ABOUT YOU?

OR THAT YOU CAN SHOOT GUNS NOW?

+"!! ZA (STEP)

OF COURSE YOU'VE **GAINED** ALL KINDS OF THINGS IN THAT TIME.

—WELL, IT'S BEEN TEN YEARS, RIGHT?

...YOU'VE *LOST* ANYTHING THAT MAKES YOU WHO YOU ARE.

...IT DOESN'T SEEM LIKE...

...BUT TO ME...

...AND YOU'VE TAKEN CARE OF ME TIME AND TIME AGAIN SINCE.

...THE ONE WITH ME WHEN I WOKE UP...

—YOU WERE...

SO TELL ME.

...YOU DIDN'T TURN YOUR *"ABSOLUTE"* INTO A LIE, DID YOU?

AND JUST NOW...

...NO MATTER HOW MUCH TIME PASSES...

...OR EVEN IF OUR SITUATIONS CHANGE—

WHAT IS IT EXACTLY THAT'S DIFFERENT ABOUT YOU?

......

I STILL... HAVE FAITH IN WHAT YOU SAID BACK THEN.

DON'T ASSUME THAT BECAUSE YOU'RE NOW AN ARISTO-CRAT...

LET ME SAY THIS.

SO WHAT IF YOU'RE A MEMBER OF SOME DUKEDOM?

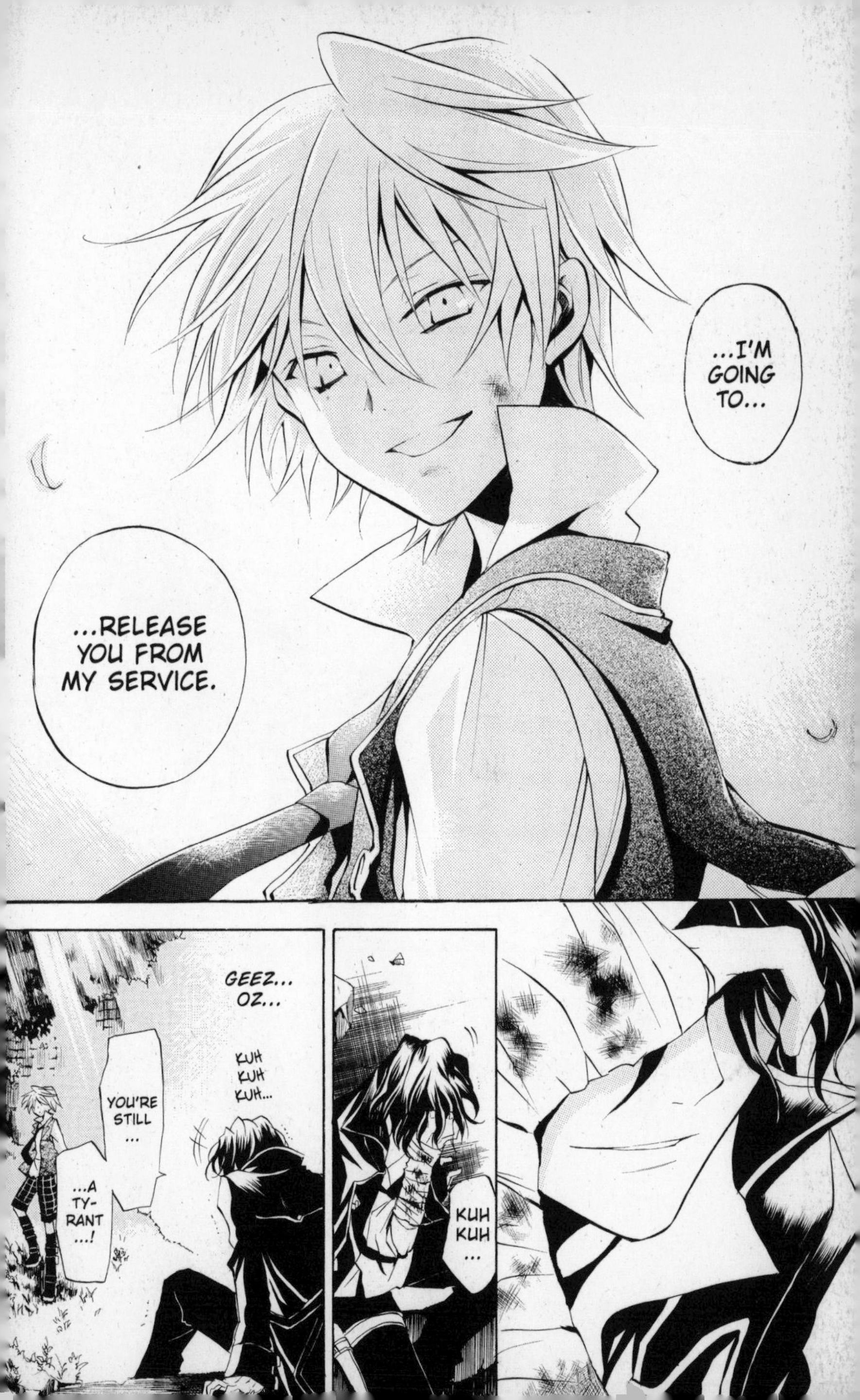
...I'M GOING TO...
...RELEASE YOU FROM MY SERVICE.
GEEZ... OZ...
KUH KUH KUH...
KUH KUH ...
YOU'RE STILL ...
...A TY-RANT ...!

...BETRAYED VESSALIUS, YOU DO REALIZE...?

I...

-SIGH-

I'M...... NO LONGER PURE.

AS LONG AS IT'S STILL WHAT YOU WANT!

IT'S NO PROBLEM.

HERA (GRIN)

ZA (STEP)

YET...

—— EVEN SO...

—— IF YOU CAN STILL FORGIVE ME...

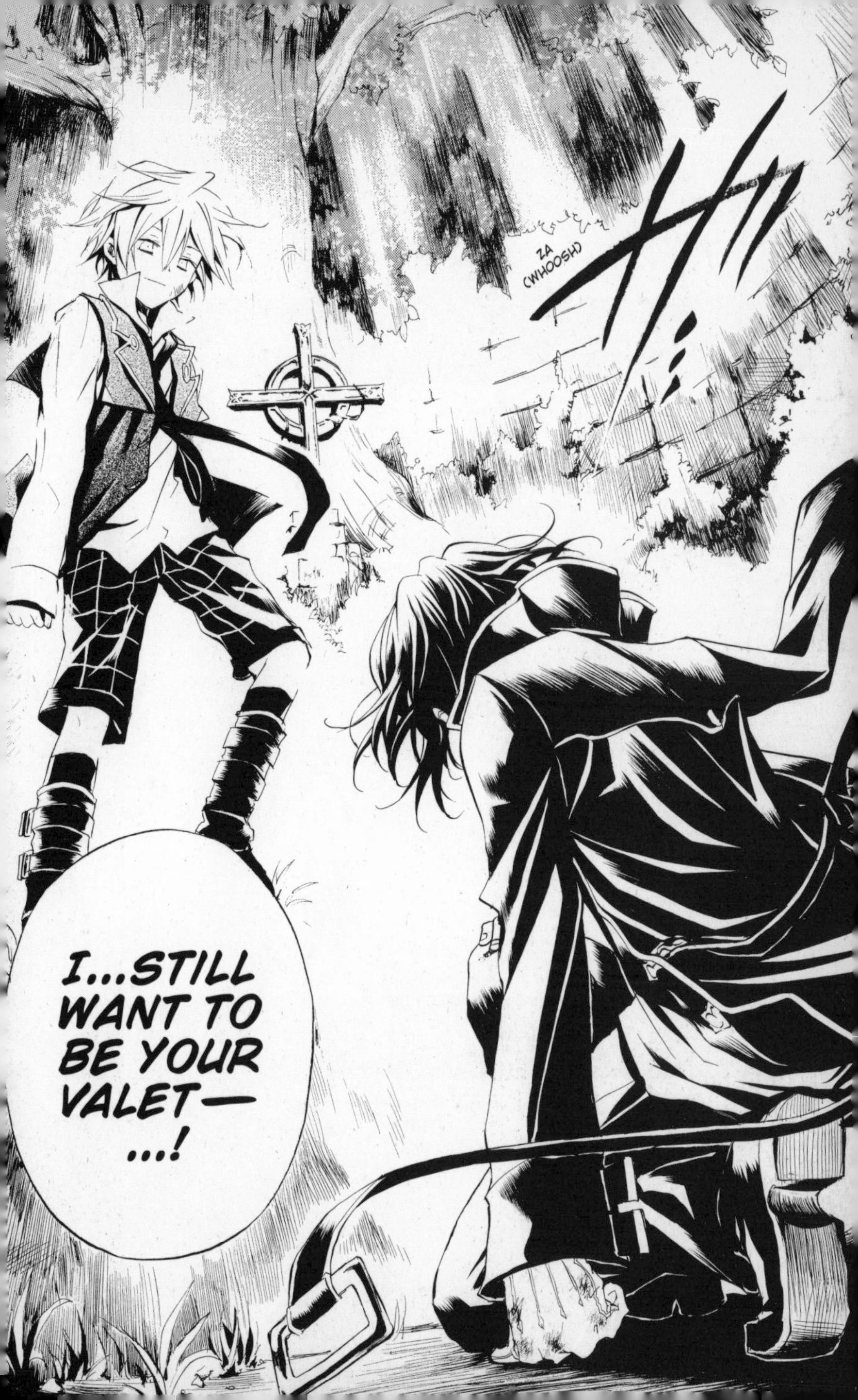
ZA
(WHOOSH)
I...STILL WANT TO BE YOUR VALET— ...!

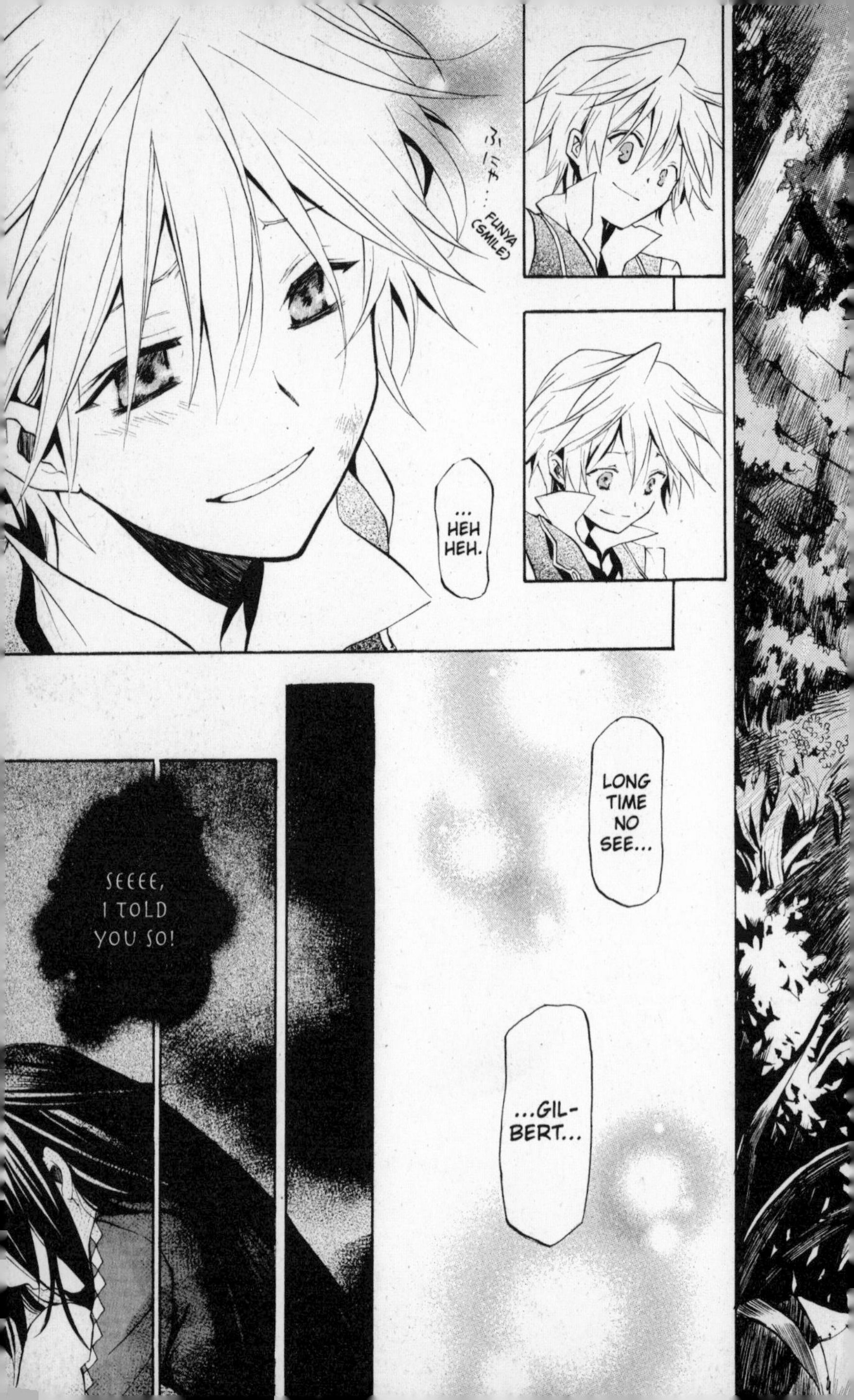
ふにゃ…
FUNYA (SMILE)
...HEH HEH.
LONG TIME NO SEE...
...GIL-BERT...
SEEEE, I TOLD YOU SO!

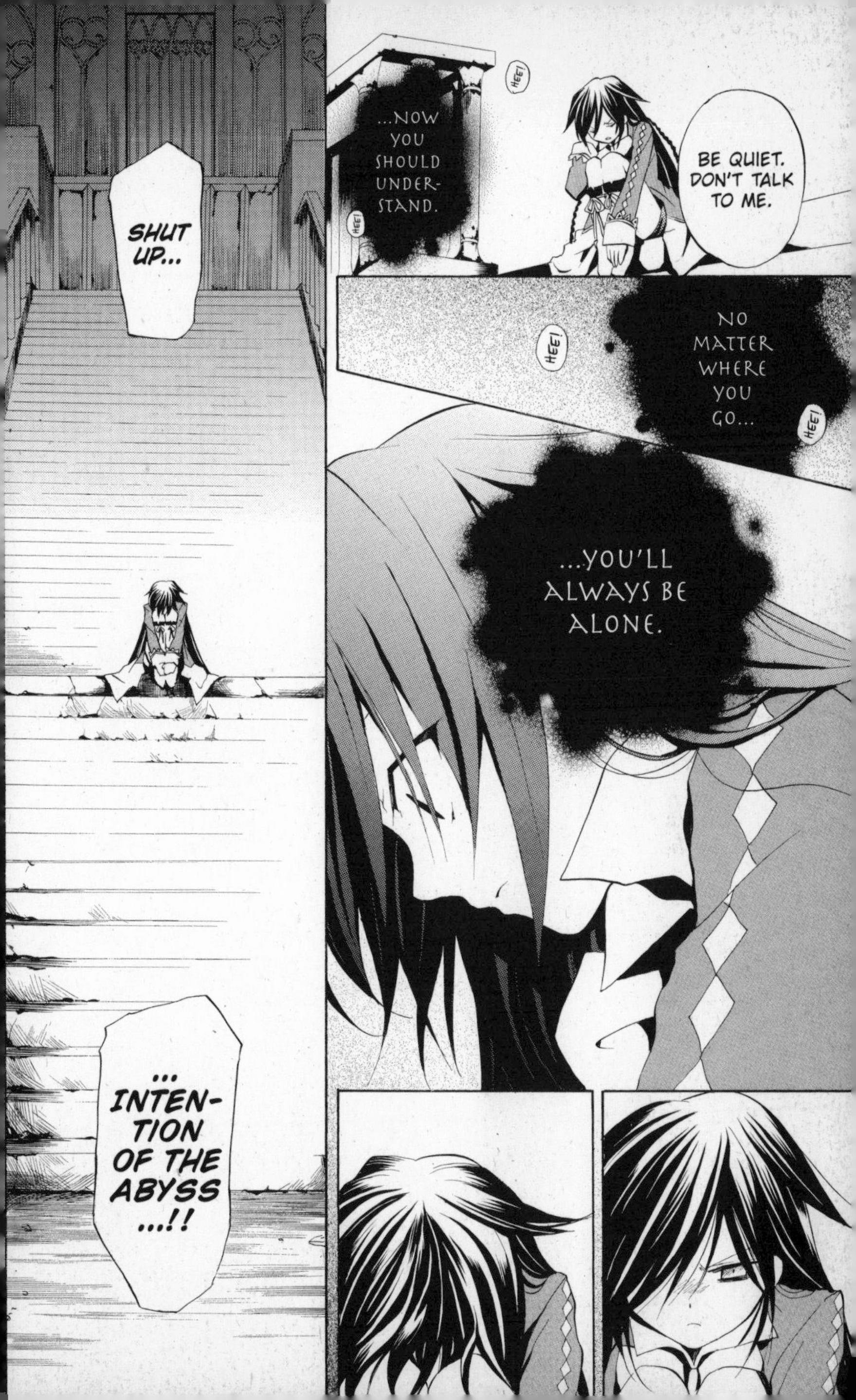
BE QUIET. DON'T TALK TO ME.
HEE!
...NOW YOU SHOULD UNDER-STAND.
HEE!
HEE!
NO MATTER WHERE YOU GO...
HEE!
...YOU'LL ALWAYS BE ALONE.
SHUT UP...
...INTEN-TION OF THE ABYSS...!!

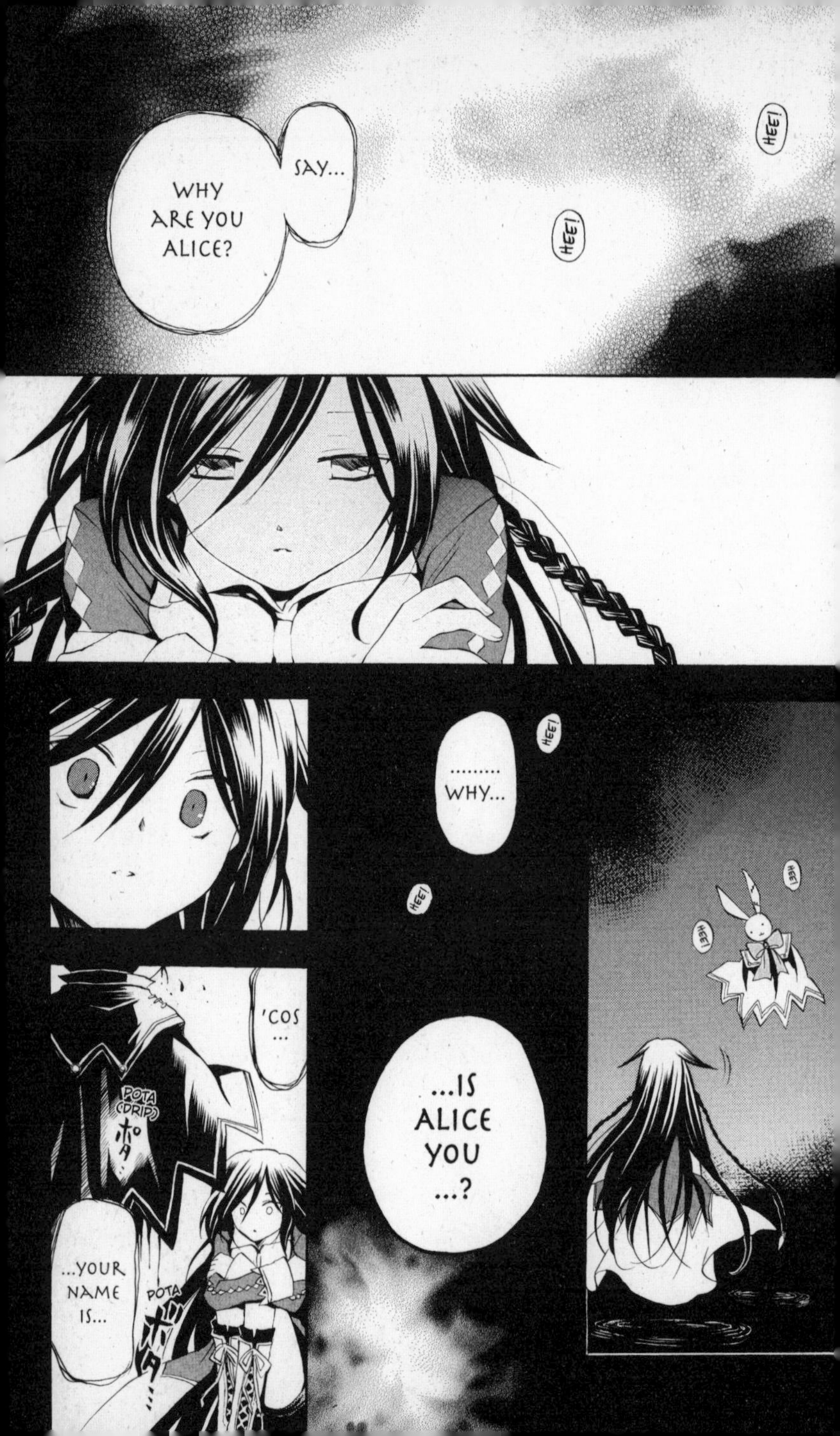
HEE!
HEE!
SAY...
WHY ARE YOU ALICE?
HEE!
HEE!
....
WHY...
HEE!
HEE!
...IS ALICE YOU ...?
'COS ...
POTA (DRIP)
...YOUR NAME IS...
POTA

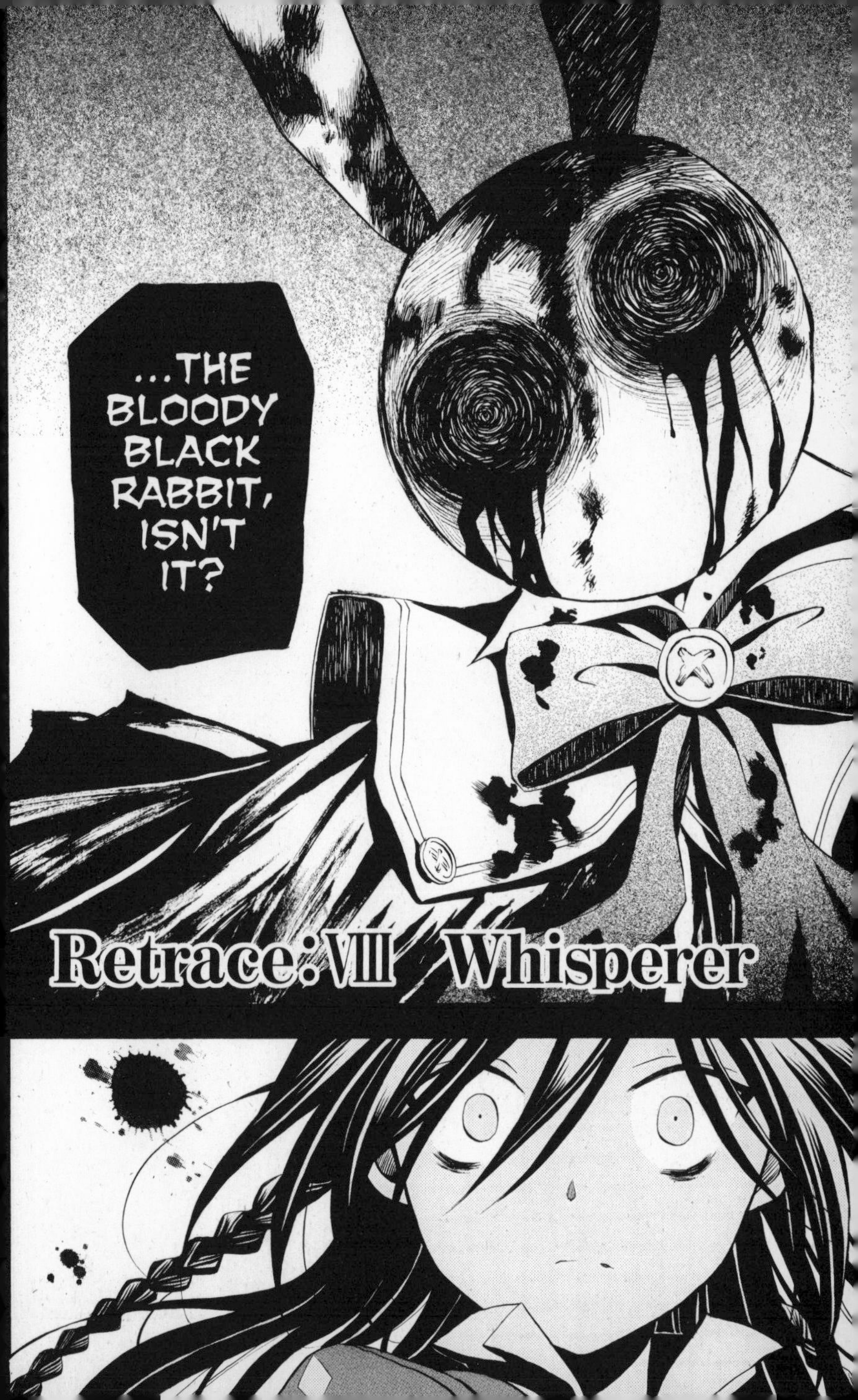
...THE BLOODY BLACK RABBIT, ISN'T IT?
Retrace:VIII Whisperer

ALICE!!

......

OZ
...

SU
(CREACH)

YOU
ALL
RIGHT?

...WAS THAT
A DREAM...?

YOU
LOOK
REAL
PALE...

115

PAN
(SLAP)

DON'T TOUCH ME SO CASUALLY ...!

...WHERE'S RAVEN?

OH YEAH...

...HE'S WAITING FOR US AT THE TOMB.

......

SO OF COURSE, IF ALICE ISN'T THERE—

AFTER ALL, WE THREE CAME HERE TO INVESTIGATE IT, RIGHT?

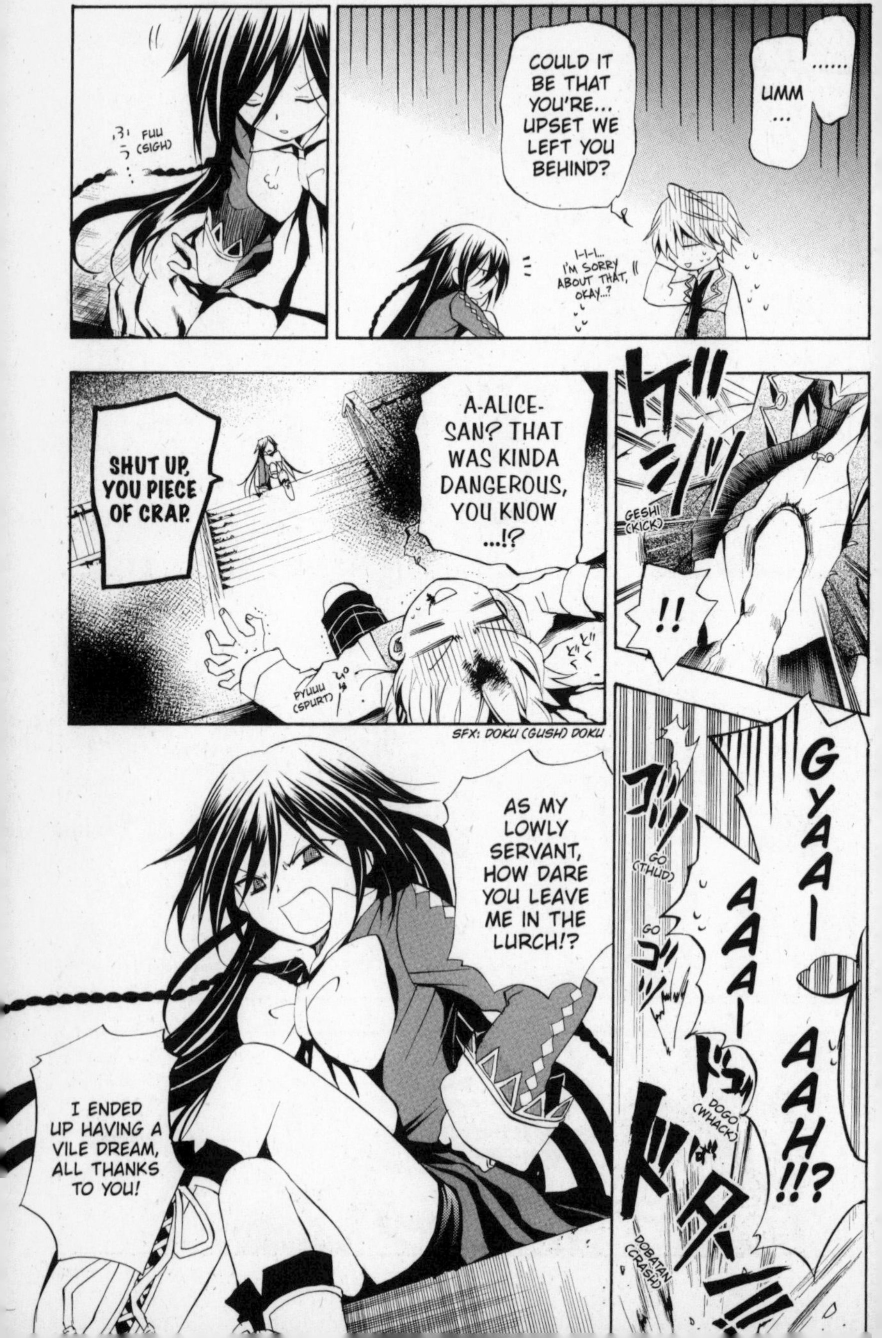
......
UMM ...
COULD IT BE THAT YOU'RE... UPSET WE LEFT YOU BEHIND?
I-I-I... I'M SORRY ABOUT THAT, OKAY...?
FUU (SIGH)
GESHI (KICK)
!!
A-ALICE-SAN? THAT WAS KINDA DANGEROUS, YOU KNOW ...!?
SHUT UP, YOU PIECE OF CRAP.
PYUUU (SPURT)
SFX: DOKU (GUSH) DOKU
GYAA—AAA—AAH!!?
GO (THUD)
GO
DOGO (WHACK)
DOBATAN (CRASH)
AS MY LOWLY SERVANT, HOW DARE YOU LEAVE ME IN THE LURCH!?
I ENDED UP HAVING A VILE DREAM, ALL THANKS TO YOU!

...SO...

KACHA (KACHAK)

MAN, HOW COOL

...YOU HAVEN'T ASKED RAVEN ABOUT THE DETAILS YET, I TAKE IT?

...I MEAN, YOU SHOULDN'T LEAVE STUFF LIKE THIS LYING AROUND, SILLY GIL...

KACHA

KA (CLICK)

HURRY UP AND TAKE ME THERE ALREADY!

EEEHN, I'M SOR-RYYY!

......

WELL... THAT'S TRUE...

TOKO (TMP)

SO I FIGURED YOU'D UNDER-STAND A BIT MORE IF WE LISTENED TOGETHER.

TOKO

ALICE, YOU DON'T KNOW MUCH ABOUT *THIS* WORLD, RIGHT?

NOPE.

—BUT THAT'S JUST ONE REASON.

TRUTH IS...

...I ALSO... WANTED TO SORT THINGS OUT IN MY HEAD FIRST.

EH-HEH-HEH! LET'S NOT GIVE THEM BACK TO HIM JUUUST YET!

I'M GLAD I WAS ABLE TO ESCAPE FROM THE ABYSS.

AND I'VE EVEN GOT GIL BACK BESIDE ME AGAIN.

...THERE ARE STILL LOTS OF THINGS THAT DON'T FEEL REAL YET...

BUT...

HEH...

NO...
I WISH WE COULD AT LEAST FIND OUT WHOSE GRAVE IT IS...

HEEEERE, SPECIAL DELIVERY!

WELL? HOW 'BOUT IT? DID YOU FIND ANY CLUES?

AH.

GIL!

......

HEY, YOU! GIMME BACK THE OTHER GUN TOO!

YOU HEARD GIL, AL—

ALICE ...?

?

SUCH WEAK VOICES... I DIDN'T EVEN NOTICE THEM AT FIRST...

...AND HAVE BEEN WAITING FOR ME ...!

...IN THESE TREES AND PETALS...

LITTLE BY LITTLE, THEY BEGAN DWELLING...

I'm home ...!

SAA (WSHH)

!

PAAA (GLOW)

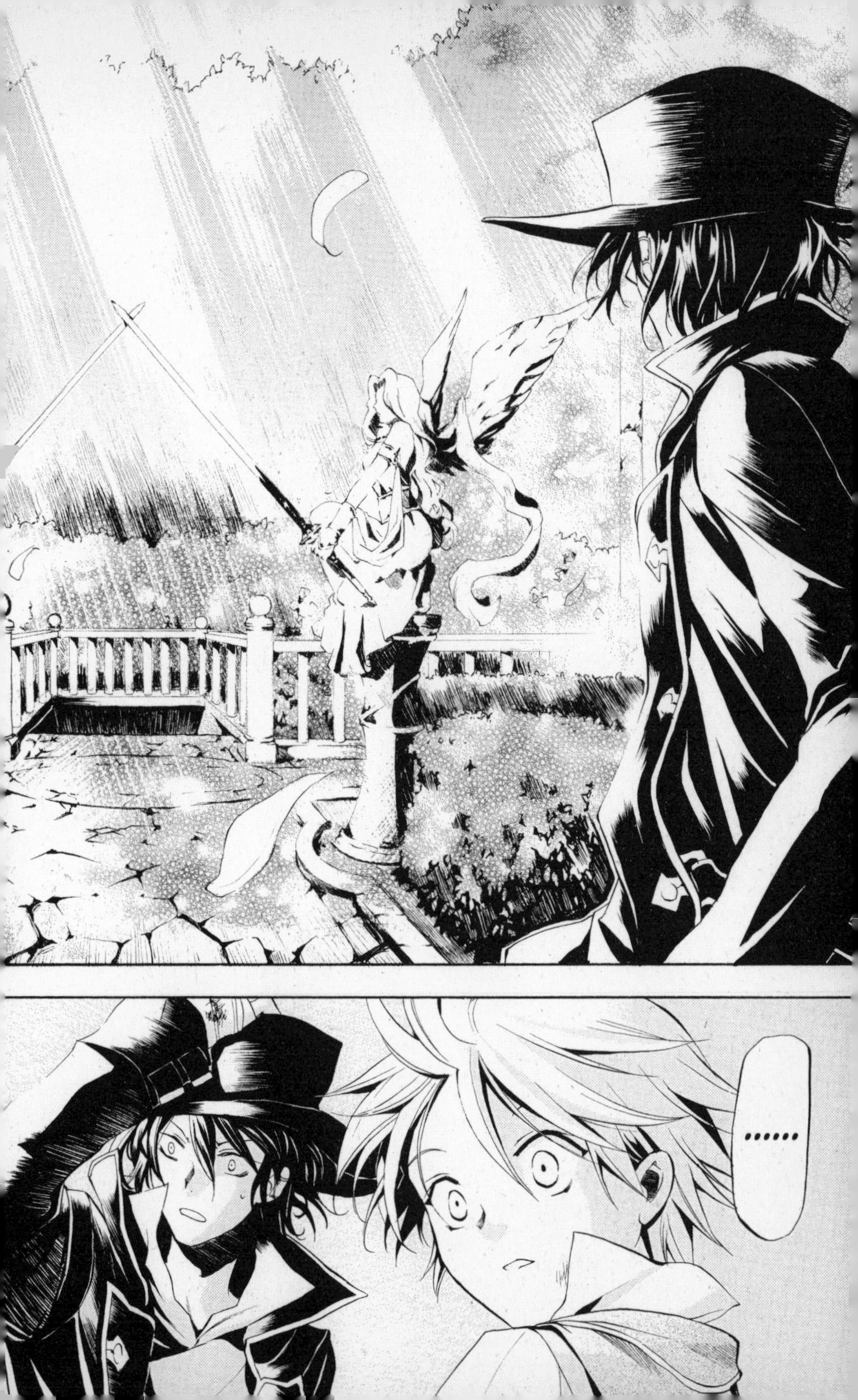
......

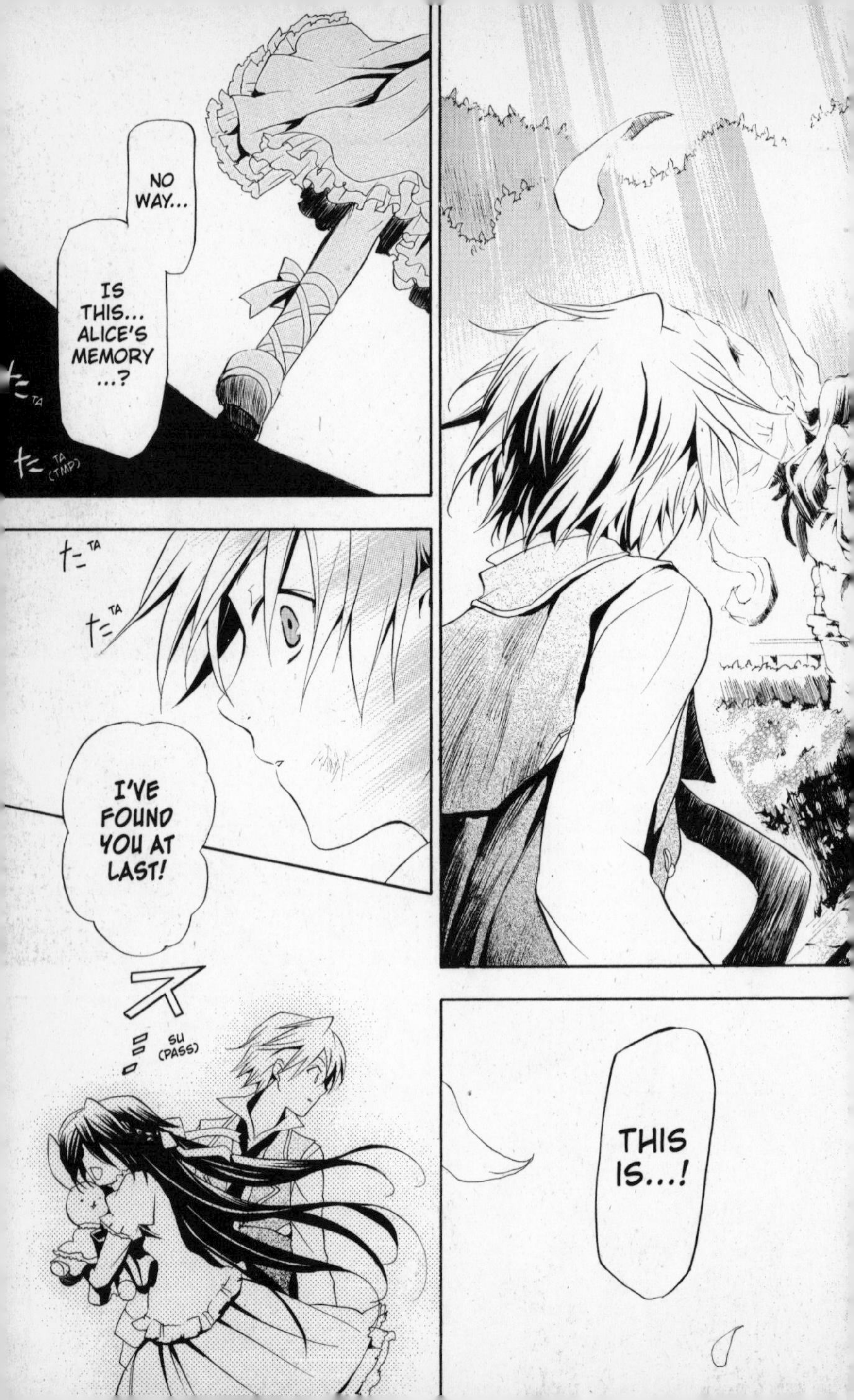
NO WAY...
IS THIS... ALICE'S MEMORY ...?
TA
TA (TMP)
TA
TA
I'VE FOUND YOU AT LAST!
SU (PASS)
THIS IS...!

A—

WHAT A NAUGHTY GIRL.

DID YOU FOLLOW ME HERE?

EH HEH HEH !!

...?

SOMEONE'S THERE...?

TA (TMP)
た
た TA
た TA
た TA
た ...

*THAT VOICE
BELONGS
TO...*

...ドクン
DOKUN [BADUMP]

...ドクン...
DOKUN

*...THE
MAN...*

*...WHO
APPEARED
INSIDE
ALICE'S
MEMORY
...!?*

*"YOU
FINALLY
CAME."*

DOKUN

DOKUN

DOKUN

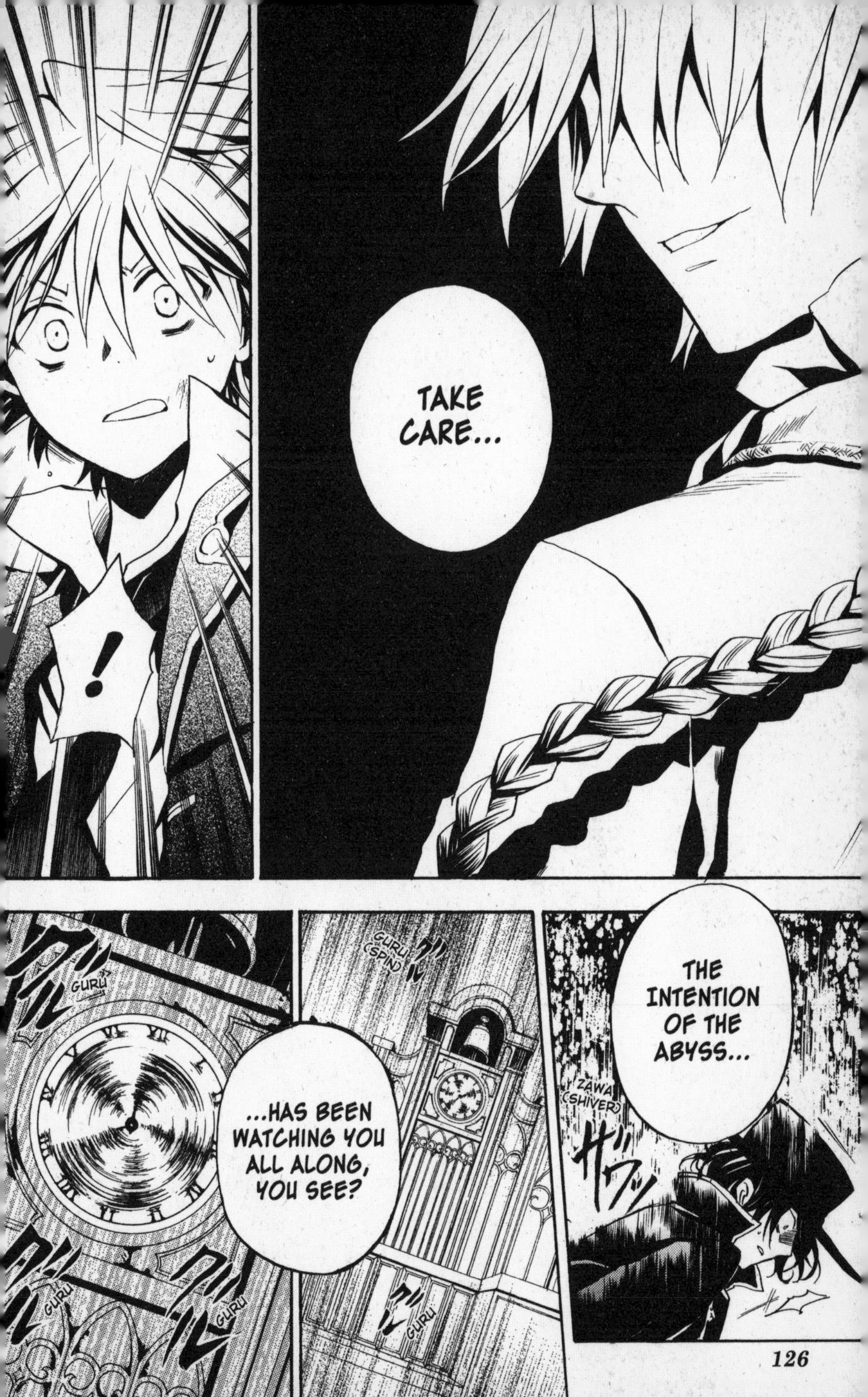
!
TAKE CARE...
THE INTENTION OF THE ABYSS...
ZAWA (SHIVER)
...HAS BEEN WATCHING YOU ALL ALONG, YOU SEE?
GURU (SPIN)
GURU
GURU
GURU
GURU

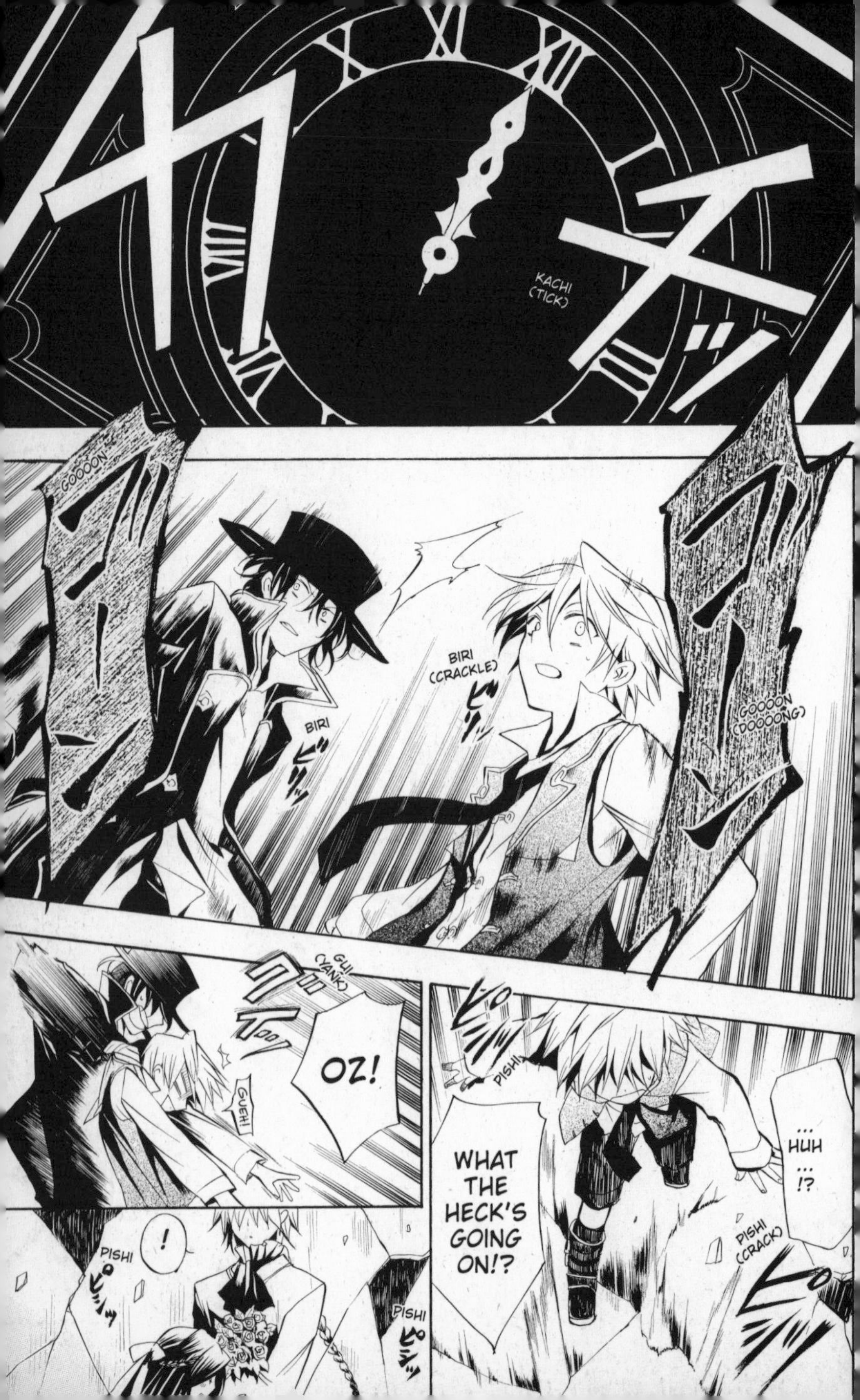
KACHI (TICK)
GOOOON
BIRI (CRACKLE)
BIRI
GOOOON (DOOOONG)
PISHI
...HUH...!?
WHAT THE HECK'S GOING ON!?
PISHI (CRACK)
GUI (YANK)
OZ!
GUEH!
!
PISHI
PISHI

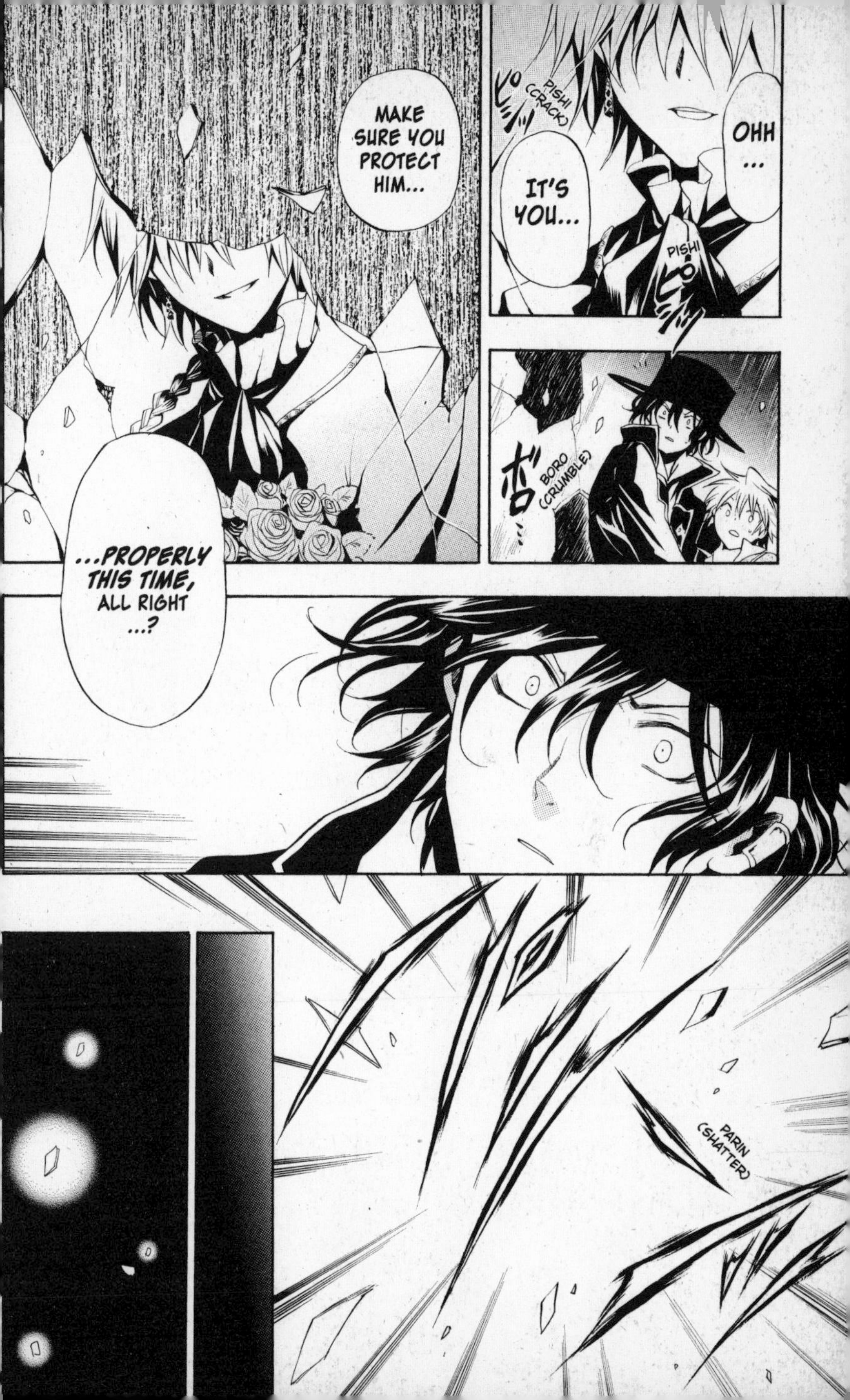
OHH ...
PISHI (CRACK)
IT'S YOU...
PISHI
MAKE SURE YOU PROTECT HIM...
BORO (CRUMBLE)
...PROPERLY THIS TIME, ALL RIGHT ...?
PARIN (SHATTER)

......

HEY... GIL... YER... CHOK... ING... ...ME...

WHAT'S... THIS INTENTION OF THE ABYSS THING—

I DON'T KNOW MUCH ABOUT IT EITHER...

HEE!

HEE!

....

ポ (POU [GLOW])

HEE! HEE!

...IT'S SUPPOSEDLY THE BEING THAT CREATED THE ABYSS AS WE KNOW IT TODAY...

...BUT

HEE!

...!
UH
...

...
IT'S A
RABBIT
!?

NO...
THAT'S
PROBABLY
A MAKE-
SHIFT
FORM...

...AAH
...

...AAH...

I'VE MET
YOU AT
LAST...

...AND IT'S
WHAT BOTH
PANDORA
AND THE
BASKERVILLES
DESIRE...!

HEE!

HEE!

HEE!

HEE!

...OKAY? SO PLEASE HURRY...

...LONG, LONG, LONG, LONG, LONG, LONG TIME...

I'VE BEEN WAITING FOR YOU.

!?

...AND COME GET ME QUICKLY?

FOR A LONG...

SO PLEASE...

AND... AND... OKAY...?

WE'LL TALK UNTIL WE GET SLEEPY...

HEE! HEE!

I HAVE MANY DOLLS READY FOR YOU, I DO!

LET'S PLAY WITH THEM, SHALL WE?

HEE!

HEE!

...MY BELOVED.

I DON'T KNOW YOU.

.... BUT MORE IMPORTANTLY...

ZOKU (SHIVER)

PAN (SLAP)

...WILL YOU LET ALICE GO?

...JUST LIKE ALL HER OTHER CONTRACTORS, YOU KNOW?

...AND SHE INTENDS TO KILL YOU...

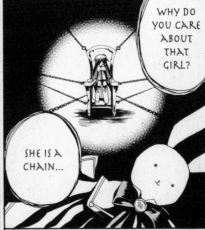

WHY DO YOU CARE ABOUT THAT GIRL?

SHE IS A CHAIN...

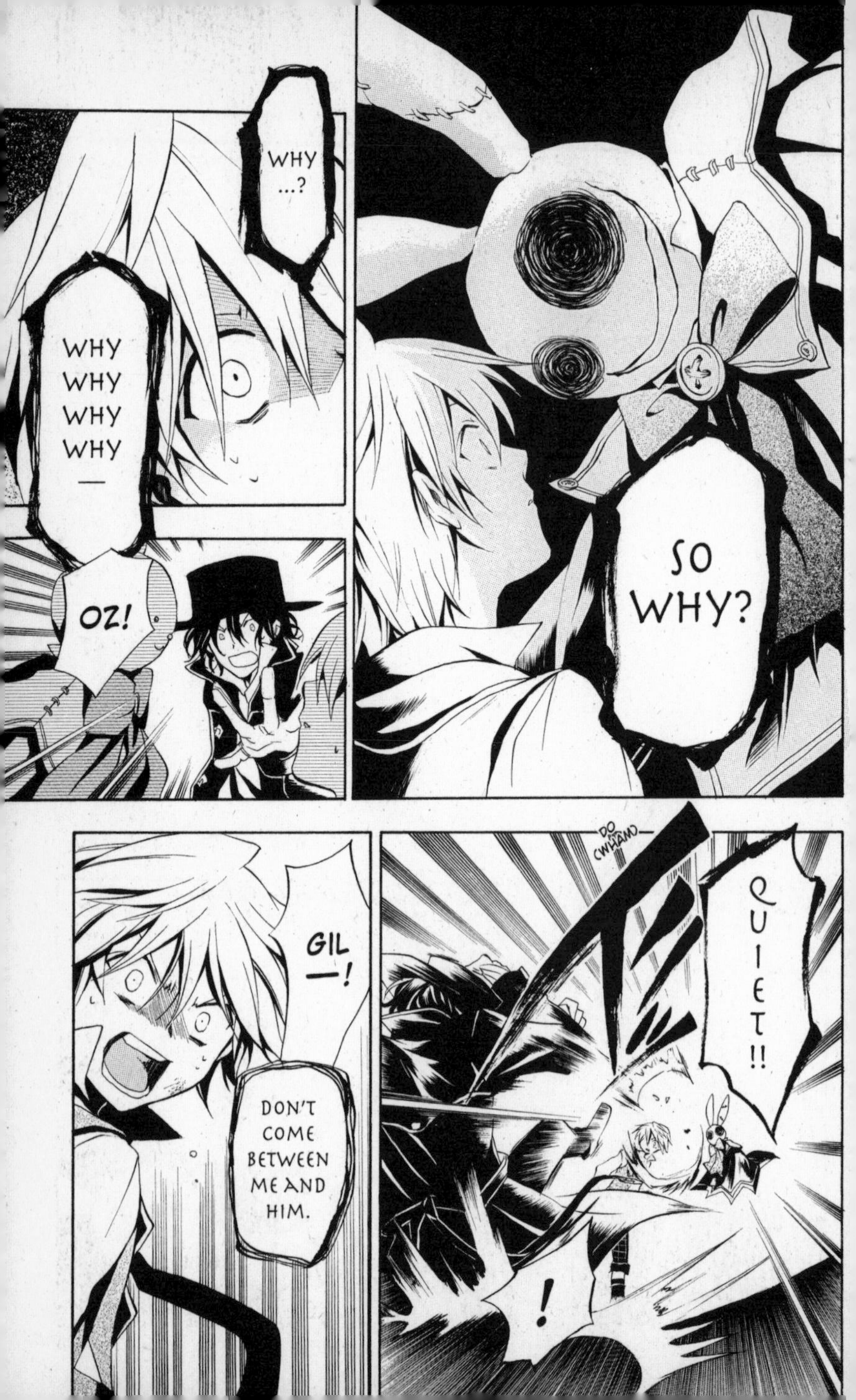
SO WHY?
WHY ...?
WHY WHY WHY WHY —
OZ!
DO CWHAM
QUIET!!
!
GIL —!
DON'T COME BETWEEN ME AND HIM.

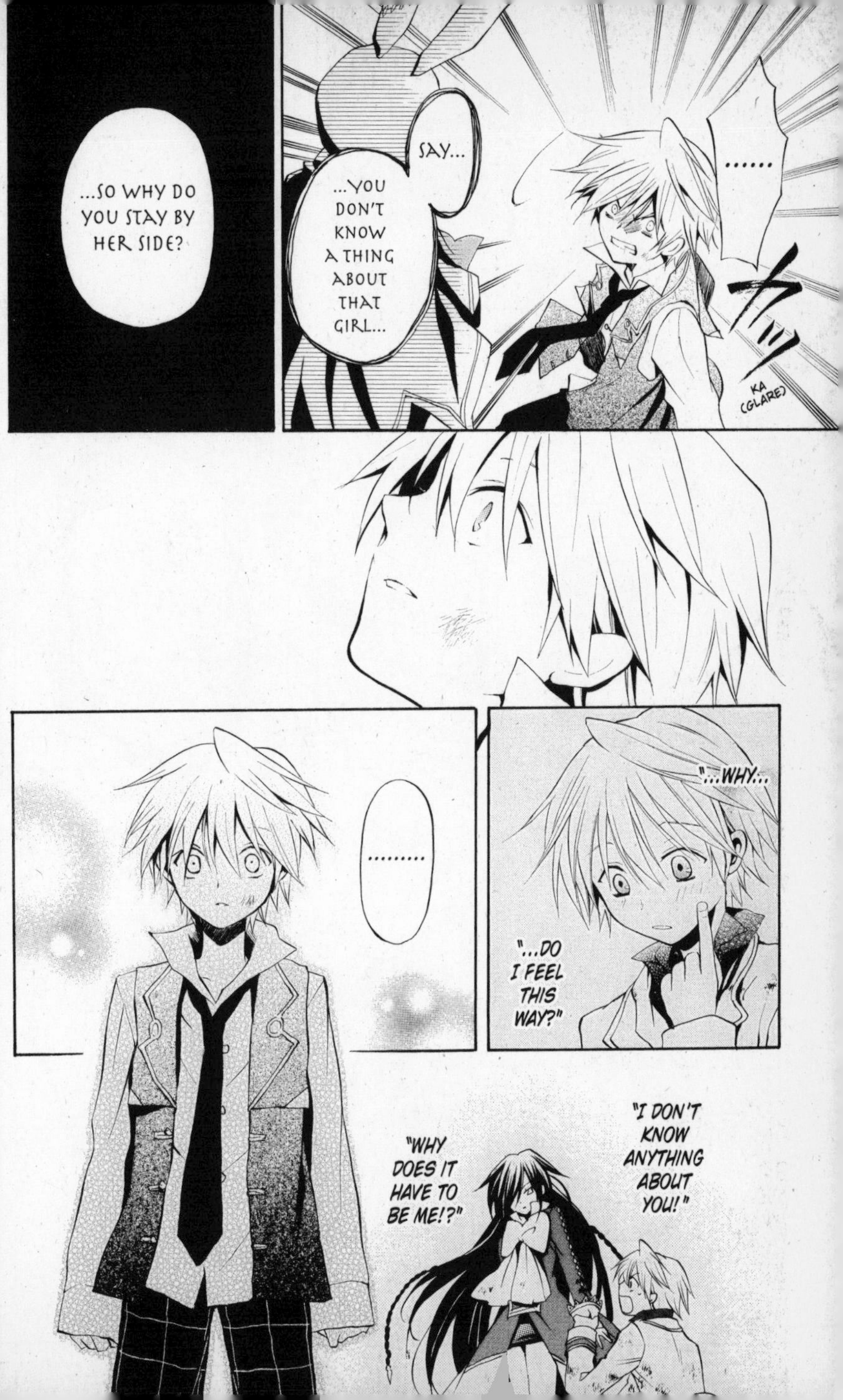
......
SAY...
...YOU DON'T KNOW A THING ABOUT THAT GIRL...
KA (GLARE)
...SO WHY DO YOU STAY BY HER SIDE?
"...WHY...
"...DO I FEEL THIS WAY?"
....
"I DON'T KNOW ANYTHING ABOUT YOU!"
"WHY DOES IT HAVE TO BE ME!?"

...WHO
DOESN'T
EVEN
KNOW...

...WHO SHE IS
OR WHY SHE
WAS BORN.

THE
REASON
...

...I'M
WITH
ALICE
...?

YES
...

SHE'S
MERELY
A BRAT
...

*FU
(WAKE)*

YET SHE
MANAGED
TO TAKE
YOU AWAY
FROM ME.

DOKUN

A
DOLL
LIKE
HER...

*GYU
(CLENCH)*

SHE
DOESN'T
DESERVE
YOU.

*DOKUN
(BADUMP)*

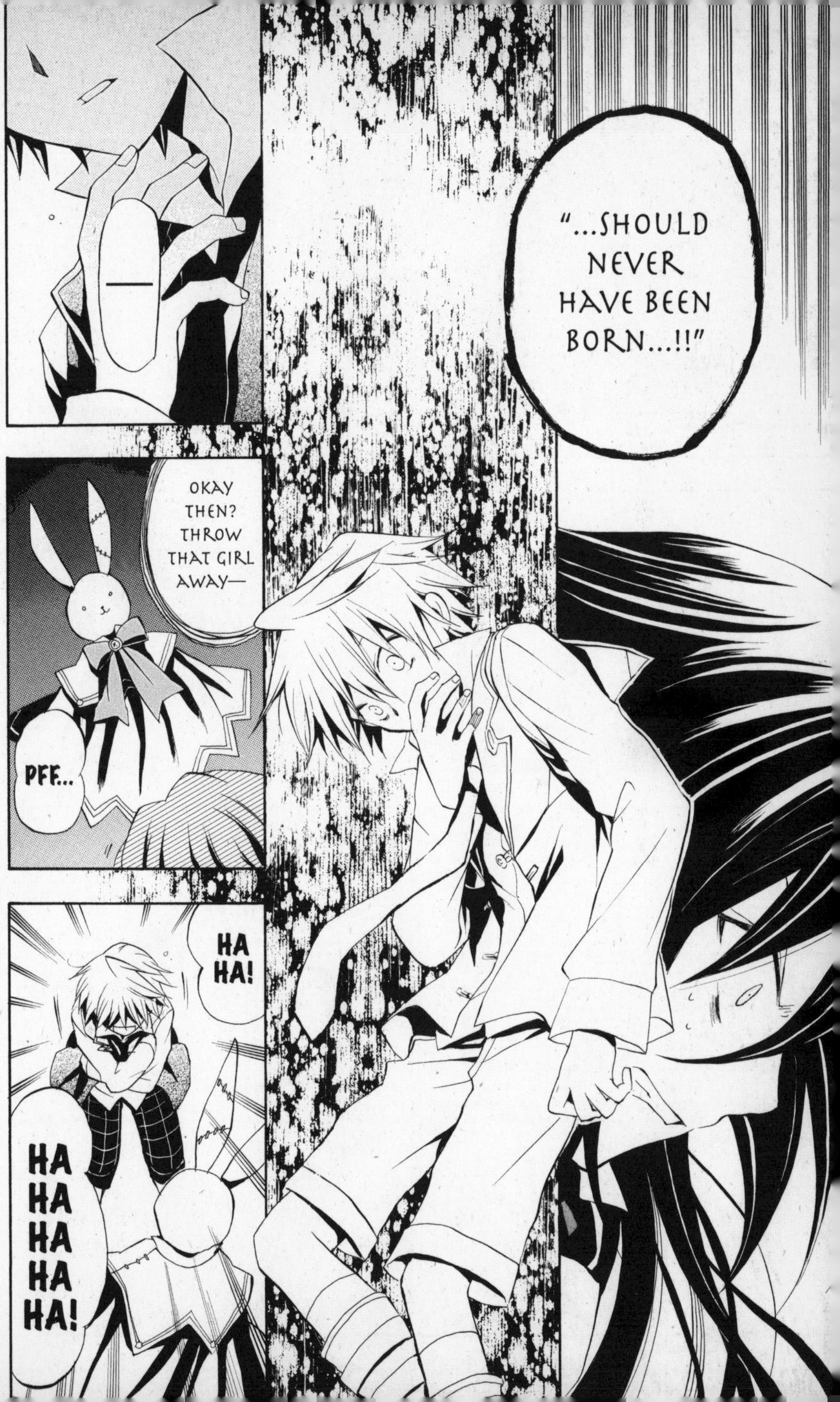
"...SHOULD NEVER HAVE BEEN BORN...!!"
—
OKAY THEN? THROW THAT GIRL AWAY—
PFF...
HA HA!
HA HA HA HA HA!

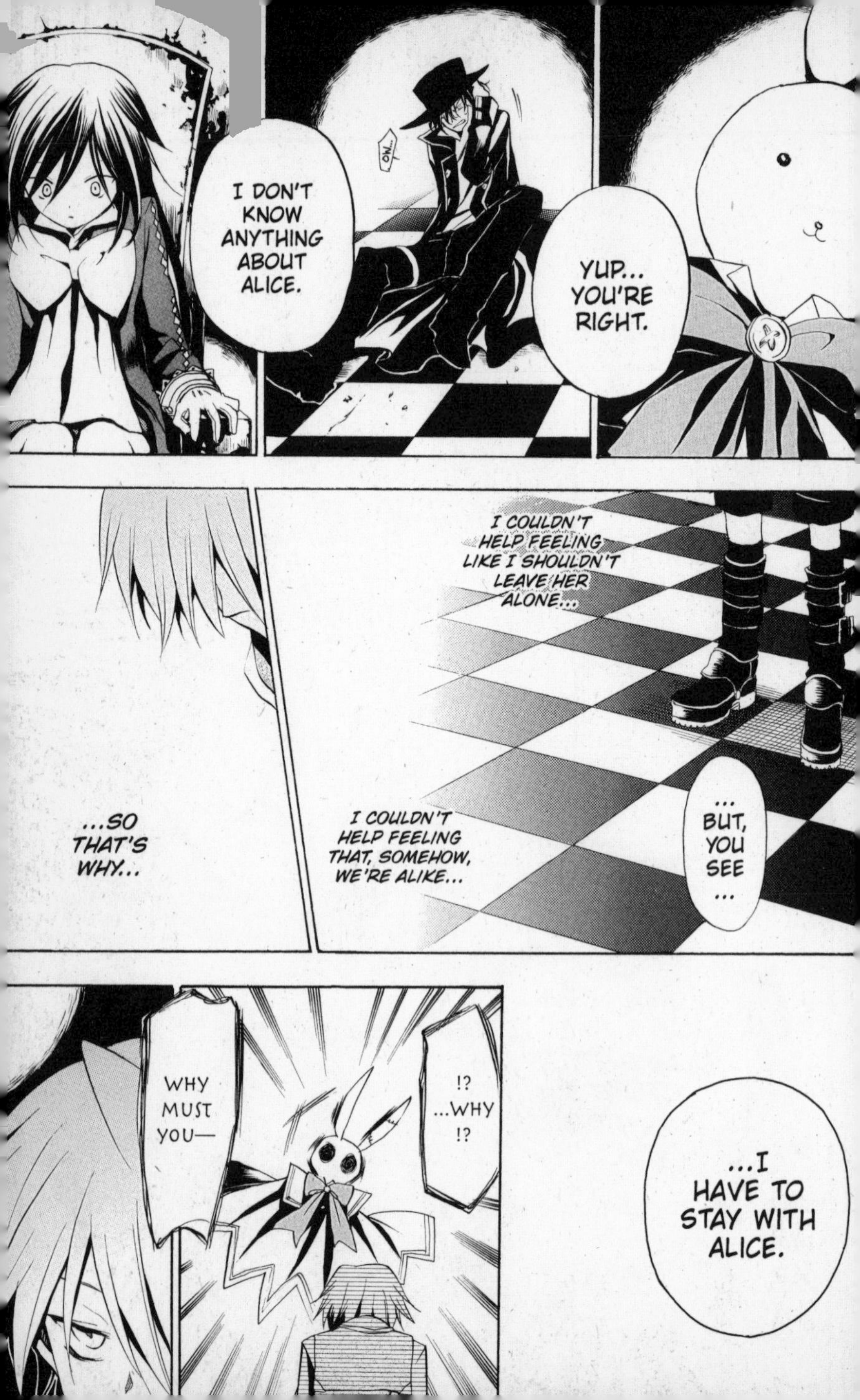
YUP... YOU'RE RIGHT.
OH...
I DON'T KNOW ANYTHING ABOUT ALICE.
... BUT, YOU SEE ...
I COULDN'T HELP FEELING LIKE I SHOULDN'T LEAVE HER ALONE...
I COULDN'T HELP FEELING THAT, SOMEHOW, WE'RE ALIKE...
...SO THAT'S WHY...
...I HAVE TO STAY WITH ALICE.
!? ...WHY !?
WHY MUST YOU—

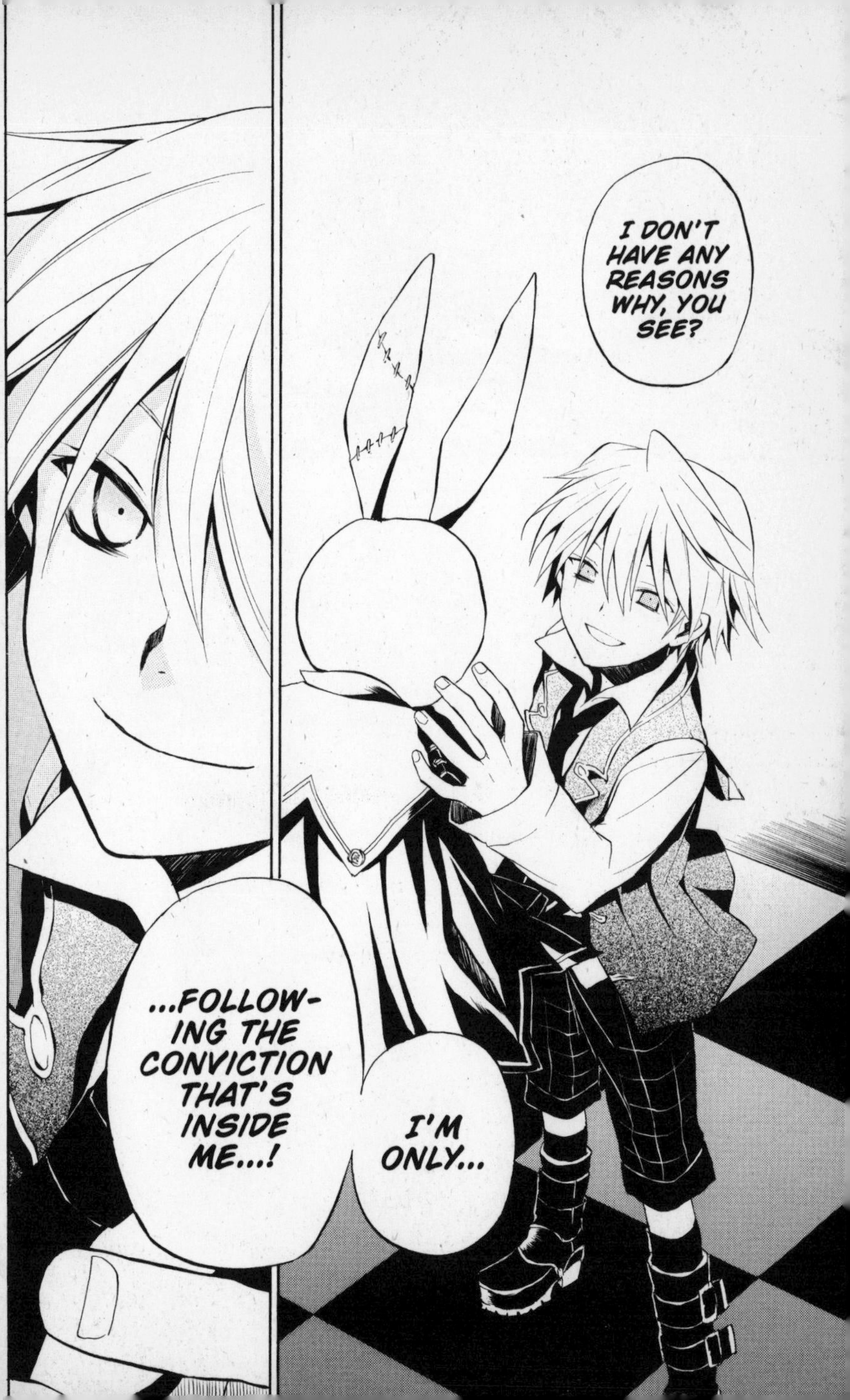
I DON'T HAVE ANY REASONS WHY, YOU SEE?
I'M ONLY...
...FOLLOW-ING THE CONVICTION THAT'S INSIDE ME...!

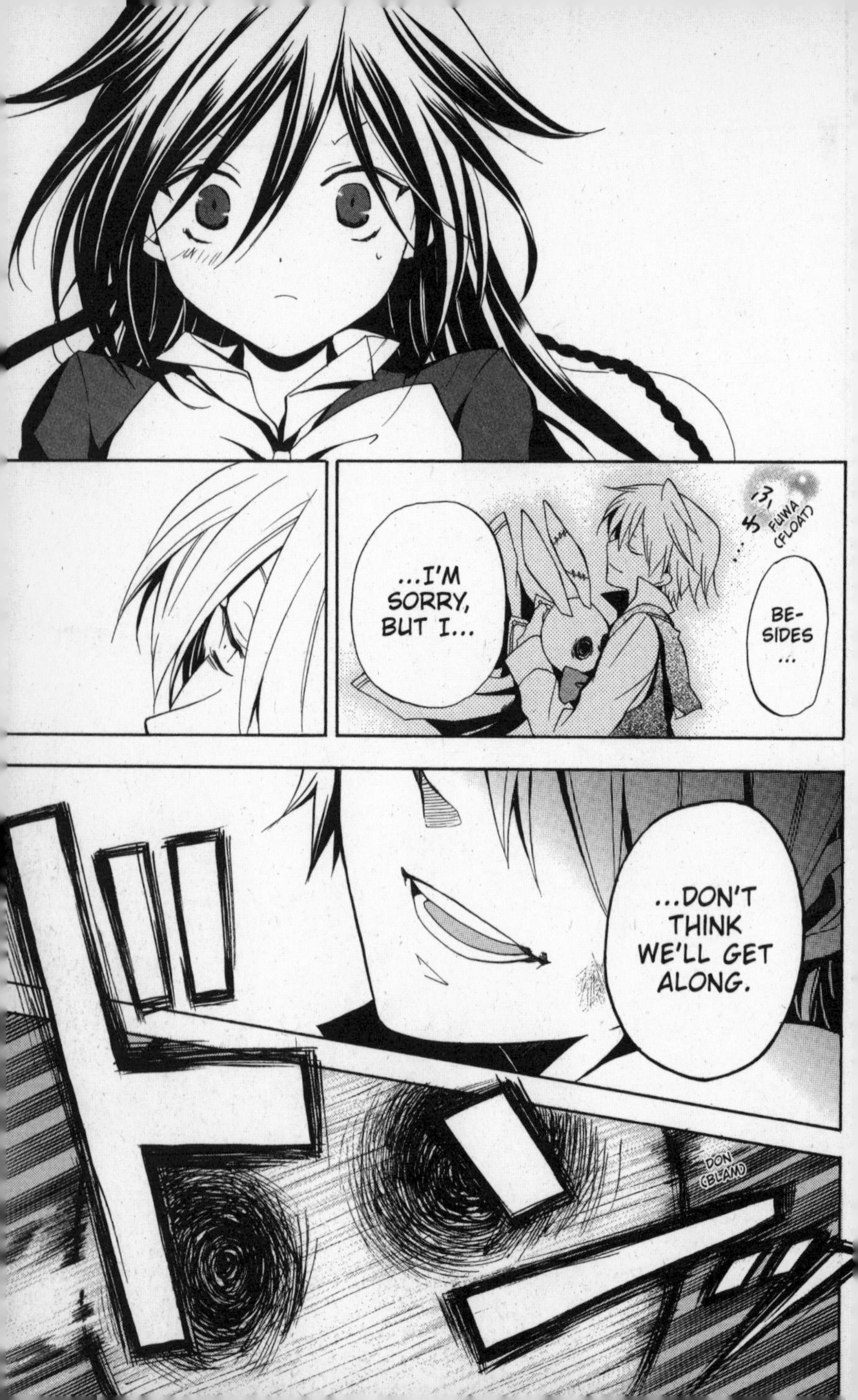
FUWA (FLOAT)
BE-SIDES...
...I'M SORRY, BUT I...
...DON'T THINK WE'LL GET ALONG.
DON (BLAM)

THANKS FOR THE INVITATION ...

...BUT THESE DAYS, I'M MORE INTO "TREASURE HUNTING" ...

...THAN PLAYING WITH DOLLS.

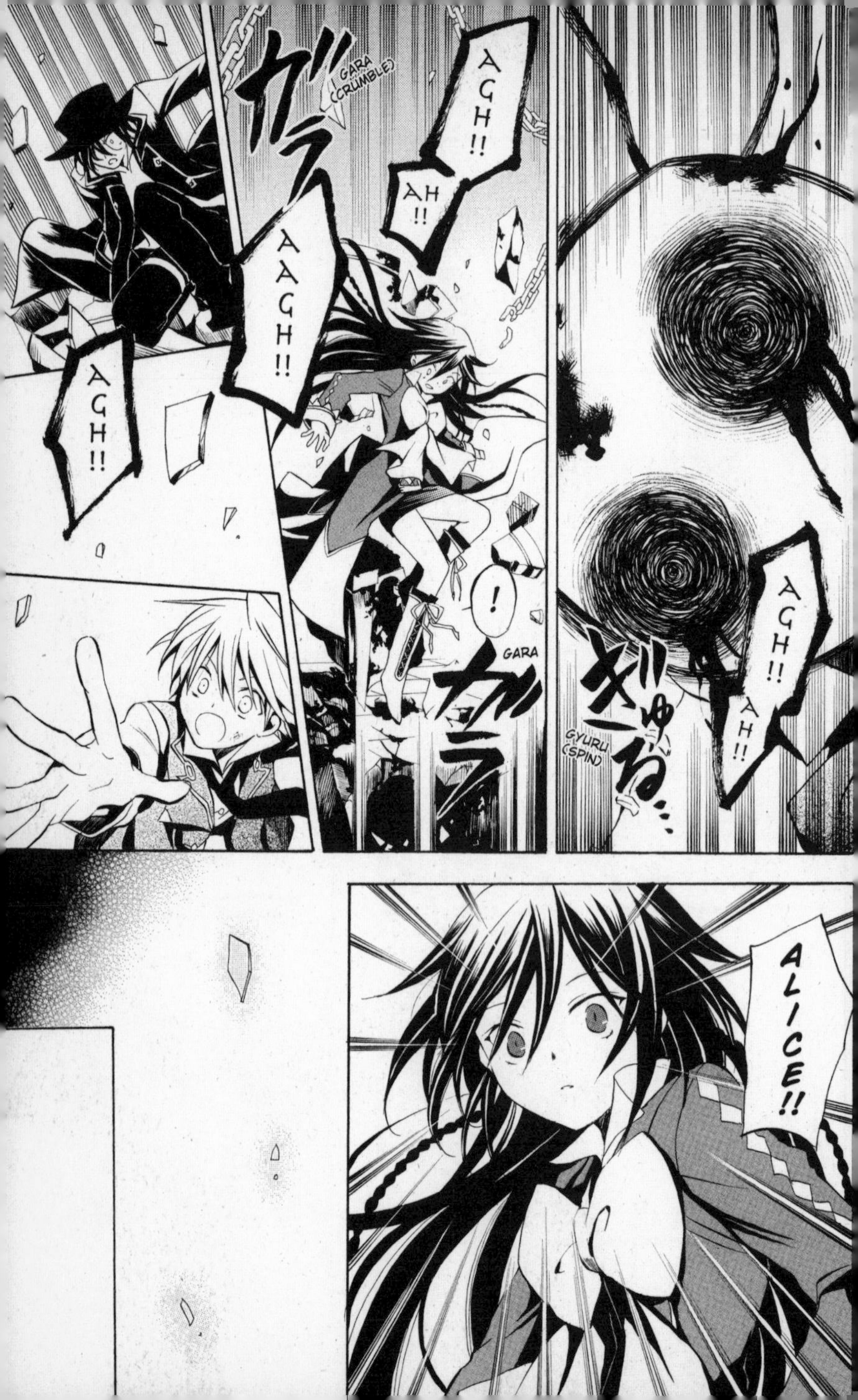
AGH!!
AH!!
GYURU (SPIN)
AGH!!
AH!!
GARA (CRUMBLE)
AAGH!!
!
GARA
AGH!!
ALICE!!

YOU...

...WILL COME TO REGRET THIS.

......ピチチチチ
(TWEETWEE)

YOU WILL COME TO RUE THE DAY THAT YOU CHOSE THE B-RABBIT OVER ME!

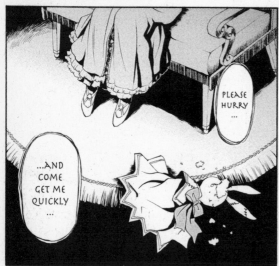

PLEASE HURRY...

...AND COME GET ME QUICKLY...

POTO (PLOP)

WELL!

SO THIS IS HOW IT IS, HMM?

HAH-HAAH~!!

I TRULY DID NOT THINK THE INTENTION OF THE ABYSS WOULD INTERVENE SO QUICKLY, BUT...

...AS THINGS ARE PROCEEDING ACCORDING TO PLAN FOR THE MOMENT...

KACHA (CLINK)

... SHALL WE RETURN ...

...TO PANDORA?

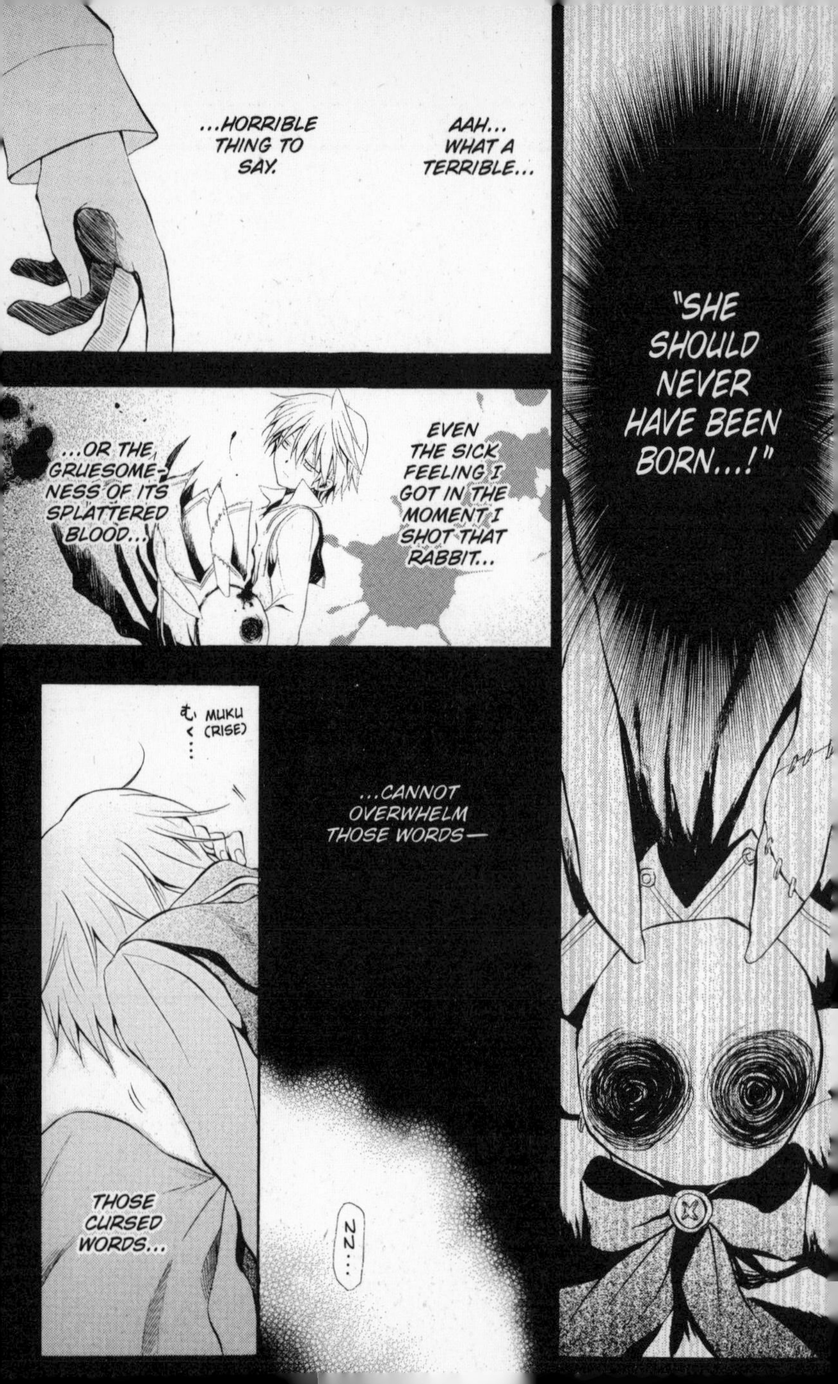
"SHE SHOULD NEVER HAVE BEEN BORN...!"
AAH... WHAT A TERRIBLE...
...HORRIBLE THING TO SAY.
EVEN THE SICK FEELING I GOT IN THE MOMENT I SHOT THAT RABBIT...
...OR THE GRUESOME-NESS OF ITS SPLATTERED BLOOD...
...CANNOT OVERWHELM THOSE WORDS—
むく... MUKU (RISE)
NN...
THOSE CURSED WORDS...

WHO WAS IT THAT UTTERED THEM TO ME...?

Retrace:IX Question

GATA
(RATTLE)

YOU'RE UP?

...IS THAT RIGHT?

PHEW...

...EH? I'M FINE...

GIL.

DOES IT HURT ANY- WHERE?

KA CLICK ♪...

...THIS IS...

MY PLACE.

GISHI (CREAK) ギシ...

WE...WERE IN ALICE'S MEMORY, WEREN'T WE?

KYORO (GLANCE) きょろ

KYORO きょろ

GATA ガタ

I MOVED US WHILE YOU GUYS SLEPT THE DAY AWAY.

GAKO (PUSH) ガコ...

HUH !?

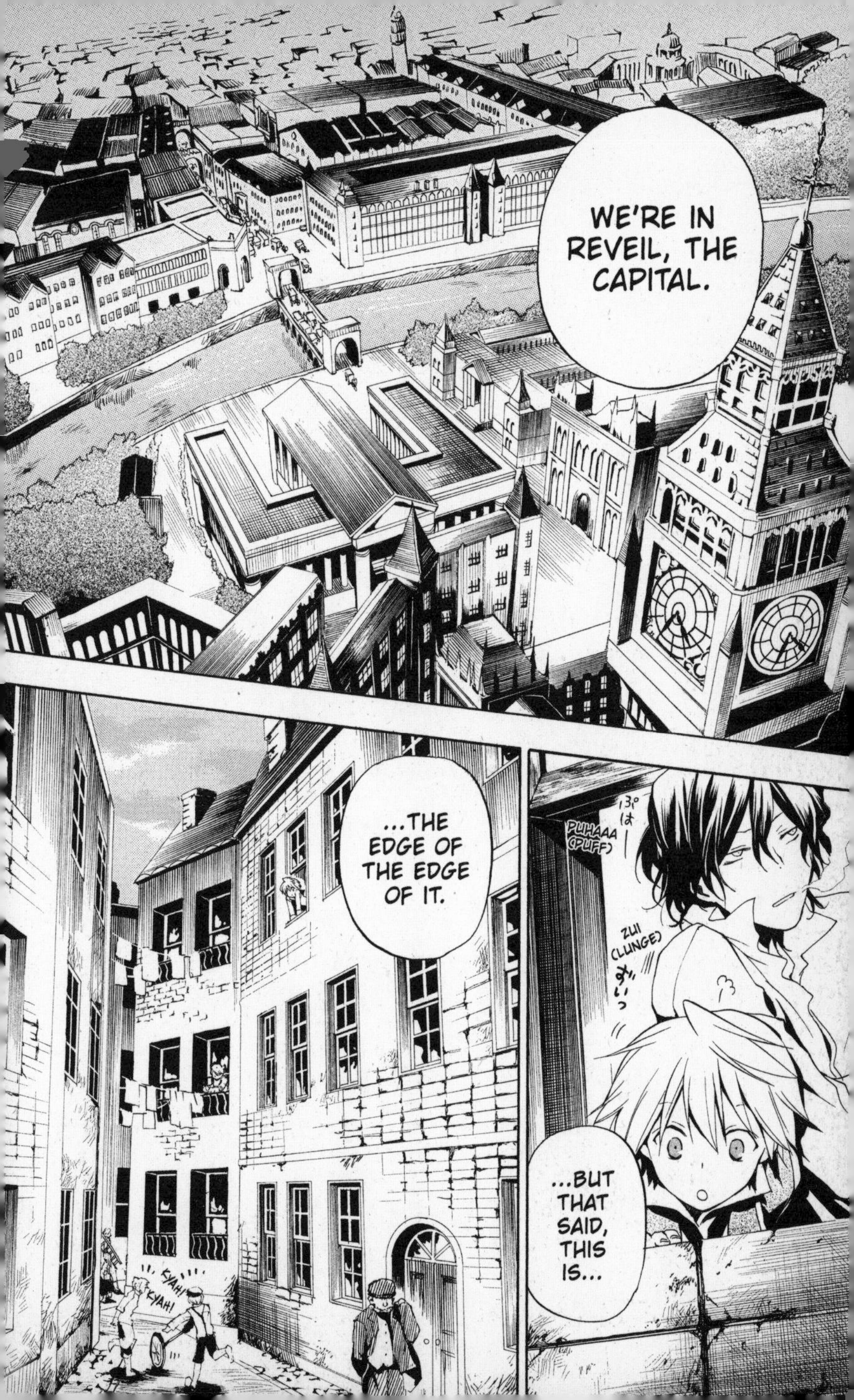
WE'RE IN REVEIL, THE CAPITAL.
ぷは
PUHAAA (PUFF)
ずいっ
ZUI (LUNGE)
...BUT THAT SAID, THIS IS...
...THE EDGE OF THE EDGE OF IT.
KYAH! KYAH!

...HE USED YOU...

FURU (SHAKE) 3, 3

FURU 3, 3

BREAK SET US UP.

THIS IS THE DUKE'S HOUSE ....?

MYYY ~!

NICE GOING THERE, RAVEN! ♡

...AS BAIT TO LURE OUT THE ENEMY...!

LETTING THE BASKERVILLES ATTACK OZ—!

......HOW COULD YOU DO THIS, BREAK...!?

FURU 3, 3

FURU 3, 3

THANKS TO YOU, I WAS ABLE TO CONFIRM AAALL KINDS OF THINGS!

FEEL FREE TO LEAVE THE REST TO US AND AWAIT FURTHER ORDERS AT HOME, 'KAAY?

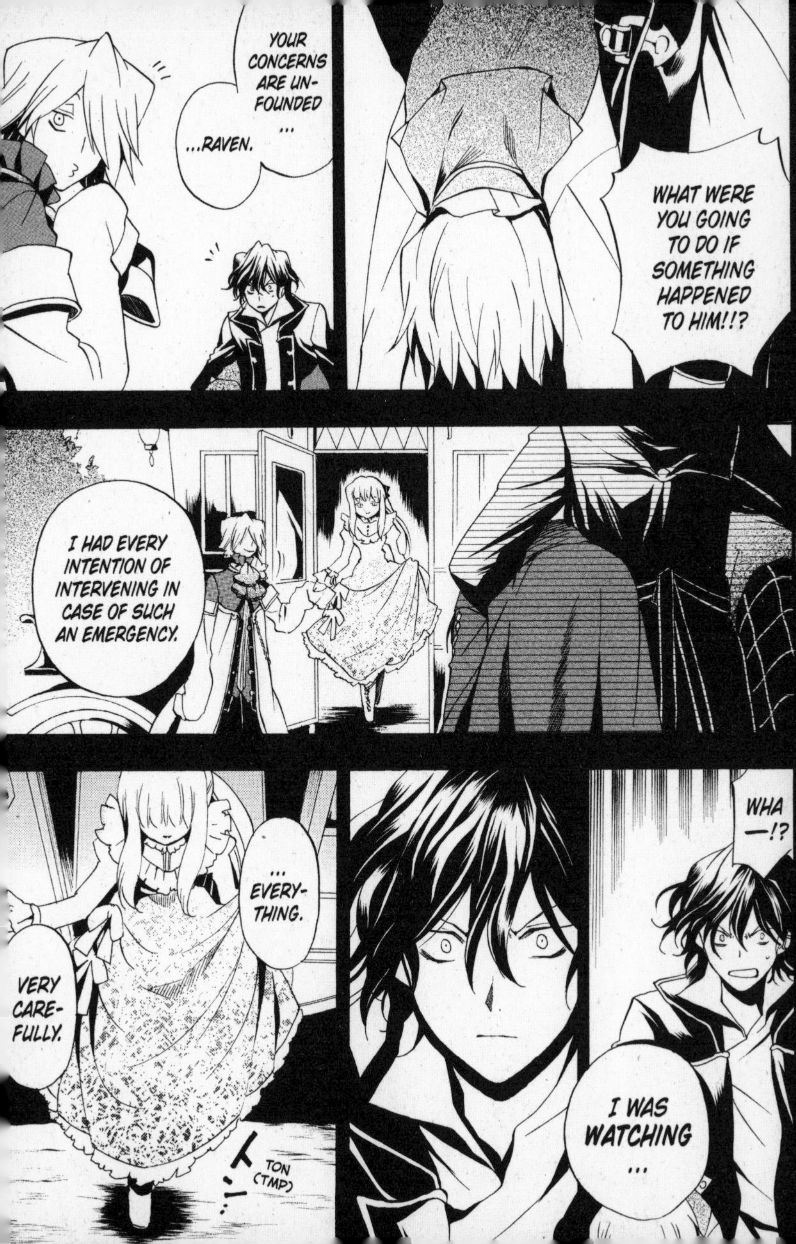
WHAT WERE YOU GOING TO DO IF SOMETHING HAPPENED TO HIM!!?
YOUR CONCERNS ARE UN-FOUNDED ...
...RAVEN.
I HAD EVERY INTENTION OF INTERVENING IN CASE OF SUCH AN EMERGENCY.
WHA—!?
I WAS WATCHING ...
... EVERY-THING.
VERY CARE-FULLY.
TON (TMP)

FROM YOUR SHADOW, YOU SEE?

....!

ZOKU (SHIVER)

FOR EXAMPLE, WHAT WAS IT NOW...

"I STILL WANT TO BE YOUR VALET!"

INDEED...

HAAAH... I KNEW THAT'S HOW OZ-KUN WOULD FIND OUT!

!!!?

DOSA (DROP)

AND AFTER WE KEPT QUIET BECAUSE RAVEN WAS SO ADAMANT ABOUT US NOT SAYING A WORD TOO...

REALLY NOW

GO (WHAM)

FURU (SHAKE)

FURU

PFFT!!

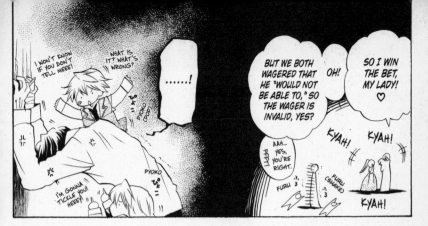

I WON'T KNOW IF YOU DON'T TELL MEEE!

WHAT IS IT? WHAT'S WRONG?

......!

PYOKO (ODD)

I'M GONNA TICKLE YOU HEEEY!

PYOKO

BUT WE BOTH WAGERED THAT HE "WOULD NOT BE ABLE TO," SO THE WAGER IS INVALID, YES?

OH!

SO I WIN THE BET, MY LADY! ♡

KYAH!

KYAH!

AAH... PFFT! YES, YOU'RE RIGHT.

FURU

FURU (SHAKE)

KYAH!

FUEH!?

...ARE YOU ALL RIGHT?

PECHI (FLICK)

....

...SEEMED A LITTLE ODD BACK THERE.

...YOU...

POOOO (DAZED)

....
I'M ALL RIGHT.

IT'S JUST THAT WHITE RABBIT, IT...

MUKU (RISE)

PYOKON (POP)

...WAS CREEPY, AND IT SCARED ME.

HOH! HOH! HOH! HOH! GOOD MORNING!

GYAAASU!!

DIE!!!

GACHAAN (GACHAAN)

BAGO (WHACK)

OH! I CAN HEAR ALICE!

GACHAN (CRASH)

WHAT THE HELL DO YOU THINK YOU'RE DOING, YOU CLOWNY BASTARD!!?

GOROON (ROLL)

DOGO (SMASH)

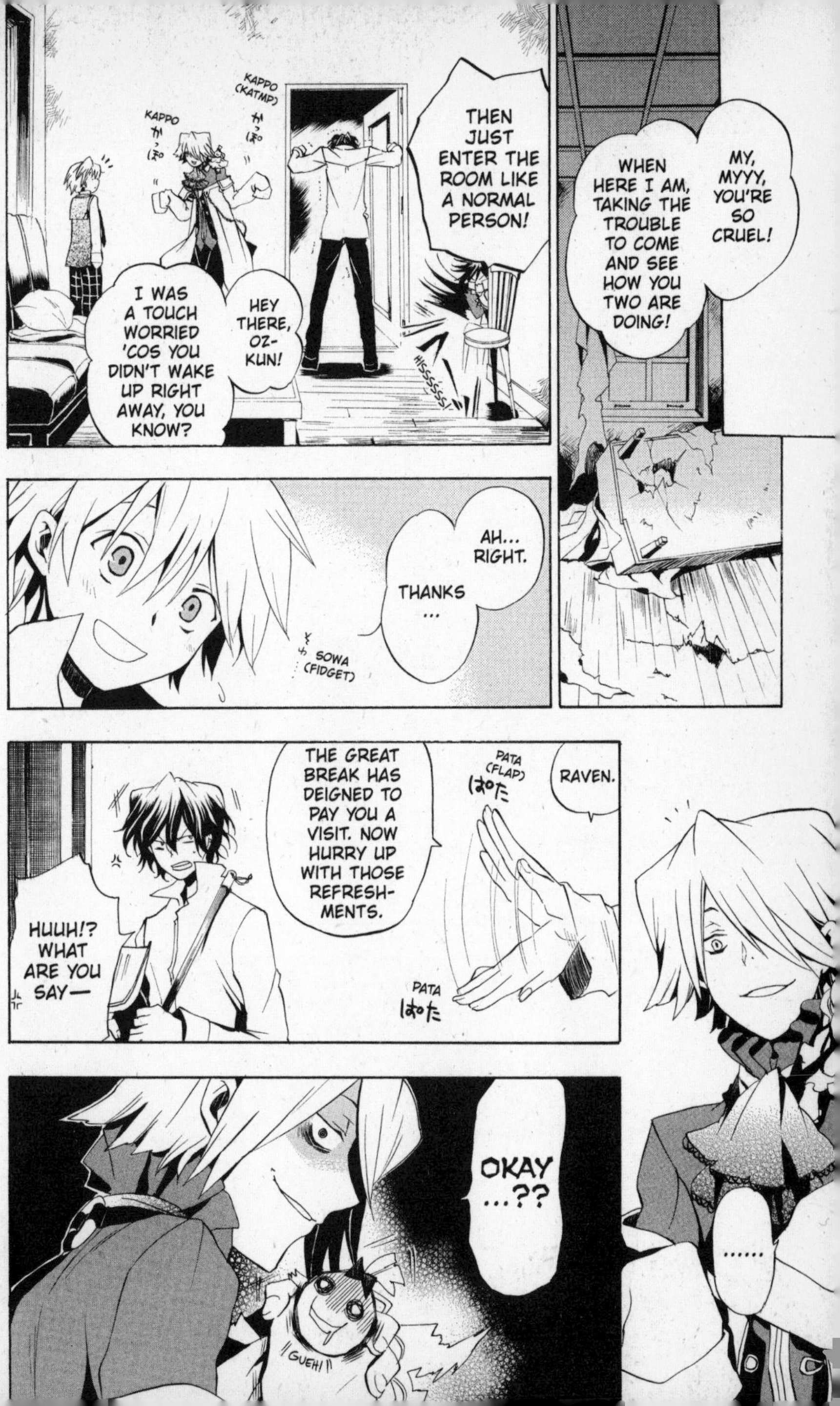
MY, MYYY, YOU'RE SO CRUEL!
WHEN HERE I AM, TAKING THE TROUBLE TO COME AND SEE HOW YOU TWO ARE DOING!
THEN JUST ENTER THE ROOM LIKE A NORMAL PERSON!
HISSSSSS!
KAPPO (KATMP)
KAPPO
HEY THERE, OZ-KUN!
I WAS A TOUCH WORRIED 'COS YOU DIDN'T WAKE UP RIGHT AWAY, YOU KNOW?
AH... RIGHT.
THANKS...
SOWA (FIDGET)
RAVEN.
PATA (FLAP)
PATA
THE GREAT BREAK HAS DEIGNED TO PAY YOU A VISIT. NOW HURRY UP WITH THOSE REFRESHMENTS.
HUUH!? WHAT ARE YOU SAY—
......
OKAY ...??
GUEH!

YOU WANT TO KNOW, DON'T YOU?

WHY LADY SHARON AND I HAVEN'T AGED?

WELL, COME AND HAVE A SIT-DOWN, OZ-KUN.

SU (SCOOCH) SU SU

DON'T BULLY GIL TOO MUCH, 'KAY?

EH? WHAT WHAT?

BOSH! (FOOMP!)

RIGHT...

...IT'S SIMPLE, REALLY.

IT'S BECAUSE WE'RE CONTRACTORS.

!

AH! HA! HA!

CHILDREN ARE THE EASIEST TO READ!

(NOT TO MENTION CONTROL...)

AAH...BUT OURS ARE NOT ILLEGAL CONTRACTS, YOU SEE?

BUT OCCA-SIONALLY...

...THE POWER STOPS A CONTRACTOR'S BODY FROM AGING, AS IN OUR CASES.

SU (SWSH)

WANT ONE?

BOSU (FOOMP)

WE USED A METHOD THAT WAS DEVELOPED BY PANDORA, SO...

...NEITHER OF US POSSESSES AN INCUSE LIKE YOU, OZ-KUN.

IT ONLY MEANS THAT OUR BODIES ARE BEING MADE TO CARRY THAT GREAT OF A BURDEN.

THOUGH OUR APPEARANCES MAY NOT CHANGE, WE'LL EVENTUALLY WEAR DOWN.

...DOES THAT MEAN YOU'RE IMMORTAL...?

HA-HA! DON'T BE SILLY! ☆

I CAN'T SPEAK FOR LADY SHARON...

...BUT I WON'T LAST ANOTHER YEAR.

OHHH... THAT WAS MUSIC TO MY EARS.

I CAN'T SAY I'M GOING TO GIVE IT UP SO EASILY, THOUGH!

WELL!

GARI (CRUNCH)

GARI

SFX: BORI (CHOMP) BORI

THERE ARE STILL...

...MANY THINGS I MUST DO.

PERO CLICK

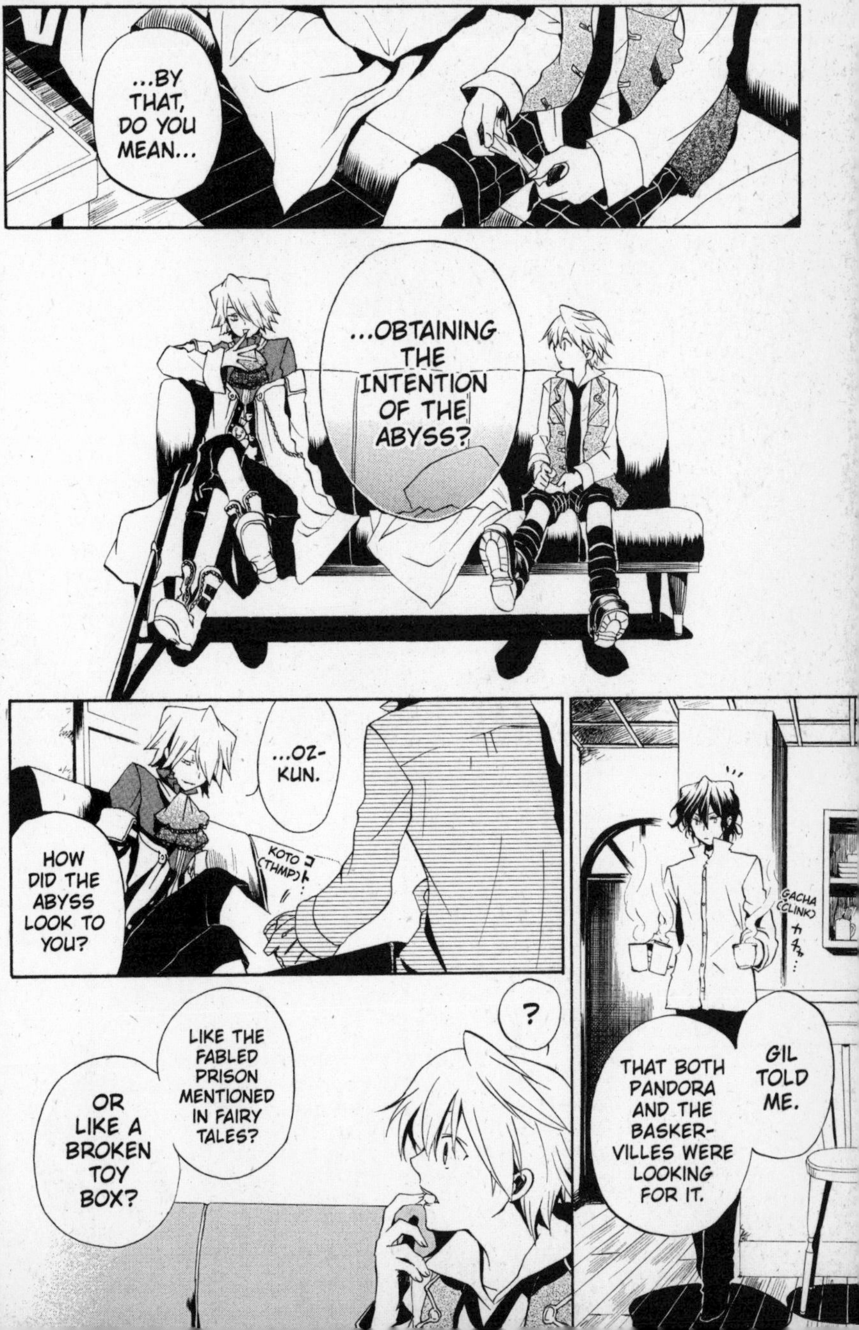
...BY THAT, DO YOU MEAN...
...OBTAINING THE INTENTION OF THE ABYSS?
GACHA (CLINK)
...OZ-KUN.
KOTO (THMP)
HOW DID THE ABYSS LOOK TO YOU?
GIL TOLD ME.
THAT BOTH PANDORA AND THE BASKER-VILLES WERE LOOKING FOR IT.
?
LIKE THE FABLED PRISON MENTIONED IN FAIRY TALES?
OR LIKE A BROKEN TOY BOX?

THAT THE ABYSS...

...IS A WOMB THAT GIVES BIRTH TO WEAPONS KNOWN AS CHAINS.

KOTO

THIS IS WHAT PANDORA BELIEVES.

THE CORE BEING THAT IS CREATING THAT DIMENSION...!

KORO (ROLL)

KORO

THAT IS WHY WE WANT THE INTENTION OF THE ABYSS.

GOKUN
(GULP)

...OZ-
KUN.

AND
...

...THE INDIVIDUAL ABSOLUTELY ESSENTIAL TO OUR PURPOSE IS YOU...

!?

PUFUUU

...AND EVEN THE "INTENTION" ITSELF APPEARED THIS TIME, I'M SURE OF IT.

BECAUSE THE BASKER-VILLES...

PUFUUU (BLOW)

~HACK~

~HACK~

HUH ....!?

...THAT PERSON IN THE RED HOOD WAS SAYING THE SAME THING.

I'M POSITIVE YOU'RE THE KEY TO OBTAINING THE "INTENTION."

KOFF!

KOFF!

KOFF!

WHY DON'T YOU TRY THINKING OF THE INTENTION OF THE ABYSS AS AN APPARATUS THAT POSSESSES IMMENSE POWER?

CURRENTLY, IT'S MALFUNCTIONING AND AFFECTING OUR WORLD.

HMM... HOW TO PUT IT...

WHAT DO YOU MEAN?

AND OZ-KUN IS JUST *THAT SORT OF* BEING!

THE RIGHT KEY IS NECESSARY TO MAKE THE MACHINE WORK PROPERLY.

SO YOU...

DO YOU UNDERSTAND?

....!

161

WHY... WOULD I HAVE SUCH—

....

...HAVE THE POWER TO COMMAND THE ENTIRETY OF THE ABYSS!

...WHO CAN SAY? WE STILL DON'T KNOW ALL THE DETAILS.

BUT PERHAPS THE REASON...

...HAS SOMETHING TO DO WITH YOUR "SIN"?

AND IT WAS ALL...!

FURA (SWAY)

...BECAUSE I HAVE THAT KIND OF POWER...?

OZ ...?

I GOT MY UNCLE AND EVERY-ONE ELSE INVOLVED...

...AND I NEARLY LOST GIL.

......

THAT'S WHY... I WAS DROPPED INTO THE ABYSS...?

BECAUSE...

GU (GRAB)

HEY ...!

UGH ...!

...MY SIN IS MY VERY BEING ...!

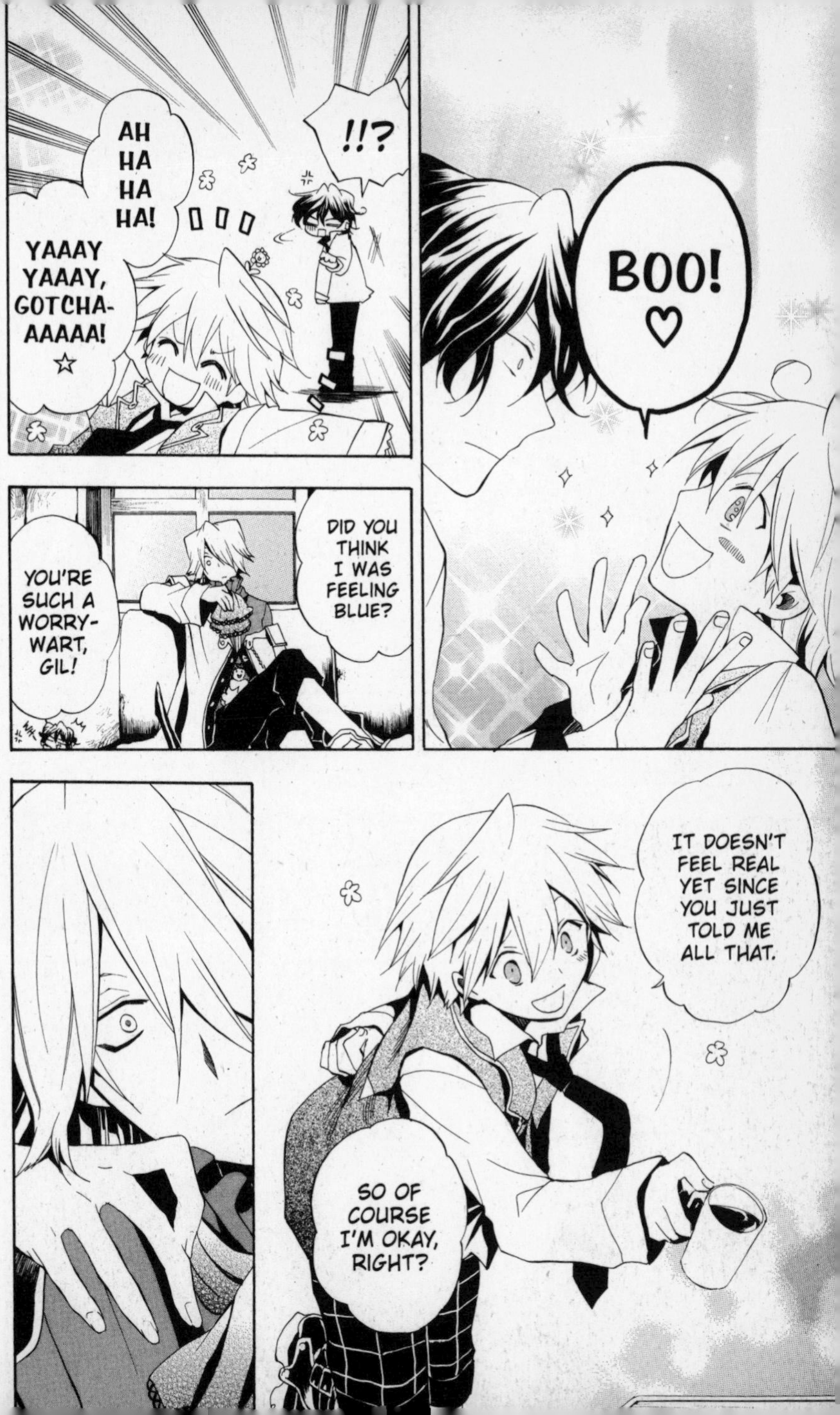
BOO! ♡
!!?
AH HA HA HA!
YAAAY YAAAY, GOTCHA-AAAAA! ☆
DID YOU THINK I WAS FEELING BLUE?
YOU'RE SUCH A WORRY-WART, GIL!
IT DOESN'T FEEL REAL YET SINCE YOU JUST TOLD ME ALL THAT.
SO OF COURSE I'M OKAY, RIGHT?

I'M GOING TO KEEP LOOKING FOR ALICE'S MEMORIES, JUST LIKE BEFORE.

...AS LONG AS GIL AND ALICE ARE WITH ME...

...I KNOW I'LL BE ALL RIGHT!

AND EVEN IF THE BASKER-VILLES SHOW UP AGAIN...

BOSU (GOOMP)

You're one freaky kid.

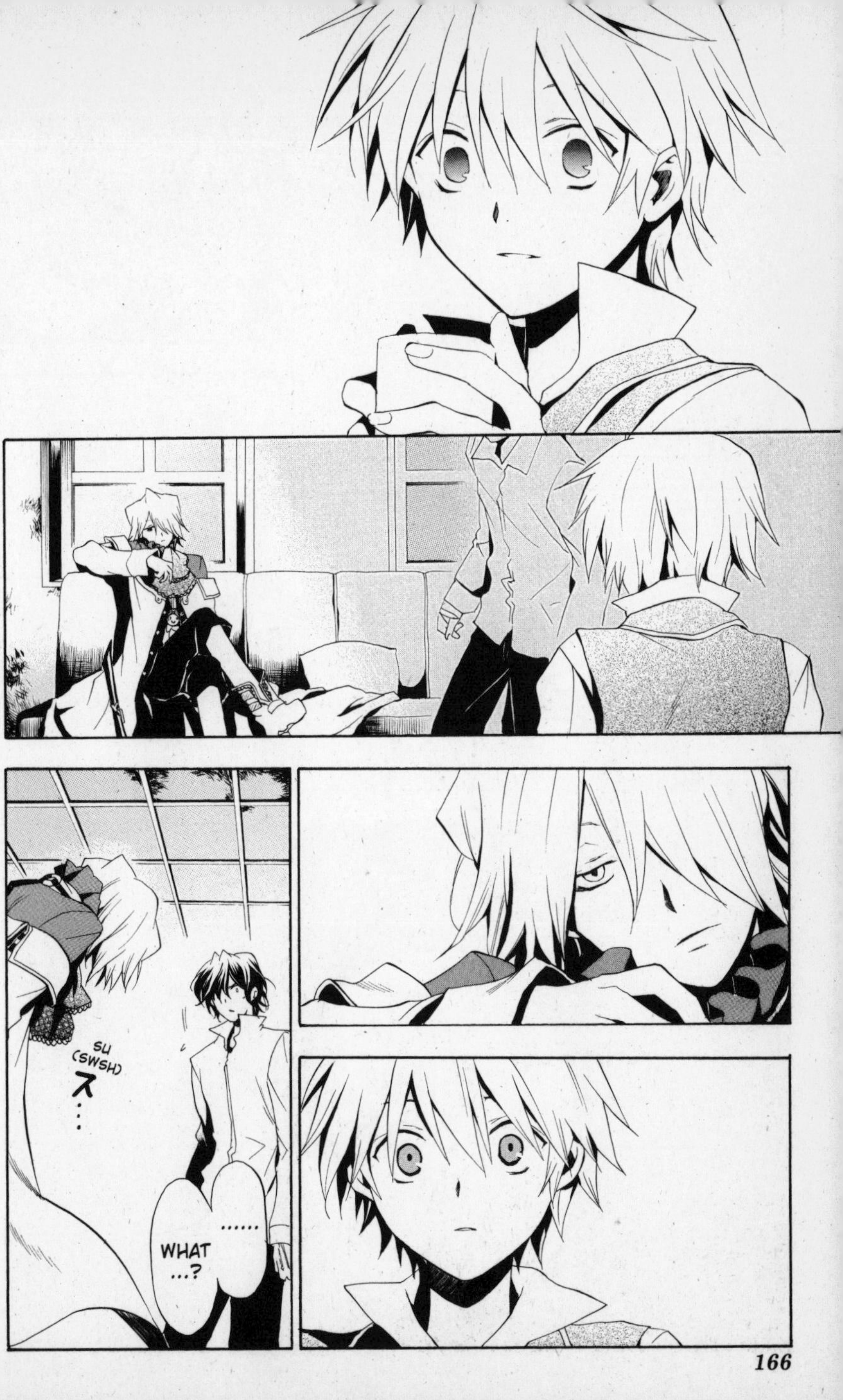
SU (SWSH)
ス…
......
WHAT ...?

...ABOUT WHAT IT WAS THAT *WARPED* YOU SO.

...I'M CURIOUS...

SAY, OZ-KUN...

HEH...

...YOU DON'T SEEM TO HAVE YET REALIZED *THAT* YOURSELF.

BUT THEN...

BR—

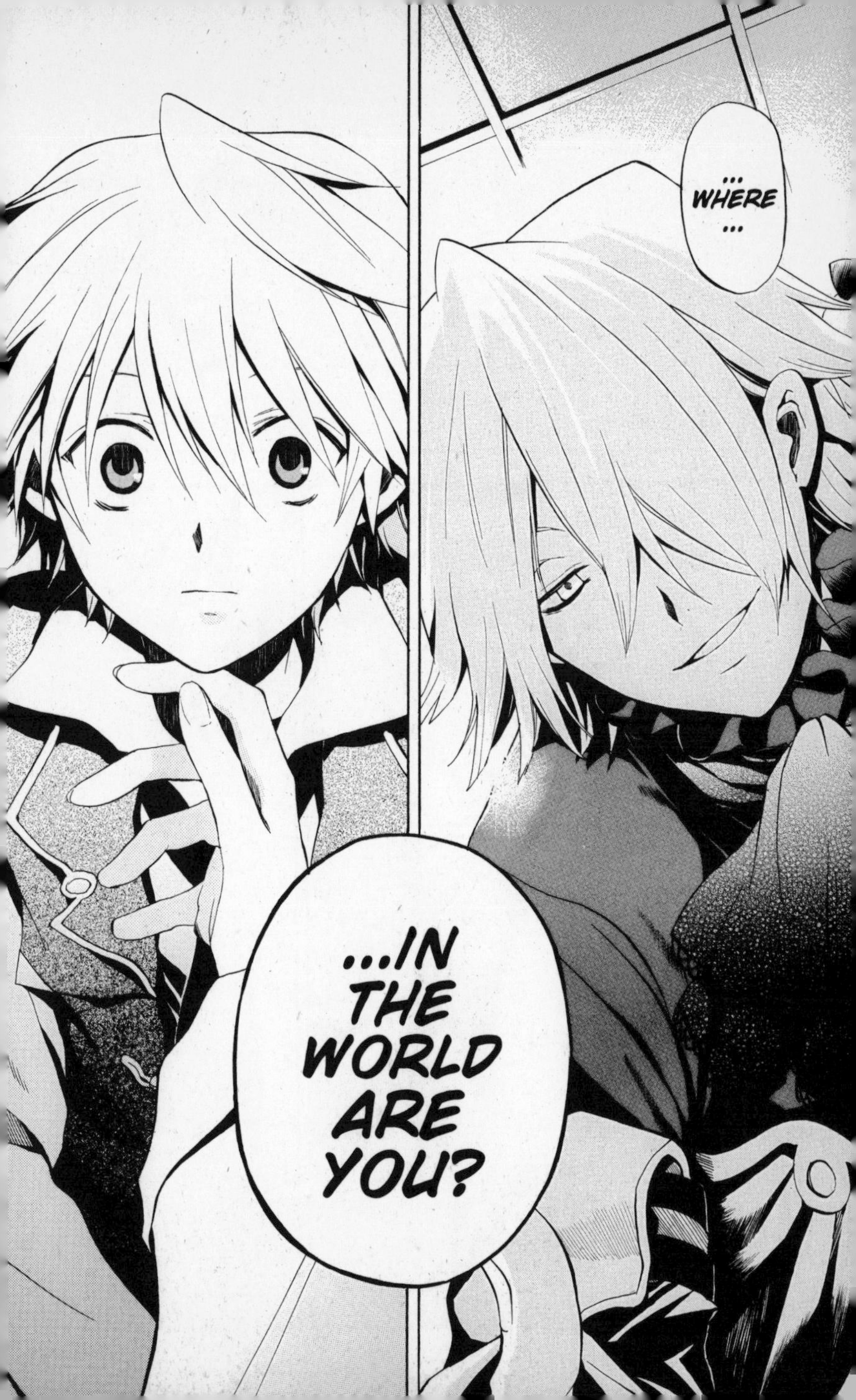
...WHERE...
...IN THE WORLD ARE YOU?

MY CLOUDED EYES...

...DON'T REFLECT YOU AT ALL, YOU SEE...?

は は HA!
HA! HA!
HA!
HA!!
HA!

AHHH! HA! HA! HA! HA!!

KUH...

YOUR EYEBALLS FINALLY ROTTED RIGHT OUTTA YER SKULL, HUH, YA CLOWNY BASTARD!!?

KUH KUH KUH KUH KUH...

IT'S SO OBVIOUS!

!?

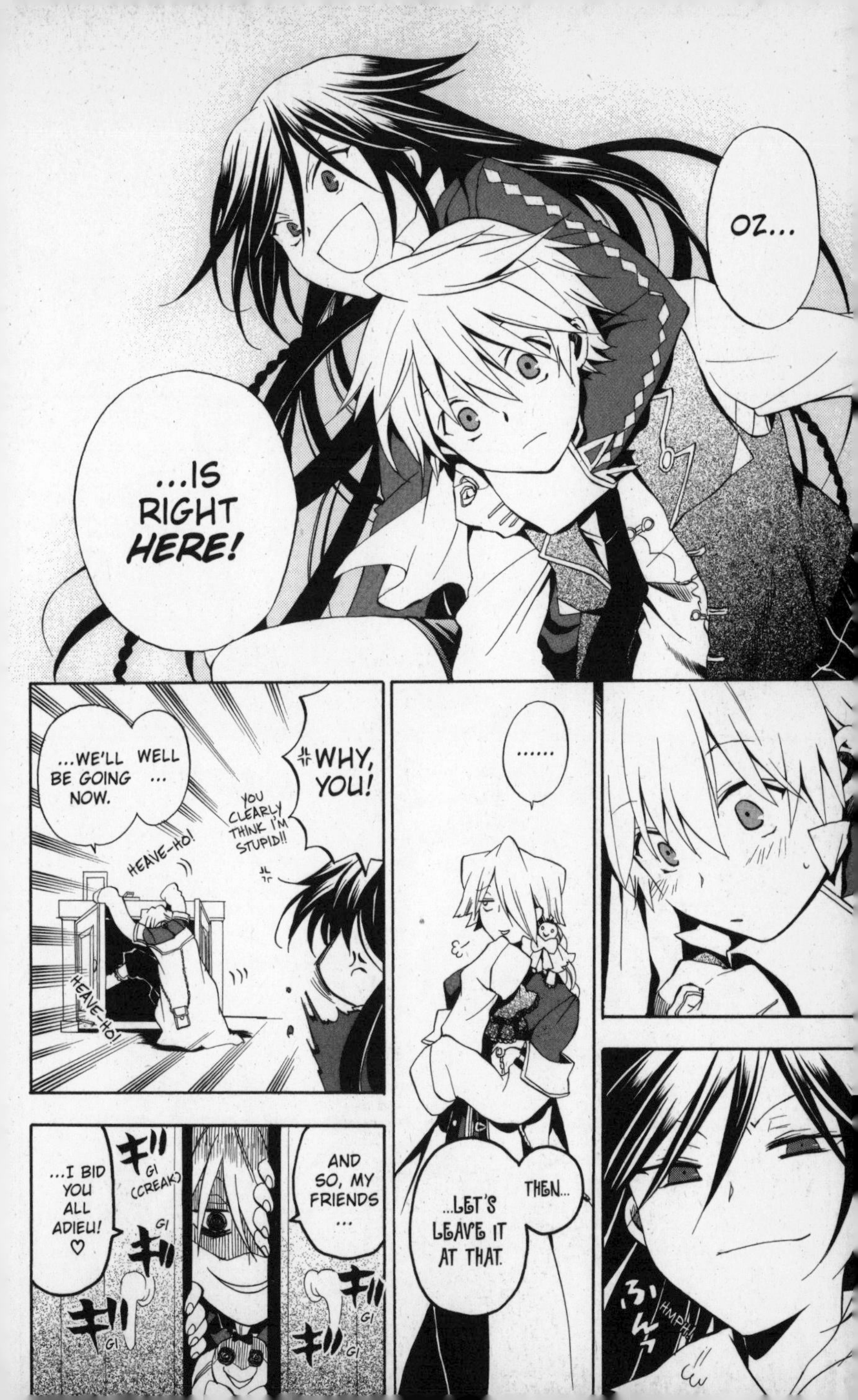
OZ...
...IS RIGHT HERE!
......
WHY, YOU!
YOU CLEARLY THINK I'M STUPID!!
WELL ...
...WE'LL BE GOING NOW.
HEAVE-HO!
HEAVE-HO!
ふん
HMPH
THEN...
...LET'S LEAVE IT AT THAT.
AND SO, MY FRIENDS ...
ギ
GI
ギ
GI
...I BID YOU ALL ADIEU! ♡
ギ
GI (CREAK)
ギ
GI
ギ
GI

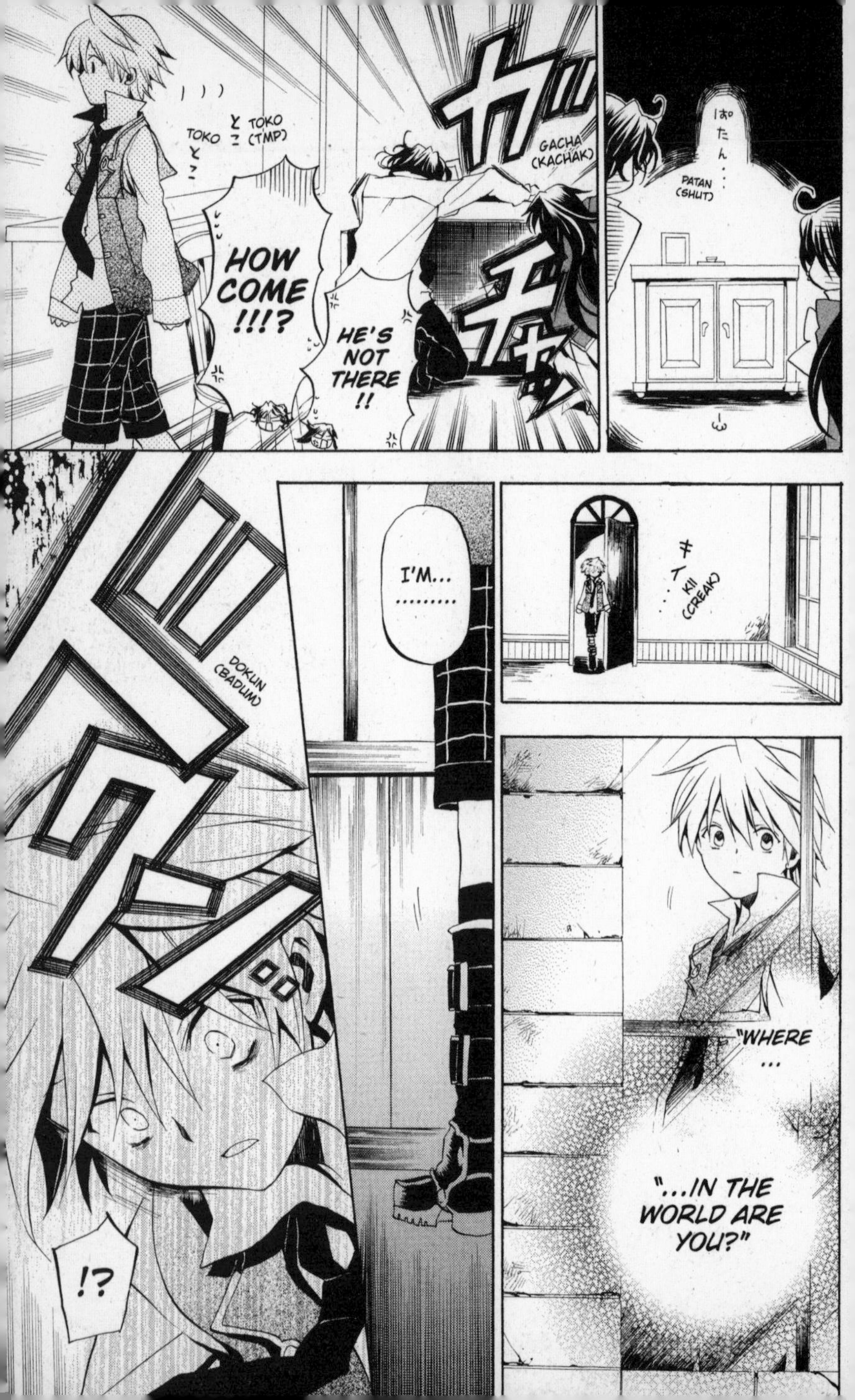
ぱたん…
PATAN (SHUT)
GACHA (KACHAK)
HE'S NOT THERE!!
HOW COME!!!?
とこ TOKO (TMP)
とこ TOKO
キィ… KII (CREAK)
I'M... ....
DOKUN (BADUM)
"WHERE ...
"...IN THE WORLD ARE YOU?"
!?

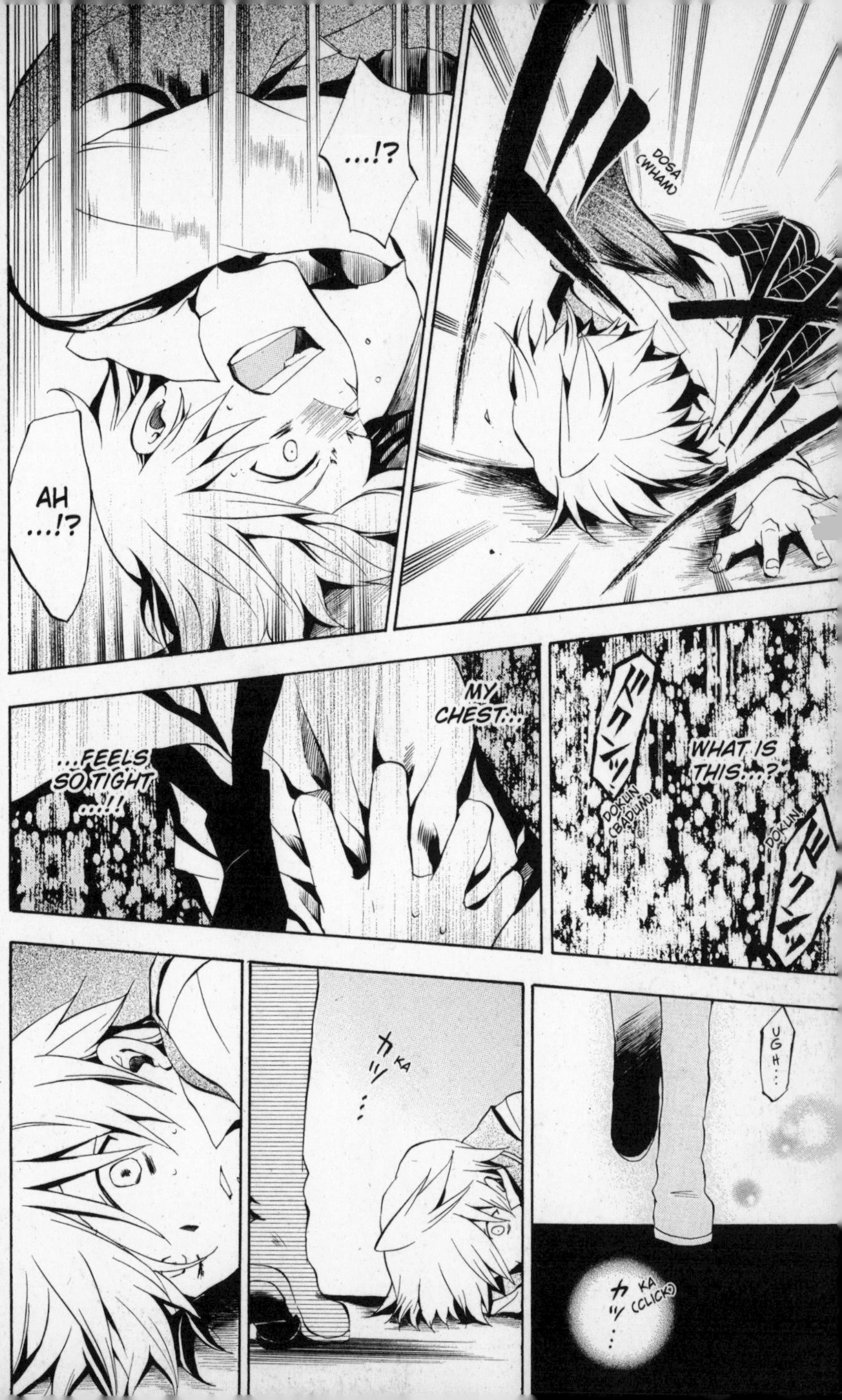
DOSA (WHAM)
...!?
AH ...!?
WHAT IS THIS...?
DOKUN (BADUM)
DOKUN
MY CHEST...
...FEELS SO TIGHT ...!!
UGH...
KA (CLICK)
KA

......?

WHO'S...
THERE...?

FU
(FAINT)

WHO'S...
THERE...?

DOSA
(THUD)

KACHI
(TICK)

!

PIKU
(TWITCH)

......IT
WOULD
SEEM...

...
HMM
...

...THAT THE
COUNTDOWN
HAS BEGUN...

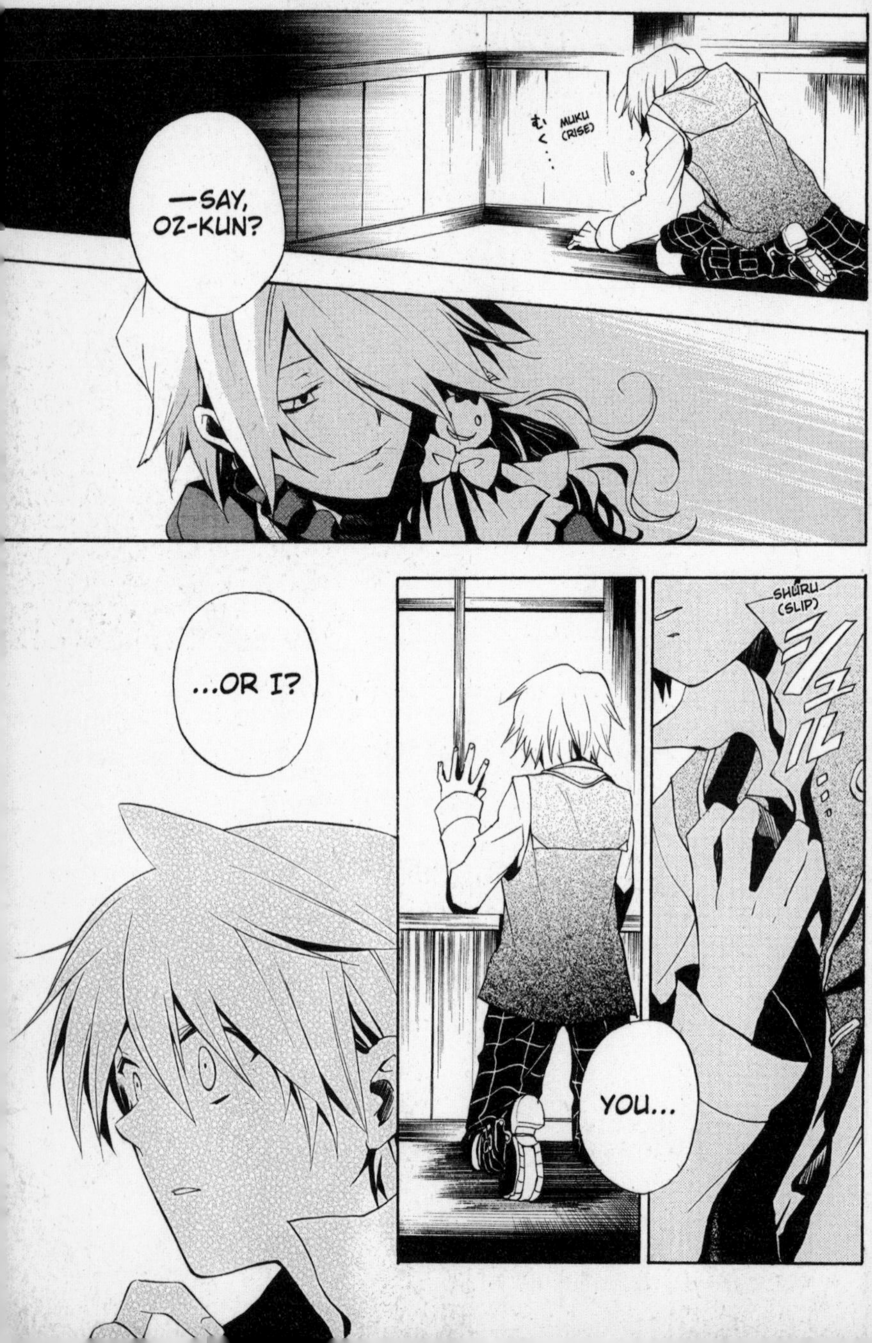
むく…
MUKU (RISE)
—SAY, OZ-KUN?
シュル…
SHURU (SLIP)
YOU...
...OR I?

YOU WILL COME TO RUE THE DAY...

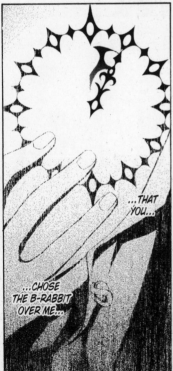

...THAT YOU...

...CHOSE THE B-RABBIT OVER ME...

TO BE CONTINUED IN PANDORA HEARTS 3

WHO WILL BE THE FIRST TO RUN OUT OF TIME ...?

Special Thanks!!

FUMITO YAMAZAKI

SEIRA YANAMI-SAN

SOICHIRO-SAN

SHINYUU-SAAAAAN ♡♡

MY EDITOR,
TAKEGASA-SAMA...
-SAMA... -SAMA...

AND YOU!!!

VOLUME 2 IS
OUUUUT!

YAHOOOOOO!!

JUN
MOCHIZUKI

MAIDORA HEARTS

♡ 1

MAIDS + SOAP OPERA!?

IS SUCH A FANTASY POSSIBLE!!?

THE THREE YOUNG SISTERS SLIP INTO ENEMY TERRITORY TO HAVE THEIR REVENGE AGAINST THE VESSALIUS DUKEDOM, WHICH TOOK EVERYTHING. THEY...DO NOT KNOW IT IS THE BEGINNING OF A LOVE-HATE DRAMA FILLED WITH SADNESS AND BETRAYAL.

VERY POPULAR, AND SERIALIZED IN MONTHLY PFANTASY (ON SALE THE 18TH OF EVERY MONTH)!

(*THIS IS NOT A REAL SERIES. JUST A PARODY OF PANDORA HEARTS BY MOCHIZUKI-SENSEI!)

C H A R A C T E R   I N F O R M A T I O N

ALICE
RECKLESS THIRD SISTER. SHE'S A MAID, BUT SHE'S BOSSY, AND KICKS BEFORE SHE TALKS. SHE'S ACTUALLY QUITE SHY.

SHARON
INTELLIGENT AND LADYLIKE SECOND SISTER. SHE PICKS UP AFTER ALICE, WHO ACTS WITHOUT THINKING. APPARENTLY SHE'S SCARY IF YOU MAKE HER ANGRY.

ADA
THE OLDEST SISTER WHO IS TIMID AND FRIGHTENED OF EVERYTHING. THERE IS APPARENTLY A REASON FOR HER LOLITA APPEARANCE ...?

OZ
DAUGHTER OF THE VESSALIUS FAMILY. A BEAUTIFUL GIRL WHOSE HEALTH IS FRAIL. AN INCIDENT CAUSES HER TO GET ACQUAINTED WITH ALICE...

GIL & BREAK
WHITE MAIDS. HOSTILE TO THE BLACK MAIDS, THE THREE SISTERS. THEIR MISTRESS IS THE DUCHESS, AND THEY ALWAYS TRY TO PICK A FIGHT WITH THE THREE.

COMMON HONORIFICS

no honorific: Indicates familiarity or closeness; if used without permission or reason, addressing someone in this manner would constitute an insult.

-san: The Japanese equivalent of Mr./Mrs./Miss. If a situation calls for politeness, this is the fail-safe honorific.

-sama: Conveys great respect; may also indicate that the social status of the speaker is lower than that of the addressee.

-kun: Used most often when referring to boys (though it can be applied to girls as well), this indicates affection or familiarity. Occasionally used by older men among their peers, but it may also be used by anyone referring to a person of lower standing.

-chan: An affectionate honorific indicating familiarity used mostly in reference to girls; also used in reference to cute persons or animals of either gender.

host   *page 6*

There are drinking establishments in Japan that hire attractive men to cater to a female clientele. A host's job typically includes pouring drinks and lavishing attention on his client, the latter of which involves a lot of sweet-talking — just like Oz in this scene!

incuse   *page 17*

An impression that is hammered or stamped, like the bust of a president on a coin.

Reveil   *page 148*

The name of the capital is derived from the French word for "alarm clock."

oden   *page 182*

A Japanese dish consisting of slices of boiled daikon radish, cubes of *konnyaku* (a kind of solidified jelly), tofu, fish cakes, hard-boiled eggs, etc., cooked in a soup stock of fish and seaweed.

PandoraHearts

I started going to the convenience store a lot after I became a mangaka. And before I knew it, I'd become friends with a middle-aged woman working part-time there. Now when I buy oden, she gives me an extra one for free!!!! Sh.........She's so niiiiiiice!! (tears)

MOCHIZUKI'S MUSINGS

VOLUME 2

PandoraHearts

JUN MOCHIZUKI

Crimson-Shell

クリムゾン・シェル

LOVE *PANDORA HEARTS*? WANT TO CHECK OUT SOME MORE OF JUN MOCHIZUKI-SENSEI'S WORK? WELL, LOOK NO FURTHER! *CRIMSON-SHELL*, MOCHIZUKI-SENSEI'S DEBUT, IS NOW AVAILABLE FROM YEN PRESS!

PandoraHearts

Look for BLACK BUTLER in
YEN *Plus*
a monthly manga anthology!

The Phantomhive family has a butler who's almost too good to be true...

...or maybe he's just too good to be human.

Black Butler

YANA TOBOSO

VOLUME 1 AND 2 IN STORES NOW!

Yen Press
www.yenpress.com

OLDER TEEN
OT

THE POWER
TO RULE THE
HIDDEN WORLD
OF SHINOBI...

THE POWER
COVETED BY
EVERY NINJA
CLAN...

...LIES WITHIN
THE MOST
APATHETIC,
DISINTER-
ESTED VESSEL
IMAGINABLE.

Nabari No Ou
Yuhki Kamatani

MANGA VOLUMES 1-3
NOW AVAILABLE

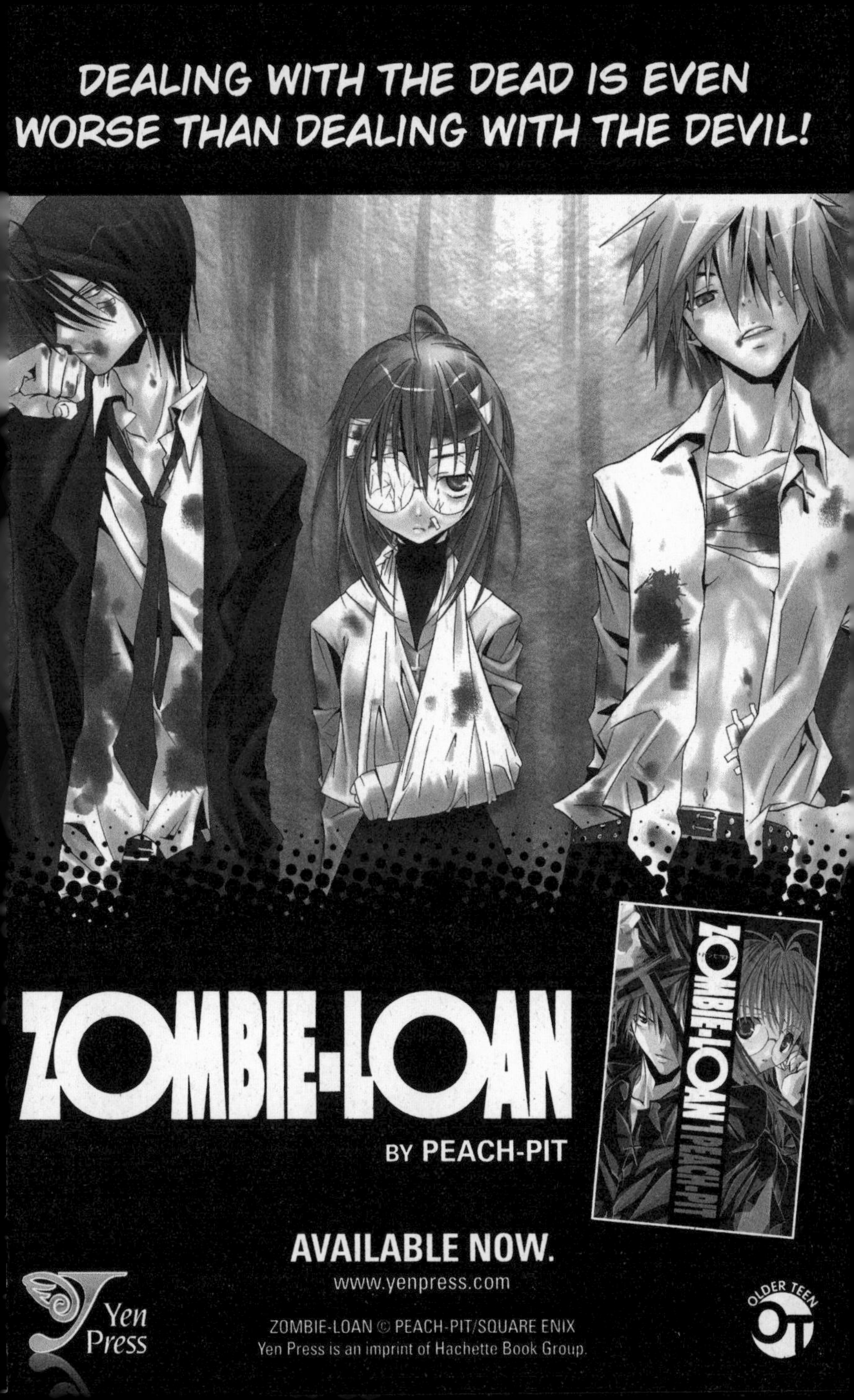
DEALING WITH THE DEAD IS EVEN WORSE THAN DEALING WITH THE DEVIL!
ZOMBIE-LOAN
BY PEACH-PIT
ZOMBIE-LOAN 1 PEACH-PIT
AVAILABLE NOW.
www.yenpress.com
Yen Press
OLDER TEEN
OT
ZOMBIE-LOAN © PEACH-PIT/SQUARE ENIX
Yen Press is an imprint of Hachette Book Group.

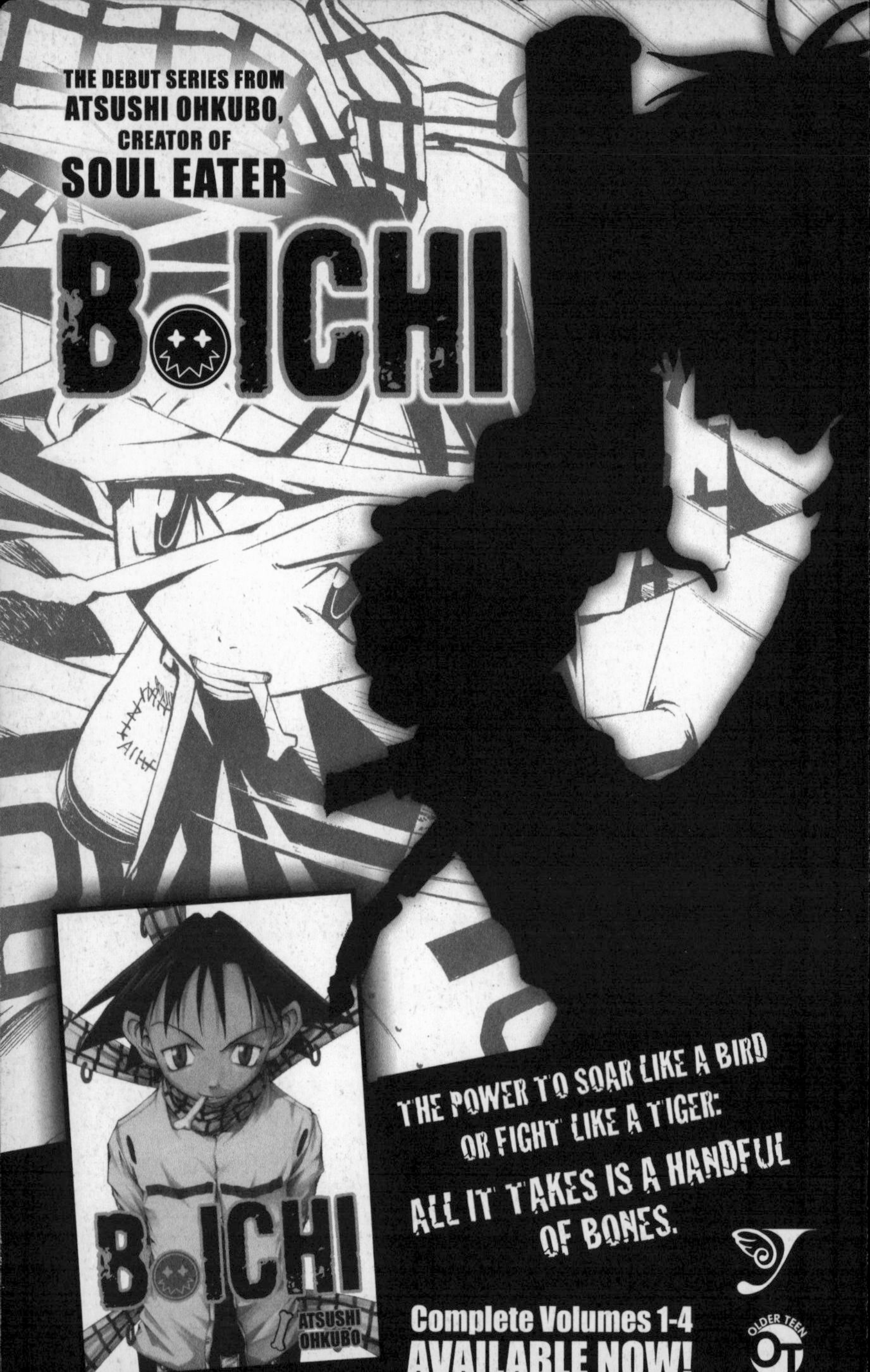

WHAT HAPPENS
WHEN YOU LOSE
AN ARM AND
GAIN A BODY?

BLACK GOD

Written by Dall-Young Lim
Illustrated by Sung-Woo Park

AVAILABLE NOW!
www.yenpress.com

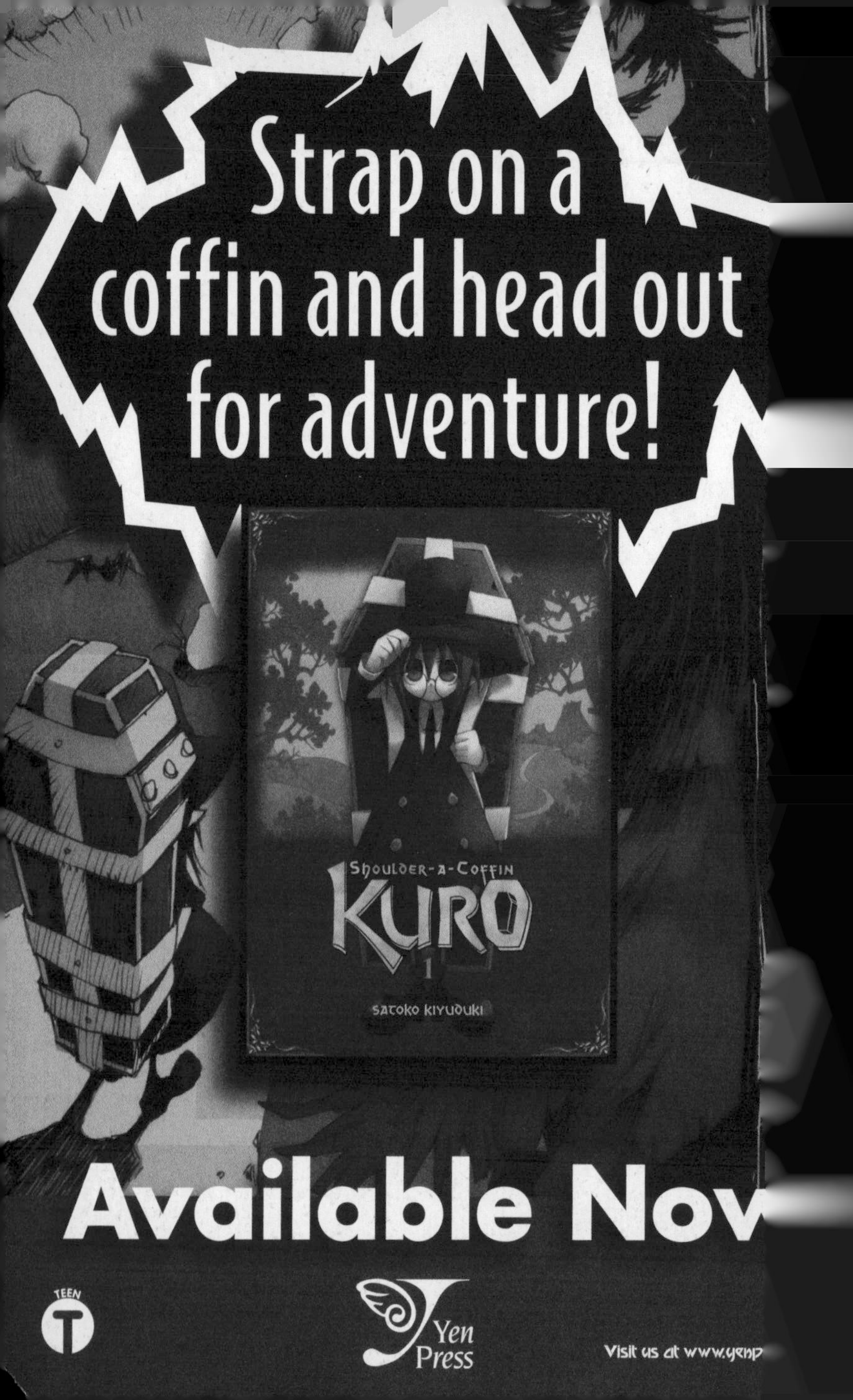
Strap on a coffin and head out for adventure!
Shoulder-a-Coffin
KURO
1
Satoko Kiyuduki
Available Nov
TEEN
T
Yen Press
Visit us at www.yenp

Kieli sees ghosts.
Harvey cannot die.
He will throw
her world into
chaos...
...and become her
one true friend.

STORY BY **Yukako Kabei**
ART BY **Shiori Teshirogi**

KIELI

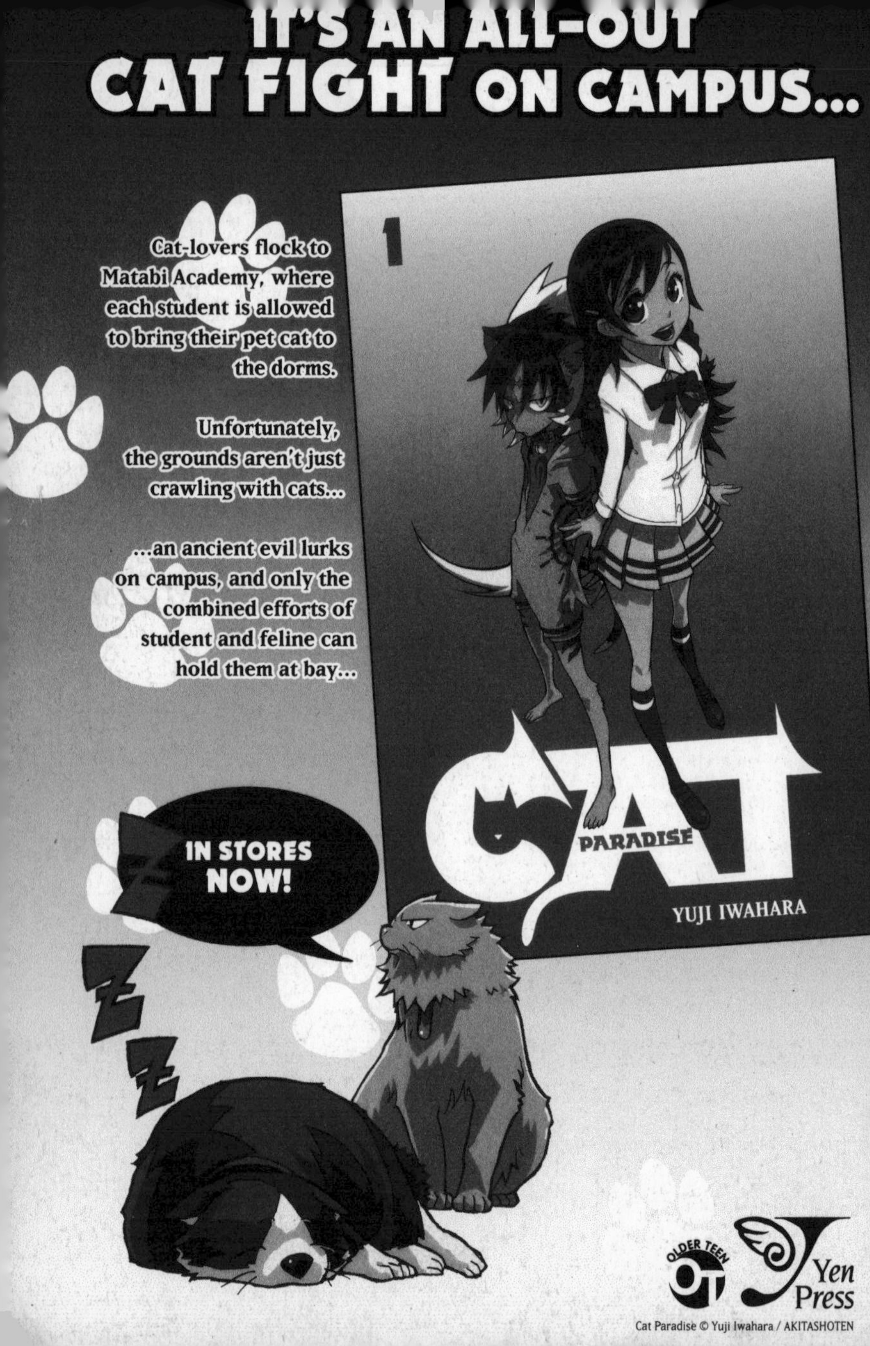
IT'S AN ALL-OUT
CAT FIGHT ON CAMPUS...
Cat-lovers flock to Matabi Academy, where each student is allowed to bring their pet cat to the dorms.
Unfortunately, the grounds aren't just crawling with cats...
...an ancient evil lurks on campus, and only the combined efforts of student and feline can hold them at bay...
1
CAT PARADISE
YUJI IWAHARA
IN STORES NOW!
Z Z Z
OLDER TEEN OT
Yen Press
Cat Paradise © Yuji Iwahara / AKITASHOTEN

PANDORA HEARTS ❷

JUN MOCHIZUKI

Translation: Tomo Kimura • **Lettering: Alexis Eckerman**

PANDORA HEARTS Vol. 2 © 2007 Jun Mochizuki / SQUARE ENIX CO.,
LTD. All rights reserved. First published Japan in 2007 by SQUARE
ENIX CO., LTD. English translation rights arranged with SQUARE ENIX
CO., LTD. and Hachette Book Group through Tuttle-Mori Agency, Inc.
Translation © 2010 by SQUARE ENIX CO., LTD.

Yen Press
Hachette Book Group
237 Park Avenue, New York, NY 10017

www.HachetteBookGroup.com
www.YenPress.com

Yen Press is an imprint of Hachette Book Group, Inc. The Yen Press name
and logo are trademarks of Hachette Book Group, Inc.

First Yen Press Edition: May 2010

ISBN: 978-0-316-07608-1

10 9 8 7 6 5 4

BVG

Printed in the United States of America